LABORS OF DIVISION

SOUTH ASIA IN MOTION

EDITOR
 Thomas Blom Hansen

EDITORIAL BOARD
 Sanjib Baruah
 Anne Blackburn
 Satish Deshpande
 Faisal Devji
 Christophe Jaffrelot
 Naveeda Khan
 Stacey Leigh Pigg
 Mrinalini Sinha
 Ravi Vasudevan

LABORS OF DIVISION

Global Capitalism and the Emergence of the Peasant in Colonial Panjab

NAVYUG GILL

STANFORD UNIVERSITY PRESS
STANFORD, CALIFORNIA

Stanford University Press
Stanford, California

© 2024 by Navyug Gill. All rights reserved.

No part of this book may be reproduced or transmitted in any form or by any means, electronic or mechanical, including photocopying and recording, or in any information storage or retrieval system, without the prior written permission of Stanford University Press.

Printed in the United States of America on acid-free, archival-quality paper

Library of Congress Cataloging-in-Publication Data

Names: Gill, Navyug, author.
Title: Labors of division : global capitalism and the emergence of the peasant in colonial Punjab / Navyug Gill.
Other titles: South Asia in motion.
Description: Stanford, California : Stanford University Press, 2024. |
  Series: South Asia in motion | Includes bibliographical references and index.
Identifiers: LCCN 2023018089 (print) | LCCN 2023018090 (ebook) |
  ISBN 9781503636958 (hardcover) | ISBN 9781503637498 (paperback) |
  ISBN 9781503637504 (epub)
Subjects: LCSH: Peasants—India—Punjab—History—19th century. | Peasants—India—Punjab—History—20th century. | Capitalism—India—Punjab—History—19th century. | Capitalism—India—Punjab—History—20th century. | Punjab (India)—Colonial influence.
Classification: LCC HD1537.I4 G555 2024 (print) | LCC HD1537.I4 (ebook) |
  DDC 305.5/630954552—dc23/eng/20230912
LC record available at https://lccn.loc.gov/2023018089
LC ebook record available at https://lccn.loc.gov/2023018090

Cover design: Daniel Benneworth-Gray
Cover art: Soni Bhalerao, *Farmer*, 2017, 24" × 13.5", Mumbai, India
Typeset by Newgen in Adobe Caslon Pro 10.5/15

Dedicated to my mother, Gurdial Kaur Gill,
for cultivating my imagination with a boundless love.

CONTENTS

	List of Illustrations	ix
	Acknowledgments	xi
INTRODUCTION	In Pursuit of Peasant Histories and Futures in Colonial Panjab	1
1	A Rule of Benevolence?: Revenue, Knowledge, and the Accumulation of Difference	22
2	Naming the Peasant: Colonial Jurisprudence and the Binding of Identity and Occupation	67
3	The Logic and Illogic of Debt: Reason and Capitalist Volatility in the New Agrarian Market	120
4	Horizons of Hierarchy: Caste, Landlessness, and the Limits of Religious Conversion	174
5	Producing a Theory of Inadequacy: Adam Smith, Karl Marx, and the Political Economy of Comparison	219
CONCLUSION	Global History and the Impermanence of Hierarchy	254
	Notes	263
	Bibliography	317
	Index	343

LIST OF ILLUSTRATIONS

MAPS

1.1 The Panjab region in the late 18th century   27

1.2 The kingdom of Maharaja Ranjit Singh, c. 1839   27

1.3 The districts of British Panjab, c. 1907   29

TABLE

1.1 Land revenue demanded and collected in Panjab, 1852–59   43

FIGURES

2.1 A blank return form used in the 1848 census of the North West Provinces   83

2.2 A sample of the returns for the 1852 census in the North West Provinces   84

2.3 A blank return form used in the 1881 census in Panjab   99

2.4 A blank copy of the certificate to be an "agriculturalist," 1901   107

2.5 A blank genealogical chart on reverse side of the certificate to be an "agriculturalist," 1901   109

2.6 A petition by a group of Mazhabi Sikhs from Gujranwala and Lyallpur for "agriculturalist" status, 1911   114

3.1 The article "Spendthrifts Ruin India" from *The New York Times*, October 7, 1900   121

3.2 A copy of a civil case judgment between a moneylender and a landholder, 1878   140

3.3 The cover page of the study of family budgets in Lyallpur by the Board of Economic Inquiry, 1934   166

4.1 A copy of a translated contract between a siri and a landowner in Ferozepur, 1932   208

ACKNOWLEDGMENTS

IF THIS BOOK IS an attempt to provide a history of the rural division of labor, then its premise ought to bear on its actual writing. And if I seek to implicate economic logic with cultural politics, such a gesture should also divulge the itinerary that produced its author. The solitary, strenuous act of putting words together—much like cultivation—has only been possible by the layered contributions of a range of gracious individuals, institutions, and *parmatma*. I have come to savor both the pleasures and difficulties I experienced during the making of this book, and thus the remaking of myself.

My primary gratitude is directed toward my parents Gurdial Kaur and Darshan Singh Gill. After arriving in Canada as migrants from east Panjab in the early 1970s, they worked in factories and taxis to provide me with a childhood full of affection, principles, and possibilities. My mother nurtured my inclinations with the utmost care, allowing me to embark on a journey of discovery without losing sight of my inheritance. Whatever qualities of thinking or speaking I have today no doubt come from her. My father demonstrated the value of quiet fortitude and diligence, and trusted me enough to find a greater purpose. Through them I drew on the spirit of my ancestors and Sikhi to endure the many peculiar tribulations of scholarly life. Their lives of struggle are a constant reminder of the power of conviction amid a litany of disparities and contingencies. This book is a rebuke of any preordained fate.

I appreciate the inspiration, instruction, and discipline instilled by my teachers over the past two decades. Gyanendra Pandey was an extremely rigorous and astute supervisor who provided the basis for me to follow a winding path. He taught me the importance of small details, asking difficult questions, and writing with elegance and empathy. I hope the prose of this book is consistent enough to indulge a few of its programmatic statements. As an undergraduate in Toronto, it felt as if I was illiterate before meeting Ritu Birla, which means she taught me how to read. I thank her for changing the course of my life by opening up a world of historical and theoretical contestations, and for staying with this project through to the end from afar. Clifton Crais was always open-minded and generous with his time, and forced me to think about my work in relation to debates in other geographies, literatures, and disciplines. I still dwell on his enticing challenge to write one beautiful sentence. For broader support and training during graduate school, I thank Jonathan Prude, Jeffrey Lesser, Christopher Krupa, Bruce Knauft, Matthew Payne, Ruby Lal, Tonio Andrade, Deepika Bahri, David Nugent, Marina Rustow, and Velcheru Narayana Rao.

A select number of people offered crucial feedback on portions of this book in various iterations as well as sage guidance on the travails of the publication process. I am indebted to Durba Mitra for her unfailing enthusiasm, insight, and innate sense of the bigger picture in all worldly matters. Rupa Viswanath asked me sharp questions with care and drew connections to numerous new and old ideas. Sheetal Chhabria helped me focus my arguments at several different points, and to think deeper about the purpose of scholarship. Manan Ahmed pushed me toward ruthless clarity while deftly navigating the politics of peer review. Ravinder Kaur offered constant intellectual warmth despite being half a world away, and recommended this press for the manuscript. Vinayak Chaturvedi gave many thoughtful suggestions on how to say what exactly I wanted to say. David Gilmartin patiently listened to me describe my raw ideas, and pointed to ways forward. Andrew Sartori directed me to be precise about where I stood on key conceptual issues. And Sunil Purushotham provided encouraging comments near the beginning of the journey. Collectively, this advice has been invaluable even where it was not followed; I now realize why scholars make that odd caveat about being responsible for their own arguments.

There is a larger group of friends and comrades who sustained my curiosity and shared their own views throughout the course of writing this book. For a poignant willingness to confront difficult questions together, I thank David Lelyveld, Balmurli Natrajan, Adeem Suhail, Rajbir Singh

Judge, Suraj Yengde, Bikrum Singh Gill, and Neilesh Bose. I also value the wisdom gained from discussions with Biju Mathew, Anjali Arondekar, Emma Heaney, Sangeeta Kamat, and Indrani Chatterjee. Early on, Gowri Vijayakumar and Lipika Kamra became supportive writing companions as we circulated drafts of our proposals with one another. From the streets of our beloved Moga to Chandigarh, Jasdeep Singh never faltered in sharing his time and talents to bridge the divide between local struggles and global scholarship. Over the years I learned a great deal about Panjab and Sikhi from Naindeep Singh, Amandeep Sandhu, Raj Kumar Hans, Randeep Maddoke, and Pritam Singh. For uplifting conversations at the right moments, I appreciate Anand Vaidya, Rohit De, Mubbashir Rizvi, Shailaja Paik, Hafsa Kanjwal, Prakash Kashwan, Inderpal Grewal, Justin Podur, Nathaniel Roberts, Vidya Kalaramadam, Anshu Malhotra, Meena Dhanda, Eric Beverley, Angela Zimmerman, Veena Dubal, Marcela Echeverri Muñoz, and Harjot Oberoi. My restless proclivity was honed in the radical activist spaces of the Toronto left in the early 2000s. From Atlanta, I have fond memories of times spent with Moyukh Chatterjee, Shatam Ray, Shreyas Sreenath, Ajitkumar Chittambalam, Debjani Bhattacharyya, Sunandan KN, Aditya Pratap Deo, Hemangini Gupta, Bisan Salhi, Sanal Mohan, Faiza Moatasim, and Guidrex Masse. My colleagues at William Paterson have provided a welcoming environment, especially Lucia McMahon, Jason Ambroise, Dewar MacLeod, Rajender Kaur, Malissa Williams, Neici Zeller, Stephen Shalom, and Richard Kearney.

The joy of writing this book was punctured by mourning the abrupt loss of two dear friends. On the one hand, MSS Pandian passed the very week I submitted my dissertation in 2014. We met on the campus of Jawaharlal Nehru University in 2011 and instantly connected over the need to put Panjabi and Dravidian politics in dialogue without recourse to Hindi or North India. After long days in the archives, I spent nearly every evening in his smoke-filled flat in Munirka Vihar, which was usually crowded with brilliant students and activists arguing, laughing, and planning. Pandian, as generous with his enthusiasm as he was sharp with his judgments, compelled me to refine the questions I wanted to pursue. On the other hand, Kavita Datla left this world in 2017. I met her in western Massachusetts during the bleak winter of 2015, where we reflected on the foibles of graduate training and scholarly trends. Kavita equally radiated warmth and wit, and was determined to find the optimism behind every turn of fortune. She not only gave me extensive feedback on the draft of an article that eventually became a chapter in this book, but provided guidance in securing my first stable job. After all of these years, I am still taken aback by the different ways Pandian and Kavita embraced me, perhaps a sign of the misanthropy and triviality of much of academic culture. While I can only speculate on how they would have engaged with this book, I will always pay tribute to their contributions to my life.

My arguments benefited from presentations at several important conferences and workshops. In particular, I thank the hosts and participants at Columbia University, Punjabi University (Patiala), Yale University, the University of Connecticut, the University of Massachusetts Amherst, New York University, the New School for Social Research, William Paterson University, and Amherst College. The Interdisciplinary Workshop in Colonial and Postcolonial Studies at Emory was a model of vibrant intellectual exchange. I also appreciate the organizers of the Annual Conference on South Asia at the University of Wisconsin-Madison, the Association for Asian Studies Annual Conference, the Lyallpur Young Historians Club, the Dalit and Minorities Organization (Amritsar), and the Jakara Movement's Sikholars Graduate Student Conference. Geraldine Forbes's comments at the manuscript workshop hosted by the American Institute of Indian Studies were heartening. Finally, I gained valuable feedback from four lively international events: The "Quest for Equity: Reclaiming Social Justice, Revisiting Ambedkar Conference" in Bengaluru in 2017; the "Karl Marx Life, Ideas, and Influence: A Critical Examination on the Bicentenary Conference" at the Asian Development Research Institute in Patna in 2018; the "Towards a Global History of Primitive Accumulation Conference" at the International Institute of Social History in Amsterdam in 2019; and the "Frontiers of Accumulation Conference" at the University of Copenhagen in 2019. These spaces helped me realize the difference between criticism and critique, and the importance of ethical engagement.

I must express gratitude to the archivists, librarians, and staff at a number of institutions across the world. Research for this book was conducted primarily at the Punjab State Archives in Chandigarh, both the

National Archives of India and the Nehru Memorial Museum and Library in New Delhi, and the British Library in London. In particular, Parminder Kaur Sandhu and Margaret Makepeace were helpful in creating a supportive research setting and tracking down stray archival leads. I also spent time reading and borrowing from the Robert W. Woodruff Library at Emory, the David and Lorraine Cheng Library at William Paterson, and the New York Public Library's Manhattan Research Library Initiative. Finally, I thank my institution's Interlibrary Loan Service—perhaps the single greatest generalized resource for sharing resources—for efficiently delivering a wide range of materials, and Geetanjali from the Panjab Digital Library for providing some of the maps. This book, as much as any other, would be impossible without such sustained yet selfless personal and impersonal contributions, a scholarly infrastructure that must be protected and indeed expanded into other domains.

I appreciate Thomas Blom Hansen, Dylan Kyung-lim White, and the team at Stanford University Press for guiding this project from manuscript to book in the midst of a global pandemic. Earlier a portion of Chapter 1 appeared as "Accumulation by Attachment: Colonial Benevolence and the Rule of Capital in Nineteenth Century Panjab," *Past and Present* 256, no. 1 (August 2022): 203–38. And parts of Chapter 4 were published as "Limits of Conversion: Caste, Labor, and the Question of Emancipation in Colonial Panjab," *Journal of Asian Studies* 78, no. 1 (February 2019): 3–22. I am grateful to the editors of both journals as well as Oxford University Press and Duke University Press, respectively, for allowing me to use my own words here. Ultimately the review process for these articles significantly improved this book. I am also much obliged to Soni Bhalerao, a wonderful artist now based in northern Maharashtra whose work I chanced upon at a gallery in Mumbai in 2017, for allowing me to use her exquisite painting on the cover. For a degree of pecuniary assistance, I thank the Research Center for the Humanities and Social Sciences at William Paterson.

Alongside my parents, the deepest source of strength to write this book came from my immediate and extended family. I thank my brother Parmbir not only for reading and helping refine all of the arguments here, but also for being the first reader of nearly everything I have ever written. I trust his instincts more than my own, and am inspired by the way he brings theoretical concerns to shape everyday life. My sisters Navkiran and Rosebir have been intensely caring, always encouraging me to pursue my passions while sharing the warmth of their own homes, families, and achievements. I am fortunate for the affection of the wider Gill, Sumbal, and Sidhu clans in Toronto, Vancouver, Amritsar, and beyond, and to be embraced by the people of Saffuwala despite a diasporic upbringing. To my partner, Anupreet, I can only express a figment of my appreciation for abetting so many commitments with an uncommon grace and confidence. And lastly, to our little Nistaar, know that I am both utterly delighted and more determined by your arrival in this perilous world. Perhaps one day you will read these words while walking the path of emancipation to make sense of our histories and futures anew.

LABORS OF DIVISION

INTRODUCTION

IN PURSUIT OF PEASANT HISTORIES AND FUTURES IN COLONIAL PANJAB

Farida, lorai dakh bijurian, kikar bijai jat,
handhai unn kataida, paidha lorai pat.

Farid, the cultivator plants acacia trees, but wishes for grapes,
he is spinning wool, yet wishes to wear silk.
—BABA FARID JI

IN THE LATE EVENING on October 20, 1893, over a hundred masked men armed with swords, hatchets, and spears gathered in the ravines outside Isa Khel in the Bannu district of Panjab. Located 260 miles west of Lahore near the Indus River, the town had a population of almost nine thousand, who were engaged mainly in cultivation and animal husbandry along with weaving and cloth trading. At around 10:30 p.m. the crowd slowly entered the main bazaar from the south and began to attack, looting and burning certain shops and homes. One of the men who was specifically targeted managed to escape only by hiding in an old well with his young son while his house was in the process of being ransacked. As the crowd moved north, they destroyed over forty buildings, killed two people, and wounded at least fifteen. Near the main intersection they were confronted by a hastily assembled police force under the command of local notables. After a brief skirmish in which thirty rounds of ammunition were fired, the authorities managed to disperse the crowd and reimpose order by midnight.

A few days later the assistant district magistrate, Herbert Casson, arrived on the scene to investigate. His report, submitted two months later, offers several curious details about the incident and its aftermath.[1] According to Casson, the attack occurred on the last night of the three-day Dussehra Festival, when most residents were distracted with liturgical recitals, musical performances, and celebratory bonfires. Such timing indicates it was not a spontaneous outburst but rather a premeditated attack, possibly with some degree of local support. The damages were initially estimated at 2.5 million rupees, though a statement provided by the victims afterward amounted to 950,000 rupees in cash, ornaments, and salable goods, which was further reduced to something under 600,000 rupees. Of the seventy-eight men arrested in the following days, twenty-one were punished with sentences ranging from a 500-rupee fine to nine years of rigorous imprisonment. Thirteen were identified as "zamindars," while the remaining eight were deemed "men of low caste." More troubling for Casson was the lethargic response of local elites, suggesting either incompetence or collusion. Although no misconduct was proved, some of these men came under suspicion and were strongly reprimanded for not having fulfilled their duties. As both a precautionary and punitive measure, five special police posts were established in the town and surrounding villages for a period of two years. Finally, Casson mentions almost offhandedly that the perpetrators were Muslims who shouted their "Muhammadan war cry of 'Ali,' 'Ali!'" as they attacked their Hindu victims.[2]

Despite all of these details—the organization of the attack; the extensive, if disputed, damages; the punishments; the doubts about loyalty; the police measures; and the fraught identities of those involved—Casson concludes the report, remarkably, by terming it a "riot" that was "purely local and politically unimportant."[3] Further confounding rumors, that outside agitators secretly instigated the crowd, that some Hindus might have joined in the looting, or that sexual indiscretions with women and boys were committed by men on both sides, failed to elicit sustained attention. The report itself contains no vernacular excerpts or follow-up commentaries, and the archival trail on Isa Khel has thus far largely fallen silent.[4] Such a curious dismissal of a fragmentary account of what seems to be communal violence in fact prompts further questions: Why did this particular incident between Muslims and Hindus *not* generate greater concern from officials in British India? How was its importance determined and compared? And what might this tell us about the shifting fortunes of identity, agriculture, and capital under colonial rule?

The discrepant response to the violence in Isa Khel lies in the unusual way the colonial state pursued the question of causality. Key to explaining its status was a measure of the motivations rather than identities of the perpetrators. This meant that although it appeared that Muslims attacked Hindus, officials surprisingly did not assign blame to a difference of religion.[5] "Religious ill-feeling had little, if anything, to do with the riot," notes Richard Bruce, commissioner of the Derajat division, a point proven by the fact that "no attempt whatever was made to desecrate religious edifices or attack public buildings."[6] Instead, the causes were identified as a straightforward reaction against land alienations, the chance to loot, and a desire to burn record books. Evidence took the form of economic data: the 19,402 acres of land mortgaged in the subdistrict in 1878 had more than tripled to 61,607 acres by 1893. With the landowners all Muslims and the moneylenders all Hindus, the conflict was nonetheless cast as one between debtors and creditors rather than communal in nature. "The hatred of the Hindu as a grasping banniah," rationalized Casson, "has much more to do with the riot than the hatred of him as a Hindu and an infidel."[7] The narrow lesson for the colonial state thus revolved around the need to protect peasants from indebtedness and to compel elites to be more diligent in their surveillance of the local population.

Beyond imperial stratagems or oscillations from religious to financial discord, what became of the riot of Isa Khel exemplifies profound issues reverberating across Panjab and the subcontinent to much of the colonized world in the nineteenth and early twentieth centuries. Denying its importance underscores important historical and historiographical possibilities for reinterpreting the politics of the past. This riot captures the changing conceptual as well as material tensions between economic logic and cultural difference under colonialism in the shadow of global capital. It also provides an opening to interrogate repetitious colonialist framings of discipline, reason, and progress from a variety of directions. In pursuit of these themes, this book investigates the history and politics of the emergence of the peasant and its implications for a new form of hierarchy in northwest colonial India and the globe. British officials regarded Panjab as a quintessential agrarian province inhabited by a uniquely diligent, prosperous, and "martial race" of cultivators. They understood the peasant to be "the predominant unit of society," insisting that the "most important consideration of all" was to implement policies designed to bring about agrarian improvement and uplift.[8] This discourse of what I term "colonial benevolence" was underpinned by an ostensibly moderate land revenue demand and protective legislation in favor of those deemed to be peasants coupled with the massive expansion of canal irrigation and extensive recruitment into the military. Such a claim can be found in other contexts too where select forms of patronage and infrastructure are still hauled out as ironclad signs of progress regardless of their authoritarian conceptualization, implementation, and deleterious long-term impact. At its center is the enduring notion that this peasantry experienced nearly a century of unparalleled prosperity. Rather than the immiserations, displacements, and insurgencies that mark other regions of British India, Panjab is seen in much of the popular and even scholarly literature as a bastion of loyalty enjoying an unrivaled period of stability and growth.

Yet the narrative of a benevolent colonialism championing a stalwart peasantry is belied when examined through the prism of how caste, labor, and capital transformed the equation of rural power. The claim that peasants remained largely unscathed if not deliberately empowered under British rule takes for granted both the category of "peasant" and the nature of agricultural production, as well the intent and operations of the colonial state. At a deeper level, it normalizes particular class and caste hierarchies by presupposing a continuity of social and economic relations from the pre- to the postcolonial. One indication of this process is the dominant interpretation of caste-based land ownership in contemporary east Panjab. According to the 2011 census, over 30 percent of the population are Dalits mainly of the Chamar and Mazhabi castes, the highest proportion in all of India. Despite mostly engaging in the labors of cultivation, however, they own less than 4 percent of the total cultivated area. Instead, the vast bulk of land is held by members of the Jatt caste, which accounts for around a third of the population.[9] A similar situation exists in the rest of pre-1947 Panjab, in Haryana, and to a lesser extent in Himachal Pradesh (India) and in west Panjab (Pakistan).[10] Such disparities are usually explained through the ahistorical alignment of identity with occupation: Jatts are peasants while Chamars and Mazhabis have been landless laborers since antiquity. The postcolonial distribution of economic and political power in the countryside is thus reinforced by colonial assumptions about the inherent and timeless qualities of rural Panjabis.

I challenge the givenness of this agrarian order and the surreptitious denial of its modern transformation by asking three interrelated questions: How did colonial racial, fiscal, and legal policies align the category of "peasant" with hereditary caste identity? What kinds of contestations over collective status, access to credit, and land ownership did this generate among different groups of Panjabis? And what did this mean for the ways that global capitalist processes became implicated in local forms of knowledge and power? In the following chapters, I defamiliarize the idea of the division of labor through an examination of the labors involved in creating and sustaining a series of ideological and material divisions: from the colonial separation of agricultural and non-agricultural tribes to the dissonance between Panjabi, Urdu, and English meanings for various aspects of cultivation, the antagonism between so-called upper- and lower-caste Panjabis, the actual division of crops between landholder and laborer, and the global conceptual split between peasant and proletarian. This book uncovers the tangled politics of how and why colonial officials and ascendant Panjabis together disrupted existing conceptions of identity and occupation to generate a new form of hierarchy in the countryside masked as traditional. The result was the creation of a modern group of hereditary landowning peasants alongside other groups engaged in cultivation yet relegated to the status of landless laborers.

Writing a history of the division of labor opens up possibilities for rethinking the conventions of at least three avenues of historical research. The first is that this book questions the very category of "peasant." Perhaps the most prominent and durable figure in modern history, peasants have long been a fount for a vast assortment of global arguments in virtually every discipline in the humanities and social sciences. All manner of colonialist, nationalist, socialist, developmentalist, and now environmentalist discourses have sought to analyze, condemn, extol, corral, and improve peasants at each position along the political spectrum. Dedicated publications such as *The Journal of Peasant Studies* and later the *Journal of Agrarian Change* rose in prominence in the 1970s due to the increasing importance of their object of inquiry.[11] After a brief intellectual interregnum, the peasant dramatically reappeared in the global public imagination in late 2020 with the massive farmer and laborer protests against a proposed set of neoliberal laws in India, leading to an outpouring of new thinking and writings.[12] Still, underlying much of this literature is the notion that the peasant simply exists everywhere, a general if not generic figure traced backward from the contested origins of modernity to the recesses of primordial times. Yet these two claims—ubiquity and antiquity—at the very least ought to provoke a pause. The obviousness of the peasant is precisely what demands reexamination in terms of what this category meant in different historical contexts, which groups came to occupy it, and how it shaped not only rural political economy but what we think we know about the past. It also means that contemporary calls for sympathy or solidarity relying on supposedly ancient pedigrees need to be critically assessed and, where appropriate, established on another basis altogether. The taken-for-granted status of the peasant is itself an element in its historical emergence.

This book also calls into question the centrality of the colonizer-colonized divide for histories of the colonial world. Such a stark, totalizing binary was in fact generated by the racial logic accompanying European conquests from the late fifteenth century onward that regarded societies in Africa, Asia, and America as inherently inferior. While anticolonial movements inverted this logic as part of their struggle to resist and expel foreign domination, generations of thinkers and writers drew on this inheritance to contest the justificatory discourses of colonialism by demonstrating the opposite, that colonized peoples were rational, accomplished, dynamic, civilized, and worthy of freedom. Indeed, postcolonial critique can be seen as an attempt to challenge the obvious as well as insidious arguments, values, and narratives that emerged through the prolonged colonial encounter.

Yet, as Frantz Fanon and Aimé Césaire trenchantly remind us, there have always been doubts about the presumed unity and coherence of those deemed "colonized." Not only did certain elite local actors ally with European powers, but others partially benefited in limited ways from colonial rule, while internal fissures over class, caste, religion, ethnicity, and language were fitfully subsumed (though never silenced) as part of most mainstream anticolonial nationalisms.[13] This book confronts the chimera of the colonized by foregrounding the competition and contradictions that developed within Panjabi society during the nineteenth and early twentieth centuries. It is therefore not another account of colonized *versus* colonizer, a repeated instance of heroic peasants fighting against the British Empire. Instead, I explore how colonialism generated a sustained, multifaceted, and unpredictable societal conflict from which certain groups identified as peasants emerged atop a new agrarian hierarchy to the exclusion and exploitation of others who were consigned to a fate of landless laboring. Racial unity might be every bit as hollow as racial inferiority.

Lastly, this book offers an alternative genealogy of the emergence and operations of global capital. If the transformative quality of the bourgeois mode of production is indisputable, the debate over its provenance, essential features, and trajectory has been equally inconclusive. Over a hundred years of intense political and scholarly writings have in various ways explored what actually constituted capitalism proper, how and where it began, and what it meant for people in different parts of the world.[14] Much of this revolved around competing interpretations of key texts from the oeuvre of Karl Marx alongside the supposedly exemplary experience of Western Europe.[15] Rather than attempt to settle this debate or dismiss it out of hand, I take inspiration from the diversity of perspectives and embrace the contingency it suggests as inherent to all forms of radical change. This requires drawing on Marx differently, not as an authoritative means to adjudicate the truth of capitalism, but as a historical figure offering profound and penetrating yet inescapably elliptical insights into the changing world he was able to witness. "Marx foresaw the foreseeable," remarked Antonio Gramsci, and not everything, everywhere, and for all time.[16] The burden of expectations—of capital to behave in universal ways and of Marx to provide universalist answers—is called into question by attending to the specificity of the transformation of Panjabi society under colonial rule. This book traces how the domains of economy and culture were in fact constituted and intertwined to generate a new, unusual, and variable form of capitalist accumulation and social hierarchy. Its point of departure is to engage in the temptation of comparison without smuggling in a modern version of the scale of civilizations. Far from a simple criticism, this book tries to think with as well as across and through Marx to make sense of a distinctive global context. That is why the events of Isa Khel cannot be understood as purely the result of financial distress, any more than they can be chalked up to religious strife.

Perhaps a final contribution of this book lies in the scope as well as approach toward historical sources. At first glance, much of what I rely on will appear familiar to historians of colonialism and agriculture: settlement reports, government circulars, famine commissions, census data, and legislative acts. I also make use of less common materials such as nineteenth-century dictionaries, statistical surveys, Christian missionary texts, local newspapers, and Panjabi proverbs. The old adage about interpretation—that two scholars can reach different conclusions from the same piece of evidence—should be conspicuous. My aim has been to critically engage this conventional archive by contrasting it with other kinds of sources and posing different kinds of questions. On the one hand, in the course of research I have uncovered certain untapped materials, from vernacular petitions for changing status and a contract between a landholder and laborer to intimate details about rural family consumption patterns. On the other hand, I draw on Sikh and Bhakti sacred verses as well as insights from a range of twentieth-century individuals such as Bhimrao Ambedkar, Mangoo Ram, Harnam Singh Ahluwalia, Muhammad Hayat Khan, and Kapur Singh. In this way, juridical rulings and quantified data are put alongside poetic supplications and personal recollections from archives in Chandigarh and New Delhi to London and beyond.

Near the end of the book, I analyze the writings of Marx along with Adam Smith, Vladimir Lenin, and Karl Kautsky as theory rather than history. A non-Europeanist engaging with ostensibly European thinkers is a deliberate gesture of refusing the boundaries of both discipline and geography, especially when those ideas have so profoundly shaped the material perception of regions such as South Asia. Indeed, their concepts have an import beyond mere accuracy; they circulate the globe through the very grammar of political economy. In this way, I confront the fundamental questions of access—Who reads whom, and writes about what?—in order to defy a hierarchy of knowledge that masquerades as neutral expertise. Monopoly has no place in historical inquiry. I therefore claim neither an entirely novel archive nor an entirely novel method. Rather, this book is an attempt to critically read across diverse genres to produce a narrative— empirically grounded and theoretically apt—that reinterprets major issues in modern Panjabi society in conversation with larger themes in global history. The tension between what constitutes the particular and the general remains abundantly indivisible.

EXPECTATIONS OF PEASANT DORMANCY AND DEATH

Until recently, the historical experience of peasants in Western Europe was widely held up as the model for the rest of the world. Its particular trajectory of dissolution and transformation inaugurated a compelling set of universal expectations. According to Eric Wolf, not only did peasants "stand midway between the primitive tribe and industrial society," but their importance was based on the conviction that "industrial society is built upon the ruins of peasant society."[17] Capitalism, in other words, was understood to both require the peasantry and bring about its end. Out of their detritus were to emerge an entirely new class of workers along with those who employed them, that is, the proletariat and the bourgeoisie. Explanations of this process have proceeded along two main lines. In the classic liberal formulation, innovations in science and technology, the erosion of religious orthodoxy, and the establishment of private property rights created a manufacturing economy that attracted rural peasants to work in urban localities. Classic Marxist accounts, on the other hand, describe how the simultaneous dislocation of the rural population, rise in commodity production, and concentration of political authority, combined with the global conquest of resources and markets, forced peasants to sell their labor-power for wages. For both interpretations, the ultimate future of the peasant was to leave the countryside—eventually, if fitfully—in order to become a worker in the city. The death of the peasantry was thus the precondition for the birth of capitalist modernity.

A crucial distinction between these two narratives was the valence given to this change as well as its horizon. For liberal interpretations, by and large, peasants becoming workers was a story of progress. The gradual, successive evolution from feudalism to capitalism, despite moments of regrettable violence, was considered either a pragmatic or inevitable triumph, producing in its wake a new relationship of free contract between workers and employers based on mutual need. The exchange of work for pay is seen as fair precisely because it is agreed upon by two rational individuals voluntarily making choices in their own best interests. It is this reciprocity, moreover, that for liberals rendered post-peasant society both largely harmonious and stable. As a result, capitalism appeared as the wholesome culmination of all that came before it.

Rather than inverting celebration into condemnation, Marxists usually offered a more intricate account of this history. While concurring with the progress involved in transforming the peasantry into the proletariat, they have also emphasized the necessary suffering, brutality, and "ruthless terrorism" required for that transformation.[18] Far from momentary, however, this specific violence was understood to reflect a general antagonism inherent to all class relations, one that becomes especially animated in periods of dramatic change. The employment contract is hardly a neutral exchange; instead, it presupposes and entrenches a deep inequality mediated by the forces of law, state, and market. Antagonism therefore continued beyond the disappearance of the peasant into a new struggle between the proletariat and the bourgeoisie. Post-peasant capitalism for Marxists was regarded as an ongoing and unfinished project. In these ways, responses to the peasant question lay at the center of competing understandings of the making of modern society.

What is significant about these two political and intellectual traditions has been for a long time their denial of the agency, activities, or even potential of peasants in the modern age. Along with articulating the dissolution of the peasant with the coming of capitalist modernity, both conventional liberals and Marxists established the notion of peasants playing little meaningful role in their own (inexorable) demise. It is as if the peasantry was absent at its own un-making.[19] Instead, change was understood to have initiated from elsewhere. To the liberal identification of a coalition of social forces with the bourgeoisie at the helm, the most crucial source of transformation was the nascent proletariat for Marxists. To whatever extent peasants may have participated in the two great European revolutionary upsurges, France 1789 and Russia 1917, the common notion is that the achievements of those struggles were due to the bourgeoisie and the worker. As a result of this intertwining of explanatory narrative with historical interpretation, a distinct image of the peasant emerged. For liberals and most Marxists alike, the peasant was a relic: an anachronism, dormant if not static, usually a force of conservatism and reaction, a flawed receptacle for outside ideology, and at best an unreliable and perhaps unworthy ally for producing a new society.[20] Despite differences over the emergence, content, and direction of modernity, both interpretations concurred on the assumed absence of peasants as subjects of history.

This unseemly consensus of peasant dormancy began to unravel in the post–World War II era of decolonization and cold war. In 1949, an overwhelmingly peasant army defeated both foreign and domestic opponents to take power in China; ten years later, another insurgency made up largely of peasants overthrew a dictatorship in Cuba. Throughout the following decades, peasant guerillas engaged in asymmetrical wars across what was then called the Third World, from Vietnam to Angola and Algeria. In India, a peasant movement initially demanding land redistribution in the area around the West Bengal village of Naxalbari escalated into an armed uprising against the state in 1967.[21] That conflict exposed the pitfalls of nationalism by laying bare the violent inequities of postcolonial society, inspiring later generations toward a form of political militancy that continues to this day. It also spurred the Indian government to redouble efforts to implement modernization programs designed by foreign institutions such as the World Bank and the Ford Foundation to lessen absolute rural poverty by increasing agricultural output.

Yet an important element common to all of these conflicts is that they were not simply gestures of peasant resistance—defensive efforts to prevent change or preserve a preexisting order—but acts of revolution, that is, positive, creative attempts to transform society.[22] These peasants were not waiting to become workers in order to assume their assigned role in a world-historical transition. Peasants *qua* peasants could observe and comprehend their situation, organize into effective military units, and use advanced weaponry and tactics to fight and occasionally defeat forces thought to be vastly superior. By disrupting the notion of peasant inertness in such decisively modern ways, these tangible political successes challenged the exclusivity of the French and Russian revolutions as paradigms of radical change and arbitrators of human progress. Liberals and especially Marxists were forced to take heed. No longer an anachronism, the peasantry could not be denied a place in the making of its own history and future.

THE DISCOVERY OF PEASANT AGENCY IN INDIA

If peasant political power was seen to emerge from the barrel of a gun, a large measure of the scholarly reexamination of peasant agency and politics was compelled by the echo of the shots. Investigations of the peasant question in India have occurred along different disciplinary paths. Economists and sociologists in the late 1960s entered into an intensive, wide-reaching debate about the classification of the peasantry, their mode of production, and the nature of agrarian capitalism. It is not without significance that this scholarship began with the Panjabi peasant. In response to the celebratory tone taken by some commentators toward the "Green Revolution"—the introduction of high-yield seed varieties, chemical fertilizers and pesticides, submersible water pumps and rapid mechanization, which dramatically increased crop output, particularly wheat and rice[23]—Ashok Rudra and his colleagues used evidence from a small study of peasants in Panjab to argue against the notion that a new class of dynamic capitalist farmers had appeared. Rather famously, they rejected the optimistic forecasts of social peace through agrarian prosperity in favor of anticipating an explicitly "Red" revolution.[24]

On the other hand, sharply critiquing their methodology as well as politics, Utsa Patnaik deployed a different criterion to measure capitalist development across several Indian states to insist on the opposite, that capitalist farmers were indeed emerging, albeit unevenly and in a historically evolutionary manner.[25] From this initial exchange, a series of responses and interventions drew in over a dozen prominent participants over the next two decades.[26] At the same time, this particular debate partially overlapped and became implicated in a much larger discussion over the precise mechanism that constituted the genesis of worldwide capitalism.[27] While the discussion about the Indian peasantry dried up somewhat inconclusively by the late 1980s, its fervor succeeded in demonstrating the importance of the peasant as a contemporary object of inquiry, one requiring distinct forms of empirical analyses, theoretical frameworks, and political narratives.

The discovery of peasant agency had an equally profound, though more gradual and enduring, impact on the discipline of history. In 1976, Eric Stokes began an important synopsis of the prevailing interpretations of colonialism in South Asia with a comment on the limits of accessing the historical peasant. He explained that the peasant archive was overwhelmingly impersonal and statistical, produced by white- or even brown-skinned desk-bound officials "entangled in a fearsome thicket of technicality." This rendered the peasant "unreachable through the intimacy of shared experience and its accompanying intuitive understanding," estranging generations of historians. Historiography, he went on, neglected to address the consciousness, experiences, and activities of peasants from within their own habitus.

Stokes critiqued the dominant scholarship by dividing historians into "neo-Machiavellians" and "neo-Marxists." Whereas the former defined British rule as a "maximum economy of effort," relying on native collaborators and in continuity with previous rulers, the latter emphasized the parasitic, extractive quality of colonial capitalism, having "struck a local bargain with feudalism" that also left Indian society largely unchanged.[28] The problem was that for both strands, "the peasantry remained an inert mass."[29] Stokes then pointed out how these positions were increasingly untenable in light of several new studies that explored different forms of peasant dynamism from the latter half of the nineteenth century. Yet although he heralded this emerging scholarship as the "return of the peasant to South Asian history," Stokes reiterated the limitations of the discipline as a whole, concluding that "the historian must content himself with the role of the humble camp follower to the sociologist and economist."[30]

A few years later, Ranajit Guha and the Subaltern Studies Collective not only furthered the critique of historiographical elitism but also proposed a dramatically new orientation toward the study of Indian history. Beginning with a reevaluation of the mass mobilizations against British rule, they argued for the importance of understanding domains of popular life neither reducible to the machinations of select personalities nor perceptible through the conventions of historical research. Appreciating the politics of the subaltern—groups denied access to power due to occupying a position of structural yet relational subordination—required a different conception of the category "political." This meant challenging the centrality of the colonial state, and most particularly its archive which rendered peasant rebellions a problem of lawlessness, by implicating historical difference within narratives of nation, community, and capital.[31] This is why histories of subalternity could not simply follow existing modes of radical scholarship in Europe, because the directions in which they led were constituted by the very marginalization and obfuscation of the subaltern. Nor was the state in the colony and its ancillary institutions identical to that in the metropolis. In other words, the venerable "history from below" approach remained the same history, only seen from a different vantage.[32] For Subaltern Studies, the colonial peasant at once fully inhabited modernity as a conscious political subject yet imagined and conducted politics in a profoundly different way. Perhaps most incisively, Guha noted that the domain of the subaltern "can be sensed by intuition and proved by demonstration," signaling an affective quality to the study of history by forcefully connecting the politics of the historian with the production of historical narratives.[33]

By insisting on the need to recognize the peasant "as a subject of history in his own right," Guha and Subaltern Studies opened up new avenues in the study of peasant history and wider questions of popular beliefs, labor relations, and knowledge practices under colonial rule.[34] They produced studies exploring the aspirations and activities of peasants in the contexts of nationalist mobilization to economic disruption and changing epistemologies.[35] At the same time, other historians also concerned with agrarian history linked regional dynamics with capitalist processes over the long *durée* to situate the Indian peasant within the broader world economy.[36] Together this body of scholarship overturned almost all of the previous assumptions about peasants serving as victims of irrational, unchanging, and naturalistic tendencies, receptacles of external ideology incapable of becoming political agents. The peasant became recognized as a crucial, distinct figure central to the making of anticolonial nationalism as much as modern capitalism. Later works have taken this critique in different directions, foregrounding how peasants conceived of their own identities or the ways peasants negotiated the unevenness of colonial capitalism or the need to broaden the definition of who is included in peasant castes.[37] More recently, scholars such as Rupa Viswanath, Tariq Ali, and Mubbashir Rizvi have provocatively reimagined the politics of rural life in different regions of the subcontinent through unfree caste regimes to the circulation of global commodities and ongoing struggles for land rights. Once peasants were acknowledged as agents rather than anachronisms, historians and anthropologists over the past four decades became pioneers instead of followers in their study.

THE INSCRUTABILITY OF PEASANT DOMINANCE IN PANJAB

Peasant domination in Panjab has been so self-evident that it warranted little sustained scholarly investigation in the years following partition and independence. Aside from the post-1960s debates over the content and potential of the Green Revolution, this peasantry has been obliquely assumed rather than directly studied. The overriding assumption of a benevolent administration, and the apparent absence of mass poverty or insurrection, largely directed scholars toward analyzing peasants through the prism of the colonial state. In 1966, Norman Barrier published a study of the legislative efforts to address the problem of peasant indebtedness in the late nineteenth and early twentieth centuries. Although he noted the state acted largely in self-interest to preserve order, he suggested "official concern" for the "alienation of land by the agriculturalist" also sprang "from a paternal attitude toward the illiterate peasantry, a feeling that the government had a responsibility to defend the rights of the poor and downtrodden."[38] While the extent to which certain laws succeeded in alleviating debt remained an open question, the proposition of the largely beneficial relationship between peasants and the British became unquestioned. Several scholars continued in this line of inquiry, examining the mindset of key officials and the conflicting priorities and actions of the administration as it consolidated and sustained its rule.[39] Despite their statist framings, these works contributed to establishing the specificity of colonialism and its claims in Panjab from the rest of colonial India.

This early historiographical emphasis on state policy led to further studies on other distinctive aspects of colonial governance that were at least indirectly related to peasants. The first is the role of canal irrigation in the making of what Imran Ali termed "a hydraulic society." Beginning in the 1880s, the administration used local labor and public funds to build hundreds of miles of canals to supply water to the drier southwestern portion of the region. This increased the area of cultivation—and therefore of taxation—from three million to over fourteen million acres, "the greatest expansion in agricultural production in any part of South Asia under the British."[40] Economic growth, however, did not correspond to social progress. For Ali, colonial developmental ambitions were thwarted by entrenched local traditions that resulted in a persistent form of feudalism rather than capitalist dynamism. In other words, the full potential of agrarian change was introduced but then inhibited by a "benevolent despotism." Thus, the main contradiction for Ali and other scholars revolved around how state-led irrigation schemes both generated rapid prosperity and maintained traditional backwardness for peasants.[41]

The second aspect of the distinctiveness of the Panjab administration focused on the politics of recruitment into the British Indian army. Assistance given by collaborating local rulers to suppress the 1857–58 revolt transformed British apprehension toward Panjabis from earlier wars (1845–46 and 1848–49) into a concerted policy of cooptation and conscription. The creation of new "military labour markets" targeted the supposedly innate martial prowess of primarily Sikhs, Pathans, Rajputs, and caste Jatts of all religions to serve as soldiers for internal patrolling, defending the frontier and imposing British rule throughout the world.[42] Not coincidentally, many of these groups were also considered naturally endowed to be peasants, so that the qualities of soldiery became conflated with husbandry. Indeed, after twenty-five years of service, ex-soldiers were given grants of land in the newly established canal colonies as part of their pensions. The peasant thereby remains unquestioned in statist studies of infrastructural development and military recruitment.

In recent years, scholarship has focused more directly on the changing texture of rural Panjab under British rule. Neeladri Bhattacharya's valuable study examines the contradictions within colonial authority and the fate of pastoral and nomadic groups amid the rise of settled agriculture. The "great agrarian conquest" was an imperial project of conceiving "a new regime of categories" alongside their haphazard, conflicting deployment in the countryside.[43] In this way, his approach is similar to Richard Saumarez Smith's district-level study of colonial recordkeeping practices and Tom Kessinger's century-long tracing of land tenures in a single village.[44] Despite a wealth of details, Bhattacharya does not question the actual composition of the peasant, nor does he substantively address the shifting politics of caste or religion, or for that matter much of vernacular Panjabi culture. His object of inquiry is the intricate workings of colonial state power—tellingly, the book opens and closes with the musings of two different officers at the beginning and end of a hundred years of British rule. As a result, the peasant is still an already-constituted figure located at the center of cultivation in these histories of modern Panjab.

In contrast to studies giving primacy to the colonial state, the field of social history has been particularly significant in investigating areas of popular beliefs and practices in Panjab. To a degree this is due to the presence of three as opposed to two major religious traditions. Sikhi not only altered the binary narrative of Hindu-Muslim relations, but the rise of Sikh power and the kingdom of Maharaja Ranjit Singh immediately prior to British rule also garnered attention as a potent political force. In fact, the undue academic emphasis on colonial manipulation is partly what prompted scholars such as Harjot Oberoi to reevaluate indigenous agency in reforming and consolidating religious identities, though not without generating important critiques.[45] This extended into studies of other aspects of social change, from rural patriarchy to gender relations and language politics.[46] Yet in these works too the peasantry is largely taken for granted. Rather than constituting an object of inquiry, the peasant appears as the implicit, unchanging subject of a region declared to be fundamentally agrarian—the societal rock upon which other social changes occurred. While there have been efforts to explore the making of the agricultural economy,[47] social histories of Panjab effectively accepted the equation of self-evident and longstanding peasant castes dominating agricultural production. As a result, while scholarship on popular life moved away from statist concerns, it still ceded the domain of material relations to fixed colonialist assumptions rather than a site of contestation among different social, political, and epistemological forces.

THE LABORS OF DIVISION

This book interrupts the obvious yet unexamined history of the peasant by tracing its emergence, contradictions, and implications in the making of a new agrarian hierarchy in colonial Panjab. The nature of my intervention is perhaps captured by revising a claim made by Dipesh Chakrabarty on the difference between modern India and Western Europe. "What distinguishes the story of political modernity in India from the usual and comparable narratives of the West," he writes, "was the fact that modern politics was not founded on an assumed death of the peasant."[48] It is my argument that Panjabi modernity and many similar regions of the Global South were in fact founded on the *birth* of peasants as we now know them. By attending to struggles within rural society as well as between colonizer and colonized, I move beyond the commonsense notion that Panjab was merely "the showcase of Indian colonial development."[49] And I demonstrate how the peasant as the product of a recent alignment of caste with occupation introduced novel forms of exclusion and exploitation for those deemed inherently landless and forever laboring. In this way, I trouble the narrative of a self-evident, exclusive group of precolonial peasants simply enduring through the nineteenth and twentieth centuries to arrive not only intact but also entitled to their position of relative dominance in the present.

Building on the scholarship of Ritu Birla, Vinay Gidwani, and Andrew Sartori, among others, this book explores wider questions of how the operation of colonial knowledge and vernacular politics transformed society amid the tumult of a new market economy. Historicizing the landed peasant and the landless laborer denaturalizes their usual location within the story of global capital. As a figure emerging from a collision between caste and class forces under British rule, the Panjabi peasant is shown to be anything but a relic of the past—and thus an indication of the persistence of semi-feudal relations or a lack of sufficient capitalism. Rather, it is a political and economic subject born of the historical differences drawn through the fractious career of capitalism in this colony. Instead of producing an assumed uniformity across the world, capital in the nineteenth century made use of local forms of power such as caste, tribe, and religion to reproduce societies in altogether dissimilar ways. Diversity and indeed uncertainty are inherent to the rule of capital. This unpredictability is therefore central to explicating the specificity of how the Panjabi peasantry could depart from the trajectory of its fictitious counterpart in Europe without resorting to the stagism of linear progress.

Historians of capitalism in the colonial world continue to confront a bountiful double burden of thinking difference with congruence. The lessons of the emergence of the peasant in Panjab for global history thus require interrogating this very oppositional pairing. It is not simply a matter of scale, of resisting the diminutive positioning of an interesting local history within a predefined global canvas. Nor do I demand that all grand frameworks basically become more reflective by including varied experiences from across the world. While both are worthwhile endeavors, the act of turning away or seeking entry still presupposes a universal division of historiographical importance, such that Panjab must speak amid "India" and through "Asia" at "Europe" or now "America" in order to garner global attention. A reason for this disparity is the elemental vocabulary used to describe changing historical phenomena—hence the need to put pressure on the concept of "the peasant" as well as "the laborer" and even "capitalism." As a result, it is productive to trace how the actual categories of political economy were in fact formed out of contingent circumstances that nevertheless acquired the explanatory force to describe vast swaths of human society. Beyond the confines of a case study, rethinking the peasant in Panjab is a way to question what is assumed to be known of peasantries in not only England or France but Brazil, Egypt, and China, as well as the capitalist logics that appear to bind these diverse places and pasts together.

In the chapters that follow, I offer a history of the making of peasant caste identity and the politics of agrarian labor under colonial capitalism.

Chapter 1 begins by examining the politics of the East India Company's conquest and early administration of Panjab in the mid-nineteenth century. I focus on how the claim of a benevolent regime extracting "moderate" revenue generated a set of material practices that disrupted and reordered the relationship between caste identity, labor activity, and land ownership. This created a form of accumulation that was modern and capitalist yet strikingly different from the standard narrative in Europe. In Chapter 2, I chart the contradictions between the multitude of evolving vernacular terms for peasant and agricultural production amid attempts by the colonial state to assign precise cultivation practices to specific castes. This poses as well as historicizes the elusive question "Who is a peasant?" and its far-reaching answers. I show how the juridical categories of agricultural and non-agricultural tribes subsumed a fluid constellation of Panjabi and Urdu terms such as *kisan*, *kashtkar*, and *hali* to produce a singular landholding peasant against various groups now categorized as landless laborers. Chapter 3 examines the contradictory evolution of the crisis of rural debt and its various remedies. I demonstrate how the problem of indebtedness, supposedly based on notions of cultural irrationality and extravagance, shifted from excessive spending to land fragmentation to the specific alienation of peasant land. A market structured by colonial legislation empowered a new class within the castes of agricultural tribes to monopolize access to land and thereby dominate the countryside. In Chapter 4, I analyze modes of lower-caste assertion through a new agrarian division of labor. From Sikhi to the Bhakti movement, and Ad Dharm to Ambedkar-led struggles, there is a long history of subordinate groups claiming equality and dignity by converting out of Hinduism. At the same time, I contrast the religious quality of untouchability with its economic imperatives in order to show how the degrading and exploitative conditions of Dalits continued across identity reformation. Chapter 5 concludes with a broader intellectual history of how the category of "peasant" came to be associated with notions of inadequacy and an expectation of transition alongside the rise of the proletariat at the very center of the discipline of political economy. By tracing the debate between Lenin and Kautsky back to Smith and his immanent critique by Marx, I situate the valorization of manufacturing within depictions of agriculture as both an antecedent and inferior civilizational condition. The ideological and material agenda of colonialism in South Asia is thus inextricable from a global inheritance of comparison.

This book ultimately seeks to give a historical account of certain social and economic hierarchies that are presented as natural and timeless, and therefore permanent. I aim to ascribe political contestation and contingency in the making of the hereditary caste peasant atop a new agrarian order in the midst of globalizing capital. Events such as the violence in Isa Khel might thereby transcend colonial dismissal to generate deeper questions about discordant societal transformations as well as the categories through which their meanings are made and unmade. On the one hand, for Panjabi history, the peasant question is a matter of explicating the novelty of hierarchy rather than the falsity of anachronism, in order to reveal its impermanence and therefore possibilities for alternative emancipatory futures. On the other hand, the emergence of the peasant in a global perspective signals the need to re-politicize political economy itself, to implicate knowledge production and cultural difference within the shifting dynamics of capitalist change. Indeed, in an oblique way, the exquisite words of Baba Farid at the start of this introduction provide an orientation into the aporia between actions and aspirations. Nor should we forget that kikar and wool have their uses too. May this effort then bear eventual fruit.

ONE

A RULE OF BENEVOLENCE?
Revenue, Knowledge, and the Accumulation of Difference

NEARLY EVERY CONQUEST OF territory in South Asia by the East India Company was underpinned by a claim of benevolence toward those conquered. Between the victory at Buxar in 1764 and the formal annexation of Awadh in 1856, officials imagined themselves as "benevolent despots," declaring that the expansion of their empire was designed to bring stability, justice, and prosperity to the local population.[1] Central among the aspects of this purportedly progressive rule—resolving political chaos, instituting fiscal responsibility, establishing the rule of law, ending abhorrent cultural practices, securing new frontiers—was the rational determination and collection of the government's share of produce from the agricultural activity of peasants. Land revenue was at once a reason for colonialism and the means to finance it. It constituted an elementary yet restive bond between sovereign and subject, one that remains crucial to all modern societies to this day.

Perhaps the clearest instance of benevolent revenue collection was during the encounter, conquest, and early administration of Panjab, the last major independent polity east of the Indus River. A report from its first chief commissioner, John Lawrence, in 1854 succinctly articulates this claim:

> When it is remembered that this tax furnishes three-fourths of the State resources, and that it is paid by agriculturalists comprising three-fourths of the population, that their contentment and happiness is more vitally affected by the manner in which this tax is levied and administered than by any other circumstance whatever, the extreme importance of the subject is manifest.[2]

Unlike other regions such as Bengal or Madras, which had large and complicated disparities between landlords of different types as well as several layers of tenants, the Panjabi peasant appeared exceptional to colonial officials for being a simple cultivating proprietor.[3] Since this group was assumed to both hold and till the bulk of cultivatable land, devising a revenue policy in its interest was regarded as a genuine effort to bring the benefits of enlightened economic order to an otherwise hapless population.

Such a claim of benevolence might simply be dismissed as a thin veneer to legitimize British rule, regardless of whether its officials were dishonest or delusional. All imperial ventures would doubtless use similar kinds of self-justification. Yet what is remarkable about this claim is how it retains the potency to shape broader understandings of agrarian change, state formation, and the emergence of capitalism in South Asia and beyond. An implicit consensus has developed among scholars of the supposed failure of capital under colonial direction to properly transform Panjab. The early generation of post-independence historians persisted in describing the "Panjab school" of administration in largely benign terms, as a uniquely personalized and flexible system of governance that "made revenue and property settlements favoring the peasant cultivator."[4] This ossified "archaic" property relations as well as sustained the "feudal" beliefs, practices, and hierarchies of the rural population.[5] Or, in a newer iteration, a "masculine paternalism" that was nevertheless reliant on "contact and empathy" along with "moderation and protection" marked the difference of British rule in Panjab.[6] Another line of research actually commends the efforts of the colonial state to increase agricultural output through canal irrigation, while seeming to regret its inability or unwillingness to "provide a determined developmental stimulus," thus keeping "agriculture in a stagnant and backward state."[7] Even more critical works nonetheless only fault the British for bringing about "a half-baked, deleterious version of capitalism" that was "ambivalent and hobbled" and unfortunately "hamstrung" by political expediency.[8] By consolidation, stagnation, or distortion, a sense of an incomplete transformation pervades the historiography of colonial Panjab.

At the center of these arguments is the disquieting notion that colonialism somehow betrayed its own world-historical mandate. Since this peasantry was neither rapaciously exploited nor actively displaced from the countryside, it seems that capitalism in this part of the world went awry. Rather unwittingly, this sort of formulation reproduces the argument made by certain Brazilian economists in the 1960s, who, interpreting widespread poverty and inefficiency in their society as a consequence of the incomplete penetration of capital, ended up calling for *more* capitalism.[9] Such a perception draws on arguably the most paradigmatic account of the encounter between peasants and the modern state, the last few chapters of Volume 1 of Karl Marx's *Capital*. Focusing on the sixteenth century onwards in England, he describes how the rural population was systematically subordinated, dispossessed, and then evicted from their villages to eventually end up in cities as impoverished workers. Marx terms this process "primitive accumulation," a phrase that has come to encapsulate the necessary material and ideological shifts that created the conditions for the emergence of capitalism proper. A dramatic series of prerequisite changes laid the foundation for modern class relations, market exchange, and industrial production.[10] Indeed, according to Eugen Weber's influential study, rural peasants became not only French citizens but also urban proletarians in the nineteenth century owing to capitalism's operating amid and through the institutions of the state.[11] Thus, even without adherence to a Marxist methodology, the notion of an incipient, innovatory accumulation is generally regarded as a key element in the origins of global capitalism.

As a result, regions such as Panjab not undergoing this form of transformation invariably appear partial, their capitalism modified by such prefixes as "semi-," "proto-," "quasi-," or even "pre-." Despite notable exceptions, the longstanding debate over what constitutes the essential features of capitalist transition continues to animate scholarship to this day.[12] Yet the search for such a specific transition presupposes a lack of sufficient change, and often equates the non-appearance of certain bourgeois relations with the continuity of the archaic and feudal.[13] As scholars of Atlantic slavery have long shown, however, the absence of a factory-based proletariat does not automatically mean a lack of capitalism, even as the terms for plantation labor remain disputed.[14] The deeper problem with such a position is that it ignores how the operation of colonial rule, irrespective of any assumed intent or outcome, radically disrupted and reordered rural

Panjabi social and economic relations without replicating the dynamics of industrial society in the metropole.[15] In other words, this manifestation of capitalism was at once modern and divergent, a departure from the past but unlike the trajectory of Europe, a distinction replete with far-reaching differences.

The configuration of agriculture and the primacy of the peasant in Panjab up to 1947 and beyond is inexplicable as a simple continuation. Rather, I suggest it is an indication of the emergence of an altogether distinct phenomenon, one requiring its own historical analysis and theoretical location. In this chapter, I excavate the wayward logic of colonial benevolence through the politics of revenue, knowledge, and culture to offer an alternative history of agrarian capitalism. Here I analyze qualitative and quantitative data from various settlement, revenue, and administrative reports alongside the standard account of accumulation in Europe. The chapter begins with the high politics of conquest, the tangled history of how Company officers first encountered the territory and peoples of Panjab and the conflicts that led to annexation in 1849. I then explore both the internal culture of administration and the political and geographical specificities of the region that produced a form of rule that ostensibly tilted in favor of the peasant. The resolve to govern Panjab differently was an attempt to control and correct perceived cultural inadequacies through economic discipline. Next, I examine how this process generated a set of natural and human contingencies that transformed the very meaning of the category of peasant. While at first glance the results of this policy appear to substantiate the claim of a modest revenue demand with generous collections and reductions, a closer examination of its inner workings reveals a much more elaborate, invasive, and disruptive process. In order to underline the importance of this change, I then contrast the archive of settlement work with Marx's narrative of so-called primitive accumulation, to uncover the conditions as well as limitations of its universality. Together this demonstrates a history of capital in the colony that traverses the given metrics of deferral or diversion, or failure. Instead, I show how the domains of economy and culture were not only co-constituted but interwoven to produce a unique form of capital accumulation that inaugurated a radically different trajectory for the peasant in Panjab.

THE HIGH POLITICS OF CONQUEST

The Company's protracted advance westward across the subcontinent is well known in its broad if elitist contours. When its army captured Delhi on the banks of the Yamuna River in 1803, there was already considerable interest in what lay beyond.[16] The kingdom of Panjab, known as the "Sarkar-i-Khalsa," encompassed a vast, prosperous domain forcibly united after decades of internal and external warfare by Maharaja Ranjit Singh of the Sukarchakia clan in 1799. From the capital city of Lahore, its boundaries eventually extended north to Srinagar and the Kashmir Valley, west of the Indus River to Peshawar and the Khyber Pass, south beyond Multan to the Cholistan Desert approaching Sindh, and east up to the Sutlej River, as well as across to a few smaller possessions. While most of the earlier principalities within this territory were defeated and governed directly by Lahore, several maintained their status by accepting incorporation as tribute-paying vassals. Smaller Panjabi kingdoms between the Sutlej and Yamuna rivers, however, hedged their bets on the antagonism between the two rival powers. Fearing annexation by Ranjit Singh, the rulers of Patiala, Nabha, Jind, and Faridkot, among others, ceased payment of tribute and sought protective alliances with the newly arrived British.

Despite growing tensions between Ranjit Singh and the Company, both sides avoided open conflict to negotiate the Treaty of Amritsar in 1809. The former agreed to not "commit or suffer any encroachments on the possession or rights of the Chiefs in [the] vicinity" south of the Sutlej, which became known as the Native States, while the latter declared "no concern with the territories and subjects of the Rajah to the northward of the River Sutlej."[17] With this river as a border, Ranjit Singh focused on military campaigns to expand his kingdom to the north and west, while the Company consolidated its position with the Native States to the east and south.

This uneasy arrangement lasted until Ranjit Singh's death in 1839. A series of dynastic upheavals thereafter created fissures between members of the royal family, ministers of the court, and generals of various military branches. For six years, the British not only observed but actively instigated discord by cultivating relations with aspiring individuals and strengthening their forces near the border. Such machinations,

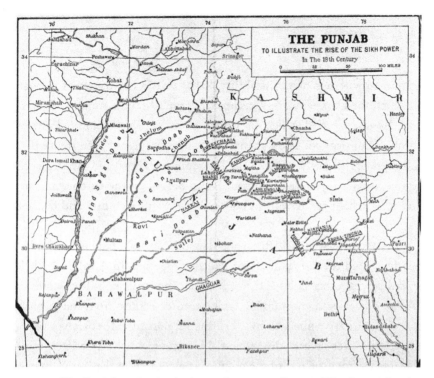

MAP 1.1 The Panjab region in the late 18th century. Source: Khushwant Singh, *The Sikhs* (London: George Allen and Unwin, 1953). Digital file from the Panjab Digital Library.

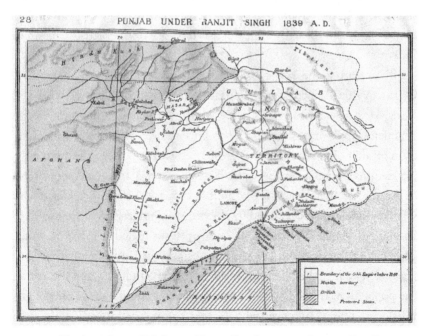

MAP 1.2 The kingdom of Maharaja Ranjit Singh, c. 1839. Source: Sita Ram Kohli and Hari Ram Gupta, *Students' Historical Atlas of India* (Allahabad: The Indian Press, 1945). Digital file from the Panjab Digital Library.

combined with a general instability, led to war in the winter of 1845–46 in which the Company army, composed largely of units from the Bengal and Bombay presidencies, prevailed over Panjab's disjointed forces through political collusion as much as military might.[18] The treaty that followed significantly reduced the kingdom's territory and army, placed Ranjit Singh's seven-year-old son, Dalip Singh, on the throne, and installed a British resident in Lahore to collect an indemnity and oversee its affairs.[19]

Yet less than two years later, a popular uprising broke out in Multan that nearly evicted the Company from Panjab altogether. In April 1848 rebels seized several other cities and much of the countryside, killing scores of British officers and encouraging widespread defections from the recently subdued military while also coordinating support from the Afghan rulers of Kabul. After defeats throughout the summer and early winter, reinforcements from the rest of the empire, as well as from the Native States, led the Company to a decisive victory near the city of Gujrat in February 1849.[20] The next month, on March 29, 1849, Governor-General James Broun-Ramsay, the Marquess of Dalhousie, issued a short proclamation stating that "the kingdom of the Punjab is at an end," deposing and exiling Dalip Singh and formally annexing his territory to the British Empire in India.[21]

By defeating the last substantial independent polity in the region, Company rule reached its spatial limits. "No longer conquering," remarked Karl Marx several years later, the Company after 1849 "had become *the* conqueror."[22] Priority now shifted to governance, which meant incorporating Ranjit Singh's kingdom with territories east of the Sutlej but retaining nominal independence for the Native States. A three-member Board of Administration, consisting of John Lawrence, his brother Henry and Charles Mansel (later replaced by Robert Montgomery), was appointed to consolidate the new province.[23] The main tasks included initiating comprehensive land revenue assessments, establishing an effective bureaucracy, disbanding the remnants of the kingdom's military, and disarming the population. In 1853, this structure was replaced by a single chief commissioner, John Lawrence, who carried the policy forward under two

MAP 1.3 The districts of British Panjab, c. 1907. Source: James Douie, *The Panjab, North-West Frontier Province and Kashmir* (Cambridge: Cambridge University Press, 1916), 223.

departments, Judicial and Financial, reflecting the priorities of the new sovereign.

Crisis returned, however, in the North West Provinces (NWP) when a revolt in the city of Meerut in May 1857 by local soldiers against their British officers spread across north India, channeling widespread resentment into a popular insurrection.[24] Yet there was wariness in much of Panjab about supporting a rebellion by the very men who had not only helped end the Sikh kingdom but were actively seeking to restore the Mughal Empire. Such a fissure in fact fractures any notion of a shared political imagination among inhabitants of South Asia for what became India. While a separate uprising occurred in the Ferozepur, Jhelum, and Sialkot garrisons, the British also received crucial military and logistical support from the Native States—their allies since 1809—that helped quell the rebellion by mid-1858. Shortly afterward, when the British Crown revoked the Company's charter to assume direct control of India, they also reappointed Lawrence as the first lieutenant-governor of Panjab in 1859. It was under his administration that the claim of benevolence became the key organizing principle of the new colonial state.

A FIT OF UNWILLINGNESS

In order to understand the intricacies of British rule in Panjab, it is important to reexamine the elements that informed the conquest itself. The late 1840s witnessed the culmination of competing arguments over what became known as the "Panjab question": the problem of what to do with the northwestern flank of the growing empire. Debates ranged over many issues: whether to keep a defensible border on the Yamuna, Sutlej, or Indus rivers; if treaties with local rulers were to be honored or overridden; and the very purpose of the Company's expansion in the subcontinent. The clearest indication of official reasoning for annexation is found in the 1849 public proclamation by Dalhousie. As with other regions of the empire, it deploys a tone of incredulity that renders Panjabis responsible for their own conquest. The proclamation begins with praise for the wisdom of (the safely deceased) Ranjit Singh, fondly invoking how "peace and friendship prevailed between the British nation and the Sikhs." This amity ended in 1845, however, when the kingdom's army attacked the British "without provocation and without cause." It is with this foundational, inexplicable betrayal that the colonial history of conquest commences.

Despite defeating the rebels, the proclamation continues, the British "generously spared the kingdom which [they] had acquired a just right to subvert" and instead signed a treaty allowing Dalip Singh his throne. The resumed good relations might have endured had treachery not occurred once more in 1848. The "seeming ingratitude of the native in revolt," argues Karuna Mantena, "provoked a deep sense of disappointment and hostility, a hostility that worked to harden racial attitudes toward non-European peoples."[25] Indeed, Dalhousie emphasized that although the British "faithfully kept their word" and "scrupulously observed every obligation," the chiefs of the kingdom "grossly and faithlessly violated the promises by which they were bound." Not only did they fail to pay the indemnity, they also "waged a fierce and bloody war" in which Company officers were captured and killed. Along with duplicity, the proclamation admonishes the savage and warlike proclivities of its people. "The whole of the Sikh people" took up arms in 1848, stated Dalhousie, blindly following their leaders down the path of disaster. In fact, Panjabis were implacable: "No punishment can deter [the Panjabis] from violence," just as "no acts of friendship can conciliate [them] to peace."[26] After twice triumphing over such deceit and barbarism, a return to the previous precarious state of affairs was simply impossible.[27]

As a product of necessity rather than design, annexation appears to have occurred unwillingly. Dalhousie insisted on the longstanding disinterest of the Company in expansion: it "desired no further conquest" and still "has no desire for conquest now." Only the trauma of the recent war compelled a change in policy. The sole means to preclude "the perpetual recurrence of unprovoked and wasting wars," Dalhousie explained, was through "the entire subjugation of a people," whom "their own government has long been unable to control."[28] British rule would therefore serve as a principled form of corrective governance. On the one hand, the new regime would abide by a certain sense of fairness: Dalip Singh would be given a pension in exile and loyal chiefs would be rewarded while the lands of those who rebelled would be confiscated, and the people would be free to practice their religions as long as they surrendered their weapons. If they "submit themselves peaceably to the authority of the British government," they could expect to be ruled with "mildness and beneficence." Yet on the other hand, Dalhousie was equally explicit in describing the force that ensured compliance with such commands. The final clause of the proclamation is unambiguous:

> But, if resistance to constituted authority shall again be attempted; if violence and turbulence shall be renewed; the Governor-General warns the people of the Punjab, that the time for leniency will then have passed away, and that their offence will be punished with prompt and most rigorous severity.[29]

According to the highest official in the country, British rule was an absolutist responsibility assumed with great reluctance in response to the perfidious erosion of cordial relations.

In a more personal medium, Dalhousie elaborated the implications of acquiring Panjab for the empire. Nine days after the official proclamation, he sent a long letter detailing his decision to a secret committee in London. After an extended (and exaggerated) account of the recent campaign, he reiterated the untrustworthiness of Sikhs. A list of names of those who had surrendered reproduced almost all the names of the notables who earlier signed treaties of peace. Even more outrageous, "no one ever thought to see the day when Sikhs would court the alliance of Affghans [sic],"[30] distressing for not only imperial equations but also the credibility of reports that depicted the two groups as unrelenting enemies. In such a dangerous situation, the future of Panjab was no longer a question of "what is desirable, or convenient, or even expedient" but was instead a matter of "national safety" and "self-defence."[31] Indeed, Dalhousie emphasized that "a strong and friendly Hindoo Government" would be "the best arrangement that could be effected for British India"—but that the "materials for it do not exist."[32] Keeping Dalip Singh on the throne would leave the British as vulnerable as before while providing continuous inspiration to those seeking their overthrow. Annexation was therefore an unwelcome but necessary strategic decision. A civilizing burden implicated in the burden of self-preservation, conquest was depicted as an imposition on the British as much as it was on Panjab.

CALCULATING OPPORTUNITY

Yet prior to the annexation proclamation, a very different set of arguments for conquering Panjab were circulating within official circles. Before the most recent outbreak of hostilities, administrators in Calcutta and London had displayed considerable interest in its territories and subjects. A trail of writings followed the British entry from the environs of Delhi in 1803, to the cis-Sutlej region in 1809, to the trans-Sutlej in 1846, and to the entire province in 1849. Several widely circulated accounts by travelers and adventurers integrated geopolitical priorities with personal reflections of journeys across what was seen as a vast region inhabited by a bewildering assortment of peoples with substantial wealth, confusing languages, and strange customs.[33] More systematic reports produced by military officers—James Browne (1797), John Malcolm (1812), Henry Prinsep (1834), W. G.

Osborne (1840), and John Briggs (1849), to name the most prominent—offer equally fascinating yet explicitly purposeful political histories of the structure of Ranjit Singh's kingdom, its relations with the British, and the religions of its peoples, especially Sikhi.[34]

One of the more striking texts in this genre is by an army field engineer named R. Baird Smith titled *Agricultural Resources of the Punjab*. Written while deployed in the 1848–49 war, his short memorandum provides a detailed analysis of Panjab's agrarian potential. The very circumstances of Smith's introduction to the region's flora are telling:

> The writer's first opportunity of noting the quality of Punjab cotton was on the eve of a general action, when he was directed by a gallant officer, more familiar with fighting than Indian farming, to 'take a company of Sappers and clear away that low thick *brushwood* in front of the line'—the brushwood in question being a capital crop of the cotton plant![35]

From this initial exposure to commercial resources through military actions, Smith went on to speculate about what awaited the British after victory. He began with the bromide that for ages Panjab had been "the battle-field of nations," either "torn by generations of intestine [*sic*] feuds" or "ruled by an oppressive, cruel and fanatical race." Yet these deprivations contrasted with its endowment of the essential elements for agricultural prosperity: "nature and capabilities of soil, profile of surface, supply of water, and habits of the cultivating class." The task of British rule would be to intervene between the past and the present. By rectifying "adverse and unsettled" conditions as well as properly managing natural resources, Panjab stood to be transformed. "Better days are coming," promised Smith.[36]

Drawing on his expertise with the canal systems in the NWP, Smith focused the rest of his text on elaborate, and at times exacting, calculations over questions of irrigation and revenue. Following convention, he divided the region by the portions of alluvial tracts named after the rivers between which they are located. The roughly 11,000 square miles of the "Baree doab" (between the Beas and Ravi rivers) contained a total of 6,211,898 potentially cultivatable acres, irrigated by 3,000 cubic feet per second of water from the Ravi. "From experience on canals in the provinces," it was known that one cubic foot of water per year is sufficient for 218 acres, so that with such a supply, "654,000 acres would be watered annually." The problem, Smith pointed out, was that most villages only water one-third of their lands, "the remaining two-thirds being either occupied by inferior crops, not requiring other irrigation than that of the usual rains, or allowed to lie fallow for the succeeding season." Thus, the supply of 3,000 cubic feet was sufficient for three times the amount actually watered, or 1,962,000 acres. In addition, the spread of canal irrigation would complement well-water irrigation by a ratio of 10 to 1, bringing another 196,200 acres to full cultivation. The total irrigated area of the Baree doab would therefore amount to 2,158,200 acres, while its effects would extend throughout the whole territory.[37]

Building a canal to fulfill this potential would cost roughly 4,000 rupees for each of the 350 miles of its length, or 1,400,000 rupees total, with an additional 20 percent to cover the interest on the capital loan and routine maintenance expenses each year. More important, to determine the potential revenue returns of this area, Smith again invoked comparable figures from the NWP. He calculated that the government could expect an aggregate return of 1,200 rupees per total square mile of territory, or 13,200,000 rupees annually—almost ten times the original outlay. Through the direct sale of water to cultivators at a rate of one rupee per acre plus miscellaneous charges, the state could further expect an additional income of 686,700 rupees per year, which would more than offset the 280,000 rupees for annual expenses and still leave a 406,700-rupee surplus. Overall, then, the enterprise of bringing canal irrigation to the Baree doab would generate a 28 percent return on the capital invested.[38] After conducting similar exercises for the Rechna doab (between the Ravi and Chenab rivers) and the Jetch doab (between the Jhelum and Chenab rivers), Smith calculated their returns at 27 percent and 25 percent, respectively.[39] Far from a self-imposed obligation, the possibility of rule here appeared as a markedly lucrative enterprise.

What is significant about Smith's analysis, aside from its optimistic projections, is that it occurred at a time when the British were engaged in suppressing rebellion in Panjab. This is an anticipatory revenue assessment, a preemptive calculation of economic possibilities not yet synchronized with political and military achievements. Smith repeatedly mentioned the limitations of his figures: data from NWP, while sufficient for general predictions, is frustratingly imprecise.[40] Nonetheless, there is also no denying or reducing the immense potential of what might have been. If the current revenue of Panjab, "popularly, and probably with tolerable accuracy," was over seventeen million rupees, it would at least double under British rule. Furthermore, within a span of twenty years, fulfilling Smith's proposals would "make the Punjab one of the most profitable and the most prosperous of the many acquisitions which have been won by the Indian army."[41] Perhaps most important, however, was the sequence and distribution of this new prosperity between the state and the population. As Smith explains,

> The strong hand of the British government will secure peace in the land; its servants will bring to its administration the experience, skill and high principle which distinguishes them; the various races forming its population will pursue peaceful courses, without interfering with each other; its agriculture—the basis of its prosperity—will be cherished, its commerce extended, and its mineral resources developed.[42]

Security, proper governance, and individual discipline were the prerequisites to an agrarian development that only British power could achieve.

The question of Panjab therefore circulated in different forms throughout the ranks of colonial authority. Where Dalhousie invoked a narrative of betrayal and indiscipline to justify annexation, junior officials such as Smith provided the painstaking calculations of its revenue possibilities. Yet these two positions were not as distinct, nor as directly oppositional, as they appeared. The former's cultural condemnations do not simply conceal the latter's economic projections, any more than an idea proceeds without its presuppositions. Nor is a public pronouncement exposed as false by revealing a private correspondence. Dalhousie obliquely recognized this intertwining. "The Sikhs themselves are warlike in their character," he repeated in his report, "turbulent and brave." But, he added, they "are not more so than the people of Rohilcund once were," referring to the Rohilla rulers of Afghan descent in the area surrounding the city of Bareilly in western NWP. If they were completely subjugated and deprived of the means to resist—and "if vigilance be exercised over them, and if they shall hereafter be governed with justice, vigour, and determination"—then there would be no reason for them not to be rendered "as submissive and harmless as the people of Rohilcund now are."[43] Deficiencies of culture, in other words, can be managed, if not overcome, through prudent economic administration. And the object of that administration, exemplified by Smith's memorandum, is the management of human and natural resources. "Castes and tribes whose habits of life have long been pastoral or predatory," Smith claimed, will, under British rule, gradually "become settled and industrious agriculturalists."[44] Rather than supplanting one or the other, economic discipline held promise for native depredations as much as cultural tropes pervaded the concern for revenue. The Panjab problem, as with every other in the colony, contained nothing purely cultural or economic.

LESSONS OF MISRULE

As a civilizing mission enacted through an economic program, the converging logic behind annexation came to the fore with the advent of full British rule in March 1849. When the Board triumvirate took charge, a bureaucratic structure supplemented the military occupation. Panjab was carved into seven divisions, each headed by a commissioner holding full criminal, civil, and fiscal authority and supported by a legion of deputies, assistants, and extra-assistants distributed throughout each district and block of territory.[45] This cohort of officers, usually handpicked by John Lawrence, constituted the veteran soldiers of the empire. A majority received formal training at Fort William College (in Calcutta) or Haileybury College and Addiscombe Military Seminary (both near London); gained practical experience in the presidencies of Bengal, Madras, and Bombay; and familiarized themselves with what were seen as similar conditions in the NWP.[46] Upon arrival in Panjab, their responsibilities varied from implementing the disarmament campaign and securing the new frontier, to establishing a criminal court and building new prisons, to drafting plans for canal construction and beginning land revenue surveys. Since only the last of these activities generated sufficient income to pay for all the others, it was in many ways the most pressing task and was conducted with the most precision. Indeed, "[l]and revenue was the foundation of imperial rule in India" as well as "the most vital instrument through which native social and economic life would be directly affected and transformed."[47] And unlike Smith's efforts from a few years earlier, limited to assessing revenue potential while encumbered by secrecy and haste, this exercise entailed an actual determination, or settlement, of the proportional division of agricultural produce between what were considered landholding peasants and the state.

The work of settlement in Panjab was not without precedent elsewhere in the empire. Every territory conquered by the Company underwent a similar, if far from identical, process of observation, measurement, and evaluation. "During the first century of British rule," notes C. A. Bayly, "land-revenue emerged as the determining discipline through which the conquerors 'knew' Indian rural society."[48] Officers serving in regions to the east and the south brought certain policies and practices with them to their new posting. In fact, it was not until 1866 that Robert Cust produced a manual for settlement activity that was based solely on the conditions in Panjab.[49] Until that point, the standard guide for all officers in north India was a lengthy text prepared by James Thomason in 1849, the lieutenant-governor of the NWP.[50] What began with concealed perplexity as the Company Empire grew in the late eighteenth century gained open confidence by the middle of the nineteenth when the Crown became sovereign.

Despite these adjacent experiences, the most significant antecedent to the revenue settlement in Panjab remained the "permanent" settlement of Bengal enacted by Governor-General Charles Cornwallis in 1793. Arguably one of the most scrutinized pieces of legislation in colonial India,[51] the attempt to create a landowning gentry that paid a fixed proportion of revenue in perpetuity not only caused severe famine and provoked widespread resistance but also laid bare the extractive basis of Company rule. Regarded by many officials as a debacle soon after its implementation, it was particularly reviled by the administrators of Panjab for estranging the local subjects, relying on rigid procedures, and making inflexibly high demands. Cust denounced its permanence, which precluded the possibility of increasing the government demand, and the flaws in method that led to the fixing of rights "in certain individuals to the utter destruction of the rights of thousands of others."[52] A generation later, Baden Henry Baden-Powell, an influential author and judge in Lahore, deemed it a "benevolent blunder" based on profound misunderstandings of native custom.[53] For officers in Panjab, the permanent settlement was the epitome of how not to govern.

In addition to an evolving administrative culture, settlement work in Panjab also contended with an unusual political and geographical context. Familiarity with the land and its people generated more than a degree of caution. Since the initial signing of a mutually-restraining treaty with Ranjit Singh in 1809, the British had witnessed his army successfully extend the frontiers of his kingdom to the north, west, and south, followed by their own direct wars in 1845 and 1848. Several accounts by British (and other European) participants in these battles describe the ferocious character, military prowess, and stubborn determination of the Sikh forces and the fortuitous nature of many of the Company victories.[54] In Dalhousie's letter, too, the resolve for annexation was underscored by a reminder to the committee in London that, for the second time, we "engaged in war with *the most formidable enemy* we have yet encountered in India."[55] In what would later inform the heavy recruitment of certain Panjabi caste and religious groups into the British Indian Army, especially Sikhs after 1858,[56] the tropes about martial valor initially inspired wariness.

Concern for issues beyond Panjab also shaped how the region was understood. During the early decades of the century, Afghan clans along the Indus—described, in terms similar to those used for Ranjit Singh's troops, as "priest-ridden fanatics, and bigoted followers of the Prophet"[57]— intermittently engaged in resistance to colonial encroachment as well as internal feuds. Their independence remained a perpetual source of instability for the British. Potential enemies further west also raised concern, including speculation of an invasion by Napoleon Bonaparte in the early 1800s and intrigue over Russian designs from the 1830s onward. After the decimation of the Company's army during the Second Anglo-Afghan War in 1842 and the ongoing defiance by Dost Mohammed Khan, the ruler of Kabul, the British abandoned efforts to extend the empire beyond the Khyber Pass.[58] Instead, after 1849, they built a network of forts linking Peshawar and Kohat to Bannu and Dera Ismail Khan from which they periodically launched attacks against their Afghan opponents and solidified a new line of defense. Panjabis recruited into military and irregular units further acted as a bulwark against those across the river, sustaining low-level warfare for much of the century. The 1901 shift in the designation "north-west" from the regions of Agra, Lucknow, and Banaras (renamed the United Provinces) to the trans-Indus territories, along with the addition "frontier," indicates the spatial reorientation toward these threats to the empire.

All of these elements coalesced to produce a conviction among officials that Panjab was to be governed differently. Yet this difference exceeds the conventional threefold division of land settlement in colonial India: *zamindari* (landlord) in Bengal, north Madras Presidency, and parts of Awadh; *raiyatwari* (cultivator) in Madras and Bombay presidencies, and Berar; and *mahalwari* (estate) in Panjab, the rest of the NWP, and the Central Provinces. Aside from the explicit permanence of the first kind of settlement, it was foremost a contract made with absentee landlords of large estates, disregarding both the various tenants and the surveying and evaluating of land productivity. The raiyatwari settlement, on the other hand, was made with individual holders of land, also assumed to be its tillers, based on precise calculations that included the possibility of default. Finally, the mahalwari, also referred to as *bhaiachara* (brotherhood) for the way it was managed in some parts, took the village as the unit for revenue and invested its population with coparcenary payment responsibilities.[59]

In Panjab, however, the coexistence and imbrication of mahalwari/bhaiachara does not fully capture the intricacies of a colonial state encountering this distinctive population and territory. Officers with decades of administrative experience confronted an agrarian society they regarded as hostile and turbulent in a newly conquered region with a precarious frontier, together implicated in a much larger theater of geopolitical intrigue. Underpinning this context, moreover, was an ideology of civilizational economics, of containing and subduing cultural failings through the patient discipline of productive enterprise. The unique politics of managing the economy could not have been more explicit. "[I]t will be the policy of the British Government," stated Lawrence in the first report after annexation, "to reduce the demand in order that the people may flourish and capital may be accumulated."⁶⁰ Revenue along with people and capital were thus regarded as unruly elements to apprehend and align in the exercise of a new kind of authority. As concern for the proper administration of Panjab intertwined with concern for the wellbeing of the empire, the priority to govern with benevolence became paramount.

BENEVOLENT EXTRACTION

A series of six reports provides the official narrative of the first decade of British rule. Authored by the Board in Lahore, submitted to Dalhousie in Calcutta, and forwarded to the Company's Directors in London, these yearly overviews contain both financial statements and extended commentaries on the results of the new policy. A clear baseline from which to measure the changes is difficult, however, owing to not only uncertainty surrounding pre-British collections but also constant shifts in the borders within which revenue was collected. Panjab as a unified geographical unit with a common polity and economy was a work in progress—externally expanding and contracting, internally including and excluding.⁶¹ Initially, the analysis of revenue was confined to the territories annexed in 1849, or roughly Ranjit Singh's old kingdom west of the Beas not including the loyalist Native States. For that area, the report mentions that the longtime chancellor of the Lahore treasury, Raja Deena Nath, provided an abstract showing the annual income at Rs. 13,318,087 in 1847.⁶² The following year, the British resident instituted a series of cursory, provisional money settlements in nearly all divisions that reduced the amount to under Rs. 8,200,000. Devastation from rebellion and its suppression interrupted the compilation of the next year's figures (though not the returns themselves), so that the same amount was recorded for the year 1849–50. The first accurate figures therefore coincide with the second year of annexation. Land revenue for 1850–51 amounted to Rs. 10,185,043; in year three it reached Rs. 10,609,757. Put differently, after an initial drop of 38 percent, the state income from land revenue remained steady for two years before increasing by 24 percent the next year and then 4 percent the year after.⁶³

Yet officials denied that linear growth was a product of rising demand. "No portion of the enhanced revenue," they insisted, "was derived from increased taxation of the land." In fact, effective revenue demand was actually *reduced* across all holdings by approximately 30 percent. Rather, the increase in state income was attributed both to the spread of cultivation (with a fortuitously bumper wheat harvest that year) and the ongoing cancellation of individual revenue-free holdings called *jagirs*.[64] In this way, the figure of income represented two intersecting trajectories: a lessening demand for revenue offset by a larger increase in the extent of revenue collectable. Demanding less from a greater number of sources and collecting with greater efficacy ultimately increased state income.

British officials in Calcutta and London regarded the new policy as an incredible and unexpected success. In a "Minute to the Court of Directors" in 1853, John Lowis describes a feeling of "wonder mixing with . . . satisfaction" upon learning of the achievements of the first administration. A sense of destiny colors the bringing of order to a violent population:

> [O]ver a territory covering, between the Beas and the Indus, more than ten thousand miles, the right moment having been seized on for the *coup d'état*, a nation of soldiers was quietly disarmed; that among a population comprising of fanatic Sikhs and fanatic Mussulmans, devotees and renegades, Jats and Goojurs, Rajpoots and Pathans, internal broils and breaches of the peace have been successfully restrained.[65]

In a similarly celebratory tone, a Minute by Joseph Dorin invokes the historical triumph of British rule. "The pacification by settlement of the Punjab," he explains, "is one of the most extraordinary episodes that has yet been added to Indian history." Against difficult odds, the Board accomplished the remarkable feat of subduing a population while imposing a novel revenue collection and did so without provoking resentment. Indeed, he even suggested that the report itself be distributed as "an instructive example" of the success that results from prudent governance.[66] Dalhousie in turn echoed these sentiments while lavishing specific praise on the conduct and foresight of the triumvirate members.[67] Finally, upon receiving the report, the Directors in London conveyed "high satisfaction" for "a wise and eminently successful administration," as "results have been achieved such as could scarcely have been hoped for as the reward for many years of well-directed exertions."[68] They added their own congratulations to the chorus and encouraged the Board to continue with its invaluable work.

Despite this unreserved praise, the administration significantly altered its practices after the first three years. With the Board replaced by a chief commissioner in 1853, boundaries were again redrawn. To the earlier territory, termed "Panjab proper," was added the districts of the cis-Sutlej (Ambala, Thanesar, Ludhiana, Ferozepur, and Simla) and trans-Sutlej (Jalandhar, Hoshiarpur, and Kangra), creating, for the first time, a single, distinct political unit between the Yamuna and Indus rivers. Although various subtractions and separations occurred over the following century and a half, this became the standard demarcation of Panjab during colonial rule.[69]

Along with consolidating boundaries, Lawrence also signaled a more explicit shift in the orientation of the state toward the project of income. The task of the new Revenue Department related "not so much to the direct interests of the Government as tax-receiver," he claimed, but "to the welfare of the agriculturalists as tax-payers." All energies directed toward revenue were intended "to secure the happiness and prosperity of the rustic population."[70] Benevolence thus imbued the prose of colonial extractions. As a corollary, Lawrence altered the method of tabulating and comparing economic data. Rather than listing the revenue demanded in a given year in one part of the report, with haphazard explanations for different reductions and remissions throughout and followed by a total figure of the state's income at the end, representation itself was rationalized. Charts now showed seven columns: "Demands," "Collections," and "Balances," with the latter sum further divided into "In train of liquidation," "Doubtful," "Irrecoverable," and "Nominal."[71] What this demonstrates is an acknowledgment of revenue as not simply an amount to be obtained but a deliberative process, a number endowed with a fixed past and invested with an expectant future. A subdivided section of balances located between demand and collection reveals both the precariousness of revenue as well as the lengths the colonial state went to quantify its generosity toward landholders.

After recalibrating both the borders and ledgers of Panjab, the figures for revenue exhibit greater depth—though not at first glance. The

A Rule of Benevolence? 43

TABLE 1.1 Land revenue demanded and collected in Panjab, 1852–59.

Year	Demand (Rs.)	Collection	Balance
1852–53	14,324,651	13,143,546	1,181,105
1853–54	15,205,700	13,919,102	1,286,598
1854–55	14,700,884	14,093,731	607,153
1855–56	14,624,259	14,158,107	466,152
1856–57	14,846,122	14,518,915	327,207
1857–58	14,516,032	14,516,032	0
1858–59	15,170,236	14,743,388	426,848

* These figures are taken from the following reports: *General report on the administration of the Punjab territories, comprising the Punjab proper and the cis and trans-Sutlej States, 1851–52 to 1852–53* (Calcutta: Calcutta Gazette Office, 1854), 138; *General report on the administration of the Punjab territories, from 1854–55 to 1855–56 inclusive* (Lahore: Punjabee Press, 1858), 30; *General report on the administration of the Punjab territories, from 1856–57 to 1857–58 inclusive, together with a brief account of the administration of the Delhi territory, from the re-occupation of Delhi up to May 1858* (Lahore: The Chronicle Press, 1858), 27; and *General report on the Punjab and its dependencies, for 1858–59* (Lahore: Hope Press, 1859), 11. The balance for 1857–58 is left blank presumably due to the upheavals of the revolt across north India that year.

second official report, 1851–52, shows that while comprehensive land revenue demand was Rs. 14,459,808, only Rs. 13,765,168 was collected, leaving a balance of Rs. 694,640, almost all of it irrecoverable. Above is a summary of the revenue activity for the next seven seasons:

On the surface, such figures show a somewhat intermittent demand matched by a gradual increase in collection and concomitant reduction in balances. Thus, it appears between 1851 and 1859, land revenue demand increased by a modest 5 percent and collections by 7 percent. Similar to the earlier discrepancy, however, these amounts conceal crucial political calculations. As Lawrence explained, the numbers are misleading for not reflecting the dynamic of purposefully reducing demand followed by a wider scope of collections. Wherever landholder discontent over revenue was registered, or even detected, authorities evinced a "scrupulous readiness" to reduce the demand, at times twice and even three times for the same district in a single season. The state's flexibility—the constant revisions to revenue rates and the various remissions granted in extenuating circumstances—in turn compromised its statistical data. "It is difficult to know with accuracy the amount of this reduction," Lawrence pointed out, "and perhaps there is no statement which can show it." He goes on:

> And the reason is this, that, while the revenue is reduced, lapses and resumptions constantly occur to cover the loss. Thus, while the lands previously taxed are being relieved, fresh lands are coming under taxation: the State gains new revenue while reducing its old revenue.[72]

Only later was the extent of the reductions and remissions accurately calculated. From 1849 to 1856, the third report claims, the state forgave no less than seven million rupees of debt. When distributed equally among all landholders, this averaged to a 25 percent "deduction made by British Government from the burdens of the people."[73] Every subsequent report went on to emphasize the numerous reductions granted by the state to landholders in various forms of distress. The following year, an official reiterated that "no sooner has an assessment been elaboratedly calculated, than it has to be altered; no sooner have engagements been entered into with the people for terms of years, then they have to be broken."[74] Even the outstanding balances were not simply negative tabulations. This was "not a residue which could not be collected" for lack of ability, according to Lawrence. Rather, it was what "the authorities refrained from collecting for fear of an undue pressure on agricultural resources."[75] An outstanding balance, in other words, was the distinguishing mark of benevolence.

A CONSPIRACY OF CONTINGENCY

If the archive of colonial agrarian relations consisted only of the annual aggregate reports, it would seem that a British policy of modesty and leniency toward the peasants of Panjab had met with serene success. In fact, this is usually taken as evidence for the claim of the "Panjab school" and its distinct form of benevolent administration.[76] Those reports, however, were based on the compilation and distillation of dozens of individual settlement reports that were much more invasive and intricate in nature and less burdened with providing a harmonious narrative. These latter reports were, as Rupa Vswananth has explored in a different context, the *un*settled accounts of settlement activity.[77] Through them, officers relate the challenges involved in assessing different environmental factors, the difficulties of measuring the qualities of the rural population, and the various methods of controlling dissent. Examining this archive of the tedious observations and activities of settlement officers provides insight into the changes instituted through an ostensibly modest revenue policy.

Along with departing from practices followed in other regions of the empire, the British contrasted their rule in Panjab most emphatically with those whom they displaced. According to an early report, Ranjit Singh's system "was a rude and simple one,"[78] reliant on a network of *kardars*, or tax collection agents, who could extract different amounts of in-kind revenue after depositing a minimum sum with the treasury. Furthermore, a significant portion of land was allocated to powerful local leaders in the form of perpetual jagirs in exchange for loyalty and a steady supply of soldiers and cavalry. Yet although a resident oversaw the financial and political affairs of the Lahore kingdom after 1846, the exact calculations used for native revenue assessment eluded Company officers. The report therefore criticizes the abuses of Ranjit Singh's system while disclosing a frustrating limit to the knowledge attainable about his finances.

Nominally, the kingdom claimed half of all agricultural produce, although the actual proportion collected varied from one-third to two-fifths, with 10 to 15 percent further deducted for cultivating expenses, waste, and fraud, as well as numerous other reductions based on political conditions, personal relationships, and environmental exigencies.[79] The amounts stipulated in the ledgers confiscated by the British in 1849 did not reflect the actual balances in the treasury, nor the history of relations between the state and landholders. "For the record of what he gave and took," the report remarks with disdain, "Runjeet Sing had trusted to his tenacious memory, aided by such primitive devices as the notching of a stick."[80]

Despite this admission of inscrutability, or perhaps because of it, the Board instituted a radically new method of measurement and calculation. In one of the earliest settlement reports of the Jalandhar district from 1851, Richard Temple relates details of this process. A British officer, accompanied by several inspectors and assistants, local *ameens* (surveyors), *patwaris* (village accountants) and *tehsildars* (sub-district revenue collectors), as well as a dozen or so servants and laborers, first conducted a broad survey to gather rough statistics on the overall revenue capacity of the area to be settled. Contiguous villages with similar physical characteristics, such as flat or hilly terrain, sandy or loamy soil, or common levels of drainage, were then grouped into units called *chuks,* each one labeled and demarcated. Within each chuk, a further division was made based on the specific quality of soil and the means of irrigation, whether from rainfall, wells, or canals. Next, "a detailed examination was made into each Chuk, and almost every village was visited by myself [Temple]." Direct observations augmented formal information, as the revenue officer personally inspected each element of the assessment to ascertain its validity. These two sets of figures, abstract and immediate, were then compared and combined in order to "frame an exact classification of each of the estates in each Chuk."[81] Within the eighty-three villages of Chuk Sutlej, for example, an acre of irrigated Class I soil was generally assessed at 3 rupees and 12 annas, un-irrigated Class II soil at 1 rupee and 7 annas, and irrigated Class III soil at 2 rupees and 6 annas.[82] In this way, a numerical chart overlaid a physical map for the whole of the district.

Following the compilation of baseline capacity came the task of determining the specific revenue rates to be applied for each type of crop grown. This required two additional figures: the average yield per acre and its average market price. Obtaining these numbers in turn entailed deeper engagement with the local population, as the pursuit of knowledge about production required an inquiry into the variables of productivity. Several early reports relate the particulars of acquiring and distilling this truth. Wherever available, statements from previous years were put alongside the figures "written down at the dictation of the village headman" and contrasted.[83] Or a revenue officer could present his own calculations to a few key interlocutors. "I showed my estimate to the Tehseeldar," explained George Barnes from the 1852 settlement of Hoshiarpur, "and desired him to point out any instance where he thought alteration necessary." For even more precision,

> I [then] associated with him, two or three respectable zemindars from the talooqua [a group of villages], whose intelligence and probity had given them a local reputation. They conferred together close to my tents—whenever

they adduced any valid reasons in support of an amendment, I generally conceded to their opinion; sometimes [however] their arguments were based on grounds which did not approve themselves to my judgement; and then, I adhered to my own estimate.[84]

Through this iterative and interactive process, with the final decision always resting with a British officer, a set of produce figures emerged.

Yet these figures were subject to still another layer of scrutiny. In a report from Ludhiana district from 1850, Henry Davidson related a critical further step. With the crops ripe in the field, "I myself," he wrote, "have caused different grains in different localities to be cut down, the land measured, and the grain weighed, my notes of the result serving for my own guidance."[85] Native numbers required British authentication. Visits to local markets, as well as references to the rates at major grain processing centers such as Lahore and, later, Ludhiana, corroborated the final version. Only after completing this elaborate series of exercises, for dozens of different crops in every grade of soil within all the chuks of each district under settlement, did a revenue officer arrive at what he could consider a reliable set of revenue rates.

Armed with these components, each parcel of land could then be computed with the general and specific figures to determine the amount payable to the state by its holder. In more painstaking detail, Temple calculated the produce returns in several charts at the end of his report. In the Kolnitah chuk of the Philor tehsil, for instance, one acre of Class I soil produced 13 *maunds* of wheat in a single season, with an average *nirikh* or market rate of 1 maund per rupee, thereby yielding 13 rupees per acre.[86] Assessed at one-quarter of the gross produce, the revenue rate was 3 rupees and 4 annas. For corn, the same chuk and class of soil produces 20 maunds per acre, but with a nirikh of 2 maunds per rupee, its yield was 10 rupees, resulting in a revenue rate of 2 rupees and 8 annas. The output for rice was 14 maunds at 2 nirikh for 7 rupees per acre for a rate of 1 rupee and 12 annas.[87] Lastly, the revenue returns—the decisive number that fulfilled the very purpose of the entire enterprise—are the application of these equations to the actual amount of land under each type of cultivation. Kolnitah chuk's 20,428 acres of wheat were *supposed* to generate 66,391 rupees for the state, while 2,064 acres growing corn should have returned 5,160 rupees and rice on just 10 acres netting 17 rupees and 8 annas.[88] The procedure for these three crops on one grade of soil in a single chuk was multiplied by scores of revenue officers across all districts across Panjab for nearly a century. Compared to the novelty of this display of mathematical and analytical might, Smith's efforts from only a few years earlier appear straightforward and quaint, even simplistic. More importantly, it was this collection of data that underpinned the British claim of a rational and moderate revenue settlement.

For all the precision, rigor, and sophistication of settlement equations, there remained aspects of agricultural production that escaped quantification. Edward Brandreth, from the 1855 report of the Ferozepur district, revealed a few of the contingencies that troubled this work. At one level, gathering even provisional data from which to base estimates and make alterations proved frustrating. "It was not an easy matter," he wrote, "to determine the relative value of the different soils." The former returns presented to him, while accurate for what landholders submitted to kardars, only showed that "each Zemeendar cultivated a proportionate share of every kind of soil." Brandreth's calculations, however, were intended to fix revenue responsibility in land to a specific individual, and therefore "showed only the total produce of the whole of his [the zamindar's] cultivation."[89] The first type of assessment offered the amount a landholder paid to the state without cultivation details, while the second stipulated the amount a particular parcel of land *was expected to generate* for both landholder and state. As a result, the two sets of figures were incongruent, with difference stemming from a divergent understanding of the purpose of revenue settlement.[90] "All I could do," conceded Brandreth, was, again, "question the most intelligent Zemeendars on the subject" to arrive at a figure with at least some semblance of authority. Intelligence to a colonial officer assessing a Panjabi could represent anything from pliability to acuity.

Natural elements also seemed to conspire against the strictures of mathematical precision. Most significant was irrigation, as a crucial means for cultivation became a critical object of inquiry for revenue officers. Since a consistent supply of water dictated the capacity of nearly any grade of soil to produce a viable crop, its measure and management was a priority.[91] Yet the importance of irrigation was almost inverse to its predictability. "I soon found," Brandreth explained, "that the irrigation of the particular year during which the measurement took place, however accurately it was ascertained, could not be received as presenting the permanent irrigation of the village."[92] Erratic rainfalls, rivers changing their course to parch or flood arable land, smaller streams drying up completely, wells throwing up brackish water, collapsing, or also drying up—these ebbs and flows of irrigation defied static certainty.

In Ferozepur, the dictates of nature actively shaped the decisions of production. "With the prospect of good rains, the Zemeendars make little use of their wells," noted Brandreth, "whereas with a bad season before them, they irrigate their fields to the utmost possible extent."[93] Deliberate subterfuge, moreover, amplified the troubles of settlement calculations. Some zamindars, "having been forewarned by the result of the settlement" in surrounding chuks, either "abstained from irrigating the usual quantity of land" capable from their wells or "destroyed the water channels" to conceal other sources of water to their fields. Less visibly cultivated land meant less revenue for the colonial administrators to demand. In such fluctuating, perplexing circumstances, the accurate evaluation of even a well proved confounding. Although Brandreth and other officers proceeded by using the abstractions of averages and medians, the quest to domesticate water remained unfulfilled throughout the nineteenth century.[94]

Indeed, the massive network of canals built in Panjab from the 1880s onward—the largest irrigation system in British India—reflects the ongoing struggle of the colonial state to wrest control of irrigation from both nature and the native population.[95] It featured so prominently because the logic of revenue collection had changed. New settlement equations meant that the British had relocated value from not only a control over people to land but also to the hypothetical output each parcel was expected to generate. Physical evasion thus no longer served to evade the grasping numerical strictures of the colonial state. A gauntlet of maps, charts, and equations extended as well as altered authority so that even contingencies were tallied into predictable entries on a ledger.

MEASURING MEN

Beyond the uncertain measures of soil, irrigation, and outputs, a far more intractable and unusual element of production animated settlement activity: the agriculturalists themselves. A short note by the Panjab government in response to a question posed by the Famine Commission in 1878 reveals the broad contours of this problem. "It frequently occurs that heavier rates are paid by the more industrious villages," admitted the report, "and lighter rates by their less skilful neighbours occupying lands of similar natural advantage." It went on:

> It is practically impossible to adjust inequalities of this nature, and it is politically inexpedient to attempt to do so. The more skilful agriculturalists pay the higher rates with more ease than their less able neighbours pay the lower rates, and also after paying the higher rates have a much larger margin of profit left to them.[96]

According to the colonial understanding of Panjabi society, agriculture was not conducted by generic, equal agriculturalists differing only in the natural environments that happened to be available to them. Rather, the agriculturalists differed in essential, immutable ways. "When differences of this nature are inquired into," the report continues, "they are found to have their origin in the *different antecedent circumstances* of each class, and not to be merely due to present differences of agricultural skill."[97] In other words, not only did these differences predate British rule, but they were based on collective as opposed to individual qualities, so that certain groups of peasants were better or worse than others.[98] More so than earth and water, the identity of those cultivating a parcel of land thus profoundly affected its productive possibilities. As a result, the most decisive responsibility of a revenue officer was the observation, measurement, and categorization of human beings.

The subject of the settlement, the person with whom the state settled the payment of land revenue, was also its object. "The character and capabilities of the cultivators," explained a revenue officer, "are every bit as much a part of the assets of an Estate, as are the soil and water on it to be worked by them."[99] Each individual settlement report contained sections discussing, with much more candor, the particulars of those groups identified as the proprietors and cultivators of agricultural land. According to Davidson, for example, "the Mussulman" inhabitants of the northern portion of Ludhiana district were "generally the worst of cultivators, deficient alike in skill and inclination," in contrast to the "widely superior [...] skill and appliances used by the Hindoo" in the southern parts.[100] More specifically, he described how "the Hindoo drives his plough with whip steadily applied, attended by his wife and children weeding the soil, and cleansing it from all hindrances." At the other end of the spectrum, "the Mahomedan, with his family confined to the mud walls of his village, will urge the plough along with, perhaps, a hookah in the other hand; forgetting the labor he is undergoing, in the charms of the drugs he is."[101] Yet this binary of religion inflected with cultural faults could also be interrupted: Hindu Rajputs were as inferior to their co-religionists as Muslim Arains were superior. For Davidson, the top of the hierarchy was occupied by Jatts, regardless of whether Hindu, Muslim, or Sikh. "The labor expended ... upon their well irrigation is astonishing," he wrote, as "night and day is heard the monotonous cry they adopt in praise of 'Rub! Rub!' [the Divine] whenever the leathern bucket filled with water mounts to the top" of the well.[102]

Along with religious and caste identity, revenue officers discussed how certain social interactions and customary understandings produced better or worse agriculturalists. For Charles Raike, the commissioner of the Lahore division who reviewed the settlement of Amritsar district, Jatts were unequivocally superior. He wrote that "the Manjha villages contain some of the finest specimens of man I have ever seen in any country." However, the authors of the report, Robert Davies and William Blyth, offered a more selective opinion. Demographically, "the mass of the agricultural population are Hindoo Juts, about 50 per cent of whom are Sikhs [sic], and 12.5 per cent were formerly in the Sikh army." Of this group, "those who have not been in [military] service are thrifty, industrious and honest." On the other hand, "those who have, are extravagant, and make bad cultivators, and besides being litigious and false, are given to intoxication." Both groups shared a mutual disdain, as the latter "are not much liked by the more peaceful portion of the community, and are styled as Boorchas [bullies]."[103]

In Ferozepur, Brandreth exercised this internal differentiation by summarily defining several castes in more pronounced ways. The Muslim "Dogurs, Bhutees and Goojurs" (Dogars, Bhattis, and Gujjars) were "utterly devoid of energy, and are the most apathetic, unsatisfactory, race of people." Arains, already lauded in Ludhiana, were indeed "first rate cultivators," but at the same time were "in general rather a litigious and discontented set," much like some of the Jatts in Amritsar. "Many of the Machees [Machhis]," he added, were "addicted to thieving" and therefore hopeless at agricultural pursuits. "Burars [Brars]" had the potential to cultivate as successfully as other Jatts, but because "they wear finer clothes, and consider themselves a more illustrious race," their quality gradually declined.[104] In different districts the very same caste thus somehow had different attitudes, attributes, and abilities. The contradiction between essential yet dissimilar qualities of certain groups was in fact central to the colonial manipulation of caste and religion. "The stereotype of the 'bigoted Julaha' was born," argues Gyanendra Pandey elsewhere, "out of the experience of events in a few specific and restricted localities—an experience that was, first, misread and then, universalised to cover diverse groups spread across a huge part of the sub-continent, and thus mythified in the interests of the colonial regime."[105] Descriptions such as these, varying in degrees of contempt and adulation, exist for every caste considered to be agriculturalists throughout Panjab.

A system of classifying people emerged in tandem with the classification of nature. Parallel to their mathematical appraisal of the environment, settlement reports were also novel exercises in measuring society.[106] Their authors doubled as incipient ethnographers, generating a unique form of knowledge that supplemented rather than supplanted history with anthropology. The "preoccupation with social order" was in fact augmented and intertwined with a "concern for revenue."[107] Simultaneous to the complementary dichotomy between Dalhousie and Smith at the time of conquest, the administration of Panjab integrated the evaluation of culture with the calculation of economic profit. Qualitative descriptions combined with quantified assessments; caste gained a numerical value; religion acquired a tangible weight; collective habits entered into the ledger—in short, culture *saturated* economy. For the colonial state, revenue had as much to do with soil quality and weather patterns as it did with the quality of men and the patterns of their social relations.

DISCIPLINING FOR A NEW DEMAND

A different type of knowledge about revenue produced through settlement activity allowed for a different practice of extraction. One of the most pivotal changes at this end of the process was the implementation of absolute monetary values. This transformed both the purpose of revenue assessment and the means for its collection. Pre-British demand in Panjab, as Indu Banga has described, was usually made proportionally on either the actual grain collected on the threshing floor (*batai*) or as a judgment of the standing crop just prior to harvest (*kankut*).[108] The new policy, however, used the equations of the settlement officer to make a demand on the abstract value a given field and its owner was calculated to be able to produce. Land combined with an ambiguous notion of labor—instead of the quantity of the crop grown upon it—now acquired definitive revenue potential. At the same time, this fixed sum was to be paid in hard currency by landholders to the state on rigid dates, often coinciding with a budgetary rather than a harvest calendar, thus increasing the importance of urban moneylenders.[109] Not only did this greatly increase the impact of precarious variations in weather—an early frost or sparse rainfall did not ordinarily change the revenue rate—but it also created a novel form and meaning of property. Once an individual became the outright owner of a parcel of land, regardless of whether a crop was even planted, they entered into a financial contract with the state. "Property rights," explains David Gilmartin, "were thus based on an implicit contract between the colonial state and the revenue payer," which "offered state-recognition of 'proprietary rights' in return for acceptance of the revenue demand."[110] Ownership was now tied to a new set of obligations.

It may not be possible to ascertain how landholders regarded paying revenue through the tethering of land to money in their own words. Accessing local perspectives in the vernacular from a largely unlettered rural population living in a humid and turbulent region in past centuries remains an abiding challenge for any historian.[111] Nevertheless, it is clear from colonial sources that many landholders immediately opposed this novel imposition. In a letter to the Board, Captain David Ross, commissioner of the Leia division, explained how zamindars were always "accustomed to pay a fixed portion of the gross produce as revenue, the actual quantity depending upon the outturn of the harvest." With the new policy, "they were afraid of money-payments, and the risk of being responsible for the full juma [payment] in unfavourable seasons."[112] The spring of 1850 witnessed unrest in several major cities as delegations arrived in Lahore to demand a reversal to in-kind payments. On the other hand, officials also noted a more discrete phenomenon of landholders leaving their fields unplowed or even abandoning their localities outright. "Landholders often evince an apparent indifference to their property," claimed one report, as they "leave their homes on the slightest pressure" with "hope and intention of returning when better times shall re-appear."[113] What officials labeled as indifference might better be described as unfamiliarity turning into opposition. Landholders rejected both inflexible demand and the notion that land, once owned, necessitated perpetual cultivation for monetized revenue payment regardless of actual output.

The Board responded in two ways. First, instead of confronting calls for reversal directly, they simply reduced the amount of cash payment to the point where it became too inexpensive to oppose. This was the most visible sign of benevolence. Whereas previously landholders might have parted with a third of their gross produce as well as paid several different additional charges, now they would be responsible for a single proportionate sum of the value of the crop grown—reduced by up to 40 percent in the first few decades. Rather candidly, Lawrence pointed out that "this is the *only* means by which a system of cash payments can be rendered popular and effective in a new country, previously accustomed to payments in kind."[114] Second, on the problem of desertions, the Board resolutely enforced proprietary discipline. Landholders "have not yet learnt that the British fiscal laws provide for the disposal of property, even temporarily abandoned by its owner, with its liabilities un-discharged." Land owned but not cultivated, and thus unproductive of the very crops needed to be sold in order to acquire the currency to pay the demand, would be confiscated and resold to a more promising candidate for revenue payment.[115] This captures the colonial imposition of new notions of property alongside individual rights and obligations. Between subsidizing consent and penalizing indiscipline, the Company slowly dissipated landholder dissent.

Besides changing the object and method of collections, the Board also began a review of all grants of revenue to individuals, called *jagirs*. No longer would the state readily alienate its income: "the first object of attention was to be the inquiry into rent-free tenures—that is, what lands were to be exempt from taxation, and on what terms."[116] Officials launched investigations into those assigned revenue, reviewed their loyalty during the two Anglo-Sikh wars of 1845–46 and 1848–49 and their overall value to the state, and then decided whether to allow them to continue. While some jagirs were renewed—mostly to some members of the former royal family, retired high-level state functionaries, and endowments for certain religious institutions—the vast majority were cancelled outright, especially if held by individuals implicated in fomenting resistance. Other jagirs were modified by reducing the collectable proportion, transferring the terms from perpetuity to the lifetime of the holder, or substituting a grant of land revenue for a cash pension. This last change tightly bound recipients to fealty by rerouting their incomes through the state. Whereas a jagir could be construed as a time-honored and well-earned privilege, a pension represented the new (and easily revocable) generosity of the government. Furthermore, the Company's sprawling military establishment obviated an independent source of troops from the rural nobility, leading to the cancellation and resumption of even more revenue-free holdings.[117] Overall state income increased by reducing the amount it preemptively relinquished.

The method of control and cooptation at the individual level was just as intricate. While a select number of former soldiers were recruited into the new army and the rest disbanded and cheaply pensioned, those leaders who actively fought against the British presented a unique challenge.[118] The decision to leave them unpunished might be seen as a sign of weakness and prompt further unrest, yet too severe a response would stoke greater resentment and possibly lead to the same result. The Board avoided both extremes by inflicting a quantity of economic retribution. Edward Thornton, commissioner of Jhelum division, related of one rebel that their landed property was left untouched, but their homes were confiscated.

"The principle" of leaving property alone, he explains, ran as follows: "The men might settle down to agricultural pursuits, while the dwelling-house ... was taken, as a mark of displeasure, and also because its confiscation compelled the rebel to resort to a meaner abode, and thus diminished his importance."[119] Social prestige thus had an economic quotient, to be measured and acted against in the interests of securing political obedience. Changing the structure of revenue payment and the means and extent of its collection thereby reconstituted the relationship between property, society, and the state.

PROVINCIALIZING ACCUMULATION

How might we understand the broader implications of revenue settlement in colonial Panjab? Rather than simply a regional variation or an anomaly of empire, what can it tell us about the supposed logic of how global processes unfold? One possibility is by juxtaposing this history with Marx's narrative of primitive accumulation. Despite important critiques, the fate, or *fatality*, of the peasant in Western Europe remains the conventional paradigm by which the difference of every other peasantry is brought to the fore.[120] Marx describes at least some of its secrets near the end of *Capital*. He writes against the autobiography of an ascendant bourgeoisie. That account, expounded by countless liberal theorists and economists in the late seventeenth, eighteenth, nineteenth, and (indeed) twentieth and twenty-first centuries, explains bourgeois dominance as the natural evolution of society, a product of their own ingenuity, dedication, and prudence coupled with the spontaneous appearance of an urban mass willing to work for wages.[121] For Marx, however, this was "anything but idyllic." Instead, "the expropriation of the agricultural producer, *of the peasant*, from the soil is the basis of the whole process."[122] His itinerary of the making of the modern proletariat in England is based on the unmaking of the English peasant.

Crucial to this process was the sardonic double-freeing of the rural population, ceasing their dependence on cultivation while denying them access to independent livelihoods. A brutal onslaught—both legislative and corporeal—enclosed customary grazing, hunting, and foraging lands; seized public commons for conversion into private property; and confiscated large

Church estates from the sixteenth to eighteenth centuries. The result was the deracination of the peasantry, leading to its near-wholesale eviction from the countryside and arrival in cities desperate to sell its own labor-power for survival.[123] Marx's genealogy of the first worker is revealing:

> Thus were the agricultural folk first forcibly expropriated from the soil, driven from their homes, turned into vagabonds, and then whipped, branded and tortured by grotesquely terroristic laws into accepting the discipline necessary for the system of wage-labour.[124]

Far from a benign, voluntary evolution, proponents of urban manufacturing worked in tandem with state authority over generations to fitfully transform peasants into proletarians.

Since Marx's time, accumulation based on separation has acquired global dimensions. In her 1913 study of the problem of declining profitability, Rosa Luxemburg reframed the scale and scope of the process. She argued that while Marx conceived of accumulation as an initial, one-time occurrence that allowed for the genesis of capitalism in Europe, it was actually an ongoing, consistent dynamic that encompassed the entire world. In order for capitalists to continue realizing profits, they require "an environment of non-capitalist forms of production" from which to extract raw materials, create commodity markets, and draw on reserve labor.[125] Societies based on agriculture fulfill this purpose, serving as the location both upon which capital enacts and from which capital extracts. In other words, capitalism necessitates as much as infiltrates its opposite. Luxemburg's notion of accumulation is predatory, ceaselessly expanding out from Europe through colonial conquest, forcibly subduing and assimilating the rest of the world to itself.[126] Capital is thus accumulated through a perpetual, unstable, and exploitative interaction between capitalist and noncapitalist world regions.

Building on this idea, David Harvey charted the wider historical and geographical aspects of capitalist development in the twentieth century. He renamed the process "accumulation by dispossession" to remove the connotations of a precise start and limited duration as well as to reiterate the importance of imposed separations. Instead of an exclusive divide between capitalist and noncapitalist regions, however, Harvey argued that capitalism had evolved through global "spatio-temporal fixes."[127] To maintain profits, it could continue to seek out and penetrate regions with undercommodified resources and markets, using multinational institutional authority to dismantle protective territorial barriers. The worldwide decline of small-scale agriculture, along with rapidly growing urbanization, epitomizes this method. Or, equally effective, it could actively destroy existent assets and devalue labor within fully capitalist regions, a project increasingly undertaken in the United States and Europe since the 1980s. According to Harvey, capitalism "can either make use of some pre-existing outside" or "it can actively manufacture it" within its own domain.[128] Space and time are thereby the two mediums through which the pursuit of surplus-value is continually reenacted the world over. Rather than strictly primitive, accumulation for Harvey is as much ongoing and outgoing as it is "cannibalistic."[129]

This narrative of accumulation—whether primitive (or originary), ongoing, or by dispossession—is what has long underpinned much of the debate over the emergence of capitalism. Beyond strictly Marxist orientations, it exerts a powerful explanatory force by providing a concise yet expansive theory of the transition from agriculture to industry, one that appears applicable everywhere.[130] Capital is usually seen to progress across the world by dominating the peasantry, either immediately by directly evicting them or gradually by encroaching and subordinating their way of life.[131] In both cases, a dynamic assumed to originate in England and then intensify and extend outward, gradually incorporating the rest of the world into its orbit, is the mark of universalization through globalization. As a result, the narrative of accumulation has stealthily generated a set of expectations for the histories of all other societies. Indeed, it is for this very reason that Harvey imprudently assumes that colonialism thwarted capital from fulfilling its mission in colonial South Asia, an instance of "a territorial logic inhibiting the capitalist logic." British rule, he states, served "to *prevent* India from developing a vigorous capitalist dynamic and thereby *frustrated* the possibilities of spatio-temporal fixes in that region."[132] Similarly, in their analysis of the relationship between capitalism and imperialism, Utsa Patnaik and Prabhat Patnaik argue that "while the peasantry was destroyed in the metropolis," the story "was entirely different in the tropical and subtropical colonies of conquest" because "[h]ere the peasantry *lingered on*."¹³³ In short, what is assumed to have occurred in Europe is taken to measure what did not occur in places such as Panjab, so that non-occurrence is equated with degrees of non-change.¹³⁴ Capitalism appears always already modern; its putative antecedents are always archaic.

Such a burden of expectation, however, can be brought into question when the supposedly universal narrative of accumulation is examined within the particular coordinates of Marx's articulation. The first imperative is to recognize the unique nature of his writings. According to Louis Althusser, there is a key distinction to draw between "the object of knowledge" and "the real object."¹³⁵ The former is the history of concepts and logic while the latter is concrete history, yet the two are routinely conflated. This has the effect of imputing Marx's conceptual explorations with the authority of definitive research. The "empiricist temptation," Althusser explains, is to read all parts of *Capital* as factual and cohesive global history. Regarding the sections on primitive accumulation in particular, he argues that they "are more the half-finished materials *for a history* than a real *historical* treatment of those *materials.*"¹³⁶ Elsewhere, Althusser is even more emphatic: "we must say that *Marx did not give us any theory of the transition from one mode of production to another.*"¹³⁷ Indeed, the literal historical experience of the peasantry in England is quite different from what Marx described.¹³⁸ Other historians too have pointed to the importance of not reading Marx as a historian of the colonial world (or of Europe) as well as of curtailing the theoretical universality of primitive accumulation.¹³⁹

From this perspective, it becomes possible to reevaluate the weight of Marx's narrative of accumulation. That these chapters appear near the end of *Capital* is itself significant. Such a placement reflects both the object of Marx's inquiry and the method of his exposition. By beginning with the commodity and proceeding to expand and introduce other concentric elements into a critique of the discipline of political economy, he signaled interest in the novelty of the bourgeois mode of production as it emerged in Europe. Marx was concerned not with a linear history of capitalism but with capital's internal configuration, its immanent contradictions, and its inherent instability. Only after dismantling the notion of a never-ending capitalism did he direct attention toward, and against, the sense of its never-beginning.[140] Primitive accumulation is therefore the result of following the long trajectory of what the rule of capital "presupposes": the logical necessity of history, of "*assuming* a primitive accumulation which precedes capitalist accumulation."[141] It occurs at the end of *Capital* to simultaneously disrupt the timelessness of capital without assigning it a discrete, causal beginning.

Beyond the configuration of *Capital*, the historiographical basis it relies on offers incisive grounds to question the status of accumulation. The relationship between proletarian and peasant becomes exceedingly important within the context of Marx's chapters. In fact, much before entering into the discussion of accumulation, he signaled in a crucial footnote the reason for using the example of the English worker to explicate this process:

> In passing, let us note that England figures in the foreground here because it is the classic representation of capitalist production, and it is the only country to possess *a continuous set of official statistics* relating to the matters we are considering.[142]

The constitution of the archive is thus central to the narrative of transition from peasant to worker.

As is well known, Marx relied on the government's Blue Books, the yearly collection of parliamentary papers, royal commissions, and official publications, named for the color of the hardcover within which they were bound. In the chapter "The Working Day" in particular, he uses various *Reports of the Inspectors of Factories*, several *Children's Employment Commissions*, and the series of *Factory Acts* to describe the trajectory of misery, degradation, and exploitation of the new working class. Initially, "capital asks no questions about the length of life of labour-power," extracting as much absolute surplus-value as possible without regard to the wellbeing of workers.[143] For example, in a report from the manufacture of lace, Marx relates:

> Children of nine or ten years are dragged from their squalid beds at two, three, or four o'clock in the morning and compelled to work for a bare subsistence until ten, eleven, or twelve at night, their limbs wearing away, their frames dwindling, their faces whitening, and their humanity absolutely sinking into a stone-like torpor, utterly horrible to contemplate.[144]

A protracted struggle of workers against their employers, entangling many different strands of British society, finally forced the government to pass laws limiting the use of child labor and shortening the working day. Although the worker emerging at the end of this half-century of class war was dramatically altered by engaging in alienated labor for the first time, and capital too proceeded to find more insidious ways of accelerating its extractions, this represents one of the earliest forms of large-scale common political action emerging through common economic experience. It was this victory, in Marx's eyes, that made the English factory workers of this period the champions of the entire modern proletariat.[145]

On the other hand, Marx also conveyed a parallel account of squalor and suffering in the countryside. In later chapters dealing with the same historical period, he made extensive use of two *Public Health* reports by Dr. Henry Hunter, a few *Reports from the Poor Law Inspectors*, and articles from the *Morning Chronicle* newspaper to relate equally vivid details. Agricultural laborers across England lived in pitiful hovels, overcrowded and dark, teeming with contagious diseases; they were fed less and worked more than prison inmates; their lords prevented them from keeping gardens to grow their own food; their rents rose rapidly and they were evicted at whim; physical punishment was as routine as drug addiction; adolescent pregnancies and illegitimate children abounded.[146] Besides death—through famine, epidemics, or sheer overwork—their only avenues of pyrrhic escape were migration to the cities or emigration to North America. In both cases, however, the ultimate destination was the same. "Surplus agricultural labourers," Marx stated, "are transformed into factory workers."[147]

What is striking about these two accounts of proletariat and peasantry is the simultaneity of their archival intertwining. We learn how the English working class endured horrors surpassing even the worst of Dante's *Inferno* in tandem with how agricultural laborers were treated as nothing more than "speaking implements" by their lords.[148] There is nothing incidental about how such exercises of observation, tabulation, and representation occurred. Rather, both were implicated in a particular set of antagonisms within English society during the turn of the nineteenth century. In response to bourgeois efforts to repeal the Corn Laws (designed to inflate wheat prices by restricting imports), the aristocracy sponsored investigations into the conditions of industrial workers, which in turn prompted the former to direct attention toward the conditions of agricultural laborers.[149] Individuals such as Lord Ashley, the Earl of Shaftesbury, encapsulated this dynamic: as a "protagonist of the aristocratic philanthropic campaign against the factories" and the exploitation of workers, he became "a favorite target" of bourgeois efforts to expose the conditions of peasants on his own estates.[150]

The cries of the factory inspectors thus *echoed* those of the public health and poor law inspectors. For Marx, this was a bitter case of thieves falling out: "the noisy and passionate dispute between the two factions of the ruling class as to which of them exploited the workers more shamelessly was the midwife of truth on both sides of the question."[151] More importantly, while knowledge about the proletariat became available through aristocratic instigation, an understanding of the peasantry resulted from bourgeois incitement. In other words, as Andrew Sartori argues, "the figure of the independent producer as the prehistory from which capital emerged is a trope generated from within capitalist society."[152] The trail of footnotes throughout *Capital* reflects the concurrent mediation of both laboring conditions by this archive.

AGAINST THE BURDEN OF EXPECTATIONS

By explicating the specific content of *Capital* along with the particular conditions for Marx's knowledge about agrarian change in England, the expectations of a universal process of accumulation can be reimagined. This is not a matter of leveling the often anachronistic accusation of Eurocentrism against his narrative. But nor is it to stubbornly insist on its unmediated worldwide unfolding, although Teodor Shanin and more recently Kevin Anderson have provocatively explored unusual capitalist trajectories by extrapolating from Marx's personal correspondence or unpublished writings.[153] Instead, I am pursuing a different line of inquiry: rather than London, what if Marx had been in Lahore or Ludhiana in the mid-nineteenth century and had to explain accumulation from that vantage point? What archive would he have used, and how would that have shaped the process he would have witnessed and described? And, what sort of narrative of global capitalism would thereby emerge?

This approach makes clear that the conventional judgment of an insufficient transformation of colonial Panjab, of its difference-as-lack, is both historically and theoretically inadequate. Its gesture of simple comparison relies on first misreading certain passages from Marx as global history and then elevating them to the status of universal theory.[154] What is thought to have occurred in Europe is taken to measure what did not occur in Panjab, so that its absence becomes a sign of stasis. Yet the emergence of this difference itself requires investigation in a way that avoids hasty verdicts of deficiency or abundance. Historians such as Kenneth Pomeranz and Dipesh Chakrabarty have shown the value of decentering the primacy of Europe in comparative analyses, and offered alternative frames of reference for making disparate historical events and experiences commensurate.[155] It is therefore no longer a matter of adjudicating the givenness of difference. Instead, by historicizing a different kind of accumulation, it becomes possible to reconceptualize how the study of the past shapes our understanding of the emergence of the modern peasant and agrarian capitalism in colonial Panjab.

Foremost is the source of materials that brings such distinct historical subjects into light. While British officers are hardly univocal in their descriptions of rural Panjabi society, there is none of the simmering, polarizing resentment between bourgeoisie and aristocracy that animated the production of knowledge about agricultural conditions in rural England. Competing groups in the metropole sought to direct institutions of state and authority toward their own interests in ways that, while not always predictable, nonetheless ended up revealing a history of exploitation and misery.[156] In Panjab, however, the administrators of a colonial state worked together to govern a population conquered and deemed backward through a program of civilizing economics. The kinds of activities they engaged in through revenue settlement—invasive studies of soil, irrigation, and crop patterns—and the quality of information they produced—revenue rates and the singular responsibility for their payment—is quite unlike anything found in Europe.[157] Except at fleeting moments, the account of the colonial countryside is largely consistent and harmonious. The lack of disputatiousness suggests the British investment in presenting themselves as a stabilizing force, such that omitting signs of discord served to legitimize their rule. The archive for the standard form of accumulation therefore might only become possible with the peculiar rise of the bourgeoisie and concomitant birth of the proletariat.

Furthermore, when Marx or any other nineteenth-century commentator speaks of the peasant in Europe, they do so with a largely ecumenical vocabulary. Whatever qualities they ascribe to *a* peasant—lazy, cunning, diligent, irrational, dumb, stubborn—it stands in for *all* peasants.[158] The presumption of equality, or at least homogeneity, lumps almost everyone in the countryside into a similar category, perhaps in anticipation of the uniformity of factory labor. However, the mix of disdain and concern English officials exhibited toward English peasants is apart from the contempt, pity, and fear of Company officers toward their newly conquered subjects. In the colonial vocabulary for Panjab, the peasantry was in fact riven with permanent differences, both petty and profound. Some peasants were much lazier than others; some were inclined to work harder; others were quick to become violent or litigious; others still were addicted to thieving, gambling, or intoxication. As economic potential in the colony meant the measuring of people as much as nature, the unique task of the settlement officer was the careful discernment and classification of these qualities. Perceived cultural distinctions, of caste and religion in particular, became fundamental principles in the political economy of Panjabi society. If, as Frantz Fanon asserted, "in the colonies the economic infrastructure is also a superstructure," then its apparent base too is permeated by conceits of culture.[159] Whatever the defects of an English peasant, they do not include the colonialist tropes of fanaticism, bigotry, or a warlike character.

Finally, there is a significant departure in the operations of the government in the metropole and colony. Throughout the struggle between the bourgeoisie and the aristocracy, the English state eventually came to facilitate an accumulation based on a series of separations. Customary practices were abolished, new methods of expropriation legitimized, and a distinct system of discipline emerged, all premised on the dislocation of the peasantry. Ending the manifold fetters of feudalism along with its alleged comforts meant the comprehensive displacement of the agricultural population that inaugurated the theme of rural-to-urban migration. Yet for the colonial state in Panjab, aware of the lessons of empire and wary of any kind of instability in a tense frontier region, the separation and movement of people was to be avoided at all costs. Instead, in an opposite way, this accumulation was an exercise of forging various attachments. Parcels of land were marked and boundaries fixed, the market value of crops established, and the population formally enumerated, all toward assigning individuals the duality of ownership rights and revenue responsibilities. Not only was migration *not* initiated by the administration, it was deliberately suppressed to confine the population to the countryside.

It thus becomes possible to recognize that the peasant that emerged after the first decades of British rule was irreducibly distinct and modern. This peasantry was forged through a new relationship with a powerful bureaucratic and disciplinary state. It struggled to follow a production cycle based on perpetual increase and expansion, and it adopted the abstraction of cash payment bound to the exclusivity of ownership. Perhaps most uniquely, its economic performance was implicated in the evaluation of its cultural and social practices, which came to generate its own set of exclusions, which will be explored in Chapters 2 and 4. In effect, what was accumulated in conjunction with capital was a novel form of state power along with social-scientific knowledge, which together produced a distinctive economic hierarchy in the colony. During the ensuing century of colonial rule—and through an accumulation of attachment rather than separation—it was this peasant that came to occupy a dominant position within rural Panjabi society.

From this vantage, then, the notion of colonial benevolence and its obstruction of capital begins to dissipate. Indeed, the deceptiveness of the question of whether or not the British were benevolent toward the peasant lies in this: an affirmative or negative answer is based on the elemental premise that frames colonialism as economically progressive. At the same time, the critique of the claim of benevolence has little to do with asserting malevolence. That sort of gesture only oscillates between the given terms of debate while leaving their thematic opposition intact.[160] By provincializing the narrative of primitive accumulation and historicizing the conquest and revenue settlement of Panjab, the difference of the Panjabi peasant is neither simply compared nor rendered incomparable to Europe. Rather, through giving that difference a history, the very burden of expectation for a unilateral (and impossible) similarity is lifted. This reveals that expectations of any kind are more the products of subsequent historical experiences and a contingent archive rather than a neutral criterion from which to measure different societies. Colonial benevolence should thus be seen as a claim produced to conceal the novelty of a discordant accumulation both crucial for the empire and yet unlike operations in the metropole. Understanding this dynamic opens up new ways to question as well as pursue the shifting conceptual and empirical grounds for comparison in global history.

TWO

NAMING THE PEASANT
*Colonial Jurisprudence and the Binding
of Identity and Occupation*

THE VAST HETEROGENEITY OF nineteenth-century Panjab presented an incessant challenge to the establishment and consolidation of East India Company rule. Governance through the idioms of reason, order, and benevolence confronted a region that appeared to offer its new conquerors only confusion and contradictions. After the Second Anglo-Sikh War in 1849, nearly 185,000 square miles were added to the Company's empire, an area one-tenth the size of its possessions in South Asia at the time and larger even than the British Isles.[1] Slightly less than half that territory came under its direct control, while the remainder was divided among several subservient yet nominally independent local rulers. In the following decades this balance would increasingly shift as more of these Native States were seized and annexed on one pretext or another. In terms of population, midcentury Panjab contained almost twenty million inhabitants, three-quarters of whom came under direct Company rule, occupying twenty-six thousand villages, two thousand towns, and a dozen major cities.[2] Only 11 percent of its people lived in urban areas, concentrated primarily in the major centers of Amritsar, Lahore, Peshawar, Ludhiana, and Multan. The rest resided in villages distributed unevenly across six alluvial tracts with borders as varied as the foothills of the Himalayas and the fringes of the Thar Desert to the Yamuna River plain and the Sulaiman Mountains.

Perhaps more confounding to officers were the many languages spoken by the peoples in this newly conquered territory. A Hindustani proverb repeated throughout the colonial record—*Har das kos paani badle, aur har bees boli*, or "every twenty miles the water changes, every forty the language"—reflects not only the diversity of vernaculars but also the bewilderment and even frustration of those tasked with categorizing them. According to the 1881 census, three-fifths of the population spoke dialects of Panjabi, by far the most common language of the region, albeit with important degrees of variation. East of the Satluj to the Yamuna, it gradually blended closer to a form of Hindustani; along the loose southern border, it was modified into Bagri (or Marwari), a dialect from Rajputana; more westward toward Multan and Dera Ghazi Khan, the language became Saraiki (or Jatki) and resembled Sindhi; turning north to the Indus Valley it was called Hindko and included many Pashto and Persian words; further upriver around Jhelum and Rawalpindi, Potwari predominated; this permeated into Dogri and Pahari along the northern hill tracts of Chamba and Mandi.[3] Such a plurality of speech, however, did not mean the mutual unintelligibility of its speakers. In fact, numerous officers and missionaries throughout the early decades of colonial rule identified Panjabi—in whatever dialect or variation—as the lingua franca of the region as a whole.[4]

Despite the prevalence of Panjabi, the Board of Administration decided to make Urdu the official language of the government bureaucracy. Spoken by only a fraction of the population and concentrated mainly in urban areas, it was the medium for high commerce, education, and political authority. In selecting Urdu, Company officials sought continuity with previous channels of influence and respectability in order to cultivate support among local elites as well as the convenience of deploying a cohort of officers already linguistically trained from service in the NWP. At the same time, Panjabi was deemed unfit for the needs of administration. Disparaged as a derivative and vulgar patois, it supposedly lacked standardization and was replete with discrepancies of script and pronunciation. It was also presumed to be exclusively associated with Sikhs and the earlier rule of Maharaja Ranjit Singh (though his court language was a form of Persianized Urdu) and was suppressed in order to consolidate the conquest and prevent anti-British incitement.[5] Thus, while English remained the language between Company men in Calcutta and London, a large intermediary group made up of revenue officials, civil judges, district commissioners, and military and police officers used Urdu to issue orders and to interact with a population that overwhelmingly spoke an array of Panjabi.

The result was a marked disconnect between the rulers and the ruled. A glimpse into this world of uncertainty is offered in an early account of the difficulties of a revenue officer. In the 1859 revised settlement of Ludhiana district, Henry Davidson commented on the problem of determining the correct terms to describe exactly who was who and did what in rural Panjab. "Much has been written on the peculiar meaning of the word 'zemindar' in different parts of India," he wrote before explaining:

> Here [in Panjab] the use of the word is very peculiar. Those, generally, who derive their livelihood directly from the soil, are not called zemindars, but "kusans." On approaching a village, and asking what people live in it, if any other race but Jats live in it, the name of the race will be given in reply. But if the population are Jats, the reply will be zemindars live there. "Zemindar log buste;" in fact the word zemindar is here only applied to the Jats.[6]

In other words, while the activity of agriculture might formally correspond to a simple occupational designation (*kusan* or *kisan*), in popular conversation it was usually mentioned in reference to caste identity (such as Jatt but several others as well), which itself could be replaced with a more general term (*zamindar*) depending on the caste but that in turn actually implied land ownership rather than laboring activity. For Davidson, and indeed scores of officers afterward, the incongruence between occupation and identity was compounded by practical contingencies and a dissimilarity of vernacular terminology.

How did British officers trained in Urdu exercise authority and control over this largely Panjabi-speaking people? Bernard Cohn has argued that acquiring knowledge of native languages, especially those considered "classical" such as Persian and Sanskrit, was crucial to achieving Company supremacy in the subcontinent. Beginning in the late eighteenth century, certain languages were studied as pragmatic instruments of daily administration as well as the means for discovering "ancient" scholastic wisdom and accessing the "authentic" customs, traditions, and laws of the people.[7] "The conquest of India was a conquest of knowledge," Cohn states, an "invasion of epistemological space" that allowed the British to classify, categorize, and fix a wealth of fluid social relations into an almost immutable hierarchy.[8] Language mastery was therefore a more elaborate project to "make the unknown and the strange knowable." It entailed a prolonged exercise of translation, simultaneously erecting and traversing barriers of cultural difference in order to transform "Indian knowledge into European information."[9]

The politics of language, however, went beyond the compilation and classification of differences of Indian culture. Instead, I argue, it sharply intersected with a politics of economy to compile and classify differences of labor—of fluid physical activities, strange productive processes, and opaque material relations. In the wake of the seemingly benevolent revenue policy for peasants seen in Chapter 1, this chapter explores the evolving discrepancy between vernacular understandings of cultivation amid attempts by the colonial state to define and order agrarian Panjab. Put differently, I trace how the question of "Who is a peasant?" was both asked and came to be answered. This places census forms, dictionaries, and grammars in conversation with vernacular proverbs, legislative acts, and local petitions. The chapter starts by examining the distinction between identity and occupation among rural Panjabis at the time of conquest, alongside the shifting, faltering British definitions for "peasant," "agriculturalist," and the "agricultural population" in early census operations. Next I explore how the plurality of proverbial articulations for peasant in the 1870s was singularized through the unique format, reach, and organization of the 1881 census. Finally, I analyze the culmination of this process in a novel legal definition for *peasant* in the Punjab Alienation of Land Act (1901), which, although contested by various groups seeking agriculturalist status, nonetheless reshaped access to the land market in the early decades of the twentieth century. As a history of the relentless yet spastic reordering of categories and their attendant material relations, this chapter sits apart from narratives of subaltern agency. Instead, it maps the quiet disruption of economic change through the attenuation of possibilities for those left outside the category of peasant. By following the slight constricting maneuvers that consolidated the marginalization of those classified as menials, vagrants, and servants, I uncover how forms of epistemological exclusion gradually consecrated a new relationship of exploitation.

AGRARIAN EPISTEMOLOGY AT THE CUSP OF CONQUEST

Any investigation into what at first glance appears to be a bygone worldview immediately confronts the problem of inadequate source material. Although the historian's familiar lament of laboring groups not producing diaries and memoirs for the sake of posterity is well known—and challenged—it nevertheless remains a significant point of departure, especially for those concerned with the histories of the colonized world. If unlettered peasants hardly leave a paper trail, what can be expected of landless laborers? Indeed, central to the possibility of writing "history from below" in Europe was the constitution of its archive. This moment in historiography proved compelling at least in part for the ways in which committed, creative historians made use of a variety of materials to conduct research into the lives and life-worlds of non-elite groups.[10] For the colony, however, a distinct set of historical and political conditions generated a very different and unexpected set of materials, one requiring an alternative historiographical enterprise.[11] As Ranajit Guha demonstrated in his study of peasant insurgency in colonial India, nearly every primary source—officer dispatches, police reports, and legal judgments but also vernacular folklore and anecdotes—was elitist in nature and usually hostile to the outlook and activities of the insurgents.[12] Yet through a particular practice of reading, there emerged a possibility for writing a history that did not simply reproduce the narrative of the colonial state or assimilate peasant insurgency as "merely an element in the career of colonialism."[13] By making use of the direct transcription of rebel utterances by officials while also inverting the valence of their secondary commentary, Guha was able to reposition the peasant rebel from object to subject in the history of anticolonial insurgency.

While this method allows for a certain access to aspects of rebel consciousness, it also presents limitations for histories of the everyday. Only the heightened intensity of an insurgency transformed colonial condescension into an active fear that prompted the writing of reports filled with long extracts, careful observations, and exaggerated claims. Times considered ordinary and issues thought of as routine did not elicit the same excessive detail and hyperbole. The division of labor in rural Panjab—the nature of its organization and the changing terms of its hierarchies as well as the texture of the lives of those in its ambit—hardly alarmed colonial authorities into producing a similar level of documentary concern. Nor did it generate a straightforwardly polarized struggle between exploited and exploiter in the sense James Scott provided for a Malaysian village in the late 1970s. Although "everyday forms of peasant resistance make no headlines," the analytic of resistance itself points to interpreting acts such as foot-dragging, pilfering, and slander as gestures of an incipient opposition to the status quo.[14] In other words, the "small arms fire in the class war" presupposes both class and war, a relationship that, while true axiomatically, is more difficult to discern and substantiate in situations where moral (and material) economies are subtly reordered rather than violated outright.[15] It is also relevant that such research and arguments rely heavily on ethnography, a methodology normally unavailable to historians. Thus, in addition to the usual restrictions of poverty, illiteracy, precarity, and the difference of the colonial gaze, the potential archive of changing agrarian relations in Panjab is more fragmentary and challenging.

A possible, albeit skewed, avenue into the earlier understandings of Panjabi agriculture comes through the existent dictionaries and grammars produced by officers and missionaries around the time of conquest. These texts capture a pivotal moment of agrarian relations, emerging as an object of inquiry and yet prior to the full onset of colonial governance. Although this genre obviously does not completely reconstruct perceptions that were eventually foreclosed, it can offer insights into forms of knowledge and methods of organization in a moment of flux. One of the first Panjabi-English dictionaries, published in 1849, was produced by an infantry captain in the Company's army named Samuel Starkey. Over four hundred pages long and lacking a preface, this text is divided into a dictionary, a basic grammar, and a series of translated colloquial dialogues.[16] While there is no explanation within the text of who exactly Starkey consulted to produce his definitions, the title page does mention the assistance of a native *jemadar* (low-level revenue official) named Bussawa Singh, perhaps recruited from one of the Native States under Company protection after 1809.[17] Intended primarily for use by officers communicating with local Panjabi interlocutors, this document makes no claim of comprehensiveness. All the translations are transliterated in Roman script and unidirectional from

English to Panjabi, covering words central to the functioning of the colonial bureaucracy and exchanges essential for acquiring useful information and conveying specific commands. As a pragmatic rather than pedagogic text, it provides a glimpse into the basic orientation of agrarian relations in the early nineteenth century.

The intricacies of definition, correspondence, and implication reveal a strikingly unique logic. Starkey translates *agriculture* into three words: *wahee, khetee,* and *kursanee*. The term *cultivation* is given as *wugdee* and *hulwaee*. And *farming* is rendered into the phrases *halee da kum* and *wahee da kum*.[18] Taken together, these definitions mean variations of the work of plowing (wahee, hulwaee) and work relating to fields (khetee), or the work done by a kisan. Yet when each of the corresponding individual nouns is defined, the result is a subtle circularity. An "agriculturalist" is a *hale* or a *hurwaee*; a "cultivator" is a *waun waone wala* or a *hulwaee kurne wala*; and a "farmer" is an *ujara chookoun wala* or a *thekha kurun wala*.[19] This set of phrases denotes a person doing a specific task—*x*-wala—as one who plows or clears land or makes such work proceed.

What is significant about this relationship is precisely the marked disjuncture between occupation and identity. Cultivation, for instance, is *not* done by a given cultivator, someone predisposed by caste or religion to cultivation, but instead simply by *one who cultivates*. Furthermore, the definition for *peasant*—perhaps the central locus of colonial discourse and discipline in the late nineteenth century—is given simply as *pind wala*, meaning a village dweller.[20] In other words, nowhere in this dictionary is a particular occupational identity given a cultural or religious connotation, nor are there any implications of who is designated to perform which kinds of work in advance. Although *landholders* are both *jumeendars* and *juts* (Jatts), somewhat anticipating Davidson's later observations discussed in Chapter 1, laborers are rendered as caste-less *mujoors*, a variant of the present-day *mazdoor*. In fact, the word *caste* is not defined at all in the dictionary. *Jat*, or more properly *jaat/jati* and distinct from the caste of Jatts, is the term used for *clan* as well as *race* and even *class*, synonyms that join "nation" and "tribe" in many parts of north India.[21] Without the automatic mediation of caste, this rendering of agrarian relations demonstrates a crucial dissonance between individuality and labor.

Captain Starkey was not alone in his linguistic interest in Panjabi. In 1833, missionaries from the American Presbyterian Church arrived in the cis-Satluj city of Ludhiana to begin proselytizing among the local population. The next year they established the region's first vernacular printing press, subsequently publishing translations of the Bible as well as various texts on language, grammar, and geography, all of which received patronage from the Company.[22] Their most important publication, however, was another first, a lengthy Panjabi dictionary in the Gurmukhi script, started by the Reverend John Newton and completed by a committee headed by Levi Janvier in 1854.[23] Similar to Starkey's work in not divulging information about the manner of its compilation, it also contains a few notable idiosyncrasies. The dictionary uses the Gurmukhi alphabet but begins with the sound "a" followed by "e" and then "o" (rather than the correct order of "o," "a," and "e"), before continuing in the standard Panjabi sequence. Also, it includes only thirty-five letters, excluding the last five of the alphabet that produce the sounds *sh, khh, gh, z,* and *lh*.[24] As a production of missionaries, this dictionary can be seen as a more comprehensive though not quite scholarly publication, discarding formal rules in favor of colloquial usages to better convey information about Panjab and Panjabis.

Designed to render the language knowable for heavenly as much as earthly purposes, Newton's dictionary offers Panjabi words in Gurmukhi transliterated into Roman script and then translated into English. *Kheti* here is rendered as "agriculture," "cultivation," and "a cultivated field," so that *kheti karnee* becomes the verb "to cultivate land." While *khet* itself is translated as "a field under cultivation" and, poetically, "a battlefield," *kisan* is both a farmer and a husbandman.[25] In a similar manner, *jimin*—pronounced colloquially, without the *z* sound for the more standard *zamin*—is "the earth," "soil," and "land" as well as "region" and "country." The entry for *jimindar* therefore reads: "a cultivator; a farmer; a landlord; [and] a landholder."[26] Parallel to Starkey, these terms share a notable absence of any cultural connotations for agrarian activities. A task is simply performed by whoever performs that task—again, cultivation by those who cultivate.

The novelty of Newton's dictionary lies in the variegated descriptions of ostensibly lower- and higher-caste groups. Beginning with the words *kamm* for "work" or "business" and *kam* meaning "deficient," "less," and "little," lines of continuity are traced through to broad segments of the population. Thus, a *kamm chalau* is given as an industrious man (though its meaning can be quite different today), and a *kammchor* is one who is unwilling to work. *Kamjor* is an adjective for weak or without strength, while *kambna* is to shake or tremble. If notions of work and status draw closer at *kamau*, defined simultaneously as an earner *and* a laborer, they seem to meet at the word *kamin*. This is rendered as not only the adjective for "deficiency" and "loss" but also the noun for "an abject person," "a menial," and "a person of low caste."[27] Its cognates are equally revealing. *Kaminpuna* is a state of meanness, baseness, and low rank, with *kamut* given as "an ignoble" or "a worthless person" and *kaminani* as "a woman of low birth." In Starkey's case, on the other hand, these terms remain both distinct and conventional: work is simply *kum* (*kam*) or *kar*, deficiency is *ghut* (*ghat*), and little is *thora*, while menial is *tueleea*.[28] Although such linkages may in fact have occurred in everyday speech, Newton's text is perhaps the first time in the English language that Panjabi words for labor were discursively associated with a broad condition of subordination. At the same time, this kind of translation is not very surprising considering that missionaries targeted precisely this group of castes for conversion to Christianity.[29]

At the other end of the spectrum, Newton offers a more elaborate description of groups identified as Jatts.[30] Initially, they are defined plainly as "the name of a caste of farmers (both Hindu and Muhammadan)." Subsequent cognate entries, however, take a rather different tone. Directly beneath *jatt* is the peculiar adverb *jatt jappha*, with the following meaning:

> Seizing and throwing down by main force, as practiced by *Jatts* and other rough plain people who are unacquainted with the arts of wrestlers, seizing suddenly in wrestling, so as to preclude trick on the part of the opponent.[31]

Not only do Jatts have a penchant for farming, but according to this statement, they also seem aptly suited to a peculiar practice of grappling. What is more, an entire gamut of words deriving from Jatt with explicitly pejorative denotations follows. Among the notable are *jatbahir*, an adjective for "ignorant, rude, clownish [and] coarse"; *jatbiddia*, given as "the ingenuity and deceit which characterize *Jatts*"; *jatall*, meaning "falsehood, quibbling, a lie"; and thereby *jatalli* to mean "a liar, one who talks nonsense." There is even a separate term for one "fabricating false and nonsensical poetic sentences," a *jatall kafia*.[32] In a somewhat contradictory way, Newton's dictionary therefore both reproduces and exceeds the parameters of Starkey's. On the one hand, it confirms the dissimilarity between occupation and identity, but on the other, it provides many more details—some clear-cut, some perplexing—about the qualities associated with certain caste groups. Not insignificantly, these latter qualities almost all derive from something other than the kinds of labor these individuals perform. Jatts are associated with farming as much as they are with jostling and joking.

Perhaps the most strictly instrumental midcentury exploration of local languages is Horace H. Wilson's *Glossary of Judicial and Revenue Terms* of 1855. In an extensive preface, he relates the frustration of Company officials, both in London and the subcontinent, who encounter vernacular words inaccurately, inconsistently, and without proper explanation in a wide assortment of administrative documents. Part of this, Wilson notes, is unavoidable and even useful, giving as an example how the word *ryot* suggests "more precise and positive notions" than "would be conveyed by cultivator, or peasant, or agriculturalist" in the southern parts of British India.[33] At the same time, however, a far greater number of cases stem from the simple indolence of officers reluctant to take the trouble of finding the equivalent words in English. Their disregard is compounded by the sheer number of languages through which the business of local government is conducted, the (chronic) suspicion of dishonesty among translators, and the unchecked repetition of errors by clerks and journalists. To begin to rectify this problem, explains Wilson, the Court of Directors issued orders in 1842 soliciting vernacular entries from administrators and specialists across the various territories of the empire.[34] After a prolonged period of collecting, comparing, and compiling, a volume spanning nearly six hundred pages and containing over twenty-six thousand words in thirteen languages written in nine different scripts was finally published thirteen years later.[35]

Although Panjabi does not figure as a separate language in this volume, the structure of Hindustani from the NWP bears enough of a resemblance to convey insights from the other side of the Yamuna. Much like Starkey, words surrounding *khet* are still neutral: *khetdar* is given as "the occupant or owner of a field," *khetihar* is plainly a "cultivator," *khetipatari* is either "agricultural labour" or "field work." Similarly, *kisan* and *kashtkar* are synonyms for the familiar husbandman or cultivator.[36] For the evaluation of specific groups, Wilson appears to follow Newton, though with important distinctions. *Kamen* here also stands for "base, low, inferior," a term applied to "artificers and servants of a village." Yet in addition to receiving allowances in grain, Wilson states that this group is given "small allotments in land, and are therefore 'minor' or inferior cultivators."[37] Their inferiority, in other words, derives at least to some degree from the small size of their landholdings. *Jat* too is explained as both an "industrious and enterprising cultivator" and "a brave and hardy race," made up of numerous Hindu, Sikh, and Muslim clans throughout the northwest of the subcontinent.[38] Their specific agricultural acumen is therefore in tandem with the more general qualities of bravery and strength. In this way, Wilson distributes notions of superiority and inferiority throughout different groups while maintaining a distance between caste identities and agrarian activities.

From these different linguistic registers, it seems clear that there was nothing indelible or inherent about the kinds of activities performed by specific groups during this period. If Starkey's text was designed as a rudimentary guide for officers in the field, Newton's was intended to equip missionaries with the ability to spread the gospel among the nonbelievers, while Wilson's facilitated the comprehension of documents by higher officials and scholars. And although any exercise of translation cannot be considered a direct conversion of form with identical content—what Wilson called transferring words "from their native garb to an English dress"—all three disclose a common theme.[39] That is, the vocabulary of agriculture is largely non-ascriptive, almost tautological, with the words for particular activities deriving from the activity itself and not a given caste group. In other words, there is no correspondence between occupation and identity. This suggests that even if rural Panjabis understood occupation and caste to be related phenomena, at this point the two were not identical and in fact entailed considerable degrees of variation based on circumstances. The answer to the (unasked) question "Who is a peasant?" would therefore not automatically be specific castes, sub-castes, or even identifiable cultural groups. Labor remained separate from the surplus of colonially defined notions of community and culture. At this critical juncture in mid-nineteenth-century Panjab, with the quest for knowledge slightly ahead of the full onslaught of colonial rule, the world of agrarian relations remained heterogeneous where it was not flexible and even fluid.

THE AMBIGUITY OF ENUMERATION

If there was no direct, comprehensive correspondence between identity and occupation in early nineteenth-century Panjab, the asymmetrical encounter with the new colonial regime introduced a dramatically different ordering of agrarian relations. Central to this wayward and uneven process was the scientific enumeration of the population through the instrument of the colonial census. To define and count subjects in an accurate way offered what one scholar terms "a panorama of Indian life," yielding immense and unprecedented powers ranging from the rational assessment and collection of land revenue, to the proportional (and disproportional) recruitment of soldiers, to the delineation and control of various castes, tribes, and religions.[40] Such calculations began with settlement activity well before the complete annexation of 1849: the earliest rudimentary figures for portions of Ludhiana district are from 1835, and a basic count of the population of Ferozepur district dates from 1841.[41] Nevertheless, the specific instrument for producing enumerative knowledge was the series of official censuses, occurring first in 1855 and followed by 1868 and then in unison across British India in 1881 and every decade thereafter until 1941 and into post-independence India.[42] It was through this medium that a new reason bolstered by force encountered and reordered the heterogeneity of rural Panjabi society. For the question of the peasant—or the myriad questions of the cultivator, the kisan, the agriculturalist, the *kheti karn vala*, the farmer—the census demonstrates the ways that enumeration aligned identity and occupation to create a novel understanding of social and economic relations.

This sequence of census dates gives the impression of a gradually progressive exercise of power, and thereby obfuscates the more subtle, irregular, or circuitous elements it brought into being. Historiographically, the first two censuses are usually downplayed or overlooked altogether, taken at best as flawed antecedents to the reliable consistency starting with the third. In other words, one can discern a slight haste to move past 1855 and 1868 to get to the main attraction of 1881.[43] Part of this stems from a disciplinary emphasis on straightforward accuracy—adopting the logic of the census itself—which contrasts the earlier reliance on aggregation and extrapolation against the "actual enumeration of the people" that is most desirable when engaged in counting. Indeed, while the 1855 and 1868 census reports are twenty-six and fifty-five pages, respectively, the 1881 report amounts to nearly five hundred pages, with an almost equal number of pages containing various tables, charts, and appendixes. Denzil Ibbetson, the author of the 1881 text, is also usually regarded as a gifted administrator, who possessed an impressive ability to compile and distill vast amounts of data into readable prose.[44] Yet what was produced in this kind of evaluation was its own anachronism, the ahistorical comparison of credibility between 1855 or 1868 and 1881. The apparent lack of accuracy or dearth of details that a census provides matters far less than its internal coherence and contemporary reception. The solution, as Kenneth Jones puts it, is to read the census "not as a data source" but "as the subject of research itself."[45] In this sense, the value of the early censuses lies in the career of the categories they inaugurate, the way certain understandings about agrarian relations came to acquire a force to restructure Panjabi society. What was consolidated from 1855 to 1881 was therefore not scientificity but the power to make a scientific claim.

Chief commissioner John Lawrence decided to comprehensively count the population of Panjab a little over five years after conquest. Following the convention established in the Bengal Presidency and the NWP, he decreed that "all persons should be numbered who might sleep in any house of every city, town, village, hamlet, and detached tenement, bearing a known name, during the night intervening between the 31st of December 1854 and the 1st of January 1855."[46] Instructions were drawn up and sent to the various districts two months in advance; each was divided and subdivided down to the village level; local commissioners drafted both English and literate native members of the bureaucracy to assist with the execution.[47] Indeed, "in many places," the reports disclosed, "the Mahomedan moollah [*mullah*], the Sikh girunthee [*granthi*] or scripture reader, the village school-master and his pupils, the petty trader, the chief cattle grazer, were selected to aid in the work of enumeration."[48] After all the entries were completed throughout the night, the returns made their way first to the local supervising officer for attestation over the next few days, then to the division commissioners in large cities for compilation and retesting over several months, and then to financial commissioner Donald McLeod in Lahore for review before appearing in the final report published by Richard Temple early the next year. The single greatest concern of the administration, that the counting would estrange and anger the local population, was quickly disproved by repeated accounts of the "alacrity and good humor" with which census officers were received in the various districts. "The utter absence of alarm among the inhabitants," writes Temple, was "truly remarkable," a sign that they "understood the work to be a statistical investigation, with no special or ulterior design."[49] As a result, the report expresses confidence in the numbers it furnishes. While some returns did raise doubts, Temple noted, the "great majority" of local authorities concurred with the "general fidelity of the census."[50] Thus, with a rigorous methodology, efficient bureaucracy, and docile population, the first census of Panjab is both presented and understood as a confident, if brief, success.

A significant consequence of this logistical and arithmetical feat is the broad categories into which the population is divided. Two notable divisions are enacted: Hindu/Muslim and agricultural/non-agricultural. On the one hand, the report finds that out of a population of 12,717,821 under direct Company rule at the time, there are 5,352,874 Hindus (which included Sikhs)[51] and 7,364,974 Muslims.[52] Besides a few additional remarks on the preponderance of Hindus in eastern districts and Muslims in western districts, and some comparisons of overall density with other territories, little is said about this stark religious binary. For the agriculturalists' split, on the other hand, Temple offered somewhat more commentary. While officially "the proportion of agriculturalists to total population is 56 per cent," he wrote, the actual number should "be greater than that shown." In fact, not only was it "probable that three-fourths subsist on agriculture," but had the proper definition been followed, no less than "four-fifths of the population would have been returned as agriculturalists." The problem appears to stem from both comprehending and applying the correct criterion, quickly mentioned as "persons deriving any part of their subsistence from the land." Such discrepancy thereby extends beyond accuracy and aggregation to the very operative categories of the census itself. Temple explained that the difficulty was the result of "enforcing attention to the definition which appears to be seldom understood by the agency employed."[53] In other words, the basis to determine who was an agriculturalist was confusing not only for the people being enumerated but for the enumerators themselves. It is only here that a sense of doubt creeps into an otherwise self-assured expression of colonial will.

The uncertainty in the absolute number and relative proportion of agriculturalists is compounded by the fact that nowhere in the report is a full explanation of the criterion for an agriculturalist given. Who exactly was an agriculturalist? What were the means for being admitted into this category? And why did this form of difference matter to colonial officials at this time? For these articulations, one must look farther east and earlier, to the census operations of the NWP in the 1840s.[54] In response to the "extraordinary errors" of previous censuses, the Court of Directors ordered that future efforts be conducted with stricter rigor "to guard against the transmission hereafter of any statement so deficient in accuracy."[55] At the local level, John Thornton, a secretary to the government in NWP, issued a series of circulars to all district collectors of land revenue (who doubled as census enumerators at the time). On October 22, 1846, he provided, among several other new guidelines, an explicit criterion for differentiating the population:

> All *persons* who derive their subsistence, in whole or in part from the land, whether in the form of wages or rent, should be shown as *cultivators,* even though they may have other sources of income.[56]

Thus, individuals were to be counted as cultivators based on deriving their subsistence as income from any activity relating to land. A year later, however, Thornton found the results unsatisfactory, complaining that "care does not seem to be generally taken in discriminating between the agricultural and non-agricultural Classes." In a circular dated November 15, 1847, he attempted to clarify his instructions by referring to the previous definition—but modified it in the process. "You will observe," he stated, that the *members of all families* who derive their support or any part of their income from the cultivation of land are to be entered as *agricultural*, whether or not they actually hold the plough or personally conduct the usual agricultural operations.[57]

All of a sudden, new elements are introduced: the members of a family are taken as a single unit; they are given the broader title of "agricultural" rather than the more specific "cultivators"; the relationship to land and agrarian activities is much more expansive; and they are now deemed a *class*. Yet a few years later, this definition was again unconsciously altered through another iteration. In a circular dated July 22, 1852, this time written by secretary William Muir, more precise directions were given for filling out census columns:

[T]hose families are to be shown as agricultural, of whom *the head* derives the whole or any part of his subsistence from the possession or cultivation of land.[58]

Presented as continuity while in fact instituting several changes, this definition now emphasized a much narrower range of activities performed by the purported head of a family as the basis for agricultural status. As Cohn notes, certain conceptual problems were thus "built into the economic categories of the census."[59] Equally remarkable is what is absent: there is no mention of castes, vernacular terms, or claims of blood, community, or culture. The slippage from single cultivators to collective agriculturalists passes as an unnoticed repetition.

In addition to written instructions, both Thornton and Muir appended blank census forms and charts with sample returns to their circular orders. The 1848 form included eleven columns along with space to record village, circle (locality), and district information (see Figure 2.1). Each family house was numbered, with the "name of the master of the house or family" standing in for its members, followed by a numerical allocation within the binaries of "Hindoos/Mahomedans," "Agricultural/Non-Agricultural," and "Males/Females." The same form was used in 1852, with slightly different wording and a new column added for officers' remarks. When filled out, it showed how a single patriarch became the metonym for a family counted and distributed across a neat row (see Figure 2.2). In the village

Number of enclosure.	Number of house or family.	Name of the master of the house or family.	Hindoos.				Mahomedan and others not Hindoos.			
			Agricultural.		Non-Agricultural.		Agricultural.		Non-Agricultural.	
			Males.	Females.	Males.	Females.	Males.	Females.	Males.	Females.

Return of the number of persons who on the night of December 31st or Poos ———————. F. S. were present in the ——————— of ——————— Pergunnah ———————

Note.—Whenever there are strangers in a house they should be entered in a separate line from the members of the family. The totals of the 2 lines would then show the number of persons in the house on the night specified.

FIGURE 2.1 A blank return form used in the 1848 census of the North West Provinces. Source: A. Shakespear, *Memoir on the Statistics of the North Western Provinces of the Bengal Presidency* (Calcutta: Baptist Mission Press, 1848), 175.

of Khundoulee, for instance, "Richpal Singh" appears as the head of an "agricultural Hindoo" family comprising four males and two females living within the two enclosures of his house, while "Khodabux" leads a "non-agricultural" family of "Mahometan" (or possibly another "non-Hindoo") religion, consisting of three males and two females with a four-enclosure house. When a version of that form was used to aggregate information from several different villages, the result was a succinct statement about those buildings, bodies, and activities important to colonial officials. Labor therefore inhabited a space between religion and gender as a constitutive organizing principle of society.

In the hands of different NWP officers, the definition of agriculturalist thereby underwent significant change during the mid-nineteenth century. From cultivators earning income from land use, to the wider class of agricultural family units, to a single agricultural patriarch deriving

No. of enclosure.	No. of house.	Name of the master of the house, or head of the family.	HINDOOS.				MAHOMETANS AND OTHERS NOT HINDOOS.				REMARKS.
			Agricultural.		Non-agricultural.		Agricultural.		Non-agricultural.		
			Males.	Females.	Males.	Females.	Males.	Females.	Males.	Females.	
1	2	3	4	5	6	7	8	9	10	11	12
1	1	Buldeo Singh,.....	3	4	0	0	0	0	0	0	
2	2	Richpal Singh, ..	4	2	0	0	0	0	0	0	
0	3	Nihal Singh, ...	2	5	0	0	0	0	0	0	
3	4	Nutthoo,.........	0	0	3	3	0	0	0	0	
0	5	Seyrhoo, ...	0	0	5	4	0	0	0	0	
4	6	Khodabux, ...	0	0	0	0	0	0	3	2	
5	7	Mohumed Khan,..	0	0	0	0	4	1	0	0	
6	8	Pohpal Singh, ...	2	3	0	0	0	0	0	0	
		Strangers, ...	3	2	0	0	0	0	0	0	Visitors from another village.
7	9	Kulloo, bhuttyara,	0	0	0	0	0	0	3	2	
		Strangers, ...	0	0	0	0	0	0	5	1	Travellers put up for the night.
		Total,...	14	16	8	7	4	1	11	5	66 total of persons.

FIGURE 2.2 A sample of the returns for the 1852 census in the North West Provinces. Source: G. J. Christian, Report on the *Census of the North West Provinces of the Bengal Presidency, taken on the 1st of January, 1853* (Calcutta: Baptist Mission Press, 1854), 14.

subsistence, the criterion shifted in whimsical ways. At the same time, parallel shifts occurred with other elements within the census. For example, the second column on the above form reflected an attempt to use "house" and "family" interchangeably: initially, officials assumed a family was simply a group that lived together; later they specified "cooking at the same *choolah* [hearth]" as the essential distinction; eventually they settled on a hybrid scheme of enclosures within a house.[60] Gender and age too fluctuated: first the separation between males and females was considered "useless" for want of accurate counting; then it was deemed necessary for adults but not for children; later, in some districts, males under the age of twelve were considered "boys" while females under ten were "girls" (based on different measures of puberty); then the distinction was discarded for a time; and finally, the official threshold for adulthood was established at age twelve for both genders.⁶¹ Amid all of this uncertainty, hardly anything in these early articulations of enumerative logic was actually logical.

More importantly, these operational shifts aligned with a changing perception of the purpose of the census and its ability to garner truth. In the beginning, Company officials were hesitant, even pessimistic about the potential of enumeration. A constant anxiety over the "carelessness or wilful concealment" by locals amplified the myriad problems of altered boundaries, omissions of rent-free holdings, repetition of discrepancies, and unsystematic methods. Indeed, beyond deceit, officials were concerned with outright native opposition. "Any census based on actual enumeration of the people," wrote Thornton in 1846, "will probably be vexatious and erroneous." Even though the census was supposed to bring about "most for the good and happiness of the people," intention and execution did not always coincide. Thornton went on to explain the disconnect:

> If the people themselves are unable to understand this, and if the diligent prosecution of the enquiry, either from the dishonesty of the Agents employed, or from the ignorant apprehensions of the people, becomes the cause of loss or injury to them, it will be better to desist at present from the enquiry, or to be satisfied with a less degree of accuracy, than might be otherwise obtained.⁶²

Around the time of the annexation of Panjab, however, the Company appeared to become more assertive and intrusive. A reversal of sorts took place, with the use of intermediaries and extrapolation from averages supplanted by a growing demand for accuracy. New rules implemented in 1851 read: "The returns should be compiled not from averages of the number of persons to a house, but from actual enumeration of the people, which should be made on a certain day to be previously fixed."⁶³ The census therefore became a universal exercise, a common form filled out by trained officers in the field throughout the territory over the course of a single night. Gone too was the fear of opposition and the insecurity and restraint it generated. "It is now well understood," declared Muir, "that the Government seeks information regarding the state of the people, in order to improve their condition, and not with a view to add to their burthens [*sic*]."⁶⁴ The possibility for accuracy thereby gained a new valence. What was initially a means to acquire greater and better knowledge of a local population for the functioning of the Company bureaucracy later became an end presented as synonymous with the improvement of that very population. Confidence replaced caution when the gathering of information *about* natives became information *for* natives. From a tool of empire, the census became an act of responsible government.

Through the intricacies of knowledge and rule in the NWP, a distinct definition of agriculturalist entered the administrative logic of Panjab. In the 1855 census, it remained largely implicit, occurring in the background of the operations, structuring some of the questions asked and some of the forms of representing the responses given. This is why Temple's figures for agriculturalists fluctuated so widely, from 50 to 80 percent of the population. Precision was elusive because it was neither urgent nor possible. Moreover, the category itself was isolated from other elements of Panjabi society. Aside from a certain notion of religious difference, no count was made of any other significant division of the population. "No detail of castes and tribes has been attempted on the present occasion," explained Temple, even though "such a classification would . . . possess much ethnological interest." What was provided, though, was a brief abstract of castes from certain districts where enterprising officers made inquiries on their own. Thus, the category Hindu was subdivided into six groupings: "Brahmins," "Jat," "Goojur," "Rajpoot," "Kumbo," and "Miscellaneous." Remarkably, this last group accounted for more than half of the entire category. Similarly, for Muslims there are seven subdivisions: "Jat," "Goojur," "Rajpoot," "Raen," "Awan," the curious combine of "Shaik-Syud-Mogul-Pathan," and, finally, "Miscellaneous." Here the latter is nearly 70 percent of the whole. Thus, in the first articulation of caste difference in the earliest official census of Panjab, "Miscellaneous" castes accounted for three-fifths of the entire population.[65] Nevertheless, whatever it might have seemed afterward, this lacuna did not impede Temple from considering the exercise both useful and successful at the time.

The report on the 1868 census expresses a rather different evaluation of efficacy. Instead of critiquing his predecessor, however, its author, John Andrew Erasmus Miller, was more aware of the limits of his own work.

After the scheduled 1864 census was cancelled by Lawrence (in his new capacity as Governor-General of India), another date was set for the night of January 10th three years later.[66] On this occasion, the administration sent much more detailed instructions seven months in advance, complete with an intricate series of checks and comparisons to ensure accuracy; it even ordered that the name of each house owner be written on an exterior wall to allow subsequent verification.[67] The population too was docile, the report repeats, accepting the census enumerators without raising an objection. Yet despite an entrenched bureaucracy with more time, resources, and preparation, Miller was considerably less sure of the statistics generated. He explained his reservations in a longwinded sentence:

> Upon the whole, *though absolute correctness cannot be claimed* for the returns of a Census even in the most enlightened countries, and still less in a Province where only 22 persons in a thousand can read and write, and where there is in common with most Eastern countries a general tendency among the people to be inaccurate in their statements of the simplest facts, the general belief among those who have had the most intimate connection with the preparation of the Returns of this Census is, that they are *for all practical purposes correct.*[68]

Tortuously combining the inherent difficulties of enumeration with low levels of literacy amid a "mendacity that is seen as constitutional to most natives," the author of the census of 1868 appeared to make do with a practical rather than absolute correctness.[69]

A major reason for Miller's pessimism was the renewed difficulties surrounding the classification of agriculturalists. In this census, the population was divided into six different classes, within which there were seventeen distinct orders, containing a total of 124 separate occupations.[70] For "Class IV—Agriculturalists," for instance, the six orders included proprietors, tenants, laborers/pastoralists, shepherds, graziers, and herdsmen, now grouped in four religions (Hindu, Muslim, Sikh, and "Others") for both male and female genders.[71] While such a minute breakdown gives the impression of rigor, it is in fact riddled with various surpluses and contradictions that belie its claims of precision. First, within each of the three main orders for agriculturalists (Proprietors, Tenants, and Labourers), there existed a sizable number of individuals not identified with a particular religion. Out of 3,245,479 total tenants, 86,389 are marked as "Others"; of 318,845 laborers, 77,034 are "Others." Crucially, this was not a matter of placing these groups within the appropriate religion or even devising a proper name for the beliefs they might have followed. Instead, these "Others" demonstrate a failure less of classifying certain individuals than of the classificatory scheme tout suite. In other words, against such unclassifiable individuals, the assertion of, say, 665,353 "Sikh proprietors" or 1,901,214 "Muslim tenants" itself becomes suspect.

The report also discloses rather flagrant errors in labeling and counting the caste of "Chumars" (Chamars). On the one hand, they were mistakenly deemed "sweepers" instead of the usual colonial designation of tanners and leather-workers, possibly through confusion with another rural lower-caste group, the Churhas.[72] At different points Miller also mentioned Chamars following a range of occupations, from laborers to shoemakers and even proprietor/tenants. On the other hand, he related that while some officers included them within the category of "Hindoos," others counted them as "Others," thereby skewing the returns for both religion and occupation. Although the short chart and memorandum explaining this last discrepancy was attached to the report, it further revealed incomplete (and implausible) figures in several districts.[73] Chamars were therefore misidentified yet connected with agriculture, miscounted yet allocated into new divisions, a part of society yet apart from it.

Finally, the category of agricultural laborers is much larger than the figures included under the class of agriculturalists. While the total number of laborers was 318,845 under that specific heading, many hundreds of thousands more were distributed throughout other quarters of the census. Laborers abounded in different guises: in Class V—Industrial, there were 616,748; Class II—Domestic contained 172,695 "servants," 240,484 "water carriers," and 502,742 "sweepers"; even Class VI—Independent included 434,962 "beggars" and, most nonsensically, 148,413 "miscellaneous others."[74] While not all were necessarily dedicated entirely to agriculture, it is more than likely that the great majority were connected in one way or another to the rhythms of agrarian production, whether as seasonal laborers for planting and harvesting or as small self-cultivators. Indeed, Miller too expressed discontent at this imprecision: "It is unsatisfactory to find so large a number recorded of persons who it was impossible to include under one or other of the headings in a very voluminous list of Occupations."[75] Amid a myriad of other anomalies and misgivings—only fourteen "money dealers" in all of Muzaffargargh district, the "manifestly absurd" dearth of "coolies" in Hoshiarpur, the problem of "salt merchants" selling more than just salt in Rawalpindi[76]—the census of 1868 was thereby shorn of its presumptive truths by its own articulations.

Such uncertainty and inaccuracy not only continued but dramatically increased in the census report of 1871. While heralded as "the first approach" to take "a general census for the whole of India at a given date," it did not entail any new enumerations for Panjab, Oude (Awadh), or Berar (eastern Maharashtra). Since those territories had recently completed internal censuses of their own, officials thought it "undesirable to incur the expense or disturb the people" so soon—an indication that previous operations had not been as untroubled as had been claimed.[77] Instead, the returns from 1868 were simply reused, albeit with a slightly different metric, and integrated into the rubric for all-India comparisons. "There seems to have been very little effort," points out Cohn of the 1871 iteration, "to make the provincial censuses comparable to each other."[78] By re-packaging the same faulty data as before, the outcome was unsurprising.

A litany of conflations and contradictions followed, only some of which were apprehended by the report's author, Henry Waterfield. The distribution of "sweeper castes" (here the vernacular is not given) into the categories of "Hindoos" and "Others" was repeated as the reason that an accurate count of religions remained elusive. Also, in several paragraphs glossing over the hereditary divisions permeating Indian society, the word "caste" is interchanged with "tribe" and also "class" and "race," thus beginning the slide toward the later formulation of agricultural tribes.[79] More explicitly, Waterfield seemed to acknowledge a few of the obviously absurd occupational classifications—forty-nine spies in Monghyr (Munger) district, twenty professional gamblers in Bengal, five pigeon-flyers in the city of Patna, thirty *budmashes* ("bad characters") in NWP, three witches in the whole country—while at the same time complaining that the enumerators missed "the distinction between insane persons and idiots."[80] For the specific question of agriculturalists, the disclosures were even more candid. Although the majority of the population of India as a whole was "directly interested in agriculture," the "precise percentage cannot be stated with accuracy." The problem, Waterfield noted, was the "impossibility, in most cases, of saying what proportion of the laborers is engaged in farming operations."[81] Moreover,

> it must be remembered that the actual number of persons engaged in tilling the soil is not limited to the number of male agricultural adults, as considerable assistance is given by women and boys, while many artisans and tradesmen own plots of land which they cultivate with the aid of younger members of their families.[82]

The figures for agriculturalists, descriptive and enumerative, yet again descended into obscurity.

What this itinerary of the first censuses in Panjab and the transfer of categories from NWP reveals is an important series of contingent shifts. At one level, confidence in the accuracy of the census began strongly in 1855, faltered in 1868, and almost completely floundered in 1871. Far from a growing faith in the progressive march of numbers, colonial officials were beset with ongoing confusion on the subjects they were attempting to classify and count. It is almost as if the greater reliance on and invocation of scientific accuracy produced a corresponding rise in doubt and frustration. On another level, occupation is throughout located as a subset of religion rather than caste. Groupings of agriculturalists and other nebulously related designations are divided between Hindus, Muslims, Sikhs, and Others, but in a way that the quality of religion does not impinge on the occupation itself. Strangely, given the minute concern for differences by settlement officers, it was almost irrelevant in the census if a proprietor or laborer is a Muslim or a Sikh. As a result, the problem of the Other was determining its proper religious designation rather than its caste or occupation. Finally, these decades witnessed the migration, and alternation, of the term *agriculturalist* from east to west. Paradoxically laden with multiple meanings through the process of its defining, the notion of the agriculturalist by the 1870s signified a peculiar dilemma in the colonial imagination. The inchoate nature of this definition prepared the ground for a confrontation between the identity/occupation divide for rural Panjabis and the patterns of life census enumerators were attempting to regiment and quantify. If the recalcitrant question of "Who is a peasant?" remained uncomfortably open up to this point, it would not remain so for long.

THE PROVERBIAL PEASANT?

While officials grappled with the discrete problems of classification and enumeration in the early decades of British rule, a markedly different body of more diffuse knowledge about Panjabi society began to accumulate. During settlement and census work especially, colonial interests gradually exceeded the ambit of the region's political history, natural geography, and economic capacity. Constantly encountering and inquiring, officers started to record their observations of various customs, beliefs, and practices of the people.[83] At first, these remained in the margins of official reports, little more than the occasional jottings of what was perceived to be exceptionally strange or exotic. The 1860 report on Amritsar district contains very few descriptions of actual Panjabis; the report on Hoshiarpur from the same year is almost entirely utilitarian.[84] Yet officers, quickly discovering the scope and value of such seemingly extraneous themes, began to collect and publish whatever became available. Much of these writings found their way into several key publications, namely Richard Temple's *Punjab Notes and Queries*, Charles Tupper's *Punjab Customary Law* series, Lepel Griffin's *The Panjab Chiefs*, and various district *Gazetteers* from the 1880s onward.[85] The voracious appetite of British knowledge production through sheer acquisition was captured by the epigram on the front cover of one series, which read: "When found, make a note of."[86]

A particularly rich set of materials within this genre appeared in the form of vernacular proverbs, sayings, aphorisms, phrases, and jokes. "The corpus of proverbs and sayings collected by colonial ethnographers in the third quarter of the nineteenth century," explains Neeladri Bhattacharya, "allows us a glimpse into the structure of dispositions that defined peasant expectations."[87] Several collections published in many of the subcontinent's languages contrasted with formal administrative writings by providing insights into the diverse textures of social life.[88] Temple, for one, immediately recognized this potential, stating that "there is no study . . . that will render the student of the natives of India so deeply conversant with their thoughts and mode of life as that of their proverbial and aphoristic lore." He went on to explain that proverbs in particular are

> habitually used on every possible occasion of daily life, especially in seasons of trouble. They are familiar to all; the women sing them as they do their household work; the men employ them for purposes of condolence and congratulation; the children are taught them as soon as they can speak; many persons largely interlard their conversation with them.[89]

This is why vernacular proverbs were not simply translated and disseminated to curious readers across the empire. Rather than appearing only in English, as with many other writings concerning the region's history and society, these collections were presented both in Panjabi and English so that the vernacular was present as the act of translation was made visible. This allowed officers to supplement their formal training in Urdu with spoken Panjabi in order to understand and communicate with the local population. The act of publishing collections of proverbs was a pedagogical enterprise with direct practical utility.

Yet communication in the colonial context was inextricable from the project of rule, the vicissitudes of conceiving priorities, conveying orders, and commanding obedience. The itinerary of one rather under-studied text, Robert Maconachie's *Selected Agricultural Proverbs of the Panjab*, made this imperative clear. In 1884, financial commissioner Edward Wace issued a directive to all district commissioners requesting the forwarding of "the best local proverbs" related to agriculture under different headings to be used in compiling a primer for instruction in village schools. After a series of delays, with scores of manuscript pages steadily arriving in Lahore, Maconachie finally distilled and codified this literature into a single volume published in 1890. Unsurprisingly, the chief result was the realization that "the rustic agriculturalist really needs little teaching as to the main points of his art," and so the British intercession into agricultural knowledge was largely superfluous. Instead, as Maconachie pointed out, "these proverbs" meant for Panjabis served to "only instruct his [sic] rulers."[90] In an earlier text, the inversion of purposes for this form of knowledge was given in more explicit terms. The introduction to Edward O'Brian's *Glossary of the Multani Language compared with Punjabi and Sindhi* plainly states: "To be able to quote an apposite proverb or saying increases one's power, and makes intercourse with the natives of the country much more cheerful than it usually is." O'Brian then gave a chillingly euphemistic example of using a proverb to placate an otherwise aggressive native:

> In kutcherry [*katchairi*, local courthouse] if you refuse a Jat's request and tell him the proverb "a miser is better than a liberal because he refuses at once," he goes away with a laugh instead of appealing to all the divine powers and eventually being hustled out by the orderlies.[91]

In blatant terms, this exemplifies the violence beneath the acquisition of indigenous knowledge, not only as a way of understanding local society for more abstract bureaucratic forms of control but as a means to actively shape certain intimate and individual behaviors toward particular ends. For officers familiar with such vernacular idioms, the routine tasks of rule seemed to become that much more effective.

As a result, proverbs, similar to dictionaries, did not allow any direct access to everyday perspectives or the wider sensibilities of the time, nor were they transparent reflections of a given reality. Guha's critique of their elitism is also pertinent, albeit in the form of a subtle and variegated bias rather than open class hostility.[92] Besides their sly purposes, the conditions for producing such collections were often as circuitous as they were opaque. O'Brian's text, for example, was commissioned in 1873 and was the work of several officers, with the assortment of materials first translated by one Abdul Rahman from Muzaffargarh and then sent for correction and confirmation to Ghulam Murtaza from Jhang before publication in 1881.[93] There is also very little indication in these texts of the castes, religions, genders, or classes of those interviewed, and thus those excluded, or the nature of the conversations between officer and informant. What these proverbs did make possible, however, was to mark another moment—of non-change—in the relationship between (circumscribed) vernacular understandings of agrarian production and colonial categories of identity and occupation.

From that perspective, Maconachie's collection becomes a useful entry point into the realm of agrarian relations in the later nineteenth century. His volume contains over one thousand proverbs divided into seventeen thematic chapters, from "On the merits of various soils" to "On careful expenditure" and "On tribal characteristics." Each was first written in Panjabi with the Nastaliq script, then transliterated into Roman script, followed by a translation into English. Although the proverbs' authors were not disclosed—district commissioners worked in conjunction with "local notables"—the locality of their providence was provided. Consider the following eight proverbs:

Las zemin hai bahut sukhhali,   Drained land is effortless,
Malhar minh na mange <u>hali.</u>   the <u>cultivator</u> does not ask for rain. [Rawalpindi, 2]

Kheti <u>kirsan</u> kat le,   O <u>cultivator</u>! Reap your harvest,
jab jane pak jae,   when it has ripened,
Sonche bhule se tere,   [Or else] because of your forgetfulness,
chiri janwar khae.   birds and animals will consume it. [Hissar, 135]

Bhadon ki dhup dekhkar,   In [the month of] Bhadon, when he saw the sun,
<u>Jat</u> faqir hoya.   the <u>peasant</u> became a faqir. [Rawalpindi, 77]

Bhadon marya,   [If sunshine in the month of] Bhadon strikes,
<u>Jat</u> faqir.   The <u>Jat</u> [loses hope and] becomes a faqir. [Jalandhar, 77]

As nind <u>kasan</u> nun mandi,   Hope and sleep are detrimental to an <u>agriculturalist,</u>
Chor nun mandi khansi,   a cough is detrimental to a thief,
Bahuta biyaj shah nun manda,   excessive interest is detrimental to a lender,
Pandat nin maudi dasi.   And a concubine is detrimental to a Pandit. [Jalandhar, 186]

Kheti kar <u>kirsana</u>,   Cultivate, O <u>farmer</u>,
Je chahe khatiya khana.   if you desire to reap what you sow. [Ambala, 188]

Wahi <u>kirsan</u> kare kheti,   The <u>zemindar</u> cultivates well,
Jisdi bahar jawe roti.   whose meal goes out to the field. [Jalandhar, 198]

Aurat ko masan,   An evil spirit to a woman,
Sahukar ko <u>kirsan</u>.   As a <u>cultivator</u> to the moneylender. [Karnal, 221]

Several aspects of these proverbs are striking.[94] First, intrinsically, there is a lyrical beauty to their rhythm and meter, something almost entirely lost in the English translation. The metaphors used and the connections made draw powerfully on local objects and their ideological environments. When ripened crops are paired with consumption in the second proverb, or kheti with *roti* (literally, unleavened flatbread but standing in for food more generally) in the seventh proverb, a relationship is at once established and disrupted by the intervening claim. It will be birds who consume the crops if action is not taken; cultivation, which produces the wheat used in making roti, will only prosper if meals are eaten diligently in the fields. At the same time, there is humorous dread of natural forces, of unexpected climate wreaking havoc on planned cycles of planting, irrigating, and harvesting. For the sun to shine during the month of Bhadon (which spans from mid-August to mid-September), when the fields are most in need of monsoon rains, is to render the peasant not simply a beggar (as in the original) but an impoverished mendicant, gloomily contemplating the mysteries of the divine. There is also the implication of women leading to ruin of men, a common theme in much of this literature. An inadvertent physiological act such as coughing is made analogous to visiting a prostitute, while evil spirits haunt a woman as a cultivator does a moneylender, implying the need to avoid such presumed misdeeds. Yet the assertion of any moral injunction suggests the occurrence of its opposite. At least some kisans must have slept in excess, neglected their fields, or lived beyond their means for proverbs to encourage rising early, being industrious, and living modestly. Multiple subtleties and layers of meaning are thus left out through the translation from Panjabi to English.

These proverbs also illustrate a myriad of differences over the question of the agrarian subject between languages. In Rawalpindi district, *hali* is translated as "cultivator." In both Hissar and Karnal, however, it is a *kirsan* that is a cultivator. On the other hand, in Ambala, *kirsan* means farmer, while in Jalandhar, it stands for zamindar. Yet also in Jalandhar, the variant of *kasan* is given as agriculturalist. Even more perplexing is that a Jatt in the third proverb from Rawalpindi is considered a peasant, whereas in the next one from Jalandhar, the same term is brought over into English untranslated, so that a Jatt is simply a Jatt. In another sense, even within the same district, there is specificity to the use of different Panjabi terms. In that fourth proverb from Jalandhar, though the word *kirsan* was available and would not affect the meter, it was a Jatt that became a faqir from lack of rain. Or, to take the same earlier proverb in Rawalpindi, a hali too could have become an impoverished mendicant, but, again, Jatt was chosen. Throughout the rest of Maconachie's text, many more Panjabi words—*kisan, hali, Jatt*—are both used differently *and* given different English meanings—cultivator, plowman, peasant—so that there is no consistent format either within each district for certain terms or for their translation. Importantly, this variation is not a function of synonyms but of differences emanating from diverse understandings of agriculture as conceptualized by the various unidentified Panjabi interlocutors.

Finally, and more broadly, this series of discrepancies reflected a persistent heterogeneity of agrarian relations. By the 1880s, despite two formal censuses and countless settlement operations, not only did the colonial state continue to be confounded by the complexity of rural laboring contributions but their efforts had also not yet succeeded in arriving at a singular definition for a peasant. Nor was there a fixed meaning for peasant in Panjabi. If the British appeared to cohere around the word *agriculturalist* while constantly invoking many other cognates, Panjabis were even further from a consensus, with no one term achieving the remotest preeminence. This suggests that at the popular level, a plurality of subjects engaged in various agrarian labors rather than a singular hierarchy corresponding to a fixed division. This is not to claim that agriculture was a realm of equality without barriers of entry or cultural prerequisites or that it occurred harmoniously between different individuals and groups. Instead, the variety of vernacular agrarian subjects points to the fact that there was no obvious, axiomatic association between identity and occupation in this period. When rural Panjabis conceived of agrarian activities, the material labors stood apart from the abstract qualities of the individuals taking part. Conversely, when a colonial officer inquired about who is an agriculturalist (or a cultivator, or a peasant), the answers were not known or understood ahead of time. Thus, even if cultivation had shifted from one who cultivates to cultivators proper, the latter at this point still did not imply a fixed group of castes understood to be inherently agrarian.

COMMUNITIES OF BLOOD AND LABOR

Amid this persistently fluid heterogeneity, the colonial state carried out its most formidable census to date under the supervision of Ibbetson during the night of February 17, 1881. This is part of what Arjun Appadurai marks as the pivot of the 1870s, as a shift from earlier concerns with physical and ecological issues to the standardization and "un-yoking" of human groups.[95] In the report's preface, its author explains the difference of this operation from previous efforts. Whereas the censuses of 1855 and 1868 were "meagre" and reliant on received local answers without a record of the actual experience of enumeration, the 1881 effort "collected, compared, and consolidated" a wealth of information in order to interpret Panjabi society as a whole. "When a lusty male in the prime of manhood tells you that he is 15 years of age," instructs Ibbetson through a demeaning example, "or a tottering elder that his winters number '20 to 30,' it is necessary to exercise your own judgement in the matter."[96] The result was to be a comprehensive, enduring statement of the "sociological keys" of Panjab and Panjabis useful both to the government and the general reader.[97] Ibbetson in fact justifies the enormous length of his report as a necessary corrective not only for the "loss of administrative powers," but also for the needs of both European scientific research and the "students of sociology" in India. The 1881 census, he states, is "an Indian blue-book,"[98] invoking the collection of domestic parliamentary papers, royal commissions, and official reports published by the British government and put to use in Karl Marx's *Capital*, as mentioned in Chapter 1. Indeed, Ibbetson's text is no mere antiquarian colonial-era document. Reflecting its impact, parts of the report still remain in publication to this day, with reprints of his chapter on "The Races, Castes, and Tribes of the People" available in Indian bookstores and routinely relied on by scholars across the world.

The explanatory force of this text is a product of both the unprecedented scope of its operations and the sheer accumulation of details. Between English superintendents, supervisors, and enumerators and various Panjabi accountants, village headmen, and return-counters, the census employed over 120,000 individuals, surveying a territory divided into nearly fifty-three thousand blocks, and spanned over three years from inception to publication.[99] At the same time, the level of specificity far surpassed previous efforts. In terms of occupations, for instance, the 1868 census divided the population into 124 separate categories; in 1881, Ibbetson found 9,038, a tally that was eventually reduced to 2,975.[100] Caste too gained new prominence as an object of inquiry. While officially ignored in 1855, certain castes had been counted only as subsets within the religious divide between Hindu and Muslim, numbering no more than eight (plus a large "Miscellaneous" category). In 1881, on the other hand, Ibbetson counted 8,392 distinct caste groups.

Such astoundingly minute divisions were made possible by the new form adopted by enumerators to record different characteristics of the population. After the columns for marriage status, gender, age, and religion, three new ones appeared—"Original caste or tribe," "Clan," and "Got or family"—followed by mother tongue, birthplace, occupation, education, and infirmities (see Figure 2.3).[101] The binary of agriculturalist/non-agriculturalist from earlier forms seems to disappear, replaced by an intricate series of values to be filled out by the enumerator and then calculated by a regional superintendent. In other words, it was no longer adequate for an individual to declare themselves an "agriculturalist," however infrequently and unclearly that happened. A British officer would now combine smaller atoms of information to make that particular determination independently. From these narrower inquiries, the report presents the total "Agricultural class" comprising of landowners, tenants, joint cultivators, agricultural laborers, and graziers. This category accounts for 54 percent of the population of men over the age of fifteen, with 22 percent given as "Industrial," around 5 percent each for "Labouring" and "Distributing," and 9 percent relegated as "Unproductive," with a similar breakdown given for women above the age of fifteen as well.[102] A new specificity thereby accompanies the assignment of an individual to a given category.

Beyond numerical allocation, the report more importantly carried out the logic of a new "ethnographic state" by providing both a theory for caste and a vast collection of descriptions.[103] Ibbetson spent a considerable amount of time explaining the nature of caste difference in Panjab and its relationship to England. He began by emphasizing the difficulty of his endeavor: "It is almost impossible to make any statement whatever regarding any one of the castes" in one part of the province that "shall not presently

*Tahsil*______ *Village* *Circle No.*______ *Block Letter*______ *Name of Enumerator*______
*House No.*______ *Description.*______

1	2	3	4		5	6	7			8	9	10	11	12	
Serial No. of Inmate.	NAME.	Condition, *i. e.*, whether married, unmarried, widow or widower.	Male.	Female.	Age last birth-day.	RELIGION, CASTE OR TRIBE, CLAN, GOT, &C.				Mother tongue.	* † ‡ Place of birth.	Occupation of men; also of those boys and females whose work is brought regularly to market.	*Education.* (1) Not under instruction but can read and write. (2) Under instruction.	*Infirmities.* (1) Unsound mind. (2) Deaf mutes from birth. (3) Blind. (4) Lepers.	
						Religion and sect.	Original Caste or Tribe.	Clan.	Got or Family.						

* If a European British Subject, add British subject. † If a foreigner, state of what country. ‡ If of mixed European and Asiatic parentage, add Eurasian.

FIGURE 2.3 A blank return form used in the 1881 census in Panjab. Source: Denzil Ibbetson, *Report on the Census of the Panjab, taken on the 17th of February 1881*, vol. 1 (Calcutta: Superintendent of Government Printing, 1883), 436.

be contradicted with equal truth" in some other part.[104] Nevertheless, the illogicality of caste could hardly be allowed to impede the tasks of rule. Ibbetson then went on to make an unconventional claim about origins.[105] He wrote that caste is far more a social practice of the region than a religious institution of Hindus; it is riven with variations, instabilities, and outright contradictions; and it is anything but perpetual or immutable. At its base, it is an antagonism between descent and calling—"community of blood and community of occupation," in his words—common to all human societies. That an English coal-heaver's son was plainly and obviously not equal to the son of an English nobleman extended the insight back to the metropole. Indeed, Ibbetson actually universalized the much-quoted fourfold division of castes, stating that "William Priest, John King, Edward Farmer, and James Smith are but the survivals in England of the four *varnas* [castes] of Manu."[106]

If caste was a matter of labor rather than biology, however, there was something peculiar about the division of labor in Panjab. All societies are liquid rather than solid, declared Ibbetson, invoking the themes of motion and fluidity over simple, rigid hierarchy. Yet "the only real difference between Indian societies and that of other countries" is that "the liquid is much more viscous."[107] The materiality of Panjabi society is thicker and less pliable than the English. To continue Ibbetson's example, in an earlier epoch a priest was perhaps a Brahmin or perhaps an ancestor of the eponymous William. In the nineteenth century, however, in India it was a Brahmin who must be a priest, while in England it was one who chose to enter the priesthood.[108] Between the two lay the difference of individual willpower and decision-making. A superior society was therefore one that was flexible enough to recognize the right of autonomous persons to decide their fate, even if it required the callous fiction of "choosing" to heave coal or clear gutters. Viscosity was the metric to construct a distinctive scale of civilizations through the allocation of labor.

Following this rather contradictory explanation, Ibbetson dedicated the rest of his report to ethnographic descriptions. Panjabi society was divided into three overarching categories: "Landowning and Agricultural," "Professional and Mercantile Caste," and "Vagrants, Menials, and Artisans." Within each of these are the names of different castes (*jaat/jati*), such that, among others, the first contains Jatts, Rajputs, and Pathans; the second Brahmins and Saiyads; and the third Julahas, Churhas, and Chamars.[109] Following a few more qualifications, Ibbetson then defined the history, locality, and innate characteristics of several dozen clans (*got/gotra*) within each jati. Entries ranged from a few sentences to nearly a page and were organized according to regional distribution. A typical entry for one of the eighty-nine distinct Pathan tribes was as follows:

> The Naser claim descent from Hotak, a grandson of Ghilzai; but the Hotak say that they are a Biloch clan, and merely dependents on them. They speak Pashto, but differ from the Ghilzai in physique. They are the least settled of all the *pawindahs* [larger tribal category], and winter in the Derajat and summer in the Ghilzai country, having no home of their own. Their chief wealth is in the flocks and herds, and they act as carriers rather than as traders. They are a rough sturdy lot, but fairly well behaved.[110]

Here are descriptions for three of the more numerous Jatt clans:

> The Chhadhar are found along the whole length of the Chanab [Chenab] and Ravi [river] valleys, but are far more numerous in Jhang, where they have for the most part retuned themselves as Rajputs. They claim to be descended from Raja Tur Tunwar. They say that they left their home in Rajputana in the time of Muhammad Ghori and settled in Bhawalpur, where they were converted [to Islam] by Sher Shah of Uchh. Thence they came

to Jhang, where they founded an important colony and spread in smaller numbers up the Chanab and Ravi. Mr. Steedman describes them as good agriculturalists, and less given to cattle-theft than their neighbours.

The Varaich is one of the largest Jat tribes in the Province. In Akbar's time they held two-thirds of the Gujrat district, though on less favourable terms than those allowed to the Gujars who held the remainder; and they still hold 170 villages in that district. They have also crossed the Chanab into Gujranwala where they held a tract of 41 villages, and have spread along under the hills as far as Ludhiana and Maler Kotla. They do not always even pretend to be Rajputs, but say that their ancestor Dhudi was a Jat who came into India with Mamud Ghaznavi and settled in Gujrat, where the tribe grew powerful and partly dispossessed the original Gujar lords of the soil.

The Sahi [. . .] claim descent from a Solar Rajput who went to Ghazni with Mahmud, and returned to found the tribe, settling on the Ravi [river] near Lahore. They are found in any numbers only in Gujrat and Sialkot. They have, in common with the Sindhu and Chima of these parts, some peculiar marriage customs, such as cutting a goat's ear and marking their foreheads with the blood, making the bridegroom cut off a twig of the Jhand tree (*prosopis spicigera*) and so forth; and they, like most of the tribes discussed in this section, worship the Jhand tree.[111]

And, finally, here are descriptions for three "vagrant" and "menial" castes:

The Harni: This again is one of the most criminal castes of the Province . . ., a greater number of them are registered under the Criminal Tribes Act than of any other caste except the Sansi. They are found in the districts lying under the hills from Ludhiana to Sialkot, and also in Firozpur and Faridkot. They are said to have been Rajputs driven from Bhatner by famine, who were employed by the Rai of Raikot in Ludhiana for purposes of theft and to harass his enemies. [. . .] Their chief crimes are burglary and highway robbery, to effect which they travel in gangs, often under the disguise of carriers with pack-oxen. Their women also wander about as pedlars to pilfer and collect information. They are all returned as Musalman.[112]

The Musalman Chuhra: Almost all of the Chuhras west of Lahore are Musalmans, and they are very commonly called Musalli or Kutana, the two terms being apparently almost synonymous, but the Kutana being chiefly used in the south-west and Musalli in the north-west. [. . .] But it appears that in many parts the Musalman Chuhra continues to be called a Chuhra so long as he eats carrion or removes night-soil, and is only promoted to the title of Musalli on his relinquishing those habits, the Musalli being considered distinctly a higher class than the Chuhra. On the other hand the Musalli of the frontier towns does remove night-soil. On the Peshawar frontier the Musalli is the grave-digger as well as the sweeper, and is said to be sometimes called Shahi Khel. . . .

The Khatik: This also is a caste of Hindustan, and is found in any numbers only in the Jamna [Yamuna river] zone, Patiala and Sirsa. But it apparently followed our troops into the Panjab, and is found in most of the large cantonments or in their neighbourhood. [. . .] They form a connecting link between the scavengers and the leather-workers, though they occupy a social position distinctly inferior to that of the latter. They are great keepers of pigs and poultry, which a Chamar would not keep. At the same time many of them tan and dye leather, and indeed are not seldom confused with the Chamrang. The Khatik, however, tans only sheep and goat skins (so at least I am informed by some Lahore Khatiks and Chamrangs) using salt and the juice of the Mandar (*Calotropis procera*), but no lime; while the Chamrang tans buffalo and ox hides with lime, and does not dye leather.[113]

The real power of Ibbetson's report, the source of its authority and (continuing) influence, thus rested on the vivid descriptions it provided of hundreds of distinct caste groups. Three aspects of this compendium are particularly relevant. First is the defining of individuals through collective racial tropes. Naser Pathans were *all* "rough" and "sturdy," yet, crucial to the colonial state, "well behaved"; Chhadhar Jatts *as a group* were less given to thieving than others; Harnis *together* not only committed crimes but were one of the "most" criminal castes. Furthermore, Ibbetson wove details about certain labors with levels of status, such that groups became identifiable through the particular activities of their members. If the Muslim Chuhra's rank depended on whether or not they ate carrion or removed human feces, the Khatik's was based on keeping pigs and using lime as a dye, while the Varaich were axiomatically "holders" of vast lands and villages, even if they initially dispossessed the nomadic Gujars. Finally, what this accomplished was the formal alignment of caste (and clan and tribe) with occupation. Groups identified with certain qualities and activities were located within the three categories of the report. In this way, all Varaichs were not only marked as Jatts but, more consequentially, as "Landowning and Agricultural." Churhas, on the other hand, became inherently and exclusively "Menial." For the first time, enumeration coincided with classification so that the logic of abstract numbers intersected the politics of caste-as-occupation descriptions.

Despite the abundance, reach, and novelty of the 1881 census, its author was forthright about its limitations. If Temple was confident about his report and Christian hesitant about his, Ibbetson was modest and even at moments critical of the accuracy of the figures he had produced. It is not insignificant that the least satisfactory portions of the report, as he mentioned, dealt with occupations in general and agricultural work in particular. This was due to what was acknowledged as the inapplicability of the English system of classification for the radically different structure of the Panjabi agrarian economy. Not only did members of the same caste perform widely different types of activities, such as the Churhas, who dug graves and swept; or the Khatiks, who kept animals and dyed leather; or the Chamars, who were shoemakers but also might till fields as tenants. More fundamentally, Ibbetson admitted that "every one or almost every one of them [these castes and others] works in the fields either continuously or at certain seasons." "It is hardly an exaggeration," he continued, to say that in many parts of rural Panjab, *"almost every adult male in a village* excepting the shop-keeper *does more or less field-work"* of one kind or another.[114] While this might in fact have been an overstatement—and one that neglected the labors of women altogether—it nonetheless signaled a larger crisis for the very enterprise of the census. If "it was clear you could know a man by his caste,"[115] as Nicholas Dirks claims colonial officials believed by the late nineteenth century, what could *not be known* was the various labors he was supposed to perform. Thus, if the scientific enumeration of the people was constantly hobbled by qualifications, reductions, and exceptions, what remained of the validity of its results? Defining an agriculturalist through a(ny) relationship to land and labor confronted divisions already made by aligning specific castes with discrete occupations. The result was perpetual disarray, what Ibbetson acknowledged as "a *reductio ad absurdum*"—the claims of certitude constantly undercut by disclosures of endless confusion and doubt.[116]

WRIT AGRARIAN

Absurdity, or the illogicality of attempting to align caste and labor through the census, did not reduce the force of these exercises, much less lead to the paralysis of the colonial state. In fact, the simultaneity of pursuing "imperial empiricism" and recognizing "ultimate inscrutability" further propelled officials both in their acquisition and application of knowledge as power.[117] Perhaps the clearest enacting of the definition of a peasant was the juridical restructuring of access to the land market. In the last decades of the nineteenth century, a tremendous expansion of canal irrigation across the western desert plains, combined with the establishment of new villages populated by land grantees—amid the sharp rise in worldwide cotton and wheat prices due to the American Civil War (1861–65)—generated an unprecedented cycle of what appeared to be agrarian prosperity.[118] At the same time, the fixing of land ownership with revenue responsibilities, along with the influx of commodity production and consumption, led to the growing specter of "peasant" indebtedness and the consequent fragmentation and alienation of landholdings, a topic that will be explored in Chapter 3. Spurred by what became known as the Deccan Riots in parts of Maharashtra in 1875 and precipitated in part by the alarmist writings of a settlement officer named Septimus Thorburn, the administration in Panjab resolved to confront economic distress and social unrest through a particular form of legal redress.[119]

On June 8, 1901, the Punjab Alienation of Land Act went into effect throughout the province, excluding the Native States, municipalities, military cantonments, and the districts of Simla, Hazara, and Peshawar. In comparison to previous legislation, such as the voluminous Punjab Tenancy Act of 1887 and the Punjab Revenue Act of 1887, it was relatively short, numbering just eleven pages with three substantive headings containing twenty-three sections. While the official purpose was stated as placing "restrictions on the transfer of agricultural land in the Punjab with a view to checking its alienation from the agricultural to the non-agricultural classes," the Act actually brought about a far more profound transformation of social and economic relations in the countryside.[120] Crucially, it reintroduced the earlier, pivotal bifurcation of society, this time articulated through the idiom of tribe.[121] Now all Panjabis became classified as members of either "agricultural tribes" or "non-agricultural tribes." Through this binary, three conditions for authorizing the sale of agricultural land were established. A transaction was only legitimate if either "the alienor [seller] is not a member of an agricultural tribe," or, if the alienor was an agriculturalist, then if "the alienee [buyer]" either "holds land as an agriculturalist in the village where the land alienated is situated," or "is a member of the same tribe or of a tribe in the same group."[122] What this meant was that supposed non-agriculturalists could freely sell but not buy land, as those designated as agriculturalists could only sell to other agriculturalists. The circulation of agricultural land, in other words, was to remain within the circuit of agriculturalists. The Act also notably limited mortgages to twenty years regardless of interest accumulation and repayment schedules, banned the forced selling of agriculturalists' land (except, explicitly, for recovering government revenue arrears), and invested district commissioners with the final authority to authorize or override any land transaction without explanation.[123]

Inescapably, the Act returned to the question of who exactly counted as an agriculturalist. For this iteration, however, the answer had perhaps the greatest ramifications, as status now became the basis for access to the market of commoditized land. Within the Act itself, this criterion was laid out in characteristically convoluted terms:

> The expression "agriculturalist" means a person holding agricultural land who either in his own name or in the name of his ancestor in the male line was recorded as the owner of land or as a hereditary tenant or as an occupancy-tenant in any estate at the first regular settlement, or, if the first regular settlement was made in or since the year 1870, then at the first regular settlement or at such previous settlement as the Local Government may, by order in writing, determine.[124]

Here an agriculturalist meant not only land ownership or two forms of recognized tenancy, but a recording of these details at the time of the first settlements a half century earlier, as well as an exclusive privileging of male lineage. Moreover, the year 1870 serves as a kind of cutoff: claims of peasant status would automatically be recognized if based on evidence prior to that date, while they would be suspect and require further verification if afterward. As a result, the law invested certain patriarchal relationships identified within a narrow window of time with the authority to shape material processes.

Mere definition, however, was far from sufficient to quell the myriad uncertainties of connecting blood and labor to the land. Indeed, the rigor of this criterion only mirrored its arbitrariness, leaving various details— Which specific documents? Whose exact descent? Why that date?—open to interpretation and counter-interpretation. To convey at least a semblance of order—and avoid utter confusion—the Act importantly also authorized local officials to determine in advance certain caste/ethnic groups ("tribes") as *inherently agricultural* for their respective districts. In a special edition of the *Punjab Gazette* published a few weeks before the Act came into effect, a table recorded several tribes in each of the twenty-seven districts as "agricultural." Multan district, for example, lists sixteen different tribes, while there were nine in Amritsar and only seven in Jhang. Rajputs, Jatts, and Pathans were ubiquitous; Biloch were recognized in most of the western districts; and Tagas only in Delhi, Kolis in Kangra, and Maliars in Rawalpindi. In Ferozepur a distinction was made between Mussalman Jatts and Other Jatts, while Ghakkars in Sialkot were qualified as Mehars Ghakkars in Jhelum.[125] This skewed correspondence meant that only particular tribes were authorized to participate equally in the buying and selling of land in specific districts. Collective cultural identity, determined through various contradictory and even capricious means, thereby shaped individual economic agency.

Despite the appearance of structure and precision, fixing the identity of agriculturalists nonetheless remained a troublesome enterprise. In particular, the premium placed on early settlement records prompted a flood of requests from concerned applicants seeking to alter their official standing. A circular issued on November 20, 1903, by the director of land records to all local officers attempts to address this latest contingency. "It is necessary for the attesting officer to ascertain who the alienee is" to verify that

Certificate granted to persons who claim to be "agriculturists" as
defined in Section 2 (1) of Act XIII of 1900.

                Serial No.   of 19   , dated   19 .

Certified that————————, son of——————, caste————,
resident of——————, is recorded as holding the land noted on the reverse
as an ___owner___ in village——————, tahsil——————, in the
      occupancy tenant
Settlement Record of 18   , and that——————, son of——————,
caste————————, resident of——————, is a direct descendant in the
male line of the above-named, in the manner shown by the genealogical tree on
the reverse, which is a true copy from the Settlement Record of 18 , or which
has been deposed to by——————   .

                                Signed.

                                                        Office or Sadr Kánúngo.

(Office Seal.)   Attested.

                                                        E. A. C.,

                                           Tahsildar or Naib Tahsildar.

FIGURE 2.4 A blank copy of the certificate to be an "agriculturalist," 1901. Source: "Certificate granted to persons who claim to be 'agriculturalists' as defined in Section 2 (1) of Act XIII of 1900," in *Handbook of Alienation of Land Acts and Circular Orders* (Lahore: no publisher, no date), 26, serial 533, Punjab State Archives, Chandigarh, India.

a buyer was indeed an agriculturalist in order to authorize a land transaction.[126] The eternal problem of deceit also stalked this process: another circular explained the difficulty of an alienee claiming a name not recognized as a subdivision of a notified tribe, or, "when a Harni claims that Harnis are Rajputs."[127] For both of these issues, officials distributed a form to be filled out by anyone seeking to purchase land (see Figure 2.4). Titled "Certificate granted to persons who claim to be 'agriculturalists' as defined in Section 2 (1) of Act XIII of 1900," it contained a short, self-declaratory paragraph with implied questions, places for witness signatures, date requirements, and an official government seal, along with space on the reverse side for drawing a genealogical tree. The first sentence of the form appears as follows:

> Certified that _____, son of _____, caste _____, resident of _____, is recorded as holding the land noted on the reverse as an owner/occupancy tenant in village _____, tahsil _____, in the Settlement Record of 18__, and that _____, son of _____, caste _____, resident of _____, is the direct descendent in the male line of the above-named, in the manner shown by the genealogical tree on the reverse, which is a true copy from the Settlement Record of 18__, or which has been deposed to by _____.[128]

In one long, discursive motion, a series of propositions sequestered and aligned certain elements to make a new statement of identity. A single man descending from another man and belonging to a caste within a given locality was one part of the equation for establishing agriculturalist status. The other part was genealogical, requiring the construction of a peculiar kind of family tree (see Figure 2.5). At its apex stood a number for a parcel of land, followed by an originary male ancestor, traced through various branches of male lineage and ending with the single male applicant. Appearing dispersed yet culminating at the very same point, this underscores the primacy of existing property recognized through patriarchal ownership for the possibility of acquiring more. Through these two measured, exacting methods of establishing singular identity and familial genealogy lay the basis for an individual's eligibility for economic exchange.

The politics of the Act and its attendant documents produced a new logic for the question of the peasant. On the one hand, its categories seemed to mimic aspects of the censuses from 1855, 1868, and 1881, with a return of the agriculturalist/non-agriculturalist binary and the increased value given to caste membership. The blank spaces of the form can be seen as census-like questions rhetorically posed to the applicant. On the other hand, while censuses were largely filled out by colonial officials and used as an instrument of administration, the Act restructured the very laws of the land market, while the certificate was designed to be filled out and used by individual applicants. Indeed, the same circular instructed applicants to make two copies of each certificate: one to be deposited in the district

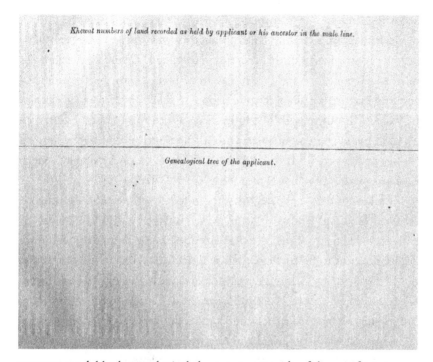

FIGURE 2.5 A blank genealogical chart on reverse side of the certificate to be an "agriculturalist," 1901. Source: "Certificate granted to persons who claim to be 'agriculturalists' as defined in Section 2 (1) of Act XIII of 1900," in Handbook of Alienation of Land Acts and Circular Orders (Lahore: no publisher, no date), 27, serial 533, Punjab State Archives, Chandigarh, India.

headquarters, with the second to "remain in the possession of the person in whose favour it has been granted."[129] Moreover, patriarchal lineage became a distinct means to establish claims of hereditary land ownership. Genealogy here implied the opposite of Michel Foucault's articulation—not as a mundane, inglorious, or nonlinear narrative but an explicit demonstration of origins and originary decent.[130] Finally, by bringing together all of these disparate elements, the Act imputed certain Panjabi identities with the authority to conduct exchanges. The answer to the question of who was an agriculturalist now determined who would be able to access the market for agricultural land.

At the same time, and perhaps unintentionally, the Act all but sealed the condition of those excluded from the possibility of claiming and acquiring land. While its formal objective may have been to prevent urban moneylenders from seizing lands through distressed sale by agriculturalists, the consequences of this prevention extended far beyond the confines of debt relations.[131] Another circular from June 5, 1901, by the financial commissioner to all district commissioners sheds light on a subtle play of words. Throughout this lengthy text, agricultural tribes referred to as "zamindars" were contrasted with all non-agricultural tribes, termed "banias and others."[132] If "banias" was a colloquial term for moneylenders, however, what, or who, was meant by "others"? This was where the wider implications of the Act's categories began to become perceptible. The criterion of "holding" land as either an owner or tenant would have automatically excluded many of the up to 80 percent of the rural population Temple earlier believed to be participating in agriculture. Also, none of the lists of districts with agricultural tribes included any of the groups classified as vagrants and menials by Ibbetson. Chamars or Churhas or dozens of other groups contributing to agricultural production were further relegated as "non-agricultural." And, finally, the certificate requirement for stipulating caste membership, along with proving paternal land rights from the first settlements, only underlined the impossibility of acquiring agriculturalist status. This, then, is how exclusionary categories intersected with exploitative practices, as the denial of peasant status precluded land ownership to confirm the fate of laboring as landless.

A PETITION FOR STATUS

Within the confines of these narrow, and narrowing, parameters, various Panjabis nonetheless attempted to improve their economic position by elevating their social status. After 1901, several groups petitioned the government claiming to have been miscategorized and seeking a corrected recognition as members of an agricultural tribe. This allowed them to access the land market as well as limit mortgage terms and prevent forced alienations. Importantly, the last two benefits only applied if the opposite party was defined as non-agriculturalist (a standard alibi for urban moneylenders), while the first benefit referred to the ability to buy from other similarly defined agriculturalists. Agriculturalists, in other words, were only safeguarded from mortgage default and land seizures when at the hands of those deemed non-agriculturalists. For officials implementing this binary classification amid a plurality of personalities and practices, the phenomenon of the rural moneylending agriculturalist—or, the peasant who also lent—represented another ongoing dilemma, as will be discussed in Chapter 3. Still, to be legally defined as a non-agriculturalist meant automatically incurring severe constraints on the mobility of one's capital and the availability of government protection. By pointing out simple errors, pleading for special consideration, and applying for reclassification, some Panjabis manipulated the definitions of agrarian status that shaped their material possibilities. Even if occurring through colonial avenues, making a claim to the category of agriculturalist in the early decades of the twentieth century became a means of contestation for certain landholding groups.

Several short petitions demonstrate both the range and basis by which Panjabis asserted agricultural status. In September 1907, a group of Arains wrote to the deputy commissioner of Muzaffargarh protesting their exclusion from the list of agricultural tribes for that district. Their letter was passed along to the commissioner of the Multan division, who forwarded it to a secretary to the financial commissioner, Evelyn Robins Abbott, who then raised the question directly with yet another secretary in Lahore. After quickly considering the evidence—the original petition mentioned there were 2,725 Arains owning approximately 19,694 acres in Muzaffargarh and that the caste had already been notified in neighboring districts of Dera Ghazi Khan, Mianwali, and Multan—a new gazette notification recognized that those "belonging to the Arain tribe shall be deemed to be an 'agricultural tribe'" in November.[133] More contentious, on the other hand, was the altering of classifications amid shifting boundaries. In April 1914, another commissioner of Muzaffargarh, Isa Charan Lall, raised an objection to the peculiar disenfranchisement of Awans. The problem was that "Awans of the Leiah Tahsil [in the Mianwali district], who were members of an agricultural tribe before 1909," as he wrote, "have ceased to be so since then on account of the transfer of that tahsil to this district [Muzaffargarh]," which did not recognize them as agricultural. In other words, agriculturalist Awans automatically became non-agriculturalists when the territory in which they lived changed administrative jurisdiction. To make the case for their readmittance, Lall provided a chart listing the number of individuals, estates, and acres owned in three other tahsils.[134] By June, Awans thus became agriculturalists once again. In similar fashion throughout the decade, various castes made arguments for recognition, or re-recognition, under the Act. Among others, Ahairs living in Delhi in 1903, Koreshis from Gujranwala in 1908, and Kakezais in Jhelum in 1910 all succeeded in acquiring the status of an "agricultural" tribe.[135]

Occasionally, attempts by individual Panjabis for recognition by the colonial state adopted a more personal tone. In a petition filed the day before the passing of the Act, Dost Muhammad Khan of Hazara district argued that he and his family faced bankruptcy due to their ineligibility for its protections. He explained that while nearly twelve thousand *ghumaons* (acres) of land owned by two of his close relations, Fateh Khan and Ilahi Khanam, had been conditionally mortgaged to pay off a Rs. 40,000 debt to Sardar Harjit Singh, the accumulated interest had added a further Rs. 140,000 to their burden. As a result, Khan and his family now owed a total of Rs. 180,000, an impossible amount to repay. In response, Singh had filed a suit in the Rawalpindi district court to recover either the full outstanding balance or clear title to the land. With a decision expected in late June 1901, Khan warned that "the petitioner's family would be ruined" if the judge ruled in favor of Singh. This dire situation stemmed from the fact that Hazara district was exempt from the Act, rendering families like Khan without access to its provisions and therefore remaining at the mercy of moneylenders. If, however, the Act were extended to Hazara (or a special inclusion granted to Khan's family), then the most they would have to endure would be a twenty-year forced lease of their land to Harjit Singh.[136] From rural Hazara through the colonial bureaucracy to the financial commissioner in Lahore, Khan was in effect arguing that the mere act of living in an exempted district should not disqualify him from the benefits of "being" an agriculturalist. Although the file does not include a decision on whether Khan's appeal was accepted, what is clear is how at least one Panjabi—holding an exceptional amount of land—understood, appropriated, and redeployed the Act's initial claims against its own inconsistencies and limitations.

A sharper yet more oblique demonstration of the debate over both categories and consistency is evident in the recognition attempts by the

Bahrupia caste in Gujrat district. In 1909, this small group's petition to be classified as Rathor Rajputs for the purposes of revenue collection was rejected by the local collector.[137] James Douie, commissioner of the Rawalpindi division at the time, also refused their appeal. In the process, he also "mooted the question of gazetting Bahrupias in Gujrat as an agricultural tribe," deciding that it too was ultimately unnecessary.[138] Three years later, however, the same group approached the officer and lawyer John Maynard to argue that the district commissioner in neighboring Sialkot had recently recognized Bahrupias as Rajputs and thereby as agriculturalists as well. Based on that development, Maynard wrote to the financial commissioner asking if "uniformity of treatment throughout the province is desirable" in order for members of the same caste to have the same status across districts.[139] The secretary, Henry Alexander Smith, abruptly rejected the call for equal treatment. "The circumstances and proclivities of the same tribe may vary in different districts," he wrote, "and it may not be advisable to gazette a particular tribe which is purely agricultural in one part of the province as an agricultural tribe in other districts."[140] Differences between castes, according to this logic, also seemed to manifest as differences within castes. Yet rather than close the file at rejection, Smith went on to make specific inquiries about this group of Bahrupias. He found that while they were classed as Rajputs as early as the 1856 settlement records for the Lahore, Gujranwala, and Sialkot districts, similar evidence was wanting in Gujrat, which proved to be a primary driver of the denial of status. On the other hand, Smith noted that Bahrupias in Gujrat owned 3,375 acres of land across eleven villages and therefore did warrant classification as agriculturalists. Even though the colonial state refused to recognize Bahrupias as Rajputs, they did acquire the status of agriculturalists, albeit through an alternate route. Denied one marker of status, they were ultimately granted another.

Even more remarkably, a group of Mazhabi Sikhs requested to be recognized as an agricultural tribe in the Lyallpur and Gujranwala districts in early 1911 (see Figure 2.6). This was unusual because, as later explored in Chapter 4, the colonial state explicitly defined their traditional caste occupation as sweeping and scavenging and thus at best menial laborers in the employ of proper landholders. Upon receiving the petition,

REVENUE AND AGRICULTURAL DEPARTMENT.
AGRICULTURE.
OCTOBER 1911, NOS. 17-25.

INCLUSION OF MAZHBI SIKHS OF THE GUJRANWALA AND LYALLPUR
DISTRICTS IN THE LIST OF AGRICULTURAL TRIBES.

File No. 34.

No. 555, dated Lahore, 4th September 1911.

From—G. F. de MONTMORENCY, Esquire, Junior Secretary to the Financial Commissioner, Punjab,
To—The Revenue Secretary to Government, Punjab.

No. 17

I AM directed to forward copies of the marginally noted correspondence.*
The Hon'ble Mr. J. M. Douie, C.S.I. The reply from Rawalpindi is not sent
as it has been ascertained that there is
only one chak of Mazhbis on the
Lower Jhelum Canal, and as proprietary
rights are not being conferred in that
colony at present, there is no need to
notify the Shahpur district Mazhbis.
In regard to the Mazhbi Sikhs of the Gujranwala and Lyallpur districts, the
Financial Commissioner recommends that they each be notified separately in
each of the two districts as an agricultural tribe in a separate group in order to
† Printed file No. 190 volume IV, page 1650. protect them against expropriation. It
was held in Mr. Maclagan's letter
No. 84-A.† (Rev & Agr.—Agri.) of 3rd May 1907, that there were no strong
grounds for holding that the Mazhbi Sikhs needed protection to prevent
their lands being alienated ; but the position has now altered, and in addition
to the yeomen and capitalists, the Mazhbis holding peasant grants will acquire
proprietary rights on the Lower Chenab Canal, and the present correspondence
gives reason to think that, without the assistance of the Act, there would be
numerous cases of expropriation.

2. Two draft notifications are forwarded.

No. 71, dated 13th March 1911.

From—Lieut. Colonel M. W. DOUGLAS, C.I.E., Deputy Commissioner, Lyallpur,
To—The Commissioner, Multan division.

No. 18

I HAVE the honour to forward a petition‡ submitted by certain Mazhbi Sikh
‡ Not printed. pensioners of this district, asking that they
may be included among the agricultural tribes
gazetted under the Alienation Act (XIII of 1900).

2. The history of the Mazhbi grants is recorded on pages 110-11, volume I, Colony
Manual. They hold one village in the Lyallpur district, three in Gujranwala, and one
on the Jhelum Canal in Shahpur.

3. The Mazhbi grantees are generally extravagant and prone to indebtedness.
They not infrequently, even in these days of prosperity, borrow from sahukars and lease
their lands out to them for the year on cash terms including the advance and interest.
There is already a tendency among nazrana-paying Mazhbis to sell their grants.

4. In common with other grantees who fulfil the required conditions the Mazhbis
will shortly be given proprietary rights, and unless they receive the protection they ask
for, it is tolerably certain that a number of them will permit themselves to be expropriated

The grants were given chiefly to improve the status of this class of Sikh and to
secure good recruits for the 23rd, 32nd and 34th Pioneer Regiments.

They are agriculturists in every sense, and their protection is politically expedient:
I have to recommend therefore that they be included among the tribes gazetted in this
district.

FIGURE 2.6 A petition by a group of Mazhabi Sikhs from Gujranwala and Lyallpur for "agriculturalist" status, 1911. Source: "Inclusion of Mazhbi Sikhs of the Gujranwala and Lyallpur districts in the list of agricultural tribes," October 1911, Punjab Government Civil Secretariat, Revenue and Agriculture Department, proceedings A, no. 17-25, file 34, 2, serial R/811, Punjab State Archives, Chandigarh, India.

Montagu W. Douglas, the deputy commissioner of Lyallpur, noted that while this group had received land grants as tenants in exchange for military service, they "are generally extravagant and prone to indebtedness."[141] Still, he concluded that Mazhabis "are agriculturalists in every sense, and their protection is politically expedient." Yet the deputy of Gujranwala, Shaikh Asghar Ali, not only argued against their inclusion but was more disparaging, stating, "The Mazhbi is the worst colonist and cultivator that one can come across." Their request, he went on, stemmed from a "desire to enhance their status by being classed with agricultural tribes, and to hide their origin." Between these two opinions revolved the fiction of legislating a group's ostensibly innate status.

When this impasse reached the desk of the financial commissioner in Lahore that September, the context within which this decision would be made had changed. Geoffrey F. de Montmorency noted that soon these Mazhabis were to be given proprietary rights in the Lower Chenab Colony, elevating their position from tenants to owners on account of their military service. Their profligate habits, however, would invariably lead to a cycle of reckless spending and excessive borrowing. Thus, "without the assistance of the Act," stated de Montmorency, "there would be numerous cases of expropriation."[142] It was also not insignificant that this group was originally given land "to secure good recruits for the 23rd, 32nd, and 34th Pioneer Regiments" of the British Indian Army.[143] He then ruled that this specific group of Mazhabis was to be notified as an agricultural tribe in these two districts—but on a separate list, so as not to be conflated with the main category of agriculturalists. In other words, the state would allow them to avail the benefits of the Punjab Alienation of Land Act without jeopardizing the fragile criterion upon which it was based. On September 26, 1911, a handful of Mazhabis thereby legally *became* agriculturalists by the stroke of a pen.

In these circuitous ways, the colonial imposition of the agriculturalist/non-agriculturalist binary produced a limited space for contestation by certain wealthy landowning or soldiering Panjabi groups. Definitions given force through the law and seemingly fixed in hard fact generated their opposite, a myriad of claims seeking greater privileges by correcting and altogether altering the basic criterion for recognition. When being a peasant could be determined, conferred, and revoked almost at whim, the contradictory and impermanent nature of the category became difficult to overlook. This also demonstrated the importance of recognition for Panjabis, as it entitled access to new avenues for legal protection and market participation. Yet what is curious about this particular struggle is that it did not elicit a direct challenge to colonial taxonomy. It does not appear that reordering the language and structure of the division of labor violated the moral economy of rural Panjabi society, toward either a more equitable appreciation of collective agriculture or a wider polarization to the point of fomenting rebellion.[144] Indeed, only groups with some existing position and resources made claims to change their status. It was this class of new peasants that later led other kinds of agitations, most prominently the demand for proprietary rights and an end to fines and restrictions on inheritance in the canal colonies that escalated into open revolt in 1907.[145] The vast majority of purportedly lower castes—Chamars, Churhas, and the rest of Ibbetson's menials and vagrants—likely did not have the means to make a demand for being recognized as agriculturalists or, if they did, were summarily rejected by colonial authorities without leaving behind a record. The Mazhabi Sikhs of Gujranwala and Lyallpur are an exception that confounds rather than confirms the rule. As a result, the discourse of correspondence between identity and occupation surreptitiously entered the political economy of Panjabi agriculture through the legal idioms of blood, tribe, and genealogy.

THE CUNNING OF AGRICULTURE

Perhaps the most basic assumption of colonial Panjabi society—that it was made up largely of peasants—now turns out to be a precarious assertion based on a more convoluted, contradictory, and inchoate history. Tracing the dissonance between Panjabi and English concepts of agrarian labor through various dictionaries, census operations, proverbs, legal definitions, and subsequent local responses thereby challenges its self-evident and timeless quality. As a result, the peasant is revealed to be a strikingly modern category, both unstable and exclusionary. A consequence of this explication is the historicizing of the peasant question itself. Well into the nineteenth century, the question of who was a peasant simply did not occur in rural Panjabi society. Instead, a range of individuals and groups unevenly conducted the various labors of agriculture without necessarily corresponding to a fixed caste hierarchy. Baba Farid's thirteenth-century invocation of Jatt at the beginning of this book points to a longer yet discontinuous and plural history. This is why determining the exact proportion of the "agricultural population" proved so troublesome for census officials from Temple to Ibbetson. Heterogeneous labor practices precluded a singular agrarian subject: a particular kind of activity did not entail a particular kind of identity, nor did identity determine activity. Kheti was done by kheti karn vale, or kisans, or halis, or perhaps Jatts but possibly also Chamars—or, all together in different capacities. By the early twentieth century, however, a new alignment between caste and labor made the notion of the peasant the exclusive domain of those fulfilling a hereditary and patriarchal criterion. Now the question of who is a peasant was asked and answered with a list of notified agricultural tribes, inaugurating the logic that it is because one *is* X that one is inherently suited to *do* Y. That so many groups sought to alter their status, either through correction or claiming it anew, reflects both the privileges the category conferred and the power of colonial law to shape material society.

At the same time, this reordering consolidated the subordination of certain groups at the bottom of the social and economic hierarchy. Early dictionaries, as well as many other sources, made clear the longstanding unequal and iniquitous relations throughout Panjabi and wider South Asian society. Specifically, the word *kamin* denotes a menial, inferior position associated with but not determined exclusively by caste, perhaps drawing on a joint philological inheritance of work (*kamm*) and deficiency (*kam*). Yet in the precolonial period, there was no precise account—no identifying, counting, and fixing—of exactly which groups occupied this position and what kinds of labors they were supposed to perform. Such heterogeneity, along with the modes of subversion it made possible, all but ended with the rise of scientific enumeration under colonial rule. The "concrete world of things," Vinay Gidwani argues in another context, is implicated in "the materiality of words as things."[146] Through the operations of the census, paradoxically growing less certain yet more determined over each iteration, *menial* becomes a noun synonymous with servants and vagrants to describe generic landless laborers defined as certain castes. Importantly, this notion not only circulated in the minds of colonial officials but was brought into being, enacted through the Punjab Alienation of Land Act and the formulation of agricultural/nonagricultural tribes. Despite both numerous official acknowledgments of Chamars, Churhas, and many others engaging in a variety of agricultural labors and the explicit purpose of the Act to only limit the influence of urban moneylending groups, those deemed menials almost always found themselves on the other side of this binary. Rendering agriculture the singular purview of peasants made up exclusively of agricultural tribes thereby marginalized those laboring within the colonial economy but left outside its epistemology.

Finally, this history also prompts a wider reconsideration of the relationship between market and non-market forces in colonial South Asia. While the inextricability of the two is both obvious and well established, the precise coordinates of their mutual reinforcement requires explication in every instance. In late nineteenth-century Panjab, the market for agriculture and land operated under a decidedly particular set of circumstances. A rule of difference permeated the process of production as well as the legal regime that organized circuits of exchanges.[147] As discussed in Chapter 1, agriculture in colonial Panjab was not conducted by generic, homogenous peasants but by individuals and groups riven with ostensibly permanent cultural differences. What this chapter reveals, on the other hand, is how the very determination of who is a peasant entailed a series of arbitrary, shifting criteria resulting in a binary division that excluded various laboring castes rendered non-agricultural. The logic underpinning this exclusion was the imputing of certain identities with the capacity to perform specific labors. Caste thus enabled some to claim peasant status, while relegating others to the status of landless laborers. This intertwining of identity and occupation entered the political economy of Panjab through a juridical restructuring of the possibilities of owning agricultural land. In particular, access to the land market was not based on simple market qualification, namely, the possession of a sufficient sum of capital to make an exchange. Rather, an individual's status determined their eligibility to engage in a transaction. Caste and the peasant status it conferred constituted the non-market qualities that sustained and shaped property relations in colonial Panjab. In this way, a new inverted continuum between identity, occupation, and land became the most important equation for rural dominance in the early twentieth century and beyond.

THREE

THE LOGIC AND ILLOGIC OF DEBT
*Reason and Capitalist Volatility
in the New Agrarian Market*

"SPENDTHRIFTS RUIN INDIA," PROCLAIMED the headline in *The New York Times* on October 7, 1900. Written by an unnamed foreign correspondent, the article described how a peculiar combination of natural and human failings was creating a dire situation in colonial India (see Figure 3.1). It began on a hopeful tone, noting that after the recent drought and famine, the coming monsoon promised a return to bountiful harvests. Yet the real problem was not a lack of rain but the culture and rationality of the people upon which it so irregularly fell. The article stated that it is "universal custom" for a man who earns approximately three dollars a month to spend upwards of three hundred on the wedding of his daughter, squandering it on such extravagances as "sweetmeats, native music, dancing and fireworks."[1] These sums were borrowed from a moneylender—a "veritable bloodsucker"—who nominally charged 24 percent interest but in practice took one anna per rupee per month, which amounted to 75 percent interest over the course of a year. Debt therefore grew rapidly, "handed down from father to son," and soon became "a terrible load which is never got rid of." Even worse, when a natural calamity did occur, people had no credit to spend on prudent expenses such as the digging of new wells or buying fodder for their animals. Instead, they hastily resorted to selling "their wives trinkets, their cooking pots, [and] the greater portion of their clothing," turning ultimately to the government for relief. Local administrators were therefore forced to intervene to "save the people in spite of themselves." "Weighed down under the burden of debt," the writer concluded, those in this predicament "have no heart, no backbone" and "make

SPENDTHRIFTS RUIN INDIA

Natives Squander all Their Savings on Family Celebrations.

PEOPLE LOADED WITH DEBT.

Money Lenders the Country's Curse—Government's Attempt at Reform Opposed.

Foreign Correspondence NEW YORK TIMES.

SIMLA, Sept. 6.—The outlook throughout the majority of the famine districts continues of a hopeful character. The rains have been on the whole copious and general, and though some parts of the country are calling out for more, others profess to have already had too much.

The crops sown with the first showers are promising well and should shortly come to maturity. When this happens hundreds of thousands of people, who for many long months past have been dependent on Government or on private charity for their daily bread, will once more be in a position of comparative affluence.

Perhaps this term indicates too much, since at no time is the peasant cultivator of India too well off. His spendthrift habits prevent it, apart from the repeated periods of scarcity which trouble him. It is the universal custom all over India for a man whose monthly income is perhaps $3 to spend as much as $300 on the marriage of his daughter. This sum he borrows from the local money lender, a veritable bloodsucker, whose minimum rate of interest is 24 per cent., which is only accorded to thoroughly well-to-do people. The ordinary peasant, small shopkeeper, or domestic servant pays one anna per rupee per mensem in the way of interest, and as sixteen annas go to the rupee it will be seen that this works out to 75 per cent. per annum. As a rule it is more than the borrower can do to pay off this interest, and so the debt goes on growing and is handed down from father to son, a terrible load which is never got rid of.

FIGURE 3.1 The article "Spendthrifts Ruin India" from *The New York Times*, October 7, 1900.

no effort to save themselves," resigned to wander listlessly in anticipation of an all-but-preordained demise.

Besides the intermittent death of the debtor, a more troubling possibility animated this concern with debt. The writer explained that not only have "people been getting more and more into debt," but "they have had decrees given against them in the law courts, their lands have been seized and given over to their creditors, and they themselves often become the paid labourers of the money lenders from whom they originally borrowed."[2] Particularly in the northwest of the country, "the wholesale suppression of the hardy agricultural class by traders and moneylenders is recognized to constitute a serious political evil," since the latter came from "the softest and most timorous class," while the "agriculturalists of the Punjab" provided "thousands of our best and stoutest soldiers." As indebtedness leads to dispossession, they were likely to "grow restless and turbulent" without a firm anchoring in property ownership and productive activity. For this reason, the writer continued, the local administration presented a bill to Viceroy Lord Curzon in Calcutta that would prevent land from "permanently passing out of the hands of the agricultural class." Despite opposition from moneylenders and lawyers, and even a few landowners worried about a reduction in credit, the writer confidently informed that it would be passed next month. By trying to "save the people from the results of their own reckless extravagance," the colonial state would simultaneously curtail potential opposition from the very peasants whose submission remained vital for the continuation of the empire.[3]

This newspaper article captures several aspects of what became known as the debt crisis between peasants, moneylenders, and the colonial state in Panjab during the late nineteenth and early twentieth centuries. According to Eric Stokes, "official opinion grew gradually obsessed by the problem of agrarian indebtedness," generating voluminous reports, polemics, studies, petitions, and private correspondence, along with various drafts of legislation.[4] Much of this material narrowly revolves around the irrational habits of peasants leading to land sales, the manipulation of civil laws by moneylending groups, and the need for the government to intervene to prevent greater instability. Over the last few decades, a substantial body of scholarship has interrogated these claims—from the function of spending habits and lending practices to the longer evolution of credit relations and popular unrest—in relation to different regions and periods in South Asia.[5] "No aspect of Indian economic history," states Sugata Bose rather starkly, "has been more written about and none left in a more confused state than the subject of rural moneylending."[6] Still, through this critical historiography, many of the simplistic and racialized assumptions about debt have been reexamined and challenged, if not overturned.

Despite the variety of approaches and arguments, however, the starting point for almost all of these investigations on peasant debt is the granting of private property rights in land. By establishing "a distinct, individual recorded title, enforceable by a modern judicial system and freely transferable by sale or mortgage," the British are understood to have initiated what turned into a crisis in the agrarian economy.[7] It is as if property rights sparked a chain reaction: bestowing peasants with land ownership led to a rise in credit, which prompted excessive spending, which triggered increasing indebtedness, which caused land sales to moneylenders, which resulted in fragmentation and displacement, which ultimately forced the government to imposed special legislation. As a result, the colonial state appears most active at either end of the sequence, "benignly" granting rights in the beginning only to hastily attempt to mitigate potential disaster at the end. The interim, meanwhile, is largely given over to the inevitable, following the unwritten yet seemingly unavoidable rules of market compulsion that effectively reproduce the theme of irresponsible agency.[8]

While the advent of private property is crucial to the emergence of the debt question, investing it with overriding importance and locating it as the seed of this problem conceals a larger history of social and material disruption and transformation. Such an explanation resembles a search for a discrete origin, an attempt to identify the singular cause from which an elaborate process inexorably unfolds. It also naturalizes the imposition of a peculiar set of capitalist relations, where the colonial evaluation of cultural attributes informed the structure of economic possibilities. Once established, this narrative assumes a familiar form, with little need to explain any of the other elements of this history or their interrelationships or internal dynamics. Indeed, and not surprisingly, the explanation of private property as the root cause of debt was first put forward by British officials in the nineteenth century. The "real and true cause of all our woe," wrote a settlement officer from Jhang district in 1882, "was the mistaken and misplaced gift of full transferable proprietary right in land to the cultivator."[9] Colonial reason in this way continues to inform the critical practice of meaning-making today.

The supposed logic of peasant debt is sustained by multiple illogics. In this chapter, I examine how and for whom the debt question developed into a problem, the conflicting outcomes of the way it was addressed, and the politics of what was naturalized and elided in the process. Turning from the juridical defining of menials as inherently non-agriculturalists in Chapter 2, it charts the fortunes of agriculturalists confronting a new yet opaque system of market volatility. I bring extensive statistical data, government reports, and legal judgments and debates to bear on untapped vernacular memorials and rural household budgets. The chapter begins by exploring how indebtedness became an object of inquiry implicated in peculiar notions of caste, religion, and community. A prolonged debate involving British officials and Panjabi elites over legislative intervention transformed the problem from general debt to land transfer to a certain kind of alienation by undisciplined agriculturalists. I then analyze the available figures for sales and mortgages across the 1901 advent of the Punjab Alienation of Land Act to show how the attempt to solve indebtedness actually empowered a particular class defined in caste terms to control the land market. Finally, I juxtapose firsthand accounts of tenant- and owner-cultivators struggling for livelihood with colonialist claims of bringing coherence and rationality to agricultural production. Far from acting as an outside force, I demonstrate how insecurity became constitutive of the colonialist reordering of labor, caste, and capital relations. This chapter is therefore not a history of debt but tracks the contradictory politics of indebtedness and their global circulation through different historical moments, conditions, and lives.

AN OBJECT OF COLONIAL INQUIRY

The practical as opposed to ideological problem of agrarian debt followed closely in the shadows of the East India Company's expansion throughout the subcontinent. After Charles Cornwallis's 1793 fixing of an impossibly high revenue demand in Bengal led to widespread defaults and famine, Thomas Munro's professedly more flexible settlement of Madras Presidency in the 1820s attempted to protect small landholders from falling into arrears, while the practice of evicting indebted peasants and confiscating lands in north India precipitated the revolt of 1857–58.[10] One of the most influential policy statements emerging from the growing official concern with peasant indebtedness came from a high court judge named Raymond West. Published in 1873, *The Land and the Law in India* was initially written as an internal government paper, but owing to the "momentous importance" of the issue, West decided to present it as a short book to the public.[11] References to this text abound in subsequent colonial reports and correspondence, as it became the anchor for various meditations on how the government ought to deal with debt.[12]

A significant aspect of West's book is the way he framed the relationship of debt to both the market and the colonial state. The dilemma revolved around determining the appropriate level of government involvement "in giving or refusing to give effect to private obligations" arising from an exchange.[13] The enforcement of contracts was in fact a key question for officials in the late nineteenth century.[14] West provided a brief history of commerce and the qualities and institutions that make it possible. On the one hand, he wrote of exchange as a primordial activity based on the mutual interests of individuals, an entirely natural process. When interrupted by occasional bouts of selfishness or violence, however, society came to recognize the need for the "prompt and strict fulfillment of promises" to ensure economic and social harmony. As West saw it,

> The absence of a remedy against knavery is opposed to all economic principles, discourages accumulation, prevents money from going to the quarters where it would be most useful, causes accommodation to cost an extravagant price, and leads to great waste of time in the contest of cunning and evasion.[15]

Yet on the other hand, such blanket enforcement could also go awry. Where "special circumstances" have arisen to disturb "the assumed equality of borrowers and lenders," he added with qualification, it is incumbent on the state to refuse to enforce those same contracts "essential in ordinary times to the general well-being."¹⁶ Differences in the capacities of individuals in particular rendered the activity of exchange dangerously lopsided. After mentioning how the inequality between seamen and miners and their employers in England required partisan state intervention, West turned his attention to his more immediate surroundings. "Still less can such an equality be assumed," he notes, "in a community split up into sections, divided by the impassable barriers of caste and hereditary occupation."¹⁷ In India, where a hierarchical society is comprised of individuals marked by inherent, immutable differences, careful manipulation ran up against ordinary fairness. Or, as West put it, "capital must be fostered, but there are other essential elements of national prosperity and safety, which must be fostered too."¹⁸

The source of this divergence for West was located squarely in religion and culture, specifically the rise of Christianity. In English society, the sanctity of the human body meant that individuals could not sell themselves into slavery, which gradually led to an acceptance of the alternative of alienating property. As land became indifferent to whosoever occupied it, commerce was given a new impetus based on a culture of equality between rational individuals. According to West, that sort of separation simply had not yet occurred in India; the conflation of individual identity with landed property had "never quite lost its hold upon the popular mind of India."¹⁹ Instead, new methods of commerce and contract were having a more perilous effect. The "embarrassed landholders of India," West stated, are "rapidly losing their paternal acres *without losing their attachment to them* [as well as] without having acquired other means of gaining a subsistence."²⁰ In other words, there was a discrepancy between the movements of economy and society, with the advancement of the former conflicting with the stasis of the latter. Imposing British laws of free exchange was therefore inappropriate for a population steeped in irrational, outmoded attachments. Without working to "improve the intellectual and moral tone of the Hindus," any rigid enforcement of contracts would be akin to "throwing them into deep water to make them learn to swim," ending in a disaster for both the local population and the empire.²¹

In terms of concrete policy, the conclusions reached by West are relatively modest and vague. He outlined several measures the government ought to adopt immediately: an outright ban on land sales without the explicit assent of local authorities; a review of all leases with terms over one year to prevent informal alienation; an automatic revenue reassessment of any land sold to discourage ownership changes; the disqualification of interest above 9 percent on amounts totaling five hundred rupees or less.[22] More tortuously, West offered a cautionary scenario of the potential ruin of three brothers jointly holding a small amount of land. If one brother decides to separate and seeks a partition, both his one-third share and the remaining two-thirds would become unviable, resulting in debt and the eventual default of all three. To prevent this outcome, West advised, the courts should either hold an auction between the brothers, with the highest bidder keeping all of the land and the other two forced to leave after being paid their proportional monetary share. Or, if none of the brothers could raise such a sum—a highly likely possibility—the three should simply recognize the benefits of remaining in a collective household and put off the decision to subdivide altogether.[23] In these ways, the paradoxically natural yet unsuitable course of fragmentation and alienation would be avoided by state intervention, keeping the patriarchal joint-family household intact for another generation. West's prescriptions were informed by the common colonial trope of discrepant temporalities—of India's present being a poorer version of England's past—wedded in this instance to a cultural inadequacy not yet suited for conducting economic affairs. British rule thus appeared as a gesture of magnanimous, if hesitant and unending, tutelage.

Within two years of the publication of West's treatise, the urgency of addressing the question of indebtedness became evident with an outbreak of violence in the western Deccan. In early May 1875, nearly a thousand small landholders rampaged through a *sahukar* (moneylender) neighborhood in the village of Supe in Pune district of the Bombay Presidency, not unlike what would happen in Isa Khel years later. After smashing the shop locks, they seized account books, debt bonds, grain, and cloth, burning them in a pile in the central square before dispersing. By early June, however, overwhelming reinforcements succeeded in reestablishing colonial order, with the arrest of 874 mostly Marathi peasants on charges stemming from over a hundred separate threats or attacks against Gujarati and

Marwari sahukars, although none were actually killed.[24] What became known as the Deccan revolt was in fact driven by a new and increasing antagonism between peasants and moneylenders.[25] A cotton boom in the 1860s led to a price slump the next decade, which, along with a series of poor harvests, created greater reliance of peasants on sahukars to pay the rising revenue demand. While the latter refused to provide credit without land as collateral in an uncertain economy, the former became more desperate to not have their properties seized by the government for nonpayment. The broader revolt itself lasted no more than four weeks, though its ramifications were felt throughout the empire and informed state policy for several decades thereafter.

At the center of the events in the Deccan was the beginning of a new contradiction between the course of the economy and the conduct of communities. The perennial theme of debt resulting from inflexible government revenue demands leading to the confiscation of land or movable property produced an agrarian system marked by greater dependency and precariousness. This is evident in the two objectives of those in revolt: according to David Hardiman, they sought "to destroy the debt bonds which the sahukars used as an instrument of oppression, and to frighten [them] into acting less oppressively in [the] future."[26] Yet unlike West's largely generic categories of "peasant" and "moneylender," the parties to this relationship were recognized as belonging to different regional and caste communities. The peasants were all poor Marathis, lower-caste Hindus, as well as some Muslims, while the sahukars were well-off Gujarati and Marwari baniyas, in addition to a few Brahmin moneylenders. How each group conducted itself in an atmosphere of economic hostility—communities of class at war—therefore exceeded the conventions of bourgeois universalism. Different perceptions of reciprocity and violation, idioms for the transmission of politics, notions of auspicious times, signs and events, and the limits imposed on the extent of violence all acquired new force in a context of dramatically changing expectations. This is also what contributed to the inability of the colonial state in the face of organized mass unrest. Not only were British officials unable to suppress the revolt, but they also remained largely aloof to the tensions that preceded it and struggled to articulate and implement possible remedies in its aftermath.

HINDU MONEY, MUSLIM DEBT

An urgent priority of the government in the wake of the Deccan revolt was to prevent similar or greater violence from happening elsewhere in the empire. This fear prompted the activities of an enterprising civil service officer named Septimus Thorburn, stationed for several years in the frontier districts of western Panjab. After conducting the first regular settlement of Bannu district from 1872 to 1879, he became district commissioner and later divisional judge in Dera Ismail Khan from 1882 to 1884, rising to commissioner of Rawalpindi and then financial commissioner of the whole province for a year before retiring in 1899. Thorburn published nine books on matters as diverse as the social life of the Pashto-speaking people in one locality, the challenges to British interests in Afghanistan and central Asia, and the conquest and early administration of Panjab.[27] Throughout these texts, he repeatedly mentioned acquiring a deep, compassionate knowledge of Panjabi society from long periods of immersion in the countryside. His claimed "evidence of experience" is contrasted to the more austere, distant, and technocratic officers who were beginning to enter the Panjab administration at that time.[28] In this sense, Thorburn epitomized the patriarchal authoritarianism of both an earlier generation of officers such as John Lawrence and Richard Temple as well as later ones such as Malcolm Darling and Frank Brayne.[29] This is a predictable genre of exhibiting concern for native wellbeing based on condescension, unilateral decision-making, and the availability (and regular deployment) of brute force.

Thorburn came to prominence in June 1884 when he wrote an internal memorandum on peasant indebtedness in Panjab. He not only claimed that the debt level was far higher than what was shown in government statistics but also held that it would soon lead to greater immiseration and instability if nothing was done about it. The origins of the problem lay in a faulty assumption made by the British when initially devising a system to govern Panjabis. "We assumed," lamented Thorburn, "that all classes must know their own interests best, and in their furtherance show thrift, intelligence and a desire for knowledge." Even when some officials "most direct in touch with the people" raised objections in favor of a more informal, personal approach, the overall policy erroneously continued as if Panjab "was inhabited by a homogenous, intelligent and aspiring people."[30] Instead, Thorburn argued, Panjabis especially in districts west of the Jhelum River were clearly divided between six million ignorant, warlike Muslim peasants and sixty thousand cunning yet weak Hindu shopkeepers, for a ratio of ten to one. The former had become indebted to the latter due to three key changes introduced by British rule: the creation of a new spirit of individualism, the application of laws ill suited for the condition of the people, and the imposition of a fixed rather than fluctuating revenue demand.[31] Thorburn then provided a vivid narrative of the new process by which a "poor Muhammadan" becomes ensnared in debt to a "grasping Hindu":

> He [the Muslim peasant] has in every case a running account with his baniah [the Hindu moneylender]. This is generally settled after each harvest, which is thus largely discounted before ripening. He pays his way fairly enough, until sickness, death of oxen, a death in his family, the failure of his crop, a case in court, or other accident occurs. He then writes a bond bearing interest either in cash or in grain; and once having done so, self-denial and the luck of several good seasons are required to extricate him.

Yet the chances of pulling out of debt and settling accounts are slim:

> Even so the creditor will not proceed to extremities so long as his debtor works for him like a bondsman. Death or working incapacity sooner or later strain or break the quasi-amicable connection which has hitherto existed between debtor and creditor. A willing slave being better as a cultivator for the creditor than an outsider, the debtor is frequently left in occupation [of the land].

All it takes in another minor calamity to shift relations even further askew:

> [T]here is an intermediate state between indebtedness involving the alienation of landed property and merely a serious debit with the baniah. At this stage the debtor signs and renews bonds and agrees to pay interest in kind at harvest time, either a share or a measure of the crop. He thus discounts the next harvest at a higher and higher rate, until he becomes, in many cases, the mere slave of his creditor.[32]

It is at this point that relations become antagonistic, where the ignorant peasant endowed with individual ownership and a high revenue demand barely retains enough grain for subsistence at harvest, while the crafty moneylender initiates legal proceedings to seize the land outright in order to hire a different, more docile tenant to cultivate it.

By the early 1880s this callous process had become troublingly common in Dera Ismail Khan. According to Thorburn, nearly every agriculturalist had incurred some degree of debt. Out of a population of approximately three hundred thousand in the district, only 23 percent owed nothing, while 13 percent were "already ruined," 10 percent "irretrievably involved," 28 percent seriously indebted and another 26 percent were in danger but could be saved.[33] In terms of land, whereas sixty thousand acres had been either sold or mortgaged in 1882 and 1883, the next year almost ninety-five thousand acres changed hands, an increase of 58 percent.[34] Although the bulk of this area continued to be exchanged between those whom Thorburn called "agriculturalists"[35] and only amounted to 8 percent of the total cultivated area, Hindu non-agriculturalists were gaining an increasing share of the market as well as acquiring the most productive and highly valued portions. At the same time, an undocumented trade in land using crop hypothecation and informal agreements flourished to the exclusive benefit of moneylenders. As a result, the Muslim peasantry—"hitherto so patient, so loyal, which sided with us from the first, and bled freely for us at Mooltan in the 2nd Sikh War, throughout the Sepoy Mutiny [. . .] and lately in Afghanistan"—was fast becoming not only dispossessed and impoverished but also discontented. Indeed, Thorburn noted, considering that Dera Ismail Khan was a frontier district, bordering a Muslim kingdom, beyond which lay Russia ("ever on the watch to embarrass us"), it was "necessary in self-interest to arrest the further degradation of the Muslim peasantry" and prevent potential sedition.[36]

In order to reverse this trajectory, Thorburn explained its causes and proposed several changes in policy. He first identified innate Muslim ineptitude, general overpopulation, and shrinking agricultural returns as "natural" forces arising inevitably out of social characteristics and the prosperity brought by British rule. The more preventable causes, on the other hand, were the ways in which contract law favors business-minded Hindus, the rigidity of the revenue system, and the estrangement of the bureaucracy from the rural population. All three combined to place peasants, already "less self-denying, less intelligent, less earnest and blighted by fatalism of their religion," at the mercy of moneylenders empowered by the institutions of the state.[37] What was needed, Thorburn stated, was restricting credit through abolishing imprisonment for debt altogether, exempting a minimum amount of land needed to support a family from seizure, rendering minor debts non-cognizable, and extending the period of repayment from three to six years. To this list he added allowing special judges to decide a reasonable amount of interest to repay, authorizing them to "go behind the bond" to examine the relations between debtor and creditor, banning professional lawyers from court procedures, preventing the seizing of draft cattle and farm implements, and avoiding issuing summons during harvest and planting periods. Finally, he continued, it is necessary to introduce a reduced, fluctuating revenue assessment in all precarious areas along with freeing officers from desk work to spend more time among the people.[38] Only this litany of prescriptions together would halt the crisis from becoming a catastrophe.

Despite the dramatic tone and extensive details of Thorburn's memorandum, the Panjab government was unimpressed, even dismissive. After some jostling between the Judicial and Home departments as to which should deal with a legal issue in a frontier area, John Andrew Grant, secretary to the financial commissioner, responded in October 1884. He mildly agreed that the amount of peasant debt was becoming notable, but immediately rejected that it had anything to do with revenue assessment. A review of several districts showed that debt actually appeared to be highest in places where the assessment was lightest, regardless of whether it was fluctuating or fixed. "The very moderation of our assessment," claimed Grant, "has tended as much as anything else to the indebtedness of the agricultural classes." He repeated the theme of benevolent rule and native indiscipline, that is, "the larger the margin of profit the greater is the credit of the zamindar," while "the greater the desire of the money-lender to get the land into his grasp."[39] As to Thorburn's specific suggestions to reform the functioning of the courts, Grant found a few recommendations useful, some of which were already in place and the rest altogether impractical.

Perhaps more importantly, Grant expressed strong disagreement over the legitimacy and efficacy of limiting the right to sell land. Not only would landowners object to the government forcing them into "a condition of irresponsible tutelage," but "if the zamindars cannot manage their own affairs no official could do it for them." Moreover, trying to prevent land sales would be detrimental, as it would reduce the availability of credit and thereby raise interest rates, which in turn would add urgency to attaching land to cash loans and thereby hasten the overall pace of insolvency and evictions. The financial commissioner therefore "doubts whether there is any reason for thinking that [. . .] any drastic legislation to meet the indebtedness of the peasantry is at present required."[40] Charles Aitchison, the lieutenant-governor of Punjab, in a reply a few months later, went further. Since the "evil" of debt was "inherent in the character and traditional habits of the people," little if anything "can be done to improve the position of the agriculturalists." Thus, "there is no hope to be looked for in usury laws," with every effort either spurring evasions by moneylenders or only making the situation worse for peasants.[41] After reviewing the recommendations and insisting that any alternation apply to all groups rather than agriculturalists alone, Aitchison concluded with Grant that Thorburn's memorandum ought to be circulated to revenue officers for limited comments pertaining only to reforming the courts.

The matter would have ended at this point, and the memorandum relegated to the archive of the colonial bureaucracy, had it not been for Thorburn's additional zeal. Dissatisfied with the government's tepid response, and perhaps following in the genre of William Wilson Hunter's cautionary *The Indian Musalmans* (1871), he went ahead and published it as a book in 1886 titled *Musalmans and Money-Lenders in the Punjab*. This version recapitulated the original memorandum, though, with the aid of rewriting and an editor, the text appeared more organized and less repetitive. The problem of indebtedness—now extended to the whole of Panjab—was again described as a challenge for the colonial state to address through reforming fixed revenue demands, land ownership rights, and civil court procedures. What was distinct, however, was the renewed emphasis on the cultural failings of caste and religious groups engaging in agriculture. Using Denzil Ibbetson's descriptions from the 1881 census, Thorburn listed various Muslim Pathan, Jatt, Rajput, Baloch, and Ghakhar inadequacies. Even "after 36 years of British rule," these groups "were, and still are, unfit" for the gift of property, being "almost as rude, ignorant, and imprudent as they were upon annexation." Given Panjabi peasants "as stupid as their own plough-oxen," Thorburn asked whether it was any mystery why they fell so desperately into debt.⁴² Drawing an analogy back to the metropole, he modified the familiar theme of natives as childlike by implicating their infantilism in financial misconduct. It was, after all, hardly their fault:

> Were the children in all the Board schools in Great Britain suddenly let loose in London, each with fifty golden sovereigns in his pocket, would it be right to blame them or the donors who had given them their holiday, if, instead of putting their money in the Savings Bank, they spent it foolishly?⁴³

What is more, these "donors" too were marked by primordial identity. It is conniving, inherently astute, yet dishonest Hindu baniyas—the equivalent of Jews in Eastern Europe—who were able to manipulate both simple peasants and colonial laws for their own enrichment.⁴⁴ When money lent with full knowledge that it would not be repaid was recovered in the form of landed property through convoluted court proceedings, Thorburn warned, the government was effectively inviting an "agrarian insurrection."⁴⁵ By collecting all of these arguments in the form of a book, and publishing it both with William Blackwood & Sons in Edinburgh and the Pioneer Press in Allahabad, he ensured that the administration would not be able to avoid his perspective on indebtedness for much longer.

Through the arguments advanced in these successive texts, Thorburn effectively transformed the question of debt in colonial Panjab. To West's abstract note on the need for government to regulate contracts between unequal, impulsive individuals, he added a new sense of affect and empiricism. Ignorant peasants, the loyal and martial hereditary sons of the soil who comprised the majority of the population, were depicted as being swindled by a small minority of pernicious moneylenders. What is more, this situation was far worse than in the Deccan, with a much higher volume of debt burdening a community riven with Muslim-Hindu antagonism and located in a dangerous frontier region. As one British officer later remarked, "If the land of the Punjaub [*sic*] had been transferred as that of the North-West Provinces has been, it is quite certain that we should not now be here."⁴⁶

For Thorburn, indebtedness became a problem of how the government should respond to the innate qualities of caste and religion impairing the ability of peasants to make responsible financial decisions. The "racialism that had thoroughly infused socials relations in feudal Europe," argues Brenna Bhandar, "was globalized with the advent of modern colonialism," which ultimately "produced and relied upon economic and juridical forms for which property law and a racial concept of the human were central tenets."[47] Money in the context of colonial Panjab was therefore anything but the universal equivalent it was envisaged to be in bourgeois society. Individuals do not relate in "purely atomistic ways" with one another any more than they purport to be equal.[48] Rather than a medium of generalized exchange rendering all difference commensurate, money played a decidedly prejudiced role in Thorburn's narrative. Certain attributes were conjured up as indelible features of different Panjabi groups and incorporated into new, volatile monetary practices. Differences-as-disabilities—of profligacy, thrift, or dishonesty—not only appeared intrinsic but were used to explain the dysfunctions of the rural economy. Without proper action from colonial officials, money that began in the hands of a Hindu could not but end up as debt upon the head of a Muslim.

IDEOLOGIES OF INTERVENTION

In this way, peasant debt gradually yet fitfully became an issue requiring serious state intervention in colonial Panjab. Despite Thorburn's second effort, what one official derided as attempting "to force the hand of the Government by publishing a book," it was still not considered a priority.[49] Upon receiving *Musalmans and Money-Lenders in the Punjab*, the Lieutenant-Governor James Lyall had almost the same response as his predecessor did to the 1884 memorandum. Besides being poorly written and unfit for an official state paper, he considered it largely a regurgitation of arguments from the discussion of the Deccan relief act. Lyall's annoyance was matched by local officers who, believing that explanations of debt in Panjab were already present in the voluminous settlement literature, disliked having to collect and summarize those points again in official correspondence. They also considered many of Thorburn's critiques of the practices of civil courts were inapplicable to Panjab, rendering his recommendations simply unnecessary.[50]

Rather fortuitously, however, Thorburn's book happened to come to the attention of the secretary of state for India, Richard A. Cross, who ordered Lyall "to give the subject his early and attentive consideration and report his conclusions."[51] This was seconded by the Viceroy for British India, the Marquess of Lansdowne (Henry Petty-Fitzmaurice), who, after witnessing the distress of agriculturalists while on tour through the NWP, echoed Thorburn's concern and asked for a prompt report on the matter for Panjab.[52] Only at this point, with pressure from both London and Calcutta, was the local administration compelled to investigate the causes and extent of indebtedness in order to come up with a solution.

Yet in the government's new emphasis on addressing the matter of debt, the question itself underwent a subtle yet significant shift. The general issue of peasant indebtedness was displaced by a more specific focus on land transfer. The problem, in other words, was overtaken by one of its consequences, a disease bypassed in the haste to conduct an autopsy. As a result, the amount, pace, and relative degree by which peasants were losing their land to moneylenders through forced sales became the focal point of the investigation. Formulating the issue in these terms, however, invited another complication. By bringing together the already ambiguous notion of peasant (and moneylender) identity with the material process of land selling, the administration was confronted with a lack of reliable statistics by which to measure these changes. "Prior to 1874–75," noted an official, "separate details for agriculturalists and non-agriculturalists were not given in the Revenue Administration Reports, and [thus] no detailed examination of the transfer to money-lenders is possible previous to that year."[53] Even after that point, whatever information was produced was scattered in various documents and therefore unavailable for convenient comparison. It was also admittedly difficult to glean supposed truths from the exaggerations, clumsiness, and inaccuracies that plagued official statistics.[54] Nevertheless, the edicts from above compelled the Panjab administration to proceed, combing through existing settlement reports and the 1878 Famine Commission, as well as ordering special rural surveys, to furnish the numerical evidence of indebted land transfer. The conclusion thereby anticipated and directed the inquiry.

With these caveats in mind, the data the administration managed to compile reveals something of both the severity and the trajectory of the problem as well as its discrepancies and elisions. The figures for land transfer were given between agriculturalists and moneylenders along an east/west division of Panjab.[55] In the eastern districts, while an average of 1,387 cases of land sales were registered to agriculturalists in 1865, none were registered to moneylenders. Sales of land to moneylenders began in 1874 with 1,679 cases, steadily increasing to 2,240 in 1879 and 2,998 in 1885. In those same years, the number of sale cases to agriculturalists grew similarly from 2,532 to 3,298 to 4,217. Parallel to the cases for land sales was the actual area of land sold. Whereas an average of 45,928 acres were sold to agriculturalists while none to moneylenders in 1865, the gap shrank to 26,289 and 24,387 in 1874, then 33,711 and 22,627 in 1879, and finally almost equal at 34,468 to 34,775 in 1885. Thus from 1874 to the end of 1885, nearly three hundred thousand acres were sold to moneylenders, amounting to 1.9 percent of the total cultivated area in these districts.

The figures in the west, on the other hand, start off similarly but gradually grow apart. In 1865 there were 1,842 cases of sales to agriculturalists with zero to moneylenders. Sales to moneylenders began in 1874 with 1,263 cases, rising to 1,769 in 1879 and then 3,836 in 1885. This remained much lower than the increases to agriculturalists, which were 2,925 to 6,124 and 8,029 in those same years. In terms of area sold, the imbalance is even greater: from 25,190 acres to agriculturalists and 0 to moneylenders in 1865, the difference swells to 34,741 and 16,930 in 1874, then 97,068 to 28,120 in 1879 and finally 127,152 to 52,154 in 1885. This constituted a little over three hundred thousand acres to moneylenders in the 1874–85 period, or 3.5 percent of the cultivated area of western districts.[56] The question of why quantified data is considered more credible than, say, qualitative descriptions replete with explicit or implicit Orientalist tropes remains a troubling problem for historians of economic life in the colony.[57] Still, it would seem that across Panjab, there was a steady increase both in the number of cases for land sales and total area sold, though the higher rate in the west was mitigated by the fact that most of the gains were accruing to other agriculturalists.

The specter of non-agricultural moneylenders acquiring land becomes evident with figures for the area of land pledged for debt. In the east, the average of 40,365 acres mortgaged to agriculturalists in the 1865–69 period fell to 28,170 acres in 1869–74 and then 25,419 in 1874–79 before climbing to 66,560 in 1879–85. For the same last three periods, however, the acres under mortgage to moneylenders went from 77,197 to 53,219 to 76,712. This amounted to a far higher figure of 9.2 percent of the cultivated area in the hands of moneylenders through sale or mortgage in these districts. The situation in the west was even more acute. The 50,058 mortgaged acres to agriculturalists in 1865–69 went down to 40,379 in 1869–74 before rising to 105,442 in 1874–79 and then leveling off at 71,785 in 1879–85. Growth for moneylenders was steeper: 31,000 to 46,300 to 103,069, representing 10.8 percent of the cultivated area. Taking east and west together, both agriculturalists and moneylenders held almost 9.7 million rupees of mortgage in 1885, a nearly 1,300 percent increase from the 694,925 rupees owed to them in 1865.[58] In contrast with absolute sales, moneylenders generally held a larger and growing share of lands under mortgage and therefore appeared to be gaining relatively more control in the countryside.

At the level of individual districts, however, the apparent clarity of these province-wide figures diminishes. Significant fluctuations in land sales and mortgage redemptions challenge the narrative of an obvious and uniform trajectory toward indebted disaster. In Gujranwala, for instance, land sales steadily increased from 1,230 acres in 1865 to 2,700 in 1876 and 4,300 in 1884, while remaining flat in Shahpur, with 2,013 acres to 2,300 and 2,500 sold in those same years. Multan district, on the other hand, witnessed the precise opposite, with the 5,573 acres sold in 1865 doubling to 11,308 the next year before sinking to 4,757 the year after, then rising to 10,580 in 1871, dropping again to 5,400 in 1874 and finally spiking to 21,800 in 1882. Amritsar too fluctuated from a low of 736 acres in 1867 and 2,100 in 1876 jumping to 30,900 in 1885, while Dera Ismail Khan climbed even more sharply, from only 625 acres in 1866 and 524 in 1872 to 46,500 in 1879, 45,700 in 1881, and 45,900 in 1884. In Sirsa, meanwhile, the amount of land sold actually decreased over time, from highs of 26,026 acres in 1865 and 35,632 in 1869 plummeting to 2,400 in 1877 and 3,000 in 1883.[59]

In terms of the extent to which lands under mortgage were redeemed by their original owners—perhaps the most informative if not inflammatory pair of figures—the data is also far from consistent. Land debt in Jalandhar district accumulated at a regular pace, with only 306 acres recovered out of 7,560 mortgaged in 1876–77, 154 from 8,289 in 1880–81, and 1,026 out of 7,339 in 1883–84. Similarly hopeless was Gujrat with 322 out of 2,284 acres redeemed, 1,013 from 3,991 and 725 from 3,243, as well as Lahore with 2,588 from 6,440, 3,919 from 12,516 and 5,441 from 10,258 during those same years. In Bannu, on the other hand, much more land was actually paid off than mortgaged in 1877–78 (13,436 acres in comparison with 1,000), which evened out the next year (3,394 redeemed to 3,051 mortgaged) before swerving completely askew the year after (only 17,541 redeemed to 189,224 mortgaged). Yet in Ferozepur district, landowners appeared to extricate themselves from debt, recovering 7,213 acres from 5,150 mortgaged in 1878–79, 5,724 from 4,441 in 1880–81, and 3,096 from 3,200 in 1883–84, as they did in Rawalpindi with 24,228 acres redeemed from only 6,809 under mortgage in 1875–76 and 6,455 from 6,980 in 1879–80.[60] These variations demonstrate that while aggregate figures show a general increase in indebtedness and land transfer, such explanations are only possible by both imposing arbitrary limits and omitting several countervailing tendencies.

Below the realm of statistics, the individual circumstances of indebtedness could be even more complicated, if not whimsical. A typical civil case initiated by a moneylender against a zamindar reveals the inner dynamics of how colonial law mediated the encounter between debt and identity. In early 1878, a man named Ramdhan brought an appeal suit against Jiwan Khan for the recovery of a debt of Rs. 700 (see Figure 3.2). The defendant admitted to borrowing money from the plaintiff but argued that the majority of the outstanding balance was interest charged at a usurious rate; he requested that the court examine the fairness of the terms of the agreement. It turns out the two parties lived in the same village in Rawalpindi district and had longstanding financial ties. Initially, Jiwan Khan had borrowed Rs. 145 and seasonally carried forward an informal balance for

Judgments of the Chief Court of the Punjab, and the High Courts of Allahabad and Bombay regarding the relations of money-lenders and agriculturists—vide paragraph 14.

Civil Judgment of the Chief Court of the Punjab, No. 110 of 1879.

RAMDHAN AND ANOTHER,—(Plffs.)—APPELLANTS,

versus

JIWAN KHAN,—(Defendant,)—RESPONDENT.

APPELLATE SIDE.

Case No. 1194 of 1878.

(PLOWDEN AND SMYTH, JJ.)

*Debtor and creditor—Money-lender and zamindar—Bond—Usurious rate of interest—Act IX of 1872, clause(1), Section 16, and Section 19—Undue influence—Act I of 1872, Section 114—Presumption.—*Plaintiff, a village money-lender, sued defendant, a zamindar, for Rs. 700 principal and interest due on a bond. Defendant admitted execution of the bond, but pleaded that the greater part of the claim consisted of interest at an usurious rate, and prayed for an examination of the accounts. It was found that the parties had had dealings as debtor and creditor for a considerable time previous to the execution of the bond : and that of the amount claimed Rs. 145 only was principal, while the remaining Rs. 555 was charged for interest. The Lower Courts therefore decreed Rs. 145 and Rs. 197-1-3 interest, total Rs. 342-1-3.

Held, per Curiam that the orders of the Lower Courts should be upheld.

Per Smyth, J.—Because, having regard to the fact that the bond was extortionate and unconscionable, and considering the relations between the parties, they were justified in the absence of rebutting proof from plaintiff in holding that the bond was executed under " undue influence " as defined in Clause (1), Section 16, of the Contract Act, and were therefore justified under Section 19 of the same Act in treating the bond as void, and in decreeing to plaintiff only the amount equitably due.

Per Plowden, J.—Because the bare facts, that the parties to a contract, the subject of litigation, are a village money-lender and a zamindar, may justify a court in presuming (within the meaning of Section 114 of the Evidence Act) that the zamindar did not give a free consent to the terms of the particular agreement, when such presumption is not inconsistent with the other facts disclosed, though there be no other evidence on the part of the zamindar to prove that he had been induced by the exercise of undue influence to consent to the terms of the particular agreement.

Special appeal from the order of the Commissioner, Rawalpindi Division, dated 27th April 1878.

K. P. Roy, for appellants.

The following judgments were delivered :—

31st March 1879.

SMYTH, J.—In this case there were dealings in the nature of a current account between the plaintiffs, who are village money-lenders, and the defendant, who is a zamindar and lambardar of the village. The dealings commenced several years ago with a principal sum of Rs. 140-10-0 due to the plaintiffs. Since the commencement of the account till the present time the items, excluding those for interest, have been few in number, consisting on the one side of four additional sums amounting to Rs. 78-14-0 received by the defendant, and on the other of two payments of Rs. 40 and Rs. 34-8-0 made by the defendant. Nevertheless a balance was struck on the account yearly, and interest added ; and the sum thus found to be due at the end of each year was carried forward into the account of the subsequent year. So matters went on till 1931 Sambat. In that year the plaintiffs took a bond for the amount due, *viz.*, Rs. 380, which was payable with interest. In 1932 Sambat, without any fresh dealings in the meantime, the bond was renewed for Rs. 457-12-0. Similarly in 1933 Sambat it was renewed for Rs. 600.

It was upon this bond for Rs. 600 with interest amounting to Rs. 100 that the suit was brought by the plaintiffs. The defendant pleaded that the amount claimed consisted for the most part of interest at an usurious rate, and he asked for an examination of the account upon which the bond was based. The Extra Assistant Commissioner on going into the account found that the amount claimed by the plaintiffs consisted of only Rs. 145 as principal, while the remaining Rs. 555 was for interest. " In " such a state of things (wrote the Extra Assistant Commissioner) the Court was bound to interfere as " it was downright cheating ; and also considering the interest exorbitant it has reduced this to one " per cent., which plaintiffs themselves allow to be fair." He accordingly gave them a decree for Rs. 145 principal, and Rs. 197-1-3 interest, or a total of Rs. 342-1-3.

In appeal to the Commissioner it was urged by the plaintiffs that the bond should be enforced, but the Commissioner dismissed the appeal, and in doing so remarked that " he (the plaintiff) had " robbed and plundered the poor creature (the defendant) in the most shameful manner."

In second appeal to this Court it is again urged that the terms of the bond should be enforced ; and the case of *Mackintosh v. Wingrove* (*I. L. R.,*4 *Cal.*, 187) was cited to show that however extortionate the bargain between the plaintiffs and the defendant might have been, if the defendant thoroughly understood and consented to it there would be no ground for the equitable interference of the Courts. But as I understand the decisions of the Lower Courts in this case, they seem to me to amount substantially to a finding that although the defendant consented to the execution of the bond, his consent

FIGURE 3.2 A copy of a civil case judgment between a moneylender and a landholder, 1878. Source: Civil Judgement of the Chief Court of the Punjab, no. 110 of 1879, Ramdhan and Another (Plaintiffs) Appellants, versus Jiwan Khan (Defendant) Respondent, appellate side of case no. 1194 of 1878, in "Agricultural Indebtedness in the Punjab," Keep With Papers (Not for Records), Revenue and Agriculture Department, proceedings no. 1–8, May 1891; Enclosure no IV, 1, National Archives of India, New Delhi, India.

several years. At some point, Ramdhan took out a registered bond for Rs. 380 with interest, which was renewed at Rs. 457 and then later at Rs. 600. It was this amount, plus another Rs. 100 in interest, which constituted the Rs. 700 demanded from Jiwan Khan in the suit. However, when the case was first heard by the local extra assistant commissioner, he denounced the terms as "downright cheating," adding that the plaintiff had "robbed and plundered the poor creature [the defendant] in the most shameful manner."[61] He reduced the amount owed to the initial Rs. 145, and then added Rs. 197 of "reasonable" interest, for a total of Rs. 342, less than half of the original claim. It was this decision that Ramdhan appealed to the Chief Court in Lahore. Yet in reviewing the case, Judge John Smyth concurred with the local officer, stating that the bond was indeed "extortionate and unconscionable." He therefore dismissed the appeal and upheld the decree of Rs. 342.[62]

The plaintiff, however, appealed the judgment a second time. Ramdhan argued it was the duty of the government to enforce a consensual agreement between two parties, regardless of the specific conditions or interest rate. Again reviewing the case a year later, Justice Smyth articulated a rather peculiar yet revealing and far-reaching understanding of authority and agency in rural Panjabi society. He found that despite the defendant consenting to the terms of the bond, his "consent was *not a free consent*." Since Jiwan Khan was subject to "undue influence," he could not be considered "a free and voluntary agent" and therefore was incapable of entering into a binding agreement.[63] This conclusion was based on two conditions. First, what was the influence Ramdhan had over Jiwan Khan? "It must be remembered," Justice Smyth explained, that "the relation between the parties was not merely that of debtor and creditor." More fundamentally, it was "of village money-lender and zamindar," a notorious and entrenched relation in this country. By definition and through a myriad of customary practices, the former had considerable power to shape the desires and decisions of the latter.

The second question asked, could it be shown that this influence was actually used? Here Smyth shifts the burden entirely. The responsibility was "on the plaintiffs to show that in obtaining the bond from the defendant they took no advantage of their position," that they "dealt with him exactly as a stranger would have done."⁶⁴ Rather than Jiwan Khan demonstrating how exactly he was influenced, it was up to Ramdhan to prove that he had not used his innate influence. With such an impossible criterion, the plaintiff could only fail, as Ramdhan's identity as a moneylender rendered him automatically in a position of superiority over a zamindar such as Jiwan Khan. By this circular reasoning, Smyth established that the defendant was not—*and could not be*—a voluntary agent, and thereby reconfirmed the reduced decree and dismissed the second appeal.

What this case demonstrates is how modern law operated differently in colonial Panjab. Civil courts were already mediating in favor of those deemed zamindars in the last decades of the nineteenth century, a marked contrast to the gloomy scenario presented in Thorburn's initial memorandum and elsewhere in British India.⁶⁵ In this specific example, although it was not mentioned in the proceedings, it is safe to assume that Jiwan Khan owned land in his village. If the judgment had gone against him or the appeals granted, it is also reasonable to believe that he would have been forced to sell at least a portion of land to pay off the Rs. 700 debt to Ramdhan. Not only did this not happen, but many of Thorburn's other criticisms were noticeably absent from the case details. Both the local commissioner and judge went "behind the bond" to examine the circumstances of the debt and imposed a sharply reduced rate of interest, while neither summoned the defendant during cultivation periods or threatened imprisonment or the seizure of land or farming implements. Unlike the Deccan and Bengal, this was far from a mechanical, distant, and "omniscient" civil court habitually passing decrees in favor of baniyas to the detriment of peasants.⁶⁶ Nor was there any mention that Jiwan Khan borrowed money to specifically pay off a revenue demand, though this cannot be ruled out. Still, what was evident was the inexorable growth of the problem of indebtedness. The figures for west and east Panjab could be made to show, despite opposing instances, a trajectory toward higher cases for land sales, more acres sold, and increasingly irredeemable mortgages. In other words, even a debt lessened (but still growing) from Rs. 700 to Rs. 342 could have been enough to force Jiwan Khan to sell some land, a predicament faced by thousands of landholders. As a result, while Thorburn's diagnosis was flawed and his prescriptions largely redundant, his conclusion of an increasingly dispossessed and potentially discontented peasantry nonetheless appears to have been true.

In this context, the project of tackling the debt problem became a different kind of priority. It was no longer a matter of assuaging an energetic, egotistical settlement officer or answering his shrill publication. Investigations into rural conditions made intervention a matter of practical governance, accountable to the highest levels. Yet if the already partisan civil courts had been ineffective in preventing mounting debt and land transfer, the solution had to be sought elsewhere. In the course of gathering empirical and juridical evidence, a new conceptualization of the peasant emerged in official discourse. Connecting notions of essential caste and religious inadequacy with occupational activity, a consensus developed around the failure of the individual zamindar to act as a rational economic agent. "Like a magnetic field," Ritu Birla evocatively argues in a different context, "the ethical cartographies of private and public could invisibly distort the meaning of material relations."[67] The Justice Smyth decision legally recognized the Panjabi peasant as innately irresponsible, unable to evaluate financial options and their implications, and thereby incapable of preserving land ownership within the properly designated agricultural community. This led to another significant shift in the problem of indebtedness. Given that there were not any reforms to be enacted at the point where debt caused land sales, the state resolved to act earlier, at the very moment of the possibility for transfer. Intervention as a formal policy now became a task not of halting the transfer of land but of preempting the alienation of peasants.

A CLASH OF VANTAGE POINTS

In less than a decade, the Panjab administration went from denying peasant indebtedness altogether to declaring a concerted effort for its prevention and amelioration. The problem too shifted from general agrarian debt to the distressed sale of land to the specific alienation of peasant land. A six-member committee was established in 1895 to study the available evidence in order to provide detailed recommendations for framing a new official policy. According to committee chair Charles Rivaz, the government now believed that "the expropriation of the class of self-cultivating land-holders in the Punjab constitutes an ever-increasing political danger which, if not arrested, is likely to grow to formidable dimensions, and that remedial action is urgently necessary."[68] The nature of this action took the form of a proposed bill designed to check the transfer of land due to indebtedness from those deemed agriculturalists. After the first drafting, the committee circulated it for feedback to various British civil officials and military officers as well as a number of Panjabi government employees, judges, and local notables. They also received dozens of unsolicited opinions from different groups across Panjab arguing for or against certain aspects of the bill. This series of responses—affirmations, warnings, questions, threats, suggestions—reveals how the legal construction of the category agriculturalist, and its investment with contradictory qualities and impulses, served to restructure the market for land. By attempting to devise a permanent solution to an ever-shifting problem, colonial law created new parameters for the cultural conduct of material exchange.

At first glance, the proposed legislation appears straightforward, clearly laying out its objectives and intentions, hardly warranting controversy. Titled "A Bill to Amend the Law Relating to Agricultural Land in the Punjab," the committee presented it to the government on September 27, 1899. The opening preamble stated that the "expropriation of the hereditary agriculturalist" is "a serious political danger" emanating from the fact that "the idea of a free transferable interest in land" is "comparatively modern in origin" and therefore "contrary both to the existing practices in most Native States and to the traditions and sentiments" of the people of Panjab.[69] To check and reverse this phenomenon, the bill introduced three key measures. First, it mandated that all permanent alienations of land be sanctioned by a local revenue officer, to be given automatically either where the alienor was not a member of an agricultural tribe or where the member of an agricultural tribe alienated to an agriculturalist in the same village or another member residing in the same district.[70] Any alienation outside of these conditions would require a special inquiry into the nature of the exchange along with additional authorization from the district commissioner.

Second, the bill imposed a limit on usufructuary mortgages—where the landholder gives up possession of land to a mortgagee in order to borrow money—to a maximum of fifteen years. During this period, the mortgagee would be entitled to whatever was produced on the land, but afterward it would revert to the original owner clear of any outstanding balance. And third, the bill banned outright the hypothecation of agricultural produce, meaning a landholder receiving money in exchange for the promise of delivering crops ahead of their harvest, sometimes for several years in advance.[71] By intervening in the politics of transfers, leases, and crops, the committee claimed to address the novelty of indebtedness in conformity with the preexisting customs of Panjabis.

A draft of the bill circulated among land revenue officials and found swift, widespread approval. Several dozen settlement officers, judicial members, and district and division commissioners gave their full support for the new law, reiterating both the importance and urgency of the issue and applauding the work of the committee. Charles Tupper, the financial commissioner and codifier of the *Punjab Customary Law* series, wrote an elaborate note of endorsement that included suggestions to clarify each section and clause. Others were more impatient, such as settlement commissioner James Wilson, who expressed a "hearty welcome" to the bill but added that he "would rather accept it as it stands than see legislation much further delayed while conflicting opinions regarding its detailed provisions are being discussed."[72]

Yet the bill also had significant detractors. Chief Judge William Clark conveyed strong doubts, warning that agriculturalists' credit would shrink as lenders would not give money without security in land or produce, while the workload of revenue officials trying to determine who was an agriculturalist would increase exponentially, paralyzing the bureaucracy. Although the disease existed, he concluded, "it is better that no remedy than a wrong one be applied." After canvassing opinions in his district, the deputy commissioner of Jalandhar Arthur Barton also cautioned against disrupting the supposedly symbiotic relationship between peasant and moneylender as well as the sacrosanct right of sale. While "the object of the act is to protect the land-owner against himself," he pointed out, "I am driven to the conclusion" that "he does not want to be so protected" and would simply continue his former borrowing practices in a more illicit manner. Even the lieutenant-governor at the time, William Young, gave his assent only grudgingly, warning of unforeseen consequences and rumors that peasants believed the bill to be "a jubilee" that would cancel all mortgages and clear all debts to restore land to its original owners.[73] Despite these reservations, a large majority of officials in Panjab supported the bill as a matter not only politically necessary but economically sound and socially responsible.

Perhaps more than any other piece of legislation, the bill invited opinions from an array of Panjabis either connected with the administrative bureaucracy or considered influential among the population. While in part this was an attempt by the committee to claim a degree of local consent for what amounted to absolutist policies—another gesture toward the so-called benevolence of the "Panjab school" examined in Chapter 1—these comments also provided officials with valuable insights into how the imposition of unprecedented changes in an already volatile, complicated and confusing atmosphere might be received. For Inam Ali, a divisional judge in Sialkot, there was "no question" that the bill would save the "ancient, sturdy and hardy but simple agricultural tribes" from dispossession by "shrewd money-lending classes," which in turn would bolster the stability and prestige of the government. Ghazanfar Ali, a tahsildar in Rawalpindi, was more emphatic about the connection between peasants and the government. He described how zamindars flock to officials when on village tours, eager to perform any kind of service while forwarding various complaints and requests for help, whereas moneylenders did their utmost to avoid attending for fear of having to endure even a nominal obligation. To allow the power of land ownership to pass from the former to the latter would therefore be a "great mistake," something the bill would arrest only if passed quickly. Concern about harm inadvertently coming to zamindars, on the other hand, was countered by Ghulam Hussain, a retired major in the army and magistrate from Jalandhar. The right to sell land was being restricted rather than annulled, he argued, while land itself would not be devalued any more than it already was when purchased under duress through mounting debt and court order. Zamindars would still be able to access money for occasional needs too, because any moneylender would readily offer advances in order to make uninterrupted profit within a fifteen-year lease.[74] The bill, according to these lower-level Panjabi officials, was a positive and necessary corrective measure that would ultimately achieve its purpose.

The committee also received more candid, idiosyncratic opinions on the bill in the form of unsolicited letters and petitions. These documents reveal how influential local notables interpreted the proposed legislation as well as articulated (and thereby attempted to reshape) the responsibility of the state toward agriculture and debt. A group of zamindars from Amritsar, Gurdaspur, and Jalandhar districts, for example, wrote a letter with over three thousand signatures explaining their support for the bill on April 19, 1900. After identifying themselves as "humble memorialists" offering their opinion "with respect and deference," they immediately switched tone to warn that agriculturalists "will be driven to the extremes of committing robbery, dacoity and other heinous crimes" if they continued to be deprived of their lands.[75] At the same time, revenue collection would decline, they added, since land left in the hands of moneylenders will either go uncultivated or diminish in output by relying on hired laborers bereft of the unique knowledge and resilience of hereditary peasants.

The letter then attempted to refute a few misconceptions about the potential drawback of the bill. To the most palpable fears over losing the right of sale, they asked a simple yet laden rhetorical question: how can agriculturalists complain about "reasonable restrictions" put on alienations by a government that gave them the very "privilege of free alienation of land" in the first place? More contentiously, the group rejected concerns over the reduction in the value of land as unimportant and immaterial. An agriculturalist does not view land as a commodity with a rising and falling monetary price, but as a perpetual source of livelihood by growing ever-useful crops, passed down "from father to son." Due to the bill, the group argued, "the progeny of the agriculturalists would [. . .] become safe from the consequences of their ancestors' lavishness." Finally, to the related problem of a reduction in credit, the group offered a more unusual rebuttal. Differing from Ghulam Hussain, they acknowledged that money would indeed become harder to access but insisted that this difficulty would actually help zamindars "learn lessons of economy" and thus "dispense with the necessity of incurring debts" altogether. On the other hand, the government should also establish agriculturalist banks to offer loans for explicitly productive purposes with reasonable terms. After some additional suggestions for improving mortgage schedules, registration policies, and retroactive application, the letter concluded abruptly with another declaration of loyalty and "ongoing prosperity to British rule."[76]

Others defended the bill but through dissimilar lines of argument. The Anjuman-i-Islamia, an educational and social service organization for Panjabi Muslims founded in Lahore in 1884, submitted an endorsement conditional on the committee implementing several technical changes. Its general secretary, Muhammad Barkat Ali Khan, expressed foremost concern over the ambiguity of the term "agriculturalist," defined in the bill at that point as anyone recorded in their own name or that of an agnate ancestor as an owner of land or hereditary tenant at the first regular settlement. Such a definition might defeat the very purpose of the legislation, since it could both include moneylenders who never engaged in cultivation but happened to own a parcel of land and exclude genuine agriculturalists who either were inadvertently misidentified at the time of settlement or had inherited land from their maternal relations.[77] To rectify this dilemma, Khan suggested stricter evaluation of hereditary and familial claims and greater discretion when using settlement records. Furthermore, he insisted on decreasing the role of revenue officers, not so much to reduce strain on the bureaucracy but to limit the expense and hassle of requiring authorization for every transaction involving land. The Anjuman was also keen to exempt what it called "self-acquired property" from the restriction on alienation, marking a distinction between inherited ancestral land and that which was purchased within the lifetime of an individual, possibly to prevent interference with charitable and religious donations.[78]

In contrast to these positions, the newspaper *Rafiq-i-Hind* and its editor, Muharram Ali Chisiiti, engaged in a public campaign of supporting the bill without qualification. Such an uncompromising stance was necessary, he wrote, because of the disparity between the forces allied on either side of the bill. Chisiiti explained that the zamindars who stood to gain the most were "simple-minded and illiterate" as well as "totally ignorant of constitutional agitation," whereas moneylenders who might lose had not only "wealth, position and education" but were "well-versed in the art of agitation."[79] Indeed, the latter were using their power to devise schemes to convince the government of popular opposition to the bill while actively confusing zamindars to believe their property rights were going to be revoked. For Chisiiti—much like Thorburn—the "dumb millions of the zemindars" were either being misled or remaining passive if not apathetic to the entire issue, "hardly aware of their interests" and therefore incapable of self-fulfilling action.[80] Over several months, his newspaper published many articles as well as testimonials from prominent local leaders, a large selection of which were reproduced and sent to the committee as evidence. In addition, Chisiiti claimed to have held public meetings throughout Lahore district to impress upon zamindars the importance of the bill and the good intentions of the government. The *Rafiq-i-Hind* position on the bill thus disparaged and bypassed zamindars in the process of claiming to support them.

Parallel to these endorsements, however, was a series of opinions opposing the bill from an equally disparate variety of angles. Perhaps most prominently, the nascent Indian National Congress sent a letter to the committee cautioning against adopting the bill. Founded in Bombay in 1885 as an explicitly loyalist association and long dominated by upper-caste and wealthy Hindus, it initially focused on fostering cooperation with the colonial administration to advocate for greater opportunities for Indians within the ranks of the civil service.[81] The Congress letter, authored by the lawyer, district commissioner, and later historian and critic Romesh Chunder Dutt, argued how despite noble intentions the bill would only make matters worse for agriculturalists. Echoing Judge Clark's doubts, he listed a familiar set of harms: restricting credit, confiscating the right of sale, decreasing land value, and reducing resources for cultivation, all leading to an ominous increase in crime.[82] Not only were agriculturalists already enjoying significant protections in Panjab, Dutt added, but the measures applied only to private debts without any provision for limiting sales due to the collection of land revenue. Was peasant debt to the government any less debilitating than to moneylenders? Instead of passing the bill in its present form, the Congress suggested the forming of another committee, this time with non-official Indian members, to study the problem anew and report its findings to the public in the near future.

More partisan critiques came from the petitions of less formal groupings in Panjab. Led by Jowahir Singh, Lal Chand, and Krori Mal, over a hundred individuals from Peshawar district petitioned that the bill was unfair toward those who lent money. In particular they argued against the limits imposed on mortgages, explaining that while one acre of land could fetch a loan of anywhere between fifty and a hundred rupees, it could only generate around three rupees of profit per year after deducting expenses and taxes, which would total at most just forty-five rupees at the end of the term limit. Thus, "no mortgagee in this ilaqa [area] can recover the principal and interest in fifteen years from the produce of the land."[83] At the other end of the province in Gurgaon district, a petition by Jia Lal Chaudhri on behalf of eighty-five individuals focused on the damaging consequences of banning crop hypothecation. Without the security of future harvests, they explained, no sahukar would give money to agriculturalists, thereby preventing the purchase of the necessities for both cultivation and daily life as well as increasing the difficulty of collecting government revenue. As a result, the sahukars "will have to leave their homes in quest of other means of livelihood," while "the agriculturalists' requirements will not be met," leading, again, to lawlessness and violence.[84] Rather desperately, both petitions requested that if the bill itself could not be stopped, then their districts should be exempted, or at least that the new rules should not apply retroactively to existing agreements between agriculturalists and moneylenders.

The most decisive critique of the bill challenged its central claim that it would end the alienation of land owned by agriculturalists. A petition by a group of over four thousand zamindars and moneylenders from Lahore district—subsequently reproduced and fraudulently resubmitted several times from different districts to the committee—captures the conflict inherent in legislating exchange through identity.[85] After a long panegyric to British rule in Panjab, it began by asking why the government would consider passing a bill that would revert agriculture back to the previous anarchic state of affairs under Maharaja Ranjit Singh. Could all the progress achieved under the British, it asked, really be abandoned at the first sign of trouble? In fact, the petition argued, the dire condition of agriculturalists "has been very much exaggerated," a product more of constant revenue reassessments, overpopulation leading to land fragmentation, and the inherent uncertainties of cultivation rather than any nefarious practice of moneylenders.[86] "[F]ounded on fallacies," the bill was not only "foredoomed to failure" but also "fraught with consequences alike disastrous to ourselves and our families, and inimical to the best interests of the Government of this Empire."[87] The reason for such cynical wariness was the petitioners' astute identification of a contradiction within its purpose. Quoting the idealistic words of a committee member, they related the purported goal of the bill:

> To obviate the political danger arising from the expropriation by moneylenders of sturdy land-holders, men who furnish the flower of the Native Army of India and who look forward, amid all the hardships and glories of a military career, to spend their declining years on their ancestral acres.[88]

Yet preventing moneylenders from taking the land of agriculturalists is not the same as keeping them on their ancestral acres because the bill only restricted the identity of the purchaser and not the act of purchasing itself. In other words, the gap created by banning moneylenders from the land market would simply be filled by a new source of lending—the agriculturalist moneylender, a wealthy zamindar-sahukar who would finance both the cultivation and consumption needs of other zamindars. As a result, the "alleged expropriation of the retired soldier" would "not be arrested but merely transformed" from "one class" in favor of "another class."[89]

Agriculturalists lending money to other agriculturalists in fact posed a uniquely intractable threat to the supposed equilibrium of the rural economy. This form of credit was more pernicious than any other because of the specific qualities associated with the identity of the lending party. The Lahore petition explains that a professional moneylender "very rarely [. . .] desires cultivating possession of the land mortgaged," instead preferring to keep the cultivator on the holding, with ownership transfer at most changing their status from proprietor to tenant. On the other hand, zamindar moneylenders who tilled their own fields "almost invariably" sought immediate possession of mortgaged land, which eventually led to the "complete and permanent severance of the late owner from the land that has descended to him from his forefathers."[90] This reflected the difference of "a certain sentimental feeling attached to landed property" to which "the ordinary economic laws of sale and purchase do not apply." According to an officer from Hissar, "no matter what price a man obtains for his land," a zamindar "considers himself the loser by the bargain," especially because "he does not like to benefit a fellow zamindar at his own loss." Besides immediately ceding possession along with ownership, even the remote possibility of buying back ancestral property—through an exceptional dint of hard work, savings, and luck—was extinguished with the knowledge that a wealthy zamindar would never part with land so fastidiously acquired whereas a moneylender might later be tempted by the right price.[91] In the simplest terms, the bill would create a situation where "the bigger fish amongst the agricultural classes will dictate their own terms and swallow the smaller fish."[92] Far from preventing the alienation of agriculturalists, the process would proceed uninterrupted as debt would still accumulate to force land transfers, with the only difference that ownership would now pass exclusively, and irrevocably, from poor to rich zamindars.

All of these opinions on the bill contributed to a remarkably contradictory image of zamindars in the late nineteenth century. Individuals and groups from different positions within the agrarian economy attempted to present their self-interest as the interest of (almost) all. While urban moneylenders and professionals not only wrote but also organized against the curtailing of their pecuniary opportunities, powerful agriculturalists quickly recognized the windfall that awaited them if the land market was reserved for them alone. Together these positions fused a series of opposing representations: zamindars were simultaneously hapless and ignorant yet appreciated and important, desperate to have access to money though unable to handle it responsibly, possessing ancient proprietary rights that were nevertheless granted and secured by a modern state. The slippage around the term *agriculturalist*, moreover, reveals both its constructed nature and the vital need to shore up and finalize its meanings in order for the bill to serve its purpose. Protecting agriculturalists—from others or themselves—presupposed knowing who exactly counted as one, a project of producing a certain quality of knowledge about primordial identity to give a legal definition the force to shape property relations. Land exemplified this tension by appearing antithetical yet implicated in the patterns of modern commerce, a quixotic means of intergenerational livelihood while at the same time owned by individuals holding the sacrosanct right to alienate. Indeed, "the notion that land requires improvement because its inhabitants are also in need of civilization uplift" was "no accident of history" but rather a mark of the colonial imbrication of culture with economy.[93] Favoring the bill therefore did not mean favoring agriculturalists in any direct, transparent way, nor did opposing it mean being simply and exclusively anti-agriculturalist.

ALIENATION FROM WHOM? AND TO WHOM?
After this extensive gathering of opinions and weighing of options, the committee submitted a final draft of the bill for approval in early August 1900. This version slightly expanded the criteria for determining an agriculturalist, made a few minor adjustments to the clauses on mortgages, and allowed crop hypothecation for one year, but by and large remained unchanged. Along with the draft submission, however, another shorter, though sharper, discussion took place among officials and elite Panjabis over the possibility of new problems emerging from this particular solution. The specter of the agricultural moneylender raised earlier acquired a novel prominence when raised internally. The cure might not be worse than the sickness; instead, some feared it would give rise to a different epidemic altogether: a law attempting to restrict a certain type of exchange could create the conditions for a more pernicious and irrepressible cycle of land alienation. In order to dispel this notion, officials again recalibrated the purpose of their intervention by uneasily combining an admission of the necessity of agrarian credit with an accusation of the irresponsible collective habits of agriculturalists. As a result, they abandoned an outright restriction on certain practices for a form of imposing measured behavioral adjustments. Doled out in appropriate doses, the treatment for debt became one of management rather than elimination.

The draft proceedings included an internal minute of dissent by the only Panjabi member of the committee at the time, a reduced but knighted son of the ruler of the princely state of Kapurthala and convert to Christianity named Harnam Singh Ahluwalia.[94] He reiterated how the arbitrary nature of the term *agriculturalist* unfairly excluded legitimate aspirants (along the lines of the Anjuman-i-Islamia), while explaining that mortgage restrictions would be easily evaded (uneasily confirming the Peshawar petition), warning against any retroactive application of the bill (against the petitioners from Amritsar, Gurdaspur, and Jalandhar), and questioning the prohibiting of pleaders from land sale cases (contra Thorburn's original recommendation).[95] The greatest drawback of the bill for Ahluwalia, however, was that its "irresistible result" would be "the creation of a large number of money-lending agriculturalists who would be enabled by the power of law to appropriate the holdings of their more indigent brethren at a greatly reduced price." Or, curiously using the same language as the Lahore petitioners, he insisted that the "monster fish in the agricultural community" would simply be "encouraged by the law to swallow smaller fish."[96] All of the government claims of protecting agriculturalists from indebtedness and alienation would end in hypocrisy, not by remaining unfulfilled but by authorizing the very processes which they sought to prevent.

Such a sweeping critique, this time by a respected loyal native prince and expressed within the officially documented proceedings, could not be easily dismissed. It prompted committee chair Rivaz to issue a lengthy reply at the next round of meetings held in October. According to him, Harnam Singh's view erroneously assumed that since landowners needed the power of alienation to borrow money for domestic and agricultural necessities, any attempt to restrict their credit would be not only harmful but ultimately futile. Yet it is precisely this unrestrained right, Rivaz argued, that provided a "direct incentive to extravagance," so that "in a large majority of cases [landowners] misuse this power and raise money for various purposes which are quite *beyond the limits of necessary or reasonable expenditure.*"[97] Indeed, the oft-repeated observation that the most prosperous areas in the province were also the most indebted indicates that borrowed money was not being spent wisely. As a result, he asked:

> If the Sikh Jat[t] of the Manjha [*sic*, Majha region] cannot resist the temptation of having recourse to the money-lender when, in his case at all events, there is clearly no question of necessity, what stronger argument can be forthcoming in support of restrictive action on the lines we propose?[98]

For Rivaz, much in the vein of the Amritsar petitioners, the goal of the government was (now) to tame the vital yet destructive nature of credit as it manifests through the irresponsible character of Panjabi landowners. Rather than completely extinguishing borrowing, the bill awkwardly sought to "restrict it to a reasonable extent," to "discourage [an agriculturalist] from raising money recklessly on his land for extravagant purposes, but to leave him ample facilities for doing so for all necessary purposes."[99] Of course, Rivaz hastily added, there were situations where this balance could not be kept, where the impulse to indebtedness overwhelmed reasoned arguments or protective measures. If a "proprietor is *hopelessly thriftless or impoverished*," it is "obviously desirable that the land in such cases should pass into the hands of some other person who can make better use of it," even as this occasional lapse into market freedom applied only to others designated as agriculturalists.[100] Nevertheless, the real purpose of the bill—or its next incarnation masked as the original—was to manage agricultural credit in order to discipline the sensibilities of agriculturalists.

Rivaz thus responded to Harnam Singh's critique by preemptive diversion. Instead of defending against the potential of creating larger fish consuming smaller ones, he insisted that the bill would change the temperature of the water and thereby the behavior of all its creatures. Now the objective was more modest, whittled down and elongated from earlier ambitions: an attempt to cultivate the virtue of responsibility by limiting without eliminating. In yet another articulation of the bill's purpose, Rivaz rehearsed the paces of the new reasoning: "Our sole justification" for restricting the right of sale of the Panjabi peasant is that "he has proved himself incapable of making proper use of this right" because "he has been unable to resist the temptation of raising money on his land" for purposes of "pure extravagance."[101] Then, sensing the shrunken scope of the bill, he asked:

> If, however, we only go so far as to prevent him from selling his land to the professional money-lender, but still allow him to sell as he pleases to any member of any agricultural tribe, what will be the result?

In other words, if the selling of agricultural land is the problem, what kind of solution is it to merely restrict the eligibly of its buyers? Rivaz's answer to his own question is telling:

> We should, by thus partially narrowing his market of free sale, depreciate the selling value of his land to some extent, but not sufficiently so to discourage him from selling except in the case of real necessity.[102]

He went on to explain that whereas an agriculturalist seeking to raise a hundred rupees could have sold an acre or so to anyone, now they would have to sell at least three acres, and that too to another agriculturalist, thereby invoking both the financial dilemmas of solvency and the sentimental attachments of honor and prestige with the intent of inducing the cautionary force of second thoughts. The civilizing mission thus turned into a project of market civilizing: the contradictory reforming of innate deficiencies through financial transactions shaped by reified social and cultural constructs.

In a curious twist of alliances and identities, another Panjabi belatedly added to the committee voiced firm support for this process by embedding it within the religious heritage of the region. The son of a minister in the old Lahore kingdom who later pledged allegiance to the British, Muhammad Hayat Khan reached the higher echelons of the administrative services then available to Panjabis and was the father of a co-founder of the Unionist Party and subsequent first indigenous premier of colonial Panjab.[103] He differed from Harnam Singh by belonging to a prominent rural family owning large tracts of land in Attock district, which he used to position himself on the committee as the representative of Muslim as well as Sikh and Hindu agriculturalists.

Hayat Khan made two arguments in favor of the bill. First, he stated that the alienation of the Panjabi peasant stemmed from not only a lack of thrift but also a "simple minded ignorance" and an "inability to fully comprehend the consequences of the contracts" entered under the "complex laws introduced by modern times."[104] British sympathy in the form of the bill was therefore indispensable to uplifting and advancing a backward and bewildered people unfamiliar with the ways of modern commerce. Second, and perhaps more importantly, he stated that the transfer of land to non-agriculturalists was explicitly against the customs of both Hindus and Muslims. According to Hayat Khan, "from time immemorial" Hindu lawgivers divided society into four castes to give every member the right to "ply their trade without interference from others," so that the "Brahmin and Kshatria were not expected to till the soil." At the same time, the Caliph Omar "prohibited his Arabian followers from possessing and even acquiring land in Egypt," deliberately "leaving it solely for the *fellahin* [peasants]," a principle upheld by all succeeding religious scholars.[105] Support for prohibiting land sales was therefore ecumenical. To the avowedly modern problem of transfer between avowedly primordial groups, Hayat Khan deployed the authority of tradition to defend the bill as a remedy in conformity with ancient Hindu and Muslim religious customs.

DECLARING SUCCESS AMID THE AMBIGUOUS AND INSCRUTABLE

For all of the opinions gathered through external solicitation and internal debate, the bill remained substantively unchanged when it passed into law as the Punjab Alienation of Land Act on June 8, 1901. In part by presenting Hayat Khan as the authentic voice of agriculturalists, Rivaz casually overruled all of Harnam Singh's concerns and queries to reaffirm the paradigm of "narrowing the opportunities for sale" in order to "remove the temptation to sell needlessly."[106] Yet the contradiction of legislating market activity through collective identity did not end with the period of formulation or consultation. A series of eight annual reports from 1901 to 1908 detail the conflicting ways the Act subsequently reshaped the economy of agrarian land and debt relations. Officials engaged in a strange exercise of at once disclosing its many failures while proclaiming it a success. On the one hand, over the first few years there was repeated mention that ordinary zamindars did not appreciate the significance of the terms "agriculturalist" or "member of an agricultural tribe." In a startling admission from 1904, the financial commissioner actually acknowledged that the "chief defect is the *wholly artificial status* of the agriculturalist *founded on nothing which is any real part of the structure of society*."[107] Confusing changes in identity and status—Was a Jatt who becomes a *faqir* (mendicant) still considered an agriculturalist? What if a Hindu tribe converted en masse into Muslim Sheikhs?—also troubled the Act's straightforward operation. At the same time, poor recordkeeping and a backlog of transactions plagued the collection of data, which thereby obstructed an accurate yearly comparison of its effectiveness.[108] Finally, moneylenders attempted to circumvent the restrictions by using surrogate purchasers and fraudulent registration, a constant source of concern that necessitated greater scrutiny of procedures and documents.[109] All of these issues were carefully documented yet left largely unresolved.

Despite these defects, on the other hand, the reports together exhibit a brazen optimism about overall progress after the Act. Without any sense of irony, officials claimed that zamindars who did not understand what it meant to be agriculturalists apparently found that membership in an agricultural tribe conferred a valuable "social distinction." Land prices had also risen from an average of seventy-eight rupees per cultivated acre in the years leading up to the Act to ninety-eight rupees in 1907. This prosperity was a sign that "amongst almost every class of the community there is the desire to acquire land."[110] Moreover, the reports continue, there was apparently an absence of difficulty in collecting revenue, wider social unrest, or even bureaucratic overwork as predicted by certain critics. Although baniyas at first remained hostile toward the Act, after a few years they too resigned themselves to it, going so far as investing their capital in more urban endeavors such as cotton milling, sugar refining, and wholesale trading while continuing to take on limited mortgages. "Above all," wrote the financial commissioner in 1908, the Act "earned the universal approval and gratitude of the hereditary landowners of the Punjab" by proving to them that the "Government sympathizes with their dearest wish, which is to hand on their ancestral land to their children's children."[111] The reports thereby overrode the various problems of the Act by invoking an assortment of claims and figures to reiterate the theme of benevolence as the ultimate sign of accomplishment.

Even more contrary than these incompatible statements was the interpretation of statistical evidence from the scores of charts appended to each report. All of the numbers, which officials admitted were unreliable, were embedded within a triumphal, progressive narrative that either minimized or overlooked anything disconcerting or rendered it a simple anomaly—a practice common to all ruling groups. Yet a closer examination of these statistics reveals contrasts and trends that show the Act to be both inconclusive and contradictory. For instance, if 47,207 transactions representing the sale of 158,638 acres of cultivated land took place throughout Panjab in 1896, there were 45,756 transactions for 152,223 acres in 1905, a rather insignificant decrease. In terms of the average sales and acreage in the five years preceding and following the Act, there was an almost identical ratio of approximately 3.4 acres sold per transaction, with 50,845 sales for 173,142 acres during 1896–1901 and 43,191 sales for 150,191 acres in 1901–1906. The results were even more perplexing when officials began keeping track of specifically agriculturalist transactions in 1902. If those deemed to belong to agricultural tribes sold 132,310 acres while buying 133,290 acres that year, the volume and gap of exchange grew to 151,041 acres sold and 152,081 acres bought in 1904 and then 152,445 acres to 156,445 acres in 1906. Agriculturalists thus continued to sell their land, only now it was purchased exclusively by other agriculturalists.

The extent of mortgages also remained unabated, with 13.5 percent of the cultivated area under mortgage in 1901, 14.1 percent in 1903, and then 13.5 percent in 1905. For redemptions the trend worsened, however, as an average of only 197,118 acres were paid off in the post-Act period compared to 235,395 acres for the pre-1901 years. Perhaps most gravely, even as the area of land redeemed by agriculturists increased, so too did their area under mortgage. While agriculturalists paid off 124,679 acres in 1902, followed by 199,179 acres in 1904 and then a spike of 301,073 acres in 1906, the area they borrowed against grew steadily from 169,585 to 194,149 to 216,954 acres during those same years, with over 95 percent of these mortgages held by other agriculturalists. As a result, not only did land continue to be sold, but agriculturalists also continued a cycle of redeeming and taking on mortgages with the difference that the transactions were now restricted to "agriculturalists."

The discrepancy in representing the Act as a success reached a climax with admissions of various kinds of manipulation. At certain moments the reports disclose how the much-heralded economic progress after 1901 was the result of arbitrary natural occurrences and deliberate political decisions. In the very first year of implementation, the slight reduction in the number and area of transfers as well as the increase in the area redeemed was admitted to be a consequence of a bumper harvest that allowed agriculturalists the "means to meet their current expenditure without the necessity of raising loans."[112] Such contingent successes grew more pronounced over the next several years. In the 1908 report, the Act's supposed limiting of sales and defaults during a time of extreme scarcity is undercut with the concession that it was only possible because of a combination of a "very liberal suspension of land revenue," the granting of government loans, an abnormally high wheat price, and an increase in military wages. In particular, suspending approximately four million rupees of revenue combined with providing over two million rupees in interest-free loans saved agriculturalists something like six hundred thousand rupees they would otherwise have had to borrow at high rates from moneylenders.

What is more, the report mentions that many zamindars evaded the Act's restrictions by putting up their homesteads as collateral to obtain money, a practice that both obscured mortgage and debt levels without appearing in any official statistics. Striking too was the fortuitous basis of the fluctuations in the area of land recovered from indebtedness. "Owing to the fact that that immigration into Australia has been prohibited," explained the deputy commissioner of Jalandhar, "large sums of money which used to be sent by the immigrants from this district for the redemption of ancestral lands are no longer remitted." However, he confidently continued, "emigrants now go further afield" so that "in a few years the figures for redemption will go up again."[113] In other words, debt levels would decrease once overseas' remittances resumed. Thus, factors that had almost nothing to do with the Act itself—surpluses, remissions, government loans, circumventions, and external incomes—were the reason for the (questionable) improvement in debt and transfer rates. How much worse might indebtedness be without a fortunate harvest, or a revenue reduction, or the possibility of migration?

A persistent dissonance thereby challenges the coherent narrative built around the Punjab Alienation of Land Act. The trajectory of its culmination and consequences was in fact erratic, contradictory, even circular. Land alienation was not a neutral, self-evident problem whose remedies could be debated and determined by a simple evaluation of effectiveness. Instead, alienation itself was a highly contingent phenomenon based on a set of shifting political calculations continuously interrupted by different conceptual, social, and natural forces. This is clear in the way the issue came to be redefined through the production and manipulation of the category of agriculturalists. The Act sought to limit both the availability of credit to reduce their expenditure as well as the eligibility of those purchasing land from them. Both of these objectives, however, became mired in duplicitous notions accompanied by confounding figures and revealing concessions. Still, sales and mortgages continued to rise as the redemption of indebted lands floundered within the increasingly polarized sphere of permitted agriculturalist exchange. Indeed, in a remarkable disclosure, the financial commissioner admitted the utter fallacy of evaluating the Act's progress by yet again altering its purpose. "The effect of the Act," he declared, "is not to be measured by the alienations or applications made under it but by *the number of undesirable alienations which it prevents—a total which no statistic can give us.*"[114] The colonial measure of success was therefore a tautology of simply asserting success by denying a consistent criterion of measurement altogether.

THINGS GO WELL IF ALL IS PERFECT

Whatever the inconsistency and indeed absurdity of colonial legislation, this attempt to address the problem of indebtedness dramatically reconfigured power relations in Panjabi society. By the end of the first decade of the twentieth century, a policy of redirecting rather than preventing the sale of agricultural land to only those who were considered agriculturalists consolidated a new rural hierarchy through caste-based control over land ownership. Amid a myriad of shifts, this intervention was underpinned by a consistent assertion of a particular kind of deficiency. A consensus emerged among British officials, and some elite Panjabis, of the need to manage the extravagant, irresponsible habits of agriculturalists. The earlier, patronizing theme of innocent and ignorant Panjabi landowners expressed by West and Thorburn morphed into a virulent and cynical condemnation of their supposedly excessive expenditure as depicted by Rivaz, the Amritsar petitioners, and the article from *The New York Times*. Although court documents do not spell out why Jiwan Khan borrowed money from Ramdhan, the assumption is that it was his own fault. Yet aligning indebtedness and alienation with a culture of indiscipline—a relationship that continues to inform understandings of Panjab as well as many other parts of the world—is belied by both admissions of the growing precariousness of rural livelihood and evidence of the wider instability and unpredictability of colonial agriculture.[115]

Returning to the period before the alienation bill became an Act, articulations of peasant indiscipline took several forms. In a settlement report from Jhang, for instance, Edward Steedman remarked that "the thrifty and unembarrassed zemindars of this district can be counted up on one's fingers." The scarcity in their numbers was a (counterintuitive) result of the abundance of their harvests and the security of their tenure. This was an ephemeral state of affairs, a mirage of progress covering up wasteful habits that would ultimately lead to collapse. Thus Steedman indignantly asked:

> To have twice as many wives as before, to eat better food, to be better clothed and housed, to ride a nag where he went formerly on foot, are the outward signs of improvement and civilization, but when we remember that all this is accompanied by debt [. . .] and that this debt is steadily increasing, how is it possible to be satisfied with things as they are?

In answering this accusation, he made an analogy to gambling—an activity of explicitly self-induced risk—in order to stave off sympathy and emphasize the irresponsibility inherent to zamindars:

> If a man draws a large prize in a lottery and follows it up by plunging into extravagances and adopting a style of living that is far beyond his income, we do not say that he is advancing in the path of civilization and steadily improving his condition. He is called a reckless prodigal, and it is universally predicted that he will go to the dogs in the shortest of periods.[116]

For Steedman, agrarian prosperity enabled these zamindars to access the destructiveness of credit, a relationship alluded to by Rivaz and later expounded upon by Darling.[117] By presenting such a dire outcome as a necessary and even fitting consequence of the reckless conduct of zamindars, the entire process of its amelioration bolstered claims of a benevolent Panjab administration.

Other reports expanded the theme of incriminating profligacy in more convoluted ways. A settlement officer from Multan repeated the criticism of agriculturalists raising the status of their transportation, saying that once there is a glimmer of a surplus harvest, "men who should be walking think they must keep their horse; those who could properly afford one or two horses, think they must keep five or six."[118] On the other hand, William Purser's report from Jalandhar identified the habit of excessiveness in family and custom. He related how certain individuals told him the reason for indebtedness was that "women, who have nothing to do, stroll into the bazaar and buy things they do not want, on credit, and thus run up accounts which their husbands cannot clear off." The paternalism of colonial rule thus found resonance with the patriarchy of the rural household. At the same time, Purser offered his own unabashedly circular reasoning, stating simply that "in the case of the improvident tribes indebtedness is, no doubt, due largely to their improvidence." More elaborately—and more self-servingly—the same report also detailed how the combination of tribal ethics and a procedural justice system amplified the burden of debt. Purser noted that "large sums of money are squandered in fighting out the most trumpery cases from the lowest to the highest courts." People would be much better off if they were summarily issued on-the-spot final decisions, but "as long as they can appeal, it is a point of honor to not admit defeat," thereby furthering a costly cycle of litigation.[119] Authoritarianism conveniently became a remedy for cultural obstinacy corrupting liberal values.

Notions of indiscipline and litigiousness established two interrelated principles that structured the debate around indebtedness. The first was to absolve government revenue demand for causing debt. Against the likes of Thorburn and others, officials argued that not only were Panjabi zamindars uniquely fortunate to be subject to a modest assessment, but the extraction of a portion of agricultural produce actually prevented their situation from worsening. Given the irresistible temptation to spend, the potential for debt grew in direct proportion to the availability of credit, which was a function of the overall profitability of agriculture. Less revenue taken therefore meant a higher surplus left to the zamindar, which automatically meant a greater likelihood, degree, and depth of debt. Second, the inherency of indiscipline implied that the tendency to become indebted could be reduced and controlled but never completely eliminated. Since this was an intrinsic deficiency, a quality of "improvidence" built into the very identity of Panjabi tribes and culture, it would remain an intractable force whatever the fiscal and legal adjustments. The clumsiness of Rivaz's response to Harnam Singh's queries reflects the attempt *to solve a problem constituted as unsolvable*. Once insulated from government fault, indebtedness and its accompanying features turned into a site of unending management.

Throughout the barrage of castigation toward irresponsible agriculturalists, however, officials at stray moments inadvertently admitted that something was amiss in the new agrarian economy they had created. Indications of the debilitating effect of rather unremarkable or unintentional expenditure undercut the cataloging of wastefulness. In Thorburn's original memorandum, for example, there was a notable absence of reckless behavior in the trajectory of how a peasant becomes indebted. Recall that an informal account with a village baniya is maintained "until sickness, death of oxen, a death in his family, the failure of his crop, a case in court, or other accident occurs." Even with these routine, unfortunate occurrences, it further took either the "death or working incapacity" of the zamindar to transform the outstanding balance into a formal bond accruing interest against landed collateral.

The precariousness of falling into debt is more elaborately, though equally naively, explicated in a report from Rohtak. Settlement officer Herbert Fanshawe wrote that "as long as a family has its proper compliment of workers, male and female, it is well-to-do." However:

> Where sons are idle, or the father becomes old while they are still boys and unable to work, or dies leaving them to the mother's care, or where there is no woman in the family or only a bad one, the home is certain to fall into difficulties.[120]

In other words, without extraordinarily perfect conditions—free of aging, sickness, or death and the right combination of people with correct mindsets—the chances of debt unfailingly increase. The above report from Jhang too betrays a rather unavoidable purpose for spending. Besides the hyperbole over horses and lurid attention to marital relations, Steedman offered a strange list of zamindar "excesses": essentially, the spending of more money on food, clothing, and shelter. Allegations of profligacy were thus repeatedly punctured by an account of prosaic if not prudent expenses.

That spending on such basic necessities raised the ire of officials lays bare the repeated claim of benevolent concern for local wellbeing.

THE IMPOSSIBILITY OF RATIONAL AGRICULTURE

This inconsistency between rhetoric and practice raises larger questions about the politics of alleging wasteful spending by zamindars. Is there such a thing as quotidian excesses or "extravagances" flowing from an emergency? Is it irresponsible to spend money on food or clothing or take on debt to cover the costs of sickness or death? Or, put differently, is a drought a rational occurrence? While there are limits to pursuing such themes from the official colonial documents,[121] a series of fascinating yet under-utilized rural studies from the 1930s offers insight into how certain landholding families struggled to organize their lives and livelihoods. The Board of Economic Inquiry, made up of a group of civil officers, published unofficial research on topics ranging from the size and distribution of family holdings; detailed surveys of dozens of villages; indexes of food prices, cattle sales, and urban wages; the costs of pressing cotton; and the supply of milk to various cities. In 1932, the Board began what became an annual series with local researchers documenting the fortunes of a varying number of families in the districts of first Lyallpur and later several others. Authored by Kartar Singh, Ajaib Singh, Labh Singh, and Faiz Ilahi, all associated with the Punjab Agricultural College (Lyallpur), the series was conceived as a way to track the trajectories of individual families of cultivators operating in a relatively stable environment (see Figure 3.3). "In order to know the true financial position of a cultivator," stated the opening preface of the first study, "one should study the whole of the business and life of the farm as one concern."[122] The families received daily visits from an investigator and kept detailed accounts of household expenses and incomes derived from farming operations and outside sources as well as the number of working days for the various family members.

For the first year of the study, the Board relocated four agriculturalist families from Jalandhar to Lyallpur, a recently established town between the Ravi and Chenab rivers and at the center of the dramatic expansion of cultivation through canal irrigation and population transfer.[123] Each family was given roughly twenty-eight acres of land along with two pairs

The Board of Economic Inquiry, Punjab.

PUBLICATION No. 40.

[GENERAL EDITOR: C. W. THOMAS, B.Sc., B.Com.]

FAMILY BUDGETS, 1932-33,
OF
FOUR TENANT-CULTIVATORS
IN THE
LYALLPUR DISTRICT

BY

SARDAR KARTAR SINGH, B.Sc. (AGRI.), N.D.D., L. AG.,
ASSOCIATE PROFESSOR OF AGRICULTURE,
LYALLPUR.

[The Board of Economic Inquiry, Punjab, does not hold itself responsible for any opinions expressed or conclusions reached by the writers.]

1934.

FIGURE 3.3 The cover page of the study of family budgets in Lyallpur by the Board of Economic Inquiry, 1934. Source: Sardar Kartar Singh, *Family Budgets, 1932–33, of Four Tenant-Cultivators in the Lyallpur District*, Board of Economic Inquiry Publication No. 40 (Lahore: The Civil and Military Gazette Press, 1934).

of bullocks and a small dwelling on the experimental Risalewala Government Agricultural Farm three miles away. Tenancy was half-*batai*, a sharecropping arrangement where the cultivators paid half of the biannual harvest as rent to the owner (in this case, the government). Although the study assigned each family a letter without disclosing the names of individual participants, it tellingly did state their religion, caste, and age information. All of the families were Muslim, three Arain, and one Jatt. Family D (Arain) had twelve members, including six adults (three men and three women), one adolescent, and five children, while Family B (Jatt) had six members, three adult men and two women with one child.[124]

For income—the bulk from cultivation but augmented by milk selling, cotton picking, carting, and casual labor—the range varied significantly. After deducting production costs, Family A earned approximately Rs. 413 from the harvest plus Rs. 22 from milk, Rs. 12 from cotton and Rs. 3 from labor for a total of Rs. 450, whereas Family B netted Rs. 257, Family C Rs. 570, and Family D Rs. 381. In terms of expenses, the study identifies eleven broad areas: housing, food, fuel, dress, medicine, light, education, religious, travel, social amusements and luxuries, and miscellaneous. Family A spent Rs. 469, mostly on food (wheat, milk, butter, sugar, a little meat, and even less fruit, Rs. 267); a supply of clothes, bedding, and shoes (Rs. 117); several trips back and forth to Jalandhar (Rs. 30); the celebration of the birth of a son (Rs. 13); and religious duties of paying the local *maulvi* and the cost of sacrificing a goat on Eid (Rs. 11). Similarly, Family B spent Rs. 406, Family C Rs. 457, and Family D Rs. 544. Taken together, food, clothing, and travel constituted 91 percent of the families' total expenditure.[125] By subtracting expenses from incomes, it turns out that three of the four families suffered deficits ranging from Rs. 19 to Rs. 163 at the end of the year. Only Family C managed to generate a surplus of Rs. 113, in large part due to a fortuitous output of wheat and the unexpected good health of their bullocks.

Dramatic fluctuations altered the families' condition over the next few years. In 1933–34, the sample group grew with the addition of a Sikh Jatt family (E) and a Muslim Jatt family (F). The results were troubling, however, as the expenses, in rupees, incurred by each family—A 528, B 439, C 449, D 556, E 465, and F 331—far outstripped the incomes earned—A 332,

B 281, C 279, D 152, E 205, and F 184. All of the families ended up in deficit, blamed this time on a downturn in the market price of wheat.[126] A year later, the number of families remained the same (with another Muslim Arain family replacing one that left the farm), while their fiscal health improved considerably. Five out of six registered surpluses ranging from Rs. 12 (F) to Rs. 227 (D), with only Family A in deficit at Rs. 89. Such a sharp reversal was attributed mainly to a doubling of the price of cotton, along with a slight reduction in expenditure on clothing and travel.[127] For 1935–36, the same families had a more mixed outcome. Both incomes and expenses increased that year, so that while families C and D generated surpluses of several hundred rupees, families A, B, and F barely broke even with less than thirteen rupees to spare, while E sustained a deficit of over eighty rupees. While no explanation was given for this year, the study mentioned that a few families benefited from rental incomes on ancestral land in their home district as well as a small rise in milk prices.[128] Thus, cumulatively after four years, half of the six families were in deficit, one did moderately well, and only two could be described as comfortably successful.

The composition of the participants was changed significantly during the 1936–37 year, possibly due to the Board's attempt to make it more representative. To the original six tenant-cultivators in Lyallpur, the study began gathering information on five owner-cultivator families (Arains, Jatts, and a Mohyal Brahmin) working an average of twelve acres from the eastern/central districts of Rohtak, Hoshiarpur, Jalandhar, and Amritsar. The sources of income also changed, as most of these families supplemented their cultivation earnings by renting out a portion of their lands to others, while one family had a member in government employment. Moreover, since the eastern families were not concentrated in one place and thus were not easily monitored, the Board paid each thirty to forty rupees to have a literate member keep their own accounts. Despite the extra incomes, however, that year only two of the Lyallpur families were solvent, while two suffered high losses and two barely broke even. For the eastern families, two out of five were in deficit, while another was saved only by collecting the study's subsidy.[129]

The next year, one of the owner families leased out all of their lands and so dropped out of the study, while another from Rasulpur began to be tracked separately due to its heavy reliance on non-cultivating earnings. Nevertheless, after deducting average expenses from incomes, all the Lyallpur families were in deficit, while the eastern families managed to stay afloat only due to the subsidy (now raised to sixty rupees), as did the Rasulpur family with additional income from one of its members' salary.[130] The study again expanded the following year, adding data on fifteen mostly Chamar families with small holdings working as laborers in the Kangra district near the Himalayan foothills. This time the outcome was even bleaker: on average the Lyallpur and Kangra families earned significantly less than they spent, while the eastern and Rasulpur families again only survived with supplemental incomes.[131]

After nearly seven years of observation and documentation, a remarkable picture of the precariousness of agriculture emerged. By the end of 1939, all but a few of the families had suffered many more years with losses rather than gains. Four of the tenant-cultivators from Lyallpur had an average cumulative deficit of almost one hundred rupees, though two managed surpluses of over four hundred rupees each. Similarly, four of the seven eastern and Rasulpur owner-cultivators had shortfalls of more than two hundred rupees, while the remaining three averaged three hundred rupees of profit. Of this latter group, however, two families did so only because of the extra funds paid by the study. Meanwhile, after just one year, nine of the fifteen Kangra smallholders had deficits of around fifty rupees each, a number rising to fourteen families if not for another form of payment made by the Board.[132] Overall, then, twenty-four out of twenty-eight cultivating families—fully 85 percent—were reduced to a condition of expenses exceeding incomes in the absence of some form of supplemental assistance.

In spite of the clarity of these contrasts, certain recalcitrant questions remain. What if a serious drought occurred in one of the study districts during this period? Or if a participating family suffered the misfortune of death or sickness for its members or livestock? Perhaps most perilously, what if the yearly deficits had in fact become debts? Presumably the Board provided loans to keep families afloat rather than force them to borrow money to cover shortfalls. If, however, like Jiwan Khan, their deficits were converted into interest-accruing bonds, the additional costs would have completely eroded any chance of a family remaining solvent, which would have likely triggered land sales and possibly even dislocation. The only difference in this context would be that the creditor to these families would have been a "fellow" agriculturalist rather than a dedicated moneylender, someone with the requisite caste credentials to purchase their land—a specious consolation for anyone forced to alienate. Thus, while these figures reflected how both uncertain and unremunerative cultivation was for these participants, their fiscal situation—much like what was revealed in the post-Act period reports—would have been much worse without the dicey benefits of avoiding accidents and receiving additional supports.

Beyond its internal revelations and elisions, the material from this set of studies challenges the wider assertions of zamindar irresponsibility. Although it uses a small number of participants operating under rather unique parameters, the authors repeatedly affirmed how these families accurately reflect the circumstances of a significant population of above average cultivators in Panjab.[133] To that end, the most consistent element across all families throughout these years was the nature of their expenditure. For those in Lyallpur, the proportion of expenses dedicated for food—almost all of it consisting of wheat, milk products, and sugar—remained between 57 and 67 percent, followed by 14 to 20 percent for clothing and 4 to 7 percent to journey to their home district. Eastern families spent slightly less for food, 53 to 55 percent, while similarly on clothing and around 9 percent for education in the place of travel. Those in Kangra paid the highest share on food, at 67 percent (most of it rice), with 12 percent on clothing and 10 percent on social expenses, an anomalously large amount explained by the fact that one family paid a bride-price of one hundred fifty rupees for the marriage of a son.[134] Nothing in any of these accounts resembles extravagance: there are no entries for grand feasts, lavish accouterments, or religious largesse—the cultivators concerned did not have the money for these anyway. Had any of the families' expenses approached excessiveness, the study's authors surely would have pointed it out. Instead, what we have is a list of more or less basic necessities consuming an overwhelming proportion of these families' budgets—and yet almost all of them ending up with deficits year after year. Not only does this refute the claim of peasant wastefulness, it also undercuts the larger premise of colonial intervention against indebtedness.

PATTERNS OF UNPREDICTABILITY

The results of this study offer an unintentional glimpse of the discordant, hostile, and overdetermined condition of cultivation under colonial rule. Kartar Singh and the other researchers assiduously avoided recording any statement from the families themselves or elaborating on what must have appeared as a conspicuous failure of the British claim of ensuring the well-being of such a large proportion of Panjab's agriculturalists. Perhaps as part of a small handful of locals allowed to enter government service or adjacent professional occupations, they could hardly be expected to critique their employers and overlords. Nor would the architects of this policy have to confront its detritus, even obliquely; Thorburn died in 1924, Rivaz in 1926. Yet although stark numbers muffle the affective dimension of consumption practices—the way these families felt about how their lives were changing within and beyond their control—they do not completely stifle the visceral sense of what was going on. A tone of modest desperation accompanies the calculations of a family falling into increasing debt while spending almost all of its income just to feed and clothe its members. This was the experience of a distinctive type of capitalism in the colony, braiding together ostensibly cultural qualities with juridical discipline to create new economic volatility. Earning a livelihood had become so precarious for "agriculturalists" that even in the best of circumstances, supplemental sources of income—subsidies, rental earnings, government employment—and favorable environmental and market fluctuations—bumper harvests, rises in commodity prices, the advent of the Second World War—were crucial to remaining solvent. And yet this too was often not enough to stave off indebtedness. What is clear is that the possibility of a peasant becoming indebted in the 1930s was not radically dissimilar to that in the 1880s.

This paradox demonstrates the importance of examining the constantly shifting parameters of the question of indebtedness. From an attempt to halt agricultural debt, then land transfers, and then the alienation of peasant land, the problem became the need to limit rural credit in order to manage the irresponsible nature of agriculturalists. The debate that culminated in the Punjab Alienation of Land Act in fact simultaneously authorized a market for land selling and used caste identity to determine who was eligible for participation in it. Rather than preventing indebtedness or eliminating the sale of land outright, alienation was instead redirected toward only those deemed members of an agricultural tribe. In this way, colonial prejudices and confusion did not merely circulate in the minds of officials; rather, those notions collided with the desires and activities of millions of Panjabis to reshape their economic relations.

Perhaps most importantly, none of the elements in the sequence of the debt problem bear any obvious or automatic relation to the next; marking the transformation of a problem is not a project of following its evolution. This is why the language of logic is especially inadequate to describe this history. It turns a highly disparate and contingent series of ideological and material struggles into a pattern unfolding from an originary, causal moment. Seasonal local loans to hold over cultivators during times of distress have a long history throughout north India, emerging in parallel with demands by various authorities for a share of agricultural produce, and may even have a place in narratives of worldwide, trans-historical debt.[135] Yet in the context of Panjab, abstract debt is more accurately expressed as indebtedness, distinct in the nineteenth century for accumulating exponentially, far beyond the possibility of repayment, and resulting in a novel crisis of land dispossession. At the same time, this economic equation is both permeated by discourses of cultural extravagance and irrationality as well as mediated by the primacy given to the caste and religious identities of those selling and buying land. Finally, the market itself functions as an unusual product of the colonial state, from enforcing civil contracts to shaping the parameters of exchange to selectively intervening through special legislation. Indebtedness here marked the forging of novel economic relationships through specific notions of individual and collective identity and rationality under colonial rule.

Thorburn's statement that zamindars, "like minors, all at once entrusted with the disposal of their property, they immediately began to squander it," thus reflects not only a condescending attitude, a crude justification for colonial rule based on drawing a line from a state of immaturity to maturity through market discipline.[136] More profoundly, it captures a premise inadvertently shared by contemporary historians who speak of peasant debt initiated by the granting of rights in private property. Regardless of a clear difference in the politics of the two positions, both adopt a colonial common sense toward the inevitability of the indebtedness problem and the trajectory it ultimately followed. An exclusive focus on causes and remedies in fact naturalizes the more unsettling problems of peasant debt. Evaluating only the success or failure of the Act to an extent absolves the colonial state and elite Panjabis from their responsibility in restructuring cultivation while also concealing the creation of a new hierarchy of class-within/through-caste. A rhetoric of irrationality underpinning legislative intervention served to obfuscate the multiplicity of forces that created conditions necessitating the taking of loans to cover unremarkable deficits. Figures from the immediate post-1901 period and studies from the 1930s reveal the contradiction of a continuing exchange of agricultural land and the increasing precariousness of agricultural solvency. This is what facilitated the consolidation of land in the hands of certain groups holding class power mobilized within caste and religious boundaries.

Immiseration, conflict, indebtedness—and not simply the ruination trumpeted by *The New York Times*—was therefore occurring in Panjab and would continue well after the Act, but not because of spendthrifts. The colonial reordering of agriculture induced a politics of indebtedness that made a large number of groups poorer and less secure while few became richer and more powerful. The materiality of the designations of "upper" and "lower" for Panjabi castes might thus more concretely be located as a product of this modern transformation rather than a millennia-old inheritance. While people like Jiwan Khan obtained respite from the usurious privations of Ramdhan, they remained susceptible to routine shortfalls, mounting debt, and land alienation to the likes of Hayat Khan. The quiet struggle for livelihood and solvency was hardly less bitter, iniquitous, or debilitating when confined to the artificial category of agriculturalists. Rural dominance was now beset by a novel yet naturalized capitalist volatility.

FOUR

HORIZONS OF HIERARCHY
*Caste, Landlessness, and the Limits
of Religious Conversion*

ON DECEMBER 12, 1935, Bhimrao Ramji Ambedkar received a letter from Sant Ram, the secretary of the Jat-Pat Todak Mandal (Association for the Breaking of Caste), inviting him to preside over its annual conference the following spring in Lahore. One of the most preeminent intellectuals at the time and the political leader of what were then variously referred to as untouchables, scheduled castes, Harijans, or depressed classes, Ambedkar went on to become the first law minister of independent India, drafting the constitution and organizing for civil rights and social reform until his death in 1956.[1] Sant Ram wrote that since no one had studied the problem of caste as deeply as Ambedkar, a public speech from him on the topic would be invaluable, adding that the "independent Harijans of Punjab are very much desirous to meet you and discuss with you their plans."[2] Ambedkar reluctantly agreed, but after obtaining a copy of his speech, the Mandal leadership became uneasy with some of its content and requested some changes. Most pressingly, they objected to passages in which he denounced the morality and sanctity of the Hindu religion and scripture and declared his intention to ultimately leave its fold. Ambedkar resolutely refused, stating that he would "not alter a comma" and accused the Mandal of duplicity before withdrawing from the conference, which was soon cancelled.[3]

On returning to Bombay with nearly a thousand printed copies of the speech, he decided to distribute it on his own under the title "Annihilation of Caste." It sold out quickly, provoking two rebuttals from Mohandas Karamchand Gandhi, to which Ambedkar issued a lengthy reply. For the second edition of the text, published in 1937, he included his correspondence with the Mandal, Gandhi's criticisms, and his own response as appendices. It has since been considered not only one of Ambedkar's most famous texts but also a radical and penetrating intervention into the nature of the problem of caste.[4]

The question Ambedkar addresses in his undelivered speech is how to understand, confront, and abolish the peculiar institution of hereditary hierarchy in Indian society. He describes a plethora of debilitations suffered by untouchables: isolation in housing, movement, and public space; exploitation through the most difficult and unremunerative occupations; restrictions on consumption, clothing, and learning; unrelenting humiliations both subtle and overt; and various kinds of symbolic and corporeal violence. Untouchability is not to be overcome by mere shifts in attitude, nor is it sufficient to rely on straightforward political or economic remedies. Of members in the Indian National Congress, he asks: "Are you fit for political power even though you do not allow a large class of your own countrymen like the untouchables to use public schools?" Similarly, of socialists who insist on the primacy of material relations: "Can it be said that the proletariat of India, poor as it is, recognize no distinctions except that of the rich and the poor?"[5] According to Ambedkar, the presumed unity of citizenship or class is undercut by a more intractable ideology of caste separation.

This phenomenon is unique to India because it is not only a division of labor, prevalent all over the world, but *"also a division of labourers"* based on fixity, graded inequality, and predestination.[6] That is why efforts at inter-caste dining and marriage have been ineffective and unrealizable, however laudable. The deeper problem, argues Ambedkar, is that such a hierarchy is sanctioned and indeed mandated by Hinduism through the sacred *Shastras*, which contain the *Vedas*, the *Puranas*, and the *Manusmriti* or the "Laws of Manu." Individual Hindus observe caste not because they are "inhuman or wrong-headed"; rather, they do so "because they are deeply religious." As a result, Ambedkar declared, "what is wrong is their religion, which has inculcated this notion of caste."[7] The solution was as succinct as it was searing: "the real remedy" was to "discard the authority of the *Shastras* and destroy the religion of the *Shastras*."[8] Only when the legitimacy of hereditary separation was overturned would there emerge the possibility of a genuinely inclusive, united, and equal society worthy of independence.

What if Ambedkar had delivered this speech in Lahore in 1936? Given the social and economic polarities of Panjabi society, his diagnosis and remedy for the sickness of caste seems incongruent with the composition of his intended audience. According to the 1931 census, over 87 percent of the population lived in villages, of which Hindus made up less than 30 percent, while the bulk of the remainder was 53 percent Muslim and 15 percent Sikh.[9] More significantly, a few years earlier a group of activists succeeded in establishing a separate religion explicitly for those considered lower castes called *Ad Dharm* or "Original Faith," drawing on the teachings of Bhagats Kabir Ji (c. 1398–1448), Namdev Ji (c. 1270–1350), and especially Ravidas Ji (c. 1450–1527). Officially this category registered over four hundred thousand adherents, nearly a third of all depressed classes in the province by some estimates, and may have included tens of thousands more who were ignored, misidentified, or coerced into declaring themselves differently.[10] Thus, not only were alternative religions without formal caste hierarchy already available in Panjabi society, but subordinate castes had effectively preempted the call to leave the Hindu faith by establishing their own distinct religion.[11] While Ambedkar recognized the scriptural critique of caste in Sikhi and even invoked Guru Nanak Ji with the Buddha as ardent opponents of the sanctity of the *Shastras*, he acknowledged neither the Ad Dharm movement nor the conditions of the largely landless agricultural laborers constituting Panjabi untouchables.[12] If caste was a perverse division of laborers as much as of labor, then the program for its annihilation appears to miss the specific logic of its operation in rural Panjab.

In this chapter, I explore the politics of emancipation through the problem of so-called lower castes freeing themselves from Brahminical Hinduism but not the constraints of lowliness or casteism in early twentieth-century Panjab. It builds on the creation of a different form of accumulation in Chapter 1 and the ways caste became a criterion for market participation from Chapter 3 to trace a longer history of popular struggle against subordination in the agrarian countryside. I draw on a wide range of sources: from early ethnographies, census figures, and medieval poetry to firsthand village surveys, a unique rural labor contract, and the only report issued by the Ad Dharm movement. The chapter starts with the first scholarly anthropological writings on village society that conceptualized the division of labor as a caste-based, religiously bounded, and pan-Indian phenomenon. Next I contrast these notions with the manifestation of hierarchy in Panjab, tracing a genealogy of radical social critique emanating from Sikhi and the Bhakti tradition during the fourteenth to seventeenth centuries. This overturned the sanctity, logic, and expression of supposedly ancient caste ideology, and gave rise to a form of rural labor relations distinct from the rest of the subcontinent. I then analyze the emergence of the Ad Dharm movement and its assertion of a separate identity and community for Panjabi Dalits in the 1930s. To bring this new sense of caste to bear on actual labor practices, I conclude by examining the fraught relationship between landed cultivators and landless laborers working side by side yet remaining profoundly separate and unequal. That a large proportion of lower castes could adopt religions other than Hinduism or start their own *and yet* remain excluded and marginalized is a stark indication of the limits of a politics centered on conversion. The antimony between emancipatory claims and a new system of exploitative relations suggests the need for a different horizon for overcoming the modern caste question.

AN INDIAN DIVISION OF LABOR?

One of the earliest and most influential studies of the division of labor and laborers in colonial India is by William and Charlotte Wiser. As American Presbyterian missionaries doubling as ethnographers in the early twentieth century, they documented their stay in a village they called Karimpur located 115 kilometers east of Agra. Together the Wisers published *Behind Mud Walls* (1930), and William later authored (solo) *The Hindu Jajmani System* (1936) based on his doctoral dissertation from Cornell University. Unlike other writings by British administrators that usually drew on horseback tours in which a large area was covered as part of official duties—notably Malcolm Darling and Frank Brayne for Panjab but also William Crooke, Edward Gait, William Hunter, Robert Russell, and

Herbert Risley—the work of the Wisers was informed by research in a single location where they stayed for five seasons between 1925 and 1930, returning for brief follow-ups in 1961 and again in 1970.[13] What has made the Wisers' writings enduring and credible for many is their formal distance from the colonial government, their university association, and their intimate research methodology.

Setting up a tent on the periphery of Karimpur, the Wisers gained access to the inner spaces and workings of the community by opening a makeshift dispensary to meet local medical needs. They combined empirical observations with intricate tables and lists along with a kind of travelogue of interactions with various caste-conscious children, women, and men and their own reflections on the possibilities of social change. As Angela Zimmerman argues in a different context, "Imperialism was the sine qua non of anthropology," because without it, "anthropologists never would have had access to the ethnographic performers, artifacts, body parts, and—in the early twentieth century—field sites that provided the empirical data that they valued above all else."[14] Nor would they have been able to conceptualize differences between societies as intrinsic and exhaustive elements to be plotted along a scientific scale of worldwide hierarchy. Indeed, William's monograph is considered the "first systematic scholarly treatment" of the social and cultural dimensions of rural labor relations and is also credited with popularizing the term *jajmani* itself.[15] Both books became classic models of the study of village India, establishing for South Asia a form of embedded, participatory ethnography that would be replicated by scores of anthropologists and sociologists over the next several decades to the present day.

To the Wisers, all relationships in Karimpur and beyond were structured by a basic, primordial binary. "In a Hindu village in North India," William Wiser wrote, "each individual has a fixed economic and social status, established by his birth in any given caste."[16] The phrase he used to describe this inborn hierarchy is "the jajmani system," based on the Sanskrit-derived Hindi word *jajman* for patron, superior, or employer with its counterpart *kam-vala*, meaning client or literally one who does work. The dynamic between the pair is a performance of unequal power concealed in plain sight. The Wisers note that "the leaders of [Karimpur] are so sure of their power that they make no effort to display it," content to dwell, dress, and eat "as simply and cheaply" as their poorer neighbors. On the other hand,

> The serving ones have learned that as long as their subservience is unquestioned, the hand which directs them rests lightly. But let there be any move toward independence or even indifference among them, and the paternal touch becomes a strangle-hold.[17]

This veiled though violent power relation is thus not simply tyrannical oppression flowing from top to bottom. According to William Wiser, there is a staggered reciprocity to jajmani relations: "Each serves the others. Each in turn is master. Each in turn is servant."[18] He lists twenty-four castes in Karimpur, from priests and carpenters to barbers, potters, leather workers, and sweepers, all connected in some way to cultivation, mapping out their duties and obligations to one another and the forms of compensation each receives. Crucially, it is Hinduism and the logic of purity and pollution that give the entire system of skewed interdependence its authority. Wiser explains that the jajmani system "has philosophical and religious sanction in the Laws of Manu which have served as a guide for the Hindu social and economic organization for almost 2,000 years."[19] He repeatedly quotes verses from the *Manusmriti* to identify the precise location of each caste and details the specific tasks they are expected to fulfill. In these two texts, the Wisers produced a scholarly representation of the village economy as a functional and largely harmonious ordering of caste groupings sustained by religious dogma. In the same year of Ambedkar's cancelled Lahore speech, William's book thus corroborated the Laws of Manu as the foundational source of the division of labor and the primeval subordination of laborers.

This interpretation of village life drew contemporaries to India who contributed valuable qualifications to the Wisers' findings. The advent of decolonization and superpower rivalry in the post–World War II period provided a unique space for the intersection of intellectual inquiry and geopolitical strategy.[20] As a consulting anthropologist to the Ford Foundation, Oscar Lewis spent eight months in 1952 and 1953 in the village of Rampur, located twenty-five kilometers west of Delhi. He argued that the reciprocal fixity of jajmani relations actually served to ensure a constant supply of labor for upper-caste agricultural operations. When lower castes occasionally asserted their claims, the supposed sanctity of the system quickly evaporated. Lewis gives the example of a group of barbers refusing to shave their patrons after a sharp reduction in their customary dues: the latter simply bought newly-available razors from the market and began shaving themselves.[21] Bernard Cohn similarly narrates the contradictory processes reshaping the relationship between Thakur landlords and Chamar laborers in a village he calls Madhopur forty-five kilometers north of Banaras. In the 1950s, the Chamars began asserting themselves by filing lawsuits and pursuing higher education and employment in the cities. At the same time, they adopted upper-caste practices, followed mainstream Vaishnava Hinduism, and discriminated against castes they considered beneath them. As Thakurs became less formal and more secular, Chamars were increasingly conservative and orthodox: "while the *Thakur* wife is coming out of seclusion," Cohn notes, "the *Camar* wife is being put into seclusion."[22] Departing from this view, Harold Gould examined another pseudonymously named village south of Faizabad in eastern Utter Pradesh in 1954–55. Based on degrees of exposure to "blood, death and dirt," he described how various castes in Sherupur were conscripted into a range of activities along a scale of purity-impurity. While critical of Wiser's claim of a millennia-long pedigree, Gould argued that jajmani was a modern yet preindustrial system "*essential* to the successful practice of rural Hinduism." Since the individual jajman "expresses the convergence of the sacred and the secular in rural economic interaction," he concluded, it constituted "a religio-economic category *uniquely adapted* to Indian civilization."[23]

Scholars who followed the Wisers' interest in jajmani and method of single-site ethnography thus reached differing conclusions about its coherence and longevity.[24] Nevertheless, together this early body of literature on village life in north India produced a powerful set of assumptions about the relationship between caste, labor, and agriculture. Villages were seen as being made up of groups with occupational roles roughly corresponding to a basic fourfold division, re-categorized by Gould as "elite-pure," "agriculturalist," "artisan," and "menial-impure."[25] While the first and second groups owned almost all agricultural land, usually as absentee zamindars but occasionally as self-cultivating proprietors, the last two served as either sharecropping tenants or precarious day laborers. "[N]o matter how poor," claims Cohn, every Thakur family in Madhopur employs at least one Chamar plowman.[26] Moreover, there appeared to be a kind of reticence or even antagonism toward laboring activity, based not on the act but the supposed spiritual defilement that accompanied it. While tilling land was considered superior to herding pigs or clearing animal (or human) excrement, it still fell short of avoiding physical exertion altogether by dealing in grain, becoming a priest, police officer, or patwari, or acquiring enough land to lease out in full. Perhaps most importantly, this arrangement of bodies, tasks, and materials was seen as mandated through a *system* named jajmani, a religiously sanctioned pan-Indian organization of human practical and spiritual affairs. Despite a few small and fewer large moments of rebellion, usually instigated by an outside force such as government schooling or civil courts, the sheer weight of divine command coupled with brute force was sufficient to ensure the broad continuity of the hierarchy.

The theme of an ancient and holistic divinely ordained caste system governing all aspects of Indian society reached its apogee a few decades later with the work of Louis Dumont. His book *Homo Hierarchicus*, originally published in French in 1966 and appearing in English translation in 1970, initiated a critical debate both over the origins of caste, religion, and hierarchy in India as well as the production of expert knowledge on the differences between Western and Eastern societies. Dumont argued that Indian society was structured religiously according to a fixed, universal principle of caste, a notion critiqued by a number of scholars who demonstrated both the contemporary variety and historical contingency of various hierarchical practices across India.[27] Challenging the timelessness as well as the singularity of caste, Nicholas Dirks emphasized the role of colonial technologies of rule in producing a common format through which Indians could be understood and controlled.[28] His arguments were preceded and followed by scholars of southern India who pointed to the vastly different spiritual, literary, and cultural resources that informed the making of local traditions and regional polities.[29] In north India, on the other hand, this debate led to investigations into the politics of varying degrees of bondage and freedom, the trajectories of specific lower-caste lives, and the ways untouchables succeeded in redefining their place in colonial and postcolonial India.[30] There have also been recent attempts to trace the evolution of caste over the long *durée*.[31] What this scholarship makes most clear is that caste neither operated as seamlessly as the Wisers and others imagined, nor continued with scriptural sanction from remote antiquity, nor had the capacity of a pan-India, all-encompassing system.

Yet in refuting these claims, the tension between hereditary identities and patterns of rural labor remains largely unexplored. As certain ethnographic accounts rendered the politics of village life a mere manifestation of an overarching system of caste, critiques of the Orientalism of these narratives tended to overlook questions of exploitation and exclusion. Even if caste was as modern as it was variable, what accounts for how dominant groups routinely invoked hereditary identity to legitimize their subordination of others within the village economy? In a fraught exchange with a headman in Karimpur, the Wisers were told that regardless of the recent conversion of low-caste Bhangis to Christianity, they remained Bhangis. "And as long as they are Bhangis," the headman warns, "they can stay in this village and do the work of Bhangis. But let them deny to us that they are Bhangis, and out they go." Later, when the Wisers attempted to encourage a few Bhangis to take up farming, they were rebuked by another leader from a cultivating caste. Why is the Sahib trying to get Bhangis to work the land, he asked? "[T]his is our right. We were born to work the land. They were born to clean up village filth. No one has the right to change this order established by God."[32] Caste identity may have been imagined or manufactured, but it continued to be a potent weapon in the arsenal of perpetuating economic disparities.

In an odd way, a pithy observation by Lewis from the 1950s still rings true. Most works on caste, he stated, are concerned with its "historical origin and development, with the rules and sanctions governing endogamy, food taboos, ritual purity, caste ranking, and the more dramatic injustices of untouchability." Thus while "there is a great deal of literature about the caste system in India, very little attention has been paid to its economic aspects."[33] In other words, it seems that greater attention has been paid to Ambedkar's opposition to divisions than his concern for laborers. The political economy of the countryside continues to be shaped by the ideology and practice of directly imprinting identity onto occupation. This is the unclaimed inheritance of the critique of the jajmani system, the persistence of determining what a person does and the resources they are entitled to by who they are understood to be.

TURNING CASTE UPSIDE DOWN
The practices of caste hierarchy in north India observed by early anthropologists appeared in sharp contrast to its logic and features in Panjab. This is in part due to the centuries of political and spiritual upheaval preceding British rule. Among the richest and most restive provinces of the Mughal Empire, Panjab witnessed a Sikh uprising by Guru Gobind Singh Ji and later Banda Singh Bahadur from the late seventeenth century to 1716, followed by a protracted struggle between different Mughal officials, local chieftains, and Afghan potentates. Invasions by Nadir Shah from Persia (1739) and multiple times by Ahmad Shah Abdali from Kabul (1747–65) further eroded what remained of imperial authority from Delhi. This gave rise to a renewed insurgency by the Sikh *misls* (fighting brigades) and the establishment of an independent kingdom by Maharaja Ranjit Singh in 1799, as briefly discussed in Chapter 1.[34] A consequence of this tumult was the disintegration of power held by traditional elites. "The effect of one hundred years of Sikh rule," explains Tom Kessinger, "was to remove a layer of *zamindars* who were never replaced."[35] Popular memory, especially in contemporary east Panjab, goes further to locate the origins of the autonomous peasantry itself in this pre-history. In any event, by losing economic entitlement, these large landholders ceased to wield the authority that they retained elsewhere as revenue collectors and rural notables, while the word *zamindar* itself acquired its distinctive meaning in Panjabi.[36]

Beyond immediate political history, another dimension of the critique of traditional hierarchy in Panjabi society was evinced through the idiom of poetry. A longer genealogy of the caste question is implicated in the north Indian Bhakti movement from the fourteenth to seventeenth centuries. This period witnessed an efflorescence of critical inquiry and expression by dozens of Bhagats ("poet-devotees") challenging a range of orthodoxies by emphasizing personal devotion, righteous individual conduct, and social equality.[37] One of its early and most prominent figures is Kabir, generally believed to have been born into a family of lower-caste Muslim weavers in Banaras in the late fourteenth century. "In the whole sweep of north Indian religion," according to one study, "there is no voice more stringent, more passionate, [and] more confident than that of Kabir."[38] Consider the following two verses:

> *Bed puran pare ka kia gun,*
> *khar chandan jas bhara.*
> *Ram nam ki gat nahi jani,*
> *kaise utras para.*
>
> What use is it to read the Vedas and Puranas?
> It is like loading a donkey with sandalwood.
> Unless you understand the essence of the name Ram,
> how will you ever cross to the other side?[39]
>
> *Jou tun brahman, brahmani jaia,*
> *tao aan baat kahe nahi aia.*
> *Tum kat brahman, ham kat sud,*
> *ham kat lohu, tum kat dudh.*
> *Kaho Kabir jo brahm bicharai,*
> *so brahman kahiat hai hamarai.*
>
> If you are indeed a Brahmin, born of a Brahmin mother,
> then why did you not come out some special way?
> How is it that you are a Brahmin, and I am of a low status?
> How is it that I am made of blood and you of milk?
> Says Kabir, one who contemplates God,
> is considered the true Brahmin among us.[40]

The first is a direct rejection (and mockery) of the value of Brahminical scripture, contrasting reciting Sanskrit texts with cultivating a personal connection to the divine, signified by comprehending Ram's name. For Kabir, salvation is not accomplished by a mere performance of reading but requires the practice of devotion in shaping an individual's spiritual journey. In the second verse, Kabir targets the ideology of inherent superiority in Hindu orthodoxy. If the supposedly superior Brahmin is born in exactly the same way as any other caste, of blood rather than milk, then what is the basis for claiming a higher or lower birth? Lowliness is detached from hereditary status and affixed to one's actions, the practice of true contemplation.

Closely following this theme is Ravidas, a leather worker also born during that period in Banaras with similarly disputed origins. He is thought to have worked with animal hides while composing poems he sang as hymns to a group of followers that included some Brahmins. It was his name, usually rendered as "Ravidasia," that came to be used by certain Sikhs of the Chamar caste, with his impact extending beyond Panjab to Uttar Pradesh, Bihar, and Maharashtra. Due to the ways Ravidas has been invoked by contemporary political parties, particularly in building temples and forming a separate Dalit religion, some scholars have concluded that "[o]f all the untouchable saint-poets," he is "by far the most important today."[41] In one verse, he questions the logic of the division between pure and impure:

> *Dudh ta bachhrai thanhu bitario,*
> *phul bhavar jal min bigario.*
> *Mai gobind puja kaha lai charavao,*
> *avar na phul anup na pavao.*
> *Mailagar berhe hai bhuianga,*
> *bikh amrit baseh ik sanga.*
> *Dhup deep naibedehi basa,*
> *kaise puj karahi teri dasa.*
> *Tan man arpao puj charavao,*
> *gur parsad niranjan pavao.*
> *Puja archa ahi na tori,*
> *kahe Ravidas kavan gat mori.*

> Milk in the teats is contaminated by the calf,
> flowers by the bees, and water by the fish.
> Mother, where shall I find an offering for the Lord?
> No other worthy flowers can be found.
> The snakes encircle the sandalwood tree,

> thus poison and nectar dwell together.
> Without incense, lamps, food offerings and flowers,
> how is your devotee to worship You?
> I dedicate my body and mind to You,
> by the Guru's grace one attains the immaculate Lord.
> Worship and offerings—I cannot do any of these,
> says Ravidas, what will become of me?[42]

Ravidas is interrupting the claim of purity, signified with milk, flowers, and sandalwood, by revealing how each item cannot avoid coming into ostensibly defiling contact with saliva, insects, and reptiles. The fallacy of untouchability is exposed by demonstrating the inescapability of touch itself. Thus the probing question at the end—of what to do with Ravidas— is directed both to the divine *and* to society at large, a sign of the untenable contradiction between exclusion and interaction. In other words, acknowledging Ravidas and what he represents is a question the people of Banaras and beyond will have to confront. This notion is carried forward in another verse:

> *Begam pura sahar ko naao,*
> *dukh andohu nahi tihi thaao.*
> *Nan tasvis khiraj na maal.*
> *khauf na khataa na taras javaal.*
> *Ab mohi khub vatan gah pai,*
> *uhaan khair sadaa mere bhai.*
> *Kaim daim sadaa paatisahi,*
> *dom na sem ek so aahi.*
> [. . .]
> *Kahe Ravidas khalaas chamaaraa,*
> *jo ham sahri so mit hamaaraa.*

> Begampura is the name of the city,
> a place without grief or anxiety.
> No worry about taxes or property,
> no fear of mistakes or downfall.
> Now I have found this most excellent place,

where there is lasting safety my companions.
Divine sovereignty is stable and eternal,
none are second or third—all are equal.
[. . .]
Says Ravidas, the emancipated tanner,
those living in this city are my friends.⁴³

Begampura, a word that means without sorrow (*be-gham*), is presented as a utopian space, linking the absence of taxes and property with no fear or grief.⁴⁴ To articulate this vision from within the city of Banaras—long considered sacred in mainstream Hindu tradition—was nothing less than insurrectionary. In a positive affirmation, on the other hand, Ravidas does away with hierarchy by collapsing second and third orders of human beings with a single, united whole. This combination produces genuine fraternity between people. The act of walking side by side—in violation of the distance prescribed by conventional Hindu regulations—allows the inhabitants of Begampura to become something almost unthinkable in a caste-ridden society: real friends.

A predecessor to both Kabir and Ravidas is Namdev, a fourteenth-century poet from the southern region of Maharashtra. Born into a tailor caste, he traveled extensively across Gujarat and Panjab, singing hymns to both an amorphous divine as well as a personified deity. For this reason, Namdev is also included in the tradition of worshipping Vishnu and is considered by some to serve "as a historical bridge between the two religio-poetic traditions" of formless Bhakti and mainstream Vaishnavism.⁴⁵ Below is one of his most emphatic verses.

Mo kao tun na bisaar tu na bisaar,
tu na bisaare ramia.
Alavanti eh bhram jo hai,
mujh upar sabh kopila.
Sud sud kar maar uthaaio,
kaha karao baap bithula.
Mue hue jao mukt dehuge,
mukt na jaanai koila.
[. . .]

Fer dia dehura naame kao,
pandian kao pichhvarla.

Do not forget me, do not forget,
do not forget me Ram.
The temple priests have doubts,
and everyone is furious with me.
Calling me untouchable they beat and drive me out,
what should I do now fatherly Lord?
If You liberate me after I am dead,
no one will know I am liberated.
[...]
The Lord turned the temple around to face Namdev,
turning His back on the Brahmins.[46]

Imploring Ram to not forget him in three successive statements signals urgency in Namdev—a demand to be addressed. The actions of the temple priests violate the individual as much as they are an affront to the divine. Crucially, Namdev insists on liberation in the present, a settling of accounts in this world rather than a deferral to the next. This is what prompts the ultimate vindication by inversion: the temple (and the divine) turns around so that a lower-caste tailor is included while elite Brahmins are excluded.

Beyond the Bhakti tradition, the most significant figure who produced a new, sustained movement and achieved far-reaching impact over the centuries is Guru Nanak (1469–1539). His importance is twofold. As the founder of the Sikh faith, he is recognized for experiencing a revelation through incarnating the divine, traveling and teaching extensively, developing a *sangat* or dedicated congregation of followers, as well as composing a large proportion of verses in the Sikh scripture called the *Adi Granth* and appointing a successor before his death. Second, it is largely through him and the early Sikh Gurus that people in the wider region accessed Kabir, Ravidas, and Namdev, since none of them created a sustained community nor committed their poems to writing. Guru Nanak was familiar with their beliefs and might have met Ravidas in person. At some point thereafter, the verses of all three (along with contributions from twelve others, including the thirteenth century Chishti sufi Baba Farid cited at the beginning of this book) were incorporated in the *Adi Granth*, compiled by Guru Arjun Ji in 1604.[47] While the languages used by various Bhagats include Brajpasha, Hindui, Khariboli, Persian, and Panjabi, they are all recorded as hymns in the Gurmukhi script.

Guru Nanak's own philosophy revolved around grasping the truth of divine existence—without attributes, timeless, self-generating—and expressing the emptiness of rituals and the fundamental oneness of life, coupled with a fierce denunciation of the deceit, hypocrisy, and injustices of the dominant religious and political order.[48] According to Nikky-Guninder Kaur Singh, his "highly structured imaginative sweep is an aesthetic and spiritual exercise in practicing truth in daily life," one that conceives of "the singular being as an all-embracing *becoming* that flows into the cosmos and seeps into the human world of motions and emotions."[49] In popular terms, it is captured in the saying: *naam japo, kirat karo ate vand chhako*, which can be rendered as a directive to "meditate on the Divine, labor diligently, and consume collectively." Concerning caste specifically, consider the following three verses from Guru Nanak:

Jaati dai kiaa hath,
sach parkhiai.
Mahura hovai hath,
mariai chakhiai.

What good is caste and class?
Let us examine the truth.
Pride in one's status is like holding poison,
by consuming it you will die.

Aakhan jor chupai nah jor,
jor na mangan den na jor.
Jor na jivan maran nah jor,
jor na raj maal man sor.
Jor na surti giaan vichaar,
jor na jugti chhutai sansaar.

Jis hath jor kar vekhai soe,
Nanak utam nich na koe.

No power to speak or power to keep silent,
no power to beg or power to give.
No power to live or power to die,
no power to rule with wealth or strategies.
No power to acquire wisdom, knowledge or reason,
no power to escape the world.
He who holds power watches over all,
Nanak, no one is high or low.

Nicha andar nich jaat,
nichi hu at nich.
Nanak tin kai sang saath,
vadia sio kia ris.

Those who are lower among the low caste,
the very lowest of the low,
Nanak seeks their company,
so why emulate the elite?[50]

Here Guru Nanak reiterates the fundamental equality of all human beings regardless of class or status. At the same time, he shifts registers to address caste arrogance. Born into a Khatri family, many of Guru Nanak's early followers were drawn from that caste, and might have carried a sense of superiority into the new sangat. In equating the pride of status with poison, and castigating the delusions of power that come with it, he specifically challenged the beneficiaries of hierarchy and their claim to divine favor. If the Lord does not recognize distinctions of any kind, individual salvation must depend on means other than inherited privilege. Inverting the status quo, Guru Nanak dismissed the patronage of the upper castes to affirm solidarity with the excluded and the dispossessed.

What these verses from Kabir, Ravidas, and Namdev along with Guru Nanak demonstrate is the profound challenge to hereditary status mounted in Panjab from the fifteenth century onward. Caste ideology was targeted and challenged, even overturned. Scripturally sanctioned hierarchy and the logic of purity/pollution were ridiculed and denounced through a radical utopian vision of justice based on divine intercession for the subordinated and the aspiration of a new bond of fraternity between equals. These verses, codified in the *Adi Granth* and publicly recited by the nascent congregation, came to inform the development of Sikhi over the following centuries. When Guru Gobind Singh inaugurated the Khalsa in the city of Anandpur in 1699, he enjoined his followers to renounce their caste affiliations, take the common surnames "Singh" and "Kaur," and drink *amrit* (consecrated sweetened water) from the same vessel, thereby physically abolishing the taint of pollution. Three out of the first five initiates were formally lower-caste—Mohkam Singh (tailor), Himmat Singh (water carrier), and Sahib Singh (barber)—while another, Jiwan Singh (sweeper), also known as Bhai Jaita, famously retrieved the severed head of the ninth Guru and composed his own verses, so that some consider him the first Dalit poet from Panjab.[51] Prior to this, the institution of *langar*, or inter-caste (and -faith) cooking and eating while seated on the floor, served to erase the notion of impurity and distinctions of rank through the collective sharing of food.[52] In the early eighteenth century, subordinate groups flocked to Banda Singh Bahadur's uprising and participated in major battles against Mughal and Afghan forces. There is even an instance of a misl made up of Sikhs originating from the Mazhabi caste led by Bir Singh Rangreta into the 1760s.[53]

This is a period when Panjabi society was being turned upside down. In the classic analyses of Christopher Hill and Ranajit Guha, inversion is a powerful, elementary modality of negating the status quo.[54] It renders profane nearly everything the existing system considers pure and profound. This atmosphere of tumult—of uncertainties and therefore possibilities—was captured in a few of the lines attributed to one of the most famous and beloved poets of Panjab, Bulleh Shah (c. 1680–1758):

Kaan lagarh nun maaran lagge,
chirian jurre dhaae,
ulte hor zamane aae.

Ghore chugan arurian utte,
gadhe khud pavaae,
ulte hor zamane aae.
Bhurian vale raje kite,
rajian bhikh mangaae,
ulte hor zamane aae.

Crows are now attacking hawks,
sparrows are defeating falcons,
upended times are upon us.
Horses are now scrounging from rubbish heaps,
donkeys themselves are loading carts,
upended times are upon us.
Those wearing coarse blankets have now become kings,
while kings are reduced to begging,
upended times are upon us.[55]

The *kaan* (crows) and *chirian* (sparrows) are symbols of the misls attacking and defeating the forces of Mughal authority as well as Ahmad Shah Abdali. The hunted have become the hunters. Their lowliness is evident in the phrase *bhurian vale*, which literally means wearers of burlap sacks but here perhaps despairingly represents the brown blankets worn by Sikh horsemen. That individuals with such humble means rose to confront and displace the ruling elites in Bulleh Shah's lifetime must have been an extraordinary, if unsettling, achievement. This upending was likened to the inversion of donkeys, the quintessential beasts of burden, now dictating the loading and pulling of carts, or prized horses, usually given the best fodder, reduced to grazing the random growths atop piles of rubbish. While debate continues over whether Bulleh Shah's tone celebrated or bemoaned what was happening around him, there is little doubt that these lines bore passionate witness to drastically changing times.

A radical set of cultural resources against caste hierarchy accompanied by a forceful politics for advocating equality and fraternity permeated early modern Panjabi society. Sikh institutions enacted the poignant visions of the Gurus and Bhagats contained in what became the *Sri Guru Granth Sahib Ji*. Rather than relying on an esoteric "sacred" language, the use of vernacular Panjabi—without prohibitions on learning or recital—ensured their wide circulation as hymns sung by individuals and together by the new congregation. Within the conceptual and material boundaries of the period, this dismantled the caste basis of the upper class and its wider hegemony.[56] No longer would the claim of divine right go unquestioned, or at least unmocked, if not directly unchallenged—if it ever did. Indeed, this partly explains why Mughal chroniclers reacted with such contempt toward Banda Singh Bahadur, describing the "large number of persons belonging to the class of sweepers and tanners, and the community of *banjaras* [herders] and others of base and lowly castes" that gathered around him as "ants and locusts."[57] They would later be more aghast that many misl leaders were Jatts and that Ranjit Singh, possibly from a pastoralist background, could rise to the status of a maharaja.

In the wake of this protracted overturning, dominance became fractured in Panjab. This was a society still unequal but without automatic recourse to an ideology of inherent or preordained hierarchy. Such egalitarianism must be qualified as well as historicized. The incisive compositions of Kabir and Ravidas and the new principles of faith articulated by Guru Nanak belong to a time of different societal polarities and potentials. In the fifteenth and sixteenth centuries, an ideology of purity, separation, and high birth buttressed the economic superiority of certain groups in the absence of the means for their transcendence. Powerful rural notables, corrupt officials, and tyrannical religious authorities could be agents of oppression without being impediments to the advent of a comprehensively new order.[58] For the vast majority, the uncertain toils of agrarian production and reproduction would continue regardless, as cultivation would not be much more secure or remunerative than other kinds of labor. Thus the clarion calls for democracy or socialism by European radicals from the mid-nineteenth century onward are no metric by which to measure the Bhakti movement or early Sikhi. It is anachronistic to foist the contemporary desire for abolishing caste onto the premodern period. Begampura, in other words, is incommensurate with the expectations of a modern political program as much as it is from the actual blueprints of Chandigarh or Islamabad.

What connections, then, can be drawn from this longer history to the period of colonial rule? It is improper to suggest that such beliefs and practices remained unchanged over centuries, and yet it is difficult to discern how they became significant in the lives of ordinary people. Still, Raj Kumar Hans has identified the source of modern Dalit expression to this radical past. "In the backdrop of the Sufis, the Sants and the Sikh movement fracturing and weakening Brahmanical ideology in the Punjab," he argues, "space became available to the Punjabi dalits."[59] Into that breach appeared figures like Wazir Singh (c. 1790–1859), among others. Hans describes Wazir as a "sant-poet" from a sweeper background who developed a large following by invoking Bhagat Ravidas to challenge caste supremacy. Similarly, Anshu Malhotra examines the life of Piro from the Gulabdasi sect in the middle decades of the nineteenth century, showcasing her poetic subversion of gender and doctrinal norms, though with more ambivalence about the inheritances of Bhakti.[60] Even later, in the time of the Ghadar Party, the Kirti Kisan Party, and the Shiromani Akali Dal between 1910 and 1940, Ali Raza describes a rather distinctive entanglement between radicalism and religion, stating that "the history of the Left in Punjab is also a history of Sikh politics in general."[61] While these individuals and movements have their peculiarities, together they should be taken as an indication of the deeper emancipatory currents circulating and convulsing within Panjabi society.

NAMING LABOR IN RURAL PANJAB

This critical genealogy illuminates what would become bitter, if opaque, contestations over caste, status, and labor in the early twentieth century. It also underpins the difference between the kind of hierarchy witnessed by the Wisers and social relations in Panjabi villages. Yet there is an initial difficulty and discrepancy in identifying the subjects that populate this history. The vocabulary of the colonial state is markedly different from the vernacular terms used by lower castes for themselves. According to a conventional colonial description, "the village servants or menials are paid by the zamindars usually in grain at the time of harvest, in return for work performed during the preceding half-year." Formally they were divided into two groups ostensibly based on caste occupations. First were those directly connected with agricultural operations, namely, the *Tarkhan* (carpenter) making and repairing wooden plows and other implements in addition to the apparatus for well irrigation; the *Kumhar* (potter) providing various earthen vessels for wells and domestic use; the *Lohar* (blacksmith) forging and sharpening plowshares along with other iron tools; the *Chamar* (leather worker) making leather bags, whips, and blinkers for bullocks; and the *Churha* (sweeper) providing brooms, baskets, and ropes. Second were a greater variety of those more distant from agriculture but still part of village life, mainly the *Nai* (barber), the *Dhobi* (washer), the *Darzi* or *Chhimba* (tailor), the *Julaha* (weaver), the *Jhinwar* or *Mehra* (water-carrier), and the *Mirasi* (musician).[62] Perhaps most strikingly, the same Brahmins who supposedly occupied the apex of the jajmani system elsewhere in India held little influence in rural Panjab, accepted and indulged but wielding few actual powers.[63]

In the first group of village menials, the first three castes were fewer in number and occupied a somewhat higher status, as they worked in their own small shops at their own pace, and increasingly took on piecework for cash remuneration. Similarly, members of the second group were also numerically few and were mostly confined to their given tasks due to the specialization of equipment and skills. The Chamars and Churhas, however, were considered the lowest and most stigmatized castes—untouchables by convention—and constituted the bulk of the menial population. Yet rarely were these groups limited to only making leather goods or weaving baskets. Instead, they served as the rural labor force, working in the fields alongside Jatt and other proprietors and receiving a share of the harvest as payment.

While colonial vocabulary simplistically aligns caste with occupation, Chamars and Churhas did not use these names for themselves, nor were they exclusively identified by them in the wider society. The Panjabi words they adopted reveal a remarkable spectrum of emerging and intertwining caste and religious identities. Significant lower-caste conversion to Sikhi is estimated to begin in the seventeenth century, to Islam even earlier, and to Christianity in the late nineteenth century. Chamar, deriving from *chamri* for skin or, more precisely, animal hides, served as a generic term for leather worker, nominally Hindu. In the northern hill areas they were sometimes termed *Dagis* or *Kolis*. Those who converted to Islam called themselves *Mochis*, closely affiliated with shoe-making, while those who became Sikh took the name *Ravidasia* after Bhagat Ravidas, which could also be given as *Ramdasia* or *Raidasia*. For a short while in the mid-twentieth century, all three, as well as some Julahas who called themselves *Rahtias* or *Kabir-panthis* after their acclaimed ancestor Bhagat Kabir, identified as *Ad Dharmi* or the followers of the Ad Dharm movement.

Churha, on the other hand, does not have an assumed etymological basis, but is presented in colonial writings as another untouchable caste of Hindu sweepers and scavengers. Converts to Islam became known as *Mussalis* or *Kutanas*, Sikhs were identified as *Mazhabis* or *Rangretas*, and Christians were termed *Masihs*. It was a regiment of Mazhabis that extraordinarily petitioned to acquire the status as an agricultural tribe in Chapter 2. Those Churhas who remained Hindu also changed their designation, preferring to be called *Valmikis* (or colloquially, *Balmikis*) after Rishi Valmiki, the assumed author of the epic *Ramayana*.[64] The two generic caste names for menial laborers thus conceal a diversity of identities in a continuous process of formation and reformation. And although today it is offensive and illegal in India to refer to anyone as either a Chamar or Churha, the word *Chamar* is still used for certain caste-oriented associations and has even been invoked positively in popular music by emerging Dalit artists in east Panjab.[65]

The term *menial* is therefore both a general and specific diminution, minimizing the various labors performed by these castes as well as underscoring their exclusion from a fixed and recognized role within the productive process. *Menial* conjures up the notion of marginality, as a periphery to the already-centered Jatt, a form of labor adjacent to the main and supposedly given work of being a peasant. At the same time, *menial* implies inchoate and provisional, an assortment of explicitly ancillary tasks without fixity or importance to the productive process. Defined as subordinate both to the landholding cultivator and to cultivation itself, the menial laborer thus occupies a position of double subalternity. The stigma of an alienated inconsequence permeates the very language by which these groups were located within the political economy of the countryside.

CONVERSION, COMPETITION AND COMMUNITY

During the late nineteenth and early twentieth centuries, these lower castes changed religious affiliations and consolidated community boundaries to gain a new kind of social and economic preponderance. Here the colonial census, as discussed in Chapter 2, was crucial in creating awareness of the relative strength of a group and the possibility of tracking its trajectory over time.[66] In the first comprehensive all-India census of 1881, undifferentiated Chamars numbered 1.4 million and Churhas 1.1 million in Panjab. This was less than Jatts (4.4 million) and Rajputs (1.7 million) and roughly equal to Brahmins (1.1 million) but more than other prominent groups such as Pathans (859,000), Gujars (627,000), and Khatris (419,000).[67] In a process that officials admitted was replete with inaccuracies, approximately 68 percent of Chamars were returned as Hindu, 25 percent as Muslim, and 7 percent as Sikh, while 58 percent of Churhas were Hindu, 37 percent Muslim, 4 percent Sikh, and 1 percent Christian. Together Chamars and Churhas constituted the second-largest caste group in Panjab and were recorded as mostly following strands of what at the time was a diverse, amorphous Hinduism.

Over the next forty years, however, the proselytizing efforts of Christian missionaries prompted various indigenous responses that transformed the act of conversion into a concerted competition. The Arya Samaj sought to reform yet preserve a version of Hinduism, launching a campaign of *shuddhi* ("purification" in Sanskrit) to "keep" lower-caste Hindus in the fold while also engaging in polemics against Christianity, orthodox Islam, and the new Ahmadiyya movement. One of their leaders, Swami Shraddhanand, went further by claiming Sikhs were in fact Hindus, belittling Guru Nanak and precipitating the public shaving of a group of Rahita Sikhs in Lahore in 1900.[68] This in turn prompted Singh Sabha activists not only to consolidate Sikh identity and membership, but also to address the contradiction between principles and practices within the community.[69] As a result of this protracted, multifaceted struggle, as well as different practices in counting, the distribution of lower castes across the major religious changed significantly in the 1921 census. Chamars (including Mochis and Dagis) now stood at 1.7 million, with those professing to be Hindus decreasing to 66 percent, Muslims remaining at 25 percent, and Sikhs increasing to 9 percent. Churhas (with Mussalis, Mazhabis, and Christians) totaled 1.4 million, with Hindus dropping to 48 percent, Muslims down to 26 percent, Sikhs rising to 7 percent, and Christians jumping to 19 percent.⁷⁰ Thus, in four decades Hindu Chamars fell from 68 to 66 percent and Hindu Churhas from 58 to 48 percent; these defectors appeared to officially leave Hinduism, mainly for Sikhi and Christianity.

A more dramatic assertion of lower-caste religious identity took place over the following decade. Rather than leaving one faith for another, however, this entailed the creation and adoption of an altogether new one. In early June 1926, a small group of Chamars met in the village of Mugowal in Hoshiarpur district to discuss ways of concentrating their power amid upper-caste cooptation and competition. The village was the birthplace of Mangoo Ram, a schoolteacher who would become the leader of the movement and an influential if somewhat overlooked figure in Panjab politics both before and after independence. In a series of interviews with the anthropologist Mark Juergensmeyer in the 1970s, Ram related the exceptional details of his life before dying at the age of ninety-four in 1980.

Born into a family of leather workers, Ram's father, who had become a successful wholesale supplier of goods to the British Indian Army, insisted that his son be educated to help with the business. Despite excelling at school, Ram was often the only untouchable student in the class, forced to sit at the back of the room or even outside, listening through an open door. In 1909, he convinced his father to send him to America in order to work and support the family through remittances. While Ambedkar was studying at Columbia University in New York, Ram picked fruit in the San Joaquin Valley in California before joining the militant anticolonial Ghadar Party in 1913.⁷¹ Reflecting on the discrimination he faced in his childhood, he fondly recalled the equality and camaraderie of the Ghadar militants, even though he was only one of two Chamars in a group of mostly Jatts. Two years later, he volunteered to smuggle weapons to Panjab to incite an uprising against British rule but was discovered en route and almost executed; he spent several years in jail and then in hiding in Manila. By 1925 Ram had made his way back to Panjab, where he founded a school and briefly worked as a teacher before turning his attention to the conditions of untouchables.⁷²

The 1926 meeting in Mugowal produced a group dedicated to articulating and organizing around a distinct narrative of lower-caste history, religion, and identity. Rather than strict piety, these individuals were inspired by a restless ambition and were "socially sensitive and politically astute."⁷³ For Ram, the history of untouchables in Panjab was a long sequence of destruction, displacement, and disappointment. As the original inhabitants of the land, they were first suppressed and enslaved by Aryan invaders, with each generation of Hindus worse than the one before and the mythical lawgiver Manu in particular denounced as a murderer. Islam at first held some liberating potential but quickly absorbed and reproduced the same logic of caste hierarchy, while Sikhi was little more than a momentary upsurge ending in tyranny. Against this past, Mangoo Ram and his followers argued that all untouchables—"chamars, chuhras, sansis, bhanjre [and] bhils"—together constituted a separate *qaum*, usually translated as "nation" but here referring to religious community, equal to Hindus, Muslims, and Sikhs.⁷⁴ To reclaim their autochthonous status, the group took the name "Ad Dharm," meaning the originary or ancient faith, and identified a quartet of figures as their founders: Valmiki, Namdev, Kabir, and especially Ravidas. In their first and only official report, they claimed that untouchables had been endowed with three qualities hitherto unrealized: *qaumiat* (community pride), *mazhab* (religion or faith), and *majlis* (organization). The group also instituted a new greeting ("Jai Guru Dev," meaning "Victory to the Divine Guru"), notion of a supreme deity (Ad Prakash or Originary Light), sacred word (*soham*, a Sanskrit term meaning "I am it"), and holy color (red, which they claimed the Rajputs had denied them).⁷⁵ By harnessing these qualities and recognizing themselves as Ad Dharmis, the group believed that untouchables would at last achieve separate parity with other communities rather than continue to be manipulated and subsumed within them.

Predictably, the new assertion provoked serious conflict with existing organizations competing for untouchable allegiance. The Arya Samaj was seen as the greatest enemy. Many Ad Dharmi leaders emerged from it or one of its affiliates (such as the Jat-Pat Todak Mandal) and were constantly enticed to return to work for lower-caste uplift within its larger neo-Hindu framework. Faced with the threat of reabsorption, Mangoo Ram focused on condemning the shuddhi campaign as a devious attempt to keep untouchables imprisoned within the grasp of Hinduism.⁷⁶ In a group whose name literally meant the "Society of Aryans," he argued, there could be no equality with non-Aryans.

On the other hand, the Ad Dharm both faced and exhibited hostility of a different kind toward the Singh Sabha movement. Here the tension was more intricate: the Sikh Gurus had explicitly denounced caste and declared the equality of all; the *Adi Granth* included verses from formerly lower-caste Bhagats venerated by all Sikhs; and Sikh institutions deliberately transgressed the boundaries of purity, pollution, and distance. Yet as Ram argued, it was also true that many untouchables—whether professing to be Hindu, Muslim, or Christian, or even Mazhabi or Ravidasia Sikh—remained largely un-touchable for both Khatri and Jatt Sikhs and that cruel and degrading treatment continued in certain forms in Sikh-dominated villages. The ostensibly lower castes still largely lived in separate areas, could not access the same wells, and were exploited for their labor; they were also at times discriminated against within some *gurduaras* through different seating arrangements and restrictions on participation in the collective preparing and consuming of food.[77] A group of Sikhs reportedly broke up a 1930 Ad Dharm rally in Nankana Sahib, the birthplace of Guru Nanak, destroying supplies, burning literature, and beating up several members.[78]

At the same time, some Singh Sabha activists recognized this contradiction within their community and directed energies toward challenging Sikhs to live up to their faith. Giani Ditt Singh, an eminent writer and formally from a Ramdasia family, published *Nakli Sikh Prabodh* ("False Sikhs Redeem Yourselves") in 1895, castigating Sikhs who continued to practice caste, while Kahn Singh Nabha's *Ham Hindu Nahin* ("We Are Not Hindus") from 1899 reiterated Sikhi as distinct from Hinduism in part through its explicit opposition to caste.[79] Their efforts were not entirely unsuccessful: in the 1921 census, over sixty thousand Sikhs refused to state their caste, compared to only twenty thousand Hindus and seven thousand Muslims, a remarkable feat given their proportion of the population.[80] There is little doubt that this was not because these people did not know their inherited position or *gotra* but that—in the tradition of Kabir, Guru Nanak, and the Khalsa—they refused to acknowledge it. Nevertheless, Ram and the Ad Dharm would not be mollified by such attempts, however sincere. To mark their separation from Sikhi, they transformed the status of Ravidas, Kabir, and Namdev. No longer were they respected Bhagats but Gurus in their own right, and thus the progenitors of an entirely new faith.

The nature of the problem of caste and Sikhi is perhaps best illustrated by a lesser-known aspect of Ambedkar's attempt to find an alternative religion for untouchables. After declaring he would not die a Hindu in 1935, he began to research different religions, meeting with their representatives and comparing their positions on caste. In the tense correspondence with the Jat-Pat Todak Mandal, Ambedkar actually speculated that his attendance at the Sikh Prachar (Propagation) Conference in Amritsar a few weeks before his cancelled speech had something to do with the committee's ignominious decision.[81] At the same time, Gandhi was said to be disturbed by the prospect of untouchables explicitly renouncing Hinduism to embrace Sikhi.[82] According to Harish Puri, Ambedkar found much to admire in the Gurus' teachings and even came close to choosing that faith in June 1936. He sent his son Yashwant Rao and several others to Amritsar for six weeks to study the situation and discuss the practicalities of a mass conversion. There was even talk of a potential marriage between Ambedkar (whose first wife, Ramabai, had died in May 1935) and a daughter from the royal family of Patiala to secure broader acceptance from the public.[83] Soon after, however, the plan was quietly dropped.

While doubts remain over his ability to reach consensus with certain constituencies among his followers, another possible explanation for the change relates to conflict within the Sikh community. On the one hand, some lower-caste Panjabis (perhaps Hindu or even Mazhabi or Ravidasia Sikh) conveyed to Ambedkar "the atrocities they suffered at the hands of the dominant community of Jat Sikhs and appealed to him to ensure that the untouchables never became Sikhs."[84] On the other hand, certain powerful Sikhs were alarmed at what this influx would mean for them. While the potential addition of sixty million untouchables to the existing four million Sikhs would raise their number fifteenfold across India, thereby drastically increasing their prominence and leverage in every sphere of life, it would also irrevocably transform the caste composition of the community. Leaders like Master Tara Singh and Baldev Singh were said to be worried that if Ambedkar and his followers converted, they would by sheer numbers gain control over Sikh religious institutions and political parties, and so might have discreetly discouraged him from following through. In his memoir published in 1972, Kapur Singh, a renowned philosopher, writer, and politician, narrates being told about a conversation between two individuals close to the situation at the time. When one asked why the mass conversion failed to take place, the other replied with vulgar rhetoric: "By making six crore untouchables Sikhs, should the Darbar Sahib be handed over to Churhas?"[85] It seems many Sikh leaders had little interest in an exponential expansion of their religion if it required a redistribution of power with those from lower-caste backgrounds. For every Ditt Singh voice urging genuine inclusion and an end to hypocrisy, there were numerous entrenched interests committed to the status quo. In this situation, the separation politics of Ad Dharm appeared to offer a greater chance for improved status and better treatment than the continuously deferred promises of equality and fraternity.

Ad Dharm's efforts bore unexpected and unprecedented results in the 1931 census. A few years before, Mangoo Ram sent a petition to the governor of Punjab demanding a separate designation: "We are not Hindus. We strongly request the government not to list us as such. Our faith is not Hindu but Ad Dharm. We are not a part of Hinduism, and Hinduism is not a part of us." The administration readily obliged, as the Ad Dharm's hostility toward the Arya Samaj as well as Gandhi and the Congress made it at best indifferent to the continuation of British rule and the rise of anticolonial nationalism. Indeed, concurring with Ambedkar on the critique of independence for a caste-ridden society, another part of the Ad Dharm program stated: "India should not be given independence until Untouchables are free and equal. Otherwise it would be a disgrace to the British rule."[86] The census results were a shock to everyone involved. Despite a campaign of intimidation "not infrequently bordering on terrorism," approximately 418,789 people identified themselves as Ad Dharmis, mainly in the districts of Jalandhar, Hoshiarpur, and Lyallpur.[87] Leaders later claimed that the actual number of people wanting to identify as Ad Dharmi was close to two million.[88]

Equally significant was the changing distribution of lower castes in the other religions. The population of Chamars (this time including Dagis,

Mochis, and Ramdasias) increased to slightly less than 1.9 million, of which Hindus were reduced to 47 percent, Muslims again remained at 25 percent, Sikhs rose to 12 percent, and Ad Dharmis became fully 16 percent. Out of 1.5 million Churhas (with Mussalis, Mazhabis, and Christians), Hindus dropped even lower to 24 percent, Muslims rose slightly to 29 percent, Sikhs more sharply to 11 percent, while Christians surged to 30 percent and Ad Dharmis now made up 6 percent. Thus, within a decade, almost one-third of Hindu Chamars and one-half of Hindu Churhas had changed their religion.[89] Between 1881 and 1931 the absolute number of Hindu Chamars actually decreased from 963,000 to 885,000 while Hindu Churhas fell even further, from 629,000 to 367,000. As Mangoo Ram noted with satisfaction, in less than five years the Ad Dharm converted roughly the same number as Christian missionaries had in fifty.[90] Thus well before Ambedkar was to give his speech vowing to convert, lower castes in Panjab had by and large already severed their ties from Hinduism, adopting Sikhi, Christianity, or their own Ad Dharm faith.

By combining existing religious figures with new doctrines and practices within a stirring historical narrative, the Ad Dharm created a distinct identity for Panjabi untouchables. Its success lay in harnessing the popular respect and devotion for Ravidas, Kabir, and Namdev into a reverence bordering on deification. Ram's comparison with Christianity is therefore more than mere boasting. Whereas missionaries had to impart a totally unfamiliar history and theology to lower castes, the Ad Dharm invoked figures already a part of the local imagination and linked to a long tradition of inquiry, critique, and assertion. An iconoclastic weaver from Banaras speaking in a familiar idiom resonated more intensely than the story of a carpenter turned messiah from Nazareth.

Yet the primacy given to figures from these specific occupational backgrounds also limited the appeal of Ad Dharm, and contributed to its eventual decline. Since most of its leadership were Chamars from Jalandhar and Hoshiarpur who exalted Ravidas in particular, the vast majority of adherents were also Chamars, Ravidasias, Dagis, and even Mochis. Despite its efforts, the Ad Dharm did not manage to overcome divides internal to lower castes to attract significant numbers of Churhas, Mussalis, Mazhabis, or Masihs. When Ram reached out to Ambedkar in 1932, supporting him against Gandhi's ultimatum over separate electorates in Pune and offering to merge Ad Dharm with his organization, the reply was noncommittal. According to Juergensmeyer, Ambedkar "wanted to join, not a separatist religious tradition, but rather an egalitarian one, which would embrace the whole of society"—hence his temporary interest in Sikhi and ultimate conversion to Buddhism shortly before his death in 1956.[91] The very elements that had informed and advanced the Ad Dharm movement thus played a role in isolating it.

After the watershed 1931 census and a surprising showing in the 1936 legislative elections, Ad Dharm leaders became embroiled in factional controversies and political maneuvering, and drifted from the task of developing their qaum.[92] Although their momentum faltered and the movement declined, Juergensmeyer points out that the Ad Dharm "established a fact which previously had been unproved." They demonstrated that "Untouchable castes were capable of mobilizing for their own benefits, and of organizing in ways that permitted them to compete under the conditions that governed the sociopolitical arena at large."[93] In little over a decade, Ad Dharm transmuted untouchability from layers of negation into the basis for a new politically informed religious community in Panjab.

DIVIDING LABOR AND LABORERS

The Ad Dharm assertion of a proud originary community did not rest entirely on refuting identification with the untouchability of Hinduism. Equally important, though receiving far less scholarly attention, was its challenge to the supposedly traditional alignment between caste and occupation. The simple, stifling equation of Chamar as leather worker or Churha as sweeper was deeply implicated—and just as debilitating—as being labeled an outcaste Hindu.[94] Two stark points coming out of the program from the 1926 meeting at Mugowal make this rejection explicit:

> 12. We are agriculturalists; we know our work well. But we are not paid enough in agricultural wages. We cannot take care of our families properly. Vacant lands should be given to the Untouchable community.
>
> 13. The government should treat agriculturalists from the Untouchable class on par with agriculturalists from other communities, especially in Lyallpur,

Sheikupura, Sargoda, Montgomery, and Multan. In these districts, there should be more land for Untouchables and more employment.[95]

This affirmation of agricultural status—emanating from the premium placed on that category in the Punjab Alienation of Land Act of 1901—raised the question of untouchable *economic* as opposed to *religious* identity.[96]

Rather fortuitously, around this time the Panjab government happened to be conducting a series of investigations into the internal dynamics of the agrarian economy. The Board of Economic Inquiry, the state-funded research body described in Chapter 3, sent interviewers to over a dozen villages for twelve months to record details of both the expenses and returns of cultivation and the patterns of consumption and reproduction by families of landholding proprietors. Just as the inhabitants of Karimpur were being studied by William and Charlotte Wiser, and Ambedkar was demanding separate electorates while Mangoo Ram was enjoying the census windfall, rural labor practices were coming under new scrutiny from the colonial state.

The most startling revelation from these studies of "peasant" cultivation was an admission of the impossibility of that very object of inquiry. R. K. Seth and Faiz Ilahi's survey of the village of Durrana Lanhana in Multan district stated the problem directly:

> It will thus appear that *it is not possible* to describe the working life of *an isolated cultivator* as such with any accuracy. It is invariably so much intermingled with that of his colleagues and members of his family that one might as well consider the combination as a unit for the purposes of the present inquiry.[97]

Agrarian production could not be reduced and singularized into the discrete labors of a lone peasant. The collective nature of the enterprise meant recognizing and tracking the contributions of different groups within the village. Instead of the jajmani system, however, the researchers termed what they observed as the *sepidari* system, a similar arrangement of castes performing various labors in exchange for shares in grain: Kumhars providing pots, Mehras carrying water, a Pandit or Mullah offering solace.

For instance, the study from Kala Gaddi Thamman in Lyallpur noted that as compensation for making and repairing one plow for a cultivating landowner, a Tarkhan received fifty pounds each of wheat and maize, one bundle of unthreshed wheat and four bundles of green fodder a year. In addition, and for several smaller duties, he would receive one rupee plus a measure of cloth at the birth of the cultivator's first son, two rupees on the marriage of a son, three rupees on the marriage of a daughter, and a quarter of a rupee on the death of a family elder.[98] Yet in Panjab this system differed for being largely a product of makeshift custom, far less formal or rigid than the representation of jajmani as a fixed law by William Wiser, wedded neither to age-old beliefs nor a religious order.[99] The performance of tasks seemed to matter more than the identity of the person fulfilling them. Also, the researchers noted that sepidari itself was declining as an organizing principle for village relations. From the late nineteenth century onward, the growth of the canal colonies and military recruitment offered greater opportunities for lower-caste mobility, while the rise of commodity production, market prices, and piecework monetized (and standardized) the process of remuneration.[100]

Beyond the village-wide constellation of castes and roles, a specific relationship captured the attention of the Board researchers. They reported a common form of labor attachment throughout Panjab called *siri*, where landholding cultivators would contract with landless laborers to provide various agricultural services for an entire season in exchange for a share of the harvest. This was not a form of tenancy with an absentee landowner, nor was there a stable list of tasks to perform or items to deliver, as in sepidari arrangements. Although sometimes termed "field laborers," siris resembled constant yet unequal companions in agricultural operations, working alongside "cultivators-proper" in every aspect of cultivation.[101]

Almost all landholding households in Panjab had some form and length of siri relations. Their payments were based on a proportion of the produce and food from the cultivator's home as well as cash advances and other types of patronage. Perhaps most importantly, the kinds of labor they performed were far removed from their caste identity. Whereas a Lohar would be translated as "blacksmith" by virtue of possessing requisite equipment, training, and capital and therefore be expected to provide plowshares and sickles, the vast majority of siris were Chamars and Churhas performing tasks unrelated to leather or sweeping. In the tedious gamut of colonial caste classifications, there is no "traditional" designation for multifarious agricultural laborers because the supposed fixity of untouchable caste-work unraveled precipitously in the countryside.

The study of Gaggar Bhana in Amritsar, for example, described how Churhas in particular diverged from their stigmatized label as sweepers, which included removing human feces (euphemistically called "night soil") from the homes of landlords. The "rural Chuhra," explained Sardar Gian Singh, "has nothing to do with the removal of night soil, which is the principle occupation of the town chuhra." The reason for this discrepancy was the unique spatial configuration of the fecal economy: there is "practically no night soil to be removed because there is no system of latrines in the villages." Instead, "when necessity arises the fields near the village are used."[102] In other words, the traditional occupation of the Churha only manifested in the confines of the modern city. In the villages of Panjab, the vast majority of Chamars, Churhas, and other lower castes performed the labors of cultivation under the sign of a siri.

What was the nature of the relationship between cultivator and siri?[103] Fortunately, the survey of Suner in Ferozepur contains a rare translated copy of an agreement signed by two individuals on June 29, 1932 (see Figure 4.1). Titled "Specimen of Agreement between Cultivating Owner and His Siri," it begins with the following sentence: "I, Chaugutta, son of Karmun—by caste weaver—am a resident of Village Suner, Tahsil Zira." Next, it states that Chaugutta has "taken a cash sum of Rs. 60" as "debt from Tehl Singh, son of Hazara Singh" to meet his "household expenses." The loan would be repaid after a full year starting from the first of Har (after the wheat harvest, mid-June) but without interest because during that period, "I will be working as siri with Tehl Singh." Chaugutta agreed to "look after his cattle and serve him generally as I am ordered," which might entail sleeping beside the cattle at night, in return for one-fifth of the grain produced from the area cultivated by one plow. In addition he would receive meals from the household of Tehl Singh but would not have access to green fodder from his land. The agreement then stipulated that if Chaugutta missed more than three days of work in the year, he would be responsible for paying the day-wages of any laborer Tehl Singh hired as a temporary replacement. If for any reason he broke the agreement, his share

APPENDIX B TO CHAPTER I
SPECIMEN OF AGREEMENT BETWEEN CULTIVATING
OWNER AND HIS SIRI

I.
App.
B.

[NOTE.—The agreement was on 8 annas Government stamp paper.]

(*Translated*).

I, Chaugutta, son of Karmun—by caste weaver—am a resident of Village Suner, Tahsil Zira. I have to-day taken a cash sum of Rs. 60, the half of which is Rs. 30, as debt from Tehl Singh, son of Hazara Singh, of Suner, Tahsil Zira, to meet my household expenses. I promise that I will repay the above-mentioned sum, on which no interest will be charged, before *Nimani* (1st of Har), 1990 (Bikrami). The interest charge has been excused for the reason that I will be working as siri with Tehl Singh. I further promise that I will continue with Tehl Singh up to *Nimani*, 1990, and will look after his cattle and serve him generally as I am ordered. My share of the produce will be one-fifth of the total grain produced from one *hal*; in fodder I will have no share. I will take my food at the house of Tehl Singh and will not absent myself from work without his permission. In case I do I shall be responsible for any wages Tehl Singh may pay during the days of my absence. If it is found necessary I shall sleep at night beside the cattle. Sick leave of only 3 days during the whole year will be allowed to me. In days of absence over and above this period, the wages of any labour that may be employed will have to be paid by me. In case I leave off work and go away before the aforesaid *Nimani*, the condition that no interest is chargeable from me, will not stand, and I shall be liable to 50 per cent. interest which along with the principal I will pay whenever the same is demanded. This document is written to serve as an evidence of the contract.

Dated 29th June 1932.

(Thumb impression of
Chaugutta)
Age : 25 years.

Witness : Atma Ram,
son of Harbans Das,
resident of Suner.

24

FIGURE 4.1 A copy of a translated contract between a siri and landowner in Ferozepur, 1932. Source: Lajpat Rai Dawar, *An Economic Survey of Suner, a Village in the Ferozepore District of the Punjab*, Punjab Village Surveys No. 9 (Lahore: The Civil and Military Gazette Press, 1936), 24.

in grain would be forfeited and he would have to immediately repay his original loan plus 50 percent interest. At the bottom are the date and name of a witness (one Atma Ram) alongside Chaugutta's age (twenty-five) and space for his thumbprint.[104]

Such a short and simple document is positively brimming with disparities of power. Chaugutta's use of the first-person pronoun indicates he is the speaker, but the voice of Tehl Singh resounds throughout. All of the declarations are duties of the former to be carried out during fixed periods for certain payments against specific consequences. Tehl Singh makes few commitments beyond the initial loan. His caste and age are not disclosed, nor is there even a place for his signature, reflecting that this document was for his use, kept in his possession to add the authority of a written contract to his considerable existing leverage in case Chaugutta became incompliant. There is also a revealing unevenness in the details of the agreement. While it clearly states the amount of money borrowed, dates for repayment and work, entitlements for food, fodder, and the harvest, and the types of penalties, it is silent on what exactly Chaugutta is supposed to do. Aside from caring for Tehl Singh's cattle, he committed to serving "generally" as "ordered." The logic of the ambiguity of laboring tasks becomes clearer against the backdrop of the calendar of agricultural operations.

Most of the village studies provide month-by-month descriptions of the labors of cultivation during a given year. In Suner, for instance, starting in the middle of June most of the fields were plowed and spread with manure while cotton was planted and the sugarcane fields irrigated from the canal; the sowing for maize began in July with regular watering from wells; after the rains in September other crops such as oilseed and chickpeas were sown; in November the sowing of wheat and some barley began; by late December the cotton crop was picked and the oilseed harvested; in January the wheat required a few well waterings; from February onward the sugarcane was pressed and its juice boiled; in March the area for sugarcane was replowed and replanted and the chickpeas harvested; canal water for sowing cotton resumed in April, which also marked the beginning of the wheat harvest; May and early June were dedicated to threshing wheat, transporting grain to market, and gathering straw; and at that point, the new year commenced with yet more plowing. Tasks for livestock fodder such as regular plowing, irrigating, harvesting, and replanting; daily animal feeding and washing; repairing fences on cotton and sugarcane fields; and clearing irrigation channels from canals also continued throughout the year. According to colonial calculations, while the average hours worked in a day ranged from just two in July to over fifteen in May, the number of workers needed per month was never fewer than three and sometimes as many as to nineteen.[105] These are the myriad labors that Chaugutta would do alongside Tehl Singh, his relatives, and perhaps others. Put differently, there was no single task that only one or the other would perform and therefore no single cultivator—hence the Ad Dharm assertion that untouchables were in fact agriculturalists.

The intertwined, indistinct quality of caste labors is evident in the everyday experiences of cultivation. According to the surveys, during the summer season (April–September), a typical day for a landholder and a siri would begin at sunrise with an empty-stomach departure for the fields. After working until roughly 8:00 a.m., they would eat a small meal consisting of *lassi* (buttermilk) and one or two *rotis* (unleavened bread) with *gheo* (clarified butter) brought to them from the cultivator's home, presumably cooked by his wife and other household women. Work resumed until around midday, when a more substantial meal of several rotis with gheo, pickled or cooked vegetables along with some *gur* (unrefined sugar) and more lassi would again be delivered, followed by more work until the approach of sunset. At that point the landholder and siri would return to eat the last meal in the former's home, or sometimes separately, consisting of the same rotis and gheo, but now with *dal* (lentils) or, on rare occasions, some goat or chicken. During the shorter days of the winter season (October–March), the number of meals would be reduced to two (at 11:00 a.m. and 6:00 p.m.) but with more gheo and sometimes barley or maize replacing wheat rotis, while during the spring harvest a fourth meal of rotis and gur would be eaten around 4:00 p.m. Only ex-soldiers had developed the habit of drinking tea by this time; opium was consumed far more regularly than alcohol.[106] In Chaugutta and Tehl Singh's situation, a Julaha and presumably a Jatt would thus eat the same food from the same source (though probably with different utensils, if used at all) for at least two out of their three daily meals.

Set against the leveling aspect of food consumption, the inequities of this relationship manifested most sharply at harvest. Here the difference of ownership conferred upon the landholder the power to pay the siri a portion of the grain they and others had produced together. The survey of Gijhi in Rohtak provides a detailed account of the expenses and returns for several cultivators. "Farmer A," for example, cultivated twenty-eight acres of land with a siri (called a "servant"). Throughout the winter and spring seasons, he spent approximately Rs. 290 on the upkeep of three bullocks, Rs. 48 on maintaining a cart, and Rs. 23 on various implements (given to sepis such as the Tarkhan and Kumhar) as well as paying Rs. 117 in land revenue. The siri received the value of around Rs. 8 in cash and slightly less than Rs. 6 in food per month (3 annas a day) for a total of Rs. 164. At harvest, the primary winter crops of wheat and chickpeas plus different fodders, millets, sugarcane, and cotton from the summer generated Rs. 1,540. After deducting expenses from the yield, Farmer A therefore netted around Rs. 898, or more than five times as much as the siri.[107] However, since part of this arrangement entitled them to the same food as cultivators, low-caste Panjabis working as siris could consume 15 to 24 percent more wheat per day than those unrelated to cultivation such as Nais and Mehras or even village Khatris and Brahmins.[108] Greater exertion and exploitation might paradoxically be accompanied by higher access to consumption. The logic of colonial revenue and the rule for calculating net assets both permitted this disparity and erased it from view. By classifying the siri as an expense for the landholder, akin to maintaining a plow or digging a well, the political economy of this relationship was effaced by the routine of keeping accounts. A human being became just another reified item on the unseen balance sheet of an agrarian enterprise.

Yet the siri was never merely an input within a process but an individual with material and social needs as well as desires and agency in a changing society. The imputed formalism of the relationship was belied by the brief disclosures of discontent and maneuvering at each end of the hierarchy in these very village surveys. Elements of wellbeing, fairness, and trust became the terrain of constant if unspectacular contestation. In Gaggar Bhana, the researcher noted that although siris "are always allowed to eat as much as they want" from the cultivator's home, "it is a common cause of grumbling among the small farmers that their labourers eat away their profits."[109] The situation could be more acute, as in Gijhi, where some landowners would force field laborers to work for low wages when they could receive higher rates outside the village. "In these circumstances it is not surprising that the relations between the zamindars and the kamins are very strained," requiring village *panchayets* (councils) to mediate. The struggle, however, was between unequal parties: despite the boldness of the kamins, "the threats of the zemindars to refuse permission to the kamins to graze their cattle in the village waste, which is the property of the owners, and *fear of starvation*, soon reduced them to submission."[110]

More obliquely, the apparent solidity of custom would bend under a shifting balance of power. At harvest laborers were entitled to an extra bundle of unthreshed wheat at the end of each day. Usually they would take a small bundle, worth a quarter of a rupee (4 annas), but if they "know that their employer cannot do without them they bring away as heavy a bundle as they can carry worth about 8 annas."[111] Beyond such slights, subversion could also be more organized and therefore more substantial. In Suner, the researcher reports that the two siris guarding the crop "of their master" had entered into "a conspiracy and managed every day to take away some grain which they kept collecting at one place." Soon they were caught, leading to a panchayet meeting where it was decided to settle the issue internally by making them return the stolen grain—amounting to over a thousand pounds—and pay a fine of ten rupees. After the resolution however, two policemen "happened to reach the village and hearing of the matter called the two culprits and, it was alleged, took [a further] Rs. 5 each from them."[112] In these and countless other ways, the apparent order and reciprocity between cultivators and siris was in fact riven with regular if not always acknowledged turmoil. Tehl Singh's contract was so askew because Chaugutta could resort to straining customary entitlements, pilfering grain, evading tasks, and even escaping the village to preserve or improve his own meager position.[113]

Cultivation in the early twentieth century Panjab thus permitted a discrete division of neither labor nor laborers. Siri participation interrupted the narrative of menial laborers as mere ancillaries in the shadow of the autonomous peasant. Throughout the colonial period and beyond, a person plowing a field or harvesting a crop would just as likely be a Jatt as a Chamar or Churha. Their relationship might better be described as an asymmetrical agreement between two caste-bound individuals—*one with land and its entitlements and the other without*—combining their labor in order to cultivate the holdings of the former. Yet even this binary is complicated by the fact that the two parties performed parallel tasks and consumed similar foods (though probably not in identical quantities) while receiving disproportionate shares from the same harvest. As noted by one researcher, in rural Panjab "social taboo on account of the neglect of observance of caste regulations is practically unknown."[114] The collective labors of cultivation therefore simultaneously disregarded and obfuscated caste hierarchy by ignoring the most obvious proscriptions on segregated exertion while strictly upholding a stark disparity in returns.

QUESTIONING THE CASTE QUESTION

The political economy of Dalit conversion in Panjab thereby challenges the conventional framing of the question of caste in colonial South Asia. It reveals a critical limit to Ambedkar's arguments from *Annihilation of Caste*. From at least the sixteenth century onward, there had already developed a culture of religious critique and social equality that overturned the dominance of Brahmins and the authority of the *Vedas*. Kabir's sublime yet devastating five-hundred-year-old wit reached further and resonated deeper among the lower castes than any modern politician's speech. The advent of Sikhi not only codified, amplified, and circulated this message but also implemented it through deliberate violations of the purity/pollution ideology. The constraints of this transformation, the persistence of ideas and practices of a certain kind of untouchability, reflected the constraints on the possibility of transforming Panjabi society in that era as well as the interests of certain powerful new beneficiaries (such as Jatts but also Khatris) of that hierarchy.

By the twentieth century, Ambedkar's call for untouchables to abandon Hinduism had been preempted not only by longstanding conversion to Sikhi, Islam, and later Christianity but also by nearly a decade of independent lower-caste organizing in Panjab. After its founding in 1926, the

Ad Dharm articulated a vision of untouchable Panjabis constituting a distinct qaum with its own history, beliefs, and traditions on par with other religious communities. It registered almost half a million adherents in a census five years before the never-delivered Lahore speech. Although its political capacity gradually waned, Ad Dharm created educational institutions and a dispersed religious network that continues to instill reverence for Ravidas and self-respect among Panjabi Dalits to the present day.[115] While Ambedkar's efforts brought untouchable issues to the forefront of a new all-India audience, much of the content of that struggle had longer, more radical, and more compelling antecedents.

Despite their differences, Ad Dharm and Ambedkar professed a common solution to the predicament of untouchables. Both believed in and attempted to bring about their emancipation in part through conversion from Hinduism into either a new or alternative faith (Ad Dharm or Buddhism). Answering the caste question with religious conversion invokes a parallel debate from nearly a century earlier in Europe. Karl Marx's 1843 essay "On the Jewish Question" analyzes the limitations of liberalism to address the problem of difference-as-discrimination by contrasting political and human emancipation. He begins by discussing how, during the nineteenth century, many thinkers argued that overcoming the religious bigotry faced by Jews in Christian Prussia required a secular state that recognized the equal rights of all its citizens. For Marx, however, this meant forcing individuals to live "a double existence"—artificially split between public citizen and private individual—to only partially relate as equals in one domain of life while continuing to experience discrimination in the other.[116] Aligning the difference of religiosity with the difference of inferiority, he points out that people "do not cease to be religious by virtue of being religious in *private*." That is why "the state can liberate itself from a constraint [such as religion] without man himself being *really* liberated."[117]

Since the exclusion of Jews persists even in an explicitly nonreligious state—for Marx this condition of secularism was epitomized by America more than France—political emancipation from Christianity does not abolish religious bigotry itself but merely displaces it from a newly constituted public sphere into a private one, where its effects become normalized features of everyday life. In this sense, the predicament of the Jew serves as a stand-in for any inequality derived from difference, religious or otherwise, that manages to live on despite its repudiation by the state. That an individual can be at once both Jew and citizen—subordinate and equal—belies the very claim to overcoming religious disparity in this manner.

The same holds true of property. The "political suppression of private property," argues Marx, "not only does not abolish private property; it actually presupposes its existence." In other words, ownership qualifications for participation in public life might end, but vast disparities in ownership itself would continue unabated. Crucially, Marx extends his argument to other forms of hierarchy, stating that the "difference between the religious man and the citizen is the same as that between the shopkeeper and the citizens, between the day-laborer and the citizen, between the landed proprietor and the citizen, between the *living individual and the citizen*."[118] Thus while the secular state "certainly represents a great progress" in denying sanction to certain discriminatory practices, it falls short of abolishing those practices themselves.[119] Inequities not only remain but are rendered natural. In contrast, Marx offers human emancipation, a horizon where the values of secularism and equality transcend the confines of the public sphere to penetrate all dimensions of social existence. It is through this prospective, aleatory politics, realized "when the real, individual man has absorbed into himself the abstract citizen," that society might achieve an expansive, holistic emancipation worthy of its potential.[120]

Of course, the distinctive history and shifting conditions of colonial Panjab does not permit any direct application of continental prescriptions. Discussions over religious conversion in fact occurred in a context markedly dissimilar to Western Europe and with even narrower parameters.[121] Lower castes might emancipate themselves in one sense by abandoning a faith that stigmatized them as inferior and impure. They might also enact this rejection openly, as Ambedkar eventually ceased to seek entry into Hindu temples and Ad Dharm created its own distinct places of worship. The postcolonial Indian state further contributed to this process, perhaps best demonstrated by making illegal the very use of caste names such as "Churha." But within the sphere of the agrarian economy, lower castes would have little choice other than to continue in the debilitating labors that structured their daily existence. A Christian Bhangi to an upper caste in Karimpur still did the work of a Bhangi. The rejection of a dominant religion by an individual could exist alongside the continuation of exclusionary and exploitative conditions. Ad Dharm's threat to convert lower castes from Hinduism or to leave Sikhi was thus not a direct challenge to the new agrarian hierarchy of rural Panjab. Indeed, both Ad Dharm and the primacy of the hereditary and singular caste peasant were novel cultural and economic productions born of the same colonial encounter.

A sign of the import of this new religion may be measured elsewhere, in the realm of dignity and the empowering of the lower castes to meet the gaze of their purported superiors. Just before concluding fieldwork in Jalandhar in the late 1960s, Kessinger revealed a brief exchange with a Chamar interlocutor who happened to be his friend and roommate. Imploring the latter to hurry up and take a set of keys from him, his unnamed friend, "while strolling slowly," replied with a steady, striking nonchalance: "Chamars don't run any more."[122] The old culture of fear-tinged deference was eroding, even as a new economy based on caste power and land ownership was being consolidated.

Perhaps the most powerful impediment to the possibility of lower-caste emancipation was the naturalization of that very hierarchy. No one was landless in Panjab until the nineteenth century because no one was landed. By aligning caste with occupation, colonial rule disrupted, reordered, and concretized a new relationship between collective identity, laboring activity, and land ownership. As cultivation became the exclusive domain of Jatts and other artificially constituted agricultural tribes, various castes diminished to the status of menials came to be identified with particular subsidiary tasks. Yet as the village surveys repeatedly showed, agrarian production was a diffuse, changing set of activities requiring contributions from a range of individuals, exemplified by the figure of the siri. The rapidly evolving technological environment throughout the twentieth century only exacerbated this polarity. Simply put, whereas land itself did not become "obsolete" and remained the critical source of rural power, every other supposedly traditional or inherent occupation eventually did: steel buckets replaced the Kumhar's clay pots while cloth from Manchester overtook the Julaha's homespun and market razors displaced the Nai's service; later, submersible pumps and tractors substituted the Mehra's water carrying and the Tarkhan's plow. All of these caste groups either found some reprieve in emerging urban industries or overseas emigration or, more likely, swelled the ranks of the landless laborers already occupied by Chamars and Churhas. Neither timeless nor hereditary, the division of labor and laborers in Panjab was a modern phenomenon yoked through colonialism to both economic imperatives and cultural categories invested with the aura of antiquity.

What Marx illuminates, then, is the contradictory ideology that underpinned material relations in early twentieth-century Panjabi society. For rural untouchables, the stigma of caste was felt not only through spiritual denigration or social distancing, or repeating the perverse injunctions of Manu. It was experienced in the routine of performing much of the same labors as a landholder while receiving only a fraction of the returns. A new qaum could not be equal to other religious communities if the extent of its demand for equality was to seek better employment conditions for its adherents from its antagonists. To a Hindu, Sikh, or Muslim landowner, a siri identifying as an Ad Dharmi or Mazhabi or Mussali remained a menial laborer. At the same time, this struggle cannot be judged against an ahistorical standard of "universal" or "human" emancipation. Higher agricultural wages and access to vacant common land continues to be a major element in the landless labor movement in east Panjab today, while in west Panjab the most prominent activism revolves around acquiring ownership rights for tenants on military-owned lands.[123] Ambedkar too was not unaware of the foundations of this inequity: as law minister of independent India, he finally abolished the Punjab Alienation of Land Act examined in Chapters 2 and 3. In this sense, the cancellation of his speech might have been ultimately, if unintentionally, productive. Instead of appearing as a pragmatic appeal directed to an audience that had already taken more radical initiatives, his text circulated elsewhere across colonial India and beyond as a poignant source of inquiry, provocation, and subversion.

Yet it is possible that at least some of Chaugutta's descendants are still working for Tehl Singh's grandchildren to this day. Material disparities between the two will continue whatever their religious parity as long as efforts for equality are confined to greater remuneration for the former while leaving unquestioned the holdings of the latter. The politics of Ad Dharm, though effective in rupturing the limits of one kind of colonial public/private difference, thus simultaneously encountered another set of limitations. While the world of caste may have been turned upside down by Guru Nanak, Kabir, and early Sikhi, losing both sanctity and tangibility, the one encountered by Mangoo Ram had its own distinctive ideology and features combined with a new tenacity. What was novel by the beginning decades of the twentieth century was a scientifically produced, fiscally bound, and legally enforced system that restructured rural relations through the colonial idiom of caste identity. Ownership of land became a consequence of the very modernity of caste. We thus still await a politics with the imaginative capacity and material force to overcome rather than overturn the recent configuration of this agrarian hierarchy.

FIVE

PRODUCING A THEORY OF INADEQUACY
*Adam Smith, Karl Marx, and the
Political Economy of Comparison*

THE UNIVERSAL CATEGORY OF the peasant goes awry sometime after the sixteenth century. This is captured by a curious marking of difference in Raymond Williams's 1976 definition from *Keywords*. The word *peasant*, which derives from the old French *pagus*, meaning country district, entered common English in the fifteenth century. At that point it was often indistinguishable from *rustic*, both words implying someone "working on the land as well as living in the country."[1] The unity and simplicity of that meaning, however, would not last. According to Williams, the word encountered a "special difficulty" during the "social and economic transformation in agriculture" between the sixteenth and nineteenth centuries. With the relationship between small landholders and aristocratic lords dissolving and a volatile new arrangement of landlords, tenants, and laborers emerging, this sense of peasant had by the late eighteenth century "virtually ceased to exist in England."[2] Not only was it no longer possible to speak of the "peasant" in the same way, but the word underwent a more important geographic as well as linguistic bifurcation. In English, along with French and Russian, *peasant* became "a loose term of abuse" for "'uneducated' or 'common' people," while in Third World usage it "still" carried the sense of "a distinct social and economic group," which, at times, also took on "heroic revolutionary connotations."[3] A pejorative for that which ceased in the West came to be a compliment for what persisted in the East.

Such a captivating definition from the metropole travels uncomfortably to the colony. The celebration of the peasant—resolute and heroic though not quite revolutionary—has nowhere been more evident in the British Empire than Panjab. But as demonstrated in Chapters 2 and 3, the very word *peasant* did not have a single equivalent in early nineteenth-century Panjabi. It might be rendered as *kisan* or *hali* or *zamindar* or even *kheti karn vala*, not to mention *Jatt*, *Arain*, or *Pathan*. These terms corresponded to individuals and groups engaged in some of the many labors of cultivation without unanimity across all regions and contexts. The "inevitable failure of translation,"[4] however, led to a paralysis of neither the colonial state nor the operations of capital. Instead, the imperatives of rule produced a new alignment between identity and activity, enacted though multiple iterations of the census and culminating in the 1901 Punjab Alienation of Land Act. Now a modern legal category—"agricultural tribe"—not only delimited certain groups as inherently suited to cultivation but also gave them exclusive rights to participate in the land market. And as shown in Chapter 4, those rendered menial laborers and landless siris only found ways to interpolate their struggle against subordination through competing religious affiliations. As a result, the singular hereditary caste-based peasant emerged as a product of the distinctive yet entangled forces of colonialism and capitalism.

The textured history of the peasant explicated in this book has no place in Williams's brief exposition. It is not part of the way he traces the evolution of the peasantry in Europe, nor its apparent prolongation in the Third World. However, this is not merely the shortcoming of a single unmistakably perceptive and influential critic. It is too convenient, and with little substance, to find presentist or technical fault with the statements of earlier thinkers. Dwelling on a contradiction is as unhelpful as dismissing it. Instead, as Andrew Sartori argues in a similar context, "there is also a history to be told about the very availability, plausibility, and purchase of political-economic concepts as modalities of claims making."[5] In other words, the way a concept acquires meaning is bound up with its subsequent analytical value and explanatory force. The landscape of peasant history therefore exceeds its strictly colonial confines to the wider condition of possibility for comparison across global contexts.

From that perspective, the real value of the discrepancy in Williams's definition lies in how it indicates the rationality of peasant difference and the universalizing of economic concepts. He assumes that a worldwide peasantry existed until a shift in certain relations brought it to an end in one part of the world while allowing it to remain in another. This formulation is uncanny, at once obvious and unsettling. Indeed, it is not an exaggeration to say that this purported asymmetry—usually posited in the language of "divergence" or "transition"—has for decades been the site of empirical and theoretical research across the disciplines of history, anthropology, sociology, political science, and economics.[6] Rather than attempting to resolve this dilemma with another, ever more comprehensive narrative, I instead explore the conceptual itinerary of its emergence. If the transformative force of capitalism is undeniable, so too is the implication of inferiority—material but also cultural and temporal—for those who appear obstinately untransformed. Equally troubling is perfunctorily mapping the binary of development/underdevelopment onto general measures of prosperity and poverty in different world regions. Why did the peasant become such an intractable problem for so many officials and scholars? How did it acquire notions of antiquity, inadequacy, and an expectation to change? And what does that mean for the way we understand the supposed logics of capital unfolding unevenly across the globe?

This chapter charts the capricious career of the peasant as an object of intellectual inquiry. Through certain moments in the genealogy of this category, I examine how different political, economic, and historicist notions shaped its modern composition and trajectory. By putting forward a set of theoretical arguments, the archive for this chapter is unusual in that it relies mainly on texts published in Europe during the late eighteenth and nineteenth centuries, excavating their contentions and interrogating their implications. I begin with the pivotal turn-of-the-century books by Vladimir Lenin and Karl Kautsky. Combining conceptual insights and empirical data with a political program, their investigations shared much but differed on the nature and direction of the changes taking place in parts of rural Europe. In plotting competing futures for the peasant question, Lenin and Kautsky established a crucial series of expectations for the transition to capitalism. I then trace this burden upon the peasant back to the foundational work of Adam Smith and the very inception of the discipline of political economy. It is at this conjuncture, I argue, that the peasant acquired a set of qualities that were the opposite of what was supposed to be its future, the worker. Smith used agriculture as a deprived backdrop to explicate how consumption based on a new division of labor unique to manufacturing was the true measure of modern wealth. Through constant assertion, comparison, and extrapolation, he assembled the raw elements of a theory of peasant inadequacy. Finally, I consider how lesser-known writings of Karl Marx offer an unconventional and far-reaching critique of political economy as an exercise of bourgeois dominance. Marx challenged Smith's method of making authoritative statements from contingent conditions in order to reveal the ideological underpinnings of what became the common sense of capitalism. Perhaps most significantly, Marx offered not an alternative answer to that same question but a way to confront the assumptions and elisions of any "timeless," "natural" order. Thus by analyzing the categories of knowledge that structure narratives of material difference, those differences and the hierarchies they entail are made conspicuous, and contestable. Alongside the specific details of historical subjects and contexts, new comparative histories of the Global South and North therefore require understanding the production, evaluation, and deployment of worldwide difference.

QUESTIONING THE PEASANT QUESTION

The year 1899 witnessed the publication of two texts that provide a crucial entry point into the contemporary study of the peasant. Lenin's *The Development of Capitalism in Russia* and Kautsky's *The Agrarian Question* inaugurated a shift in the investigation of rural economic life. Unlike earlier works dealing with peasants—largely distant and antiquarian commentaries, polemical tracts of different political persuasions, or the results of colonial encounters as seen in Chapters 1 and 4—Lenin and Kautsky adopted a different approach. Written independently although at nearly the same time, both texts were innovatively conceived and empirically grounded with an explicit focus on the peasant. Neither Lenin nor Kautsky were connected with any state authority at the time of writing, giving their works a rare degree of political autonomy. Both were carefully researched and based on extensive official and unofficial archives. Lenin in particular made abundant use of the house-to-house census material produced by the *zemstovs* (new provincial and district assemblies), which, according to one contemporary scholar, "constitute perhaps the most ample single source of data we have on the peasant economy of any country in modern times."[7] Due to their intersecting careers, combined with the circulation of their texts among a highly politicized audience, Lenin and Kautsky established much of the terrain of future scholarship.[8] Together they produced the peasant as a phenomenon requiring sustained analysis not only in Russia or continental Europe but across the world.

The significance of Lenin and Kautsky's investigations of the peasantry begins with their very formulation. Both pose the issue in the form of a question—explicitly in Kautsky's title, more diffusely though evident in Lenin as well.[9] The agrarian question—or rather, the peasant question[10]—encompasses a number of themes: the character of household labor, the impact of new agricultural technologies, the relationship between commodity production and foreign markets, the trends of peasant differentiation and land fragmentation, the future potential of capital in the countryside.[11] It is worth considering, however, how this formulation is implicated in a larger genre of political and philosophical inquiry. A series of intractable "Questions" dominated public discourse in the nineteenth century—Jewish, Women's, Negro, Irish—which also extended into the twentieth and twenty-first centuries—Southern, Palestine, Immigrant, Muslim. What does it mean for such a range of issues to be articulated in the form of open-ended questions?[12]

Intervening in debates over the interpretation of Marx's oeuvre, Louis Althusser offers the imperative that "it must first be asked *the question of its questions*."[13] Rather than simply tabulating the different elements of Marx's thought, which often results in an amalgam of degrees of influence from Immanuel Kant, Georg W. F. Hegel, and Ludwig Feuerbach,[14] he argues for thinking through the constitutive tension between a particular idea and the broader ideological field of social problems and material structures within which it occurs.[15] An idea, or a question, cannot be understood by reference to its own interiority; it is never coterminous with its content. Instead, it is to be located in relation to the wider if diffuse range of assumptions and propositions which make possible its articulation. Only when understood in this way—no longer a self-referential explanation but in unity with its conditions—can a question gesture toward an answer.[16] Investigations that pose questions are at once already posing something else in the process.

Common to all of these "questions," then, is the catachresis of their conceptualization as questions in the first place. The genre itself is an act of misnaming a puzzling, urgent problem. Consider again perhaps the most penetrating exposition of this formulation, Marx's 1844 essay "On the Jewish Question." As explored in Chapter 4, the figure of the Jew is deployed as a split between private person and universal citizen to demonstrate the limits of the liberal state. "The emancipation of the state from religion," Marx argues, "is not the emancipation of the real man from religion."[17] Rather, it is a perverse sleight of hand that erects a hollow and dependent public realm in order to leave intact all manner of inequality and inequity in the private realm. In that sense, the Jewish question is actually the problem of the Jew (as an alibi for any form of difference) for the emancipatory claims of secular liberalism. From another angle, this argument is more forcefully made in W.E.B. Du Bois's articulation of the Negro question. In *The Souls of Black Folk*, published in 1903, he not only names "the Negro Problem" as the "concrete test of the underlying principles of the great republic" after the failure of Reconstruction but evocatively states that ubiquitously "unasked question" by whites to blacks: "how does it feel to be a problem?"[18] Again, the Negro question is the problem of genuine liberty amid the contempt, exclusion, and violence of American society. Behind the tremor of a question lies the intensity of a problem.

If the peasant question is, in fact, the problem of the peasant, then what kind of a problem is it, and for whom? Here the circumstances of the turn of the century provide the outlines of an answer. In Lenin's case, 1899 offered an opportunity for the itinerant and underground revolutionary to work out a dilemma of Russian society that came to be replicated the world over. A small and nascent proletariat surrounded by tens of millions of seemingly backward peasants complicated the prospects for socialist revolution. While the peasantry represented an immediate problem of developing collective consciousness and coordinating a plan of action for the countryside, they were at the same time an abstract problem of understanding the nature of class conflict and the course of economic progress at large. These two concerns were more immediate for Kautsky, as his personal interests in agrarian matters converged with his duty as a leader of Germany's Social Democratic Party (SPD). It became evident at the end of the nineteenth century that the party required a coherent practical as well as conceptual position on agricultural society. Since "agricultural developments have given rise to phenomena which do not appear to be reconcilable with Marxist theories," Kautsky explains in his introduction, the agrarian question has also "become a central problem of theory."[19] It is this urgency that defines the peasant as not simply a question to be answered or left unanswered but a discrete yet broad political and theoretical responsibility impossible for Lenin or Kautsky to avoid.

ANTICIPATING THE HISTORY OF THE FUTURE

To urban revolutionaries, Kautsky acknowledges, "the peasant was a mystical, incomprehensible and perhaps even sinister being."[20] Implicit in the peasant problem is the notion of the class's continuity from a distant past, a primordial and unchanging way of life interrupted only by the turbulence of early capitalism. Both Lenin's and Kautsky's narratives are underpinned by a sharp sense of the temporality and potentiality of this conjuncture. "Before capitalism appeared," writes Lenin, "agriculture in Russia was the business of the gentry, a lord's hobby for some, and a duty, an obligation for others."[21] Kautsky is more precise about identifying this anterior, noting that the existing form of agricultural production in Germany and much of Europe emerged after the popular migrations and settlements of the fifth century.[22] From this remote origin, a particular value is ascribed to the social and economic organization that appears to persist over the ensuing centuries. During this time, according to Lenin, peasants "vegetated behind their medieval partitions," living an "age-old routine" of "local seclusion and insularity."[23] This resulted in "the complete isolation of the cultivator from all that went on in the world beyond the confines of his village."[24] Within that space, the rhythms of life occurred through the "indestructible" institution of the family farm, which, Kautsky explains, "not only produced its own food, but also built its own house, made its own furniture and household implements, and even constructed most of its own crude tools, tanned its own leather, worked flax and wool and made its own clothing."[25] Between isolation and self-sufficiency, the history of peasant life reflects a repetition of strictly limited activities and ambitions.

Such a condition became inadequate in contrast to the newfound possibilities of modern industrial society. Here Lenin's and Kautsky's emphases differ. Lenin is forthright in confronting what he regards as the shortcomings intrinsic to peasant life, though not only in the most obvious ways. He shares arguments about the superiority of urban industry to rural agriculture but suggests other related domains of social life that are equally problematic. In recognizing how large cities produce the "treasures of science and art," Lenin calls for the "abolition of the antithesis between town and country."[26] To the accusation that this would homogenize and invalidate these refined pursuits, his answer is clear. Such abolition is necessary precisely in order to bring these avenues of self and social development "within the reach of the whole of the people" to "abolish that isolation from culture of millions of the rural population."[27] This is an argument, in other words, against the circumscribed quality of life that isolated living and labor entails when compared to what can be achieved in a larger metropolis. Rather than accepting the timelessness of a drudging and truncated existence, Lenin embraces the arrival of the conditions that produce the possibility—in his mind—of genuine human fulfilment for the very first time.

Kautsky, on the other hand, describes more of the deprivations of peasant life at the cusp of change. "Impelled by the goad of competition," the specter of "overwork" appears as production begins to shift from immediate consumption to market exchange.[28] This leads to a situation where individual peasant households are increasingly forced to compete with large-scale agricultural enterprises. What is remarkable is not that the former at times survive and even succeed against the seemingly obvious superiority of the latter but how peasant households manage to do so. Kautsky terms this "the peasant art of starving," the ability of peasants to deploy both industriousness and frugality to prevent economic collapse.[29] Strategies include prolonging the workday and deploying child labor to maintaining the barest of houses, severely curtailing diet, and almost completely neglecting hygiene.[30] Such a minimal, indeed pitiful material existence also impinges upon the imagination. Living through privations reduces the peasant to the point where the pressure to produce atrophies the ability to think, so that "carefulness soon degenerates into meanness." After analyzing a report on peasant conditions from late nineteenth-century France, he remarks that so great is peasant hardship that "they seem even to lose utterly any capacity for pleasure."[31] For Kautsky, the endurance of peasant society occurs as a feat of desperate and self-inflicted material and mental miseries.

This is the world that is to be transformed with the advent of capitalism. Unsurprisingly, Lenin and Kautsky are in agreement with the positive devastation the new bourgeois mode of production will bring.[32] One becomes convinced of the "progressiveness of capitalism," Lenin explains, when witnessing how the "shattering to the very foundations the ancient forms of economy and life" lead to the creation of "new social classes striving of necessity toward contact, unification, and active participation in the whole of the economic (and not only economic) life of the country."[33] Kautsky is equally resolute in assessing the effects of capital: "the vagaries of the grain and cattle markets now manage to accomplish what poor harvests, fire and sword could never achieve," as "not merely temporary privation, but the alienation and ultimately the complete separation of the peasants from the source of their life and livelihood."[34] Capitalist change is therefore inseparable from dismantling and devastating peasant society.

Where Lenin and Kautsky differ most strikingly is over the precise trajectory of the impact of capital on peasant society. The future is brought to the fore by examining not only the process of change but also its direction. Lenin reads capitalism in Russia as precipitating the expansion and acceleration of the internal contradictions of peasant society toward a point of crisis. A key feature of this upheaval was "depeasantising" or the hastening of peasant differentiation, the "utter dissolution of the old, patriarchal peasantry and the creation of *new types* of rural inhabitants."[35] The countryside, in other words, would no longer remain populated by generic peasants. Instead, polarization was dividing the very content of the category into two novel, mutually antagonistic camps, "the rural bourgeoisie" and "the rural proletariat."[36] Based on landholding size, cultivation methods, and employment of outside labor, peasants of different social and economic standing were increasingly taking on the character of industrial relations. "Every crop failure," according to Lenin, "flings the masses of the middle peasants into the ranks of the proletariat," just as it catapults handfuls of successful large landholders into that of the bourgeoisie.[37] Urban class politics thus became the mirror for the unfolding dynamics of rural society.

Kautsky rejects this homology between urban and rural, at least initially. His analysis of the direction of capitalism makes explicit the unique quality of peasant production. "Agriculture," he declares, "does not develop according to the pattern traced by industry: it follows its own laws."[38] Yet from this flexible statement, Kautsky gradually becomes more ambiguous in tracing the path of capital in the countryside. Peasants were different from workers, yet the former were becoming the latter; the modern farm was a singular enterprise, but it had acquired capitalist features; and while agriculture as a whole developed distinct from industry, it was inherently inferior to the latter.[39] Throughout his text, Kautsky both asserts the polarization thesis and defends the viability of the peasant, even as he adds several qualifications.[40] At one point he even invokes an ethereal dualism not dissimilar to that found in Du Bois: "Two souls inhabit the breast of the dwarf-holder: a peasant and a proletarian," internally struggling over the course of the future without a preordained outcome.[41] The difficulty of Kautsky's position in fact reflects the bewildering complexity of the situation. With such uncertainty surrounding the process and path of change, Kautsky withdraws from affirming any single direction to instead express the multiplicity of possibilities for the question of the disappearance of the peasantry.

A UNIVERSAL END TO PEASANT SOCIETIES?
Despite what appears to be a contrast between Kautsky's openness to Lenin's dogma, such a divide takes for granted the usefulness of plurality. Articulations of multiple possibilities expand the horizon but often to the point of overwhelming the sense of sight altogether. Simply restating ambiguity does not fulfill the internal demands of analysis. In the task of devising a program for the SPD, Kautsky equivocates. Recognizing capitalism as both ineluctable and unpleasant, he remarkably concludes that "we cannot, and ought not, to impede capitalist development; but this does not mean that a proletarian socialist party has any reason to support it."

He goes on to explain the global implications of this position, noting that along with maintaining the peasantry, "it is a reactionary utopia to call upon [the SPD] to support the resistance of the indigenous peoples of the colonised countries against their expropriation."[42] The reasoning behind this opposition is telling:

> Such work *is too dirty for the proletariat to become an accessory*. The whole rotten business is one of the historic tasks of the bourgeoisie; and the proletariat should be glad not to have to soil its hands with it. There need be no worries that the bourgeoisie will neglect its duty and allow economic development to come to a standstill.[43]

By refusing to analyze the end of the peasantry, Kautsky ends up advocating for the SPD to effectively withdraw from the difficulties of analysis altogether.

Lenin's decisiveness, on the other hand, might be reread not as obstinacy but as the fulfillment of the requirements of his investigation. Although without an official sponsor, his thesis is an attempt to respond concretely to the prevailing understanding of the relationship between capitalism and the peasantry in Russia. The Narodniks, influential middle-class populists in the late nineteenth century, were foremost in opposing the onslaught of capitalism by celebrating the peasant as inherently anticapitalist and championing independent small-scale production as a viable economic alternative. Offering a twofold critique, Lenin argues that a romantic return to peasant production is neither desirable nor possible. Precapitalist production is not only "incomparably more burdensome" to the peasant, but more fundamentally it is in the midst of a radical and apparently irreversible transformation. The Narodniks, fearing that "an admission of the historically progressive nature of capitalism means an apology for capitalism," attempt to demonstrate that "this disproportionate, spasmodic, feverish development is not development."[44] The dilemma is false, Lenin points out, as soon as capitalism is understood to be simultaneously exploitative yet emancipatory, destroying the past while heralding the future in order to transform the peasant into the proletarian.

Perhaps more profoundly, the charge of Kautsky's ambiguity exceeds its context to shape the larger conceptualization of the peasant problem.

His position implies understanding peasant transformation as a global phenomenon. If within each peasant there is a competition to remain a peasant or change into a proletarian, then the future of any society is to be determined by assessing the relative strength of these two internal tendencies. From that vantage, in the late nineteenth century the struggle would appear to have long been decided in places like England, underway in Germany and Russia, while not even beginning in Panjab. Indeed, it is this formula that in part constituted the existence of peasants across the Third World during the latter half of the twentieth century as a sign of backwardness and continuity to be overcome through development and modernization.[45] Lenin, on the other hand, avoids imposing a rubric for all peasant societies by delineating the specificity of his object of inquiry. To argue that Russian peasants were undergoing a dramatic polarization—again, whatever its historical veracity—limits any worldwide explanatory pretensions.[46] Lenin makes explicit the pitfalls of doctrinal fidelity:

> Of course, infinitely diverse combinations of elements of this or that type of capitalist evolution are possible, *and only hopeless pedants could set about solving the peculiar and complex problems arising merely by quoting this or that opinion of Marx about a different historical epoch.*[47]

The "new type" of rural inhabitant Lenin describes therefore radically limits the notion of peasant continuity from the past by emphasizing the novelty of what capitalism is producing in specific context of Russia. Whereas for Kautsky the presence of the peasant in colonial Panjab might be a sign of the lack of sufficient proletarian strength within the soul of that individual, for Lenin this peasant would be an original phenomenon requiring its own historical analysis. Kautsky's claim of multiplicity thereby ends up imposing a surreptitious universalism for understanding all peasant societies.

From these intersecting yet conflicting discourses, a particular conception of the peasant emerges. Foremost, and regardless of differing emphases, the peasant enters modernity directly from antiquity. The antecedent to dramatic change is necessarily its opposite, some variation of a prolonged, even primordial stasis. There is also a given sense of the inferiority of the peasant in terms of the ability to produce as well as the quality of life. Even before peasants suffer the uncertainties of the market, they are somehow deficient and estranged, as inadequate to themselves as they are unfit for any world-historic task. Recognition of these limitations becomes widespread only with the appearance of more mature forms of "civilization," so that progress automatically implies industrialization. Finally, the peasantry carries the expectation to be transformed. Its presence is almost an affront to all that is modern, in need of both an explanation and a program for its rectification. As a result, the destiny of the peasantry is its own abrogation in order for the human content of the category to be reconstituted into the form of the worker. Through the writings of Lenin and Kautsky, the figure of the peasant appears at once ancient, backward, and always on the verge of change.

BACKWARDNESS AND THE DIVISION OF LABOR

The process of forming and fixing the peasant with inferiority and transience predates the crucible of early twentieth-century intra-Marxist debates. While Lenin and Kautsky's writings on the peasant consolidated and organized a set of qualities, imbued them with specific trajectories, and thereby established the terrain for subsequent investigations, they did not invent the ideas and vocabulary upon which their own studies relied. Indeed, the conceptualization of the modern peasant eludes a singular beginning. What is possible, and more valuable, is excavating the elemental logic that underpinned the making of the peasant problem. That line of inquiry points toward a longer *durée* of less explicit though nonetheless crucial mediations central to the discipline of political economy.

The writings of Adam Smith offer a compelling entry point into this problematic. As both economic theorist and moral philosopher, he inaugurated a new genre for the systematic study of market processes and social relations as well as the intellectual basis for advocating changes in state policies.[48] Smith's seminal *An Inquiry into the Nature and Causes of the Wealth of Nations*, composed over the span of twenty-seven years and published in 1776, is arguably the most influential treatment of the inner workings of exchange and manufacturing during a period of unparalleled tumult. Amartya Sen regards it as "monumental," while other scholars describe it as a "deep reservoir of ideas and arguments" and the "foundation for what became known as classical economics."⁴⁹ Within the context of the Scottish Enlightenment, Smith drew upon a range of predecessors and contemporaries: François Quesnay, David Hume, Francis Hutcheson, Bernard Mandeville, and John Locke, among others. In turn, he has been drawn upon differently since his death by a wider variety of thinkers such as Marx, Immanuel Kant, Jeremy Bentham, David Ricardo, and John Stuart Mill.⁵⁰ It would not be an exaggeration to say that Smith's ideas implicitly informed the attitudes and approaches of colonial officials in places like Panjab and the rest of the British Empire. Indeed, the divergent, even contradictory deployment of Smith over the centuries—by figures like Thomas Paine and Mary Wollstonecraft to Friedrich von Hayek and Milton Friedman—has spawned an entire literature dedicated to tracing both his influences and those he influenced.⁵¹

At the center of Smith's study of the principles of political economy lies a unique conceptualization of the idea of wealth.⁵² In an opening rebuke to mercantile orthodoxy that emphasized increasing exports over imports, he declares the general ability to consume, along with the labor that enables it, as the true measure of wealth. A nation is wealthy to the extent that it is able to provide its population with the "necessaries and conveniencies of life."⁵³ Consumption, as both a process and a hierarchical level, is regulated first by the quality of the labor applied and second by the ratio of the employed to the unemployed in the population. To explain this assertion, Smith offers two civilizational juxtapositions.⁵⁴ Why is it, he asks, that "among the savage nations of hunters and fishers," nearly every capable individual works strenuously to produce basic goods and yet those same nations "are so miserably poor" and afflicted with a host of desperate privations?⁵⁵ At the same time, "among civilized and thriving nations" a great many people do no useful work at all, yet the "produce of the whole labour of the society is so great" that even the poorest are "abundantly supplied" far beyond what "is possible for any savage to acquire."⁵⁶ The mere fact of hard work and high employment, while essential, are not in themselves sufficient to produce a superior standard of wealth. Measuring the wealth of nations thereby requires further elaboration.

A second juxtaposition demonstrates how Smith unpacks this conundrum. "The very meanest person in a civilized country" has access to an array of products and services that far "exceeds that of many an African king."⁵⁷ If consumption rather than acquisition is the sign of wealth, then its extent can be found in the range of goods one is able to consume. The superiority of poor Europeans to African royalty, according to Smith, is a reflection of the diverse range of options available to the former over the latter.

More significant than civilizational hierarchies is the new force that produces such a diversity of consumable options. Smith gives the example of what might be described as an itinerary of the woolen coat, an item that, "as course and rough as it may appear," is nonetheless indispensable to the lowest of day laborers in England. Its historic appearance is the result of the "the joint labour of a great multitude of workmen." The constellation includes shepherds, sorters, wool-combers, dyers, spinners, and weavers who "must all join their different arts in order to complete even this homely production." At the same time, merchants and carriers are required to transport materials between these different and distant workers and to deliver the final product to various markets. For this task of commerce and navigation, moreover, scores of shipbuilders, sailors, sailmakers, and rope-makers must also be employed in a series of complementary industries. All of these specialties further require an assortment of implements and materials to be able to work within their own fields, thus generating a layer of workers to produce supplies and repair things for other workers. Indeed, Smith exclaims, "what a variety of labour too is necessary in order to produce the tools of the meanest of those workmen!"⁵⁸ If such a tremendous ensemble is required for the production of one relatively simple item, then an adequate appreciation of even a portion of common household consumables "exceeds all computation."⁵⁹ A society's wealth thus becomes evident at the confluence of the amount and range of goods it produces.

Understood in this way, however, the formula for wealth conceals a slippage between the subject of consumption and its production. According to Smith, those commenting on the sphere of activities beginning to be labeled "the economy" have mistaken effect for cause. An expression of wealth is erroneously given as its basis. "It is not because one man keeps a coach while his neighbour walks a-foot," explains Smith, "that the one is rich and the other poor." Rather, it is "*because* the one is rich he keeps a coach, and *because* the other is poor he walks a-foot."[60] Put differently, Smith deems that alehouses are not the cause of excessive public drinking but are instead an effect of a general disposition toward drunkenness.[61] The quality of being rich or poor, or even of being an alcoholic, is always an individual measured against the backdrop of social conditions and values. Instead of a person oscillating between consumption and production, a more accurate evaluation of wealth requires both an inversion and a recasting of the subject measured. What an individual is able to consume is part of what a society is able to produce.

The wealth of a society is thus a consequence of the dynamism and magnitude of its productive processes. For Smith, such immense outputs are only possible through the novel separation, organization, and application of labor. His inquiry proceeds with what David McNally describes as "a rapture for the division of labour," a phrase Smith is credited with popularizing and possibly even coining.[62] Labor, now practiced in a different way under different conditions, is the critical element that inaugurates a new epoch. Pin-making, Smith's famous allegorical example, best demonstrates the impact of the innovations at hand. Whereas the archaic pin-maker toiling alone could barely make one pin a day, let alone twenty, the new method of distributive labor divides pin-making into eighteen discrete tasks performed by ten workers who together produce almost forty-eight thousand pins in the same period.[63] What is remarkable about this increase is not only that it is exponential, and thus unlike any pattern of growth earlier in history, but that it is also presented as replicable in all other productive endeavors. "In every other art and manufacture," Smith states, "the effects of the division of labour are similar to what they are in this very trifling one."[64] As a specific process that is nonetheless reproducible in all aspects of human society, the division of labor is Smith's conceptual pivot toward modern wealth.

THE PRODUCTIVITY OF DIFFERENCES

The notion of the division of labor presupposes difference. Labor is only meaningfully divisible if there are already differences within a society to draw upon. The fixed assignment of a unique individual to a discrete task within an increasingly complex series initiates the potential for accelerated productivity. How difference occurs and becomes productive is therefore crucial to Smith's argument. At one level it appears arbitrary, the result not of "any human wisdom" but by "a certain propensity in human nature" to "truck, barter, and exchange."[65] This oft-emphasized phrase is usually regarded as the definitive gesture of naturalizing market relations. Yet in the very next paragraph, Smith troubles any direct connection between nature and exchange. If this "propensity be one of those original principles in human nature," then "no further account can be given," as its quality of innateness by definition precludes analysis. What "seems more probable," he suggests, is that this propensity is "the necessary consequence of the faculties of reason and speech."[66] Although Smith expresses disinterest in exploring the matter further, it is significant that the practice of exchange, and the difference upon which it is based, is distanced from the nature of human beings. While approving of market exchange as a whole, he presents the propensity to do so as one that emerges through historical processes rather than a biological urge.

The initial spectrum of human difference thus has a history. Smith evocatively critiques inherited, instinctual explanations by describing the coming of age of two "most dissimilar characters," a philosopher and a street porter. For the first eight or so years of life, they are practically indistinguishable from each other, so much so that "neither their parents nor playfellows [can] perceive any remarkable difference." Yet at some point, slight peculiarities in "talents" are noticed, gradually nurtured, and slowly expanded. This leads to differentiation between the two, which widens throughout adolescence toward the point of separation. Outright difference, as expressed through hierarchy, culminates when "at last the vanity of the philosopher is willing to acknowledge scarce any resemblance." A porter comes to stand apart from a philosopher, Smith explains, "not so much from nature" but "from habit, custom, and education."[67]

The question of self-interest is also given somewhat misplaced attention in most discussions of Smith's text. The morality of the pursuit of personal benefit is less important than what deliberate, interconnected action makes possible. It is true that the triumvirate of butcher, brewer, and baker do not so much provide dinner as offer it for sale, motivated not by benevolence but "from their regard to their own interest." However, while Smith perhaps approves of their motivation, what he actually emphasizes is the profound and fruitful interdependence of all human relations. Autarky is impossible; there is no such thing as an entirely independent person free from multiple bonds with others. Instead, a person, positioned "at all times in need of the co-operation and assistance of great multitudes," is always implicated in mutual relations of dependence and benefit.[68] This endless web of necessary connections is the exact opposite of a constraint, and is therefore not to be reduced or even lamented. Forms of social interaction beyond immediate circles of personal affinity and kinship are the constitutive feature that gives rise to society itself.

From this perspective, Smith's appreciation of the historicity of an individual's unique quality becomes clear. The productivity of differences is again illuminated through a primordial scene. "In a tribe of hunters or shepherds a particular person makes bows and arrows," explains Smith, "with more readiness and dexterity than any other."[69] This superior skill in turn activates a new logic of ability coupled to interest. The producers of bows and arrows exchange them for cattle and venison, so much so that they are able to cease hunting for personal need and instead focus on becoming full-time makers of arms.[70] A similar specialization occurs in every productive activity, stimulating "every man to apply himself to a particular occupation" in order to "cultivate and bring to perfection whatever talent or genius he may possess for that particular species of business."[71] Neither rendered natural nor diminished by self-interest, differences enhance the potential of human sociality.

It is this rudimentary account of difference that Smith carries into the realm of nascent class relations. The subtle distinctions made in bounded scenarios acquire greater significance when assembled and grafted onto the dynamics of a changing society. Smith uses income—as the agent that allows wealth to be expressed in the form of the wool coat—to establish a threefold division of society. The rent of land, the wages of labor, and the profits of stock correspond to "three different orders of people": landlords, workers, and capitalists.[72] Since the first group obtains its income by inheritance rather than effort, it is destined in Smith's estimation to become indolent, "incapable of that application of mind" necessary for active public participation.[73] Flaws are also found in the second group, workers, who live according to forces beyond their control or comprehension, existing in precarious ineptitude and thus rendered negligible to societal participation. The third group, however, holds distinct advantages over the other two. Capitalists engaged in profit are better informed and are more committed and inclined to work together as a class to fulfil their interests. Whereas landlords and workers are too afflicted to participate fully in society, Smith posits capitalists as having the ability to command the direction of the whole. Difference loses its innocence once society comes to be shaped by the political dimension of economic processes.

AGRICULTURE, UNDIVIDED LABOR, AND MODERNITY

The division of labor is what distinguishes modern society from its antecedents in Smith's narrative. Elements in his formulations cohere into fixed logics that find purpose in the entanglements of impersonal relations of exchange. This binary is evident almost from the inception of Smith's discourse. Wealth brought about through a division of labor is meaningful only in contrast to its opposite, undivided labor. Smith alludes to what this "other" of the market would entail. "In that rude state of society in which there is no division of labour," he explains, people can only hope to be fulfilled by their own immediate efforts. Undifferentiated and independent, "every man endeavours to supply by his own industry his own occasional wants as they occur." As a result;

> When he is hungry, he goes to the forest to hunt; when his coat [evidently not woolen] is worn out, he clothes himself with the skin of the first large animal he kills: and when his hut begins to go to ruin, he repairs it, as well as he can, with the trees and the turf that are nearest it.

In this bleak and exhausting state of affairs "in which exchanges are seldom made, and in which every man provides every thing for himself," there is a fantastical absence of social ties.[74] It is an atomized backwardness prior to even the primitive, verging on the primeval. Pin-making, and all the relations it entails, is unthinkable.

A few stages up from this base condition is hardly any better. Without "a great town" for the bounty of the division of labor to be manifest,

Smith points out, individuals are still bound by their individuality, so that "every farmer must be butcher, baker and brewer for his own family."[75] It is significant that the faults of autonomy—as the other of interdependence—are exemplified by a rural, agricultural setting. Smith describes families scattered in innumerable villages, isolated and estranged from each other, preoccupied to the point of barely meeting basic needs. The reason is that this form of social organization precludes specialization, as each family "must learn to perform themselves a great number of little pieces of work."[76] Such tedious dedication, necessarily distributed across countless minor tasks, cannot but result in deficiencies of output, quality, and efficiency. For Smith, labor performed through division in manufacturing enterprises based in cities provides an antidote to the endemically unfocused and overburdened nature of rural agriculture.

Beyond dependency, there is a more intractable limit to agricultural production. Its object, by and large, is the production of food. Abundantly producible yet perishable, food can only be consumed in fixed quantities and at regular intervals. Smith makes a striking observation about its unique purpose and potential. "The desire of food," he states, "is limited in every man by the narrow capacity of the human stomach."[77] It is this physiological property that renders the production of food both the basis for all human civilization as well as an insurmountable barrier to its future development: a necessity that is incapable of exceeding the horizon of need. He goes on to relate another primeval moment where, gradually, the labor of one is able to provide for two, when "the labour of half the society becomes sufficient to provide food for the whole." Only at this point does it become possible for that other half of the population to pursue other interests, to begin to conceive and produce other things, to engage in satisfying an ever-expanding range of "wants and fancies of mankind." Yet here Smith offers another contrast, this one between classes, to demonstrate the curious way this difference is expressed. There are intrinsic limits to food production:

> The rich man consumes no more food than his poor neighbor. In quality it may be very different, and to select and prepare it may require more labour and art; but in quantity it is very nearly the same.

No such similarities, and therefore limits, exist between goods other than food:

> But compare the spacious palace and great wardrobe of the [rich], with the hovel and the few rags of the [poor], and you will be sensible that the difference between their clothing, lodging, and household furniture, is almost as great in quantity as it is in quality. [. . .] The desire of the conveniencies and ornaments of building, dress, equipage, and household furniture, seems to have no limit or certain boundary.[78]

In this way, Smith establishes a basic hierarchical difference between productive activities. Food production, while undoubtedly essential, is at the same time limited and limiting. Other goods, however, entail no constraints, as they can be both produced and consumed endlessly. The corn of Poland is similar to that of France and England, but, according to Smith's tastes, French silk and English woolens are far superior to any Polish cloth.[79] Anyone's hunger can be quelled by a loaf of bread, but a connoisseur's sartorial thirst is only quenched by specific delicacies.

Smith calibrates the difference of food production with the production of all other commodities to a certain way of organizing social and economic relations. The implicit questions being asked are: Where is food produced? By whom? And under what conditions? The answer points to a state of affairs without a division of labor, the possibility of specialization, or the ability to produce in perpetuity—in other words, rural peasants producing largely in isolation. Agriculture, beset with all its inadequacies, thereby constitutes the universal backdrop from which its opposite emerges. As the other of a present en route toward the future, agrarian production serves to accentuate, even exacerbate what it can never be. "The nature of agriculture," Smith declares, "does not admit of so many subdivisions of labour, nor of so complete a separation of one business from another, as manufacturers."[80] Only urban workers producing together in manufacturing enterprises make possible the goods that fulfill social needs beyond food. Pins, coats, lavish dinners, and whatever else are more than simply items to be consumed; rather, they are itineraries of the circumstances that produce them as much as indications of the level of civilization that consumes them.

THE OTHER OF THE WORKER

The ideological limitations of agriculture find their counter in the infinite potential of manufacture. More precisely, if the negative critique of agriculture indicates an affirmation of industrial production, there is also a parallel extolling of industry that relies on a debasement of agrarian production. The first articulation of the unique superiority of industry in Smith actually comes from an unlikely source: a critique of slavery.[81] Rather than any utopian humanist or spiritual opposition, however, his position rests on decidedly more pragmatic grounds. "The wear and tear of a slave [. . .] is at the expense of his master," he points out, while "that of the free servant is at his own expense."[82] In addition, the paltry amount set aside by the master for the slave's upkeep is usually squandered by a careless or cunning overseer. Since free laborers, by which Smith seems to mean manufacturing workers, are responsible for their own sustenance, this same fund is instead managed with utmost prudence. As a result, the health of slaves deteriorates quicker, requiring the master to incur greater expense in their rehabilitation and eventual replacement. Free laborers—so long as they are freely available to sell their labor, as discussed in Chapter 1—entail no such obligations.[83] But Smith faults slave productivity on another level as well. "The experience of all ages and nations," he states, "demonstrates that the work done by slaves, though it may appear to only cost their maintenance, is in the end the dearest of any." This is so because the impetus for work relies on open force without the possibility of reward. While a slave "can have no interest but to eat as much, and to labour as little as possible,"[84] a worker, on the other hand, is propelled to constantly increasing output by the lure of personal benefit. Thus, Smith argues, "the work done by freemen comes cheaper in the end than that performed by slaves."[85]

The boon that is the division of labor becomes evident when free workers replace slaves in productive enterprises. Three distinct qualities appear exclusively at the site of industrial production. Workers dedicated to a single repetitive task (or perhaps a few of the eighteen required for pins) acquire greater dexterity over time and thereby increase the amount of work performed. From the standpoint of output, efficiency demands monotony. Second, this fixity reduces the time lost moving between different tasks. "A man commonly saunters a little in turning his hand from one sort of employment to another,"[86] Smith acutely notes, an indiscretion to be gradually eliminated with the discipline of factory supervision. Finally, such singularized labor encourages workers to innovate along the productive process as well. "Men are much more likely to discover easier and readier methods of attaining any object" when "the whole of their minds is directed towards that single object."[87] The rise of machines, according to Smith, is the result of a long series of spontaneous, creative efforts of workers to reduce their own work. Whereas a slave is without incentive to develop skills or save either time or labor, and might even be punished for the attempt to do so, a worker is conditioned by the very conditions of production toward those ends.

These distinct elements find expression in the newfound possibilities of accumulation. The limitless quality of industrial goods in comparison with the finitude of agrarian foodstuffs implies, at least conceivably, that the former can be produced, consumed, and reproduced faster and forever. Yet a paradox of this theoretical boundlessness is that it requires a set of discrete, rational, and measurable boundaries for its conceptual integrity. Endless production presupposes the keeping of an accurate ledger. Agriculture as a circumscribed activity resulting in perishable goods largely disregards the same accounting strictures by virtue of its status as inherently ephemeral. Corn cannot be perpetually amassed, any more than the idea to amass it can occur. Before the deluge of modernity, "when the stock which a man possesses is no more than sufficient to maintain him for a few days or a few weeks," there was no possibility, and hence no desire, for accumulation. As Smith explains, an individual "seldom thinks of deriving any revenue from it," instead living sparingly while immersed in a cycle of laboring, consuming, and laboring once more. A radical change takes place, however, when the complexity of exchanging industrially produced goods leads to stock being gathered in quantities far beyond immediate consumption. Now, when an individual possesses stock sufficient for "months or years," there is a resultant impulse "to derive a revenue from the greater part of it."[88] Smith describes how the enterprising individual, after setting aside a small amount for necessary personal consumption, deploys the remainder of the stock (now identified as "capital") out into the world.

Circulation—"his capital is continually going from him in one shape, and returning to him in another"—thus generates the incremental differences that add up to profit.[89]

By laying out what appears as a series of elemental moments in human social and economic affairs, at times wayward and even whimsical, Smith in fact accomplishes an act of ontology masquerading as theory. A set of concepts is demarcated and defined—wealth, the division of labor, difference—and then assembled into a series of relations—interdependence, efficiency, accumulation. When these disparate qualities are then described as operating in particular, inexorable ways, *the result is the production of logic itself.* And it is the unassuming, patient exercise of explication that imbues this logic with a compelling explanatory value.

Perhaps most important are the implications of the imagined terrain upon which this process takes place. Smith's text is replete with comparisons. The constant contrast between the spheres of the urban, industrial, and thus modern, with the rural, agricultural, and thereby archaic generates the binary of worker/peasant. Moreover, this contrast is an actual *contest* unfolding in Smith's time. His account is exactly of its period, a position implicated in the contemporaneous struggle underway in British society described in Chapter 1. The concepts "worker" and "peasant" are both simultaneous and oppositional, emerging not only in practical but also epistemological antagonism to each other. As Smith's discourse consolidates the past as the other of the present, the same logic operates to posit the peasant as the other of the worker. The inner coherence and operation of these concepts are thus implicated in external forces that shaped the specific society from which they emerged. This is the implicit, unacknowledged history that trails the peasant as it traverses the world.

DISCOVERING AND CONCEALING VALUE

Between Smith's assembling of certain qualities into a logic for the peasant and Lenin and Kautsky's debate over its precise trajectory sits the work of Karl Marx. This position is not a function of simple chronology. A strictly linear ordering would actually begin with Smith, move on to Marx, and then end up with Lenin and Kautsky. Indeed, Kautsky not only met Marx and edited some of his posthumous work, but both he and Lenin were self-professed followers of his ideas—much of their polemics hinged on revoking the other's claim to being a Marxist. Rather, Marx occupies a central position due in part to the way he provides a critique of the foundational categories of political economy and their historical manifestation at specific moments and locations. Moreover, and obviously, he need not have visited or even considered colonial Panjab and its peasantry in order to bear on that history. His ideas incisively trouble the unmarked culture of economic concepts circulating across the globe. Marx's arguments therefore extend in *both* temporal directions, toward conceptualizing the peasant as inferior as well as anticipating its disappearance.

Some of Marx's most sustained commentary on Smith is found in a rather inconspicuous place, the unfinished manuscript written intermittently during the 1861–63 period and titled *Theories of Surplus-Value*.[90] The text consists of detailed, critical analyses of different concepts and thinkers, with extended excerpts from James Steuart to Thomas Hobbes, David Ricardo to Thomas Malthus, and William Petty to the Physiocrats, among several others. It also contains an outline for the full, multi-volume (and ultimately unfinished) project of *Capital*. Described by one reviewer as "an eye-witness account of the convulsions out of which the great watershed was formed which divided all streams of thought today," this text captures Marx's engagement with the discipline of political economy and its early disciples.[91]

According to Marx, Smith's greatest discovery is that labor is the source of value and stimulus for purposeful activity. The processes that result in the ascendancy of manufacturing also imbue it with an ever-expanding drive toward expansion. Marx excerpts passages where Smith explains how in a "rude state of society," the value of a product (such as a beaver skin) simply reflects the labor necessary to produce it.[92] Yet modern society transforms the equation for value. Manufacturing produces commodities, but their value is not simply equal to the labor expended on producing them. If the value of labor was a function of the price of a commodity, Marx argues, then "the workman's wage would be equal to the value of his product."[93] Instead, this equivalence is altered by the new way production is organized. Modern production arranges labor not to produce a commodity for sale directly but to perform certain activities under the auspices of a capitalist that result in the production of a commodity. This subtle shift generates a difference between what a laborer is paid and the price of a commodity. The capitalist pays wages to workers performing various pin-making tasks while selling the pins they produce on the market. It is at this moment, notes Marx, that Smith "has recognized the true origin of surplus-value."[94] Surplus does not accrue from the shrewd, mercantile selling of a commodity *above* its value but is a quality *inherent* in the structure of relations that produce commodities.

Yet at the same time, Marx argues that Smith enters into an impasse that stifles the thrust and honesty of his analysis. When wages are allied to rents and profits as the incomes of the constituent elements of society (workers, landlords, and capitalists), the result is a "general theory of surplus-value."[95] A problem emerges, however, when this theory relies on shifting relations of exchange to explain what is supposed to amount to a fixed law of exchange. Simply put, the dynamic of something more being exchanged for less—a capitalist profiting by selling unpaid labor of workers—is inexplicable. Appropriating Smith's voice, Marx writes that "he [Smith] feels that some flaw has emerged," that "somehow—whatever the cause may be, and he does not grasp what it is—in the actual result the law [of exchange] is suspended." This is because there is a tacit, furtive realization that, with the rise of manufacturing, "something new occurs."[96] A parallel conflation of surplus-value with profit and labor-power with wages compounds the confusion. The notion that capital can create surplus-value on its own, while appearing to legitimize the appropriation of the capitalist, actually ends up retuning the equation to a kind of arithmetic merchant exchange. This "makes [Smith] irresolute and uncertain," writes Marx, and "cuts the firm ground from under his feet."[97] What Marx explores extensively in the first volume of *Capital*, and what is perhaps the reason he begins with an analysis of the commodity, is summarized here in a single, capacious sentence:

> [The novelty of manufacturing arises through] labour-power itself *becoming a commodity*, and that in the case of this specific commodity its

use-value—which therefore has nothing to do with its exchange-value—is precisely the *energy* that creates exchange-value.[98]

Labor as commodity, both unprecedented and unlike any other, might therefore be understood as the basic unit of modernity. Its expression is its enactment. Smith at times nears this revelation but does not reach it. Says Marx, "Adam's twisting and turnings, his contradictions and wandering from the point," prove that "he had got himself stuck in the mud and *had* to get stuck."[99]

A CRITIQUE OF THE IDEOLOGY OF POLITICAL ECONOMY
The metaphor of Smith mired and immovable is perhaps a fitting extension into Marx's larger critique of political economy. He identifies three distinct contradictions of the entire discipline as it came into prominence in the eighteenth century. First, throughout his exposition, Smith establishes certain definitions that invest the concepts he traces with an immutable quality: differences are useful; labor is productive activity; capital is the incremental increase of stock; and so on. Yet these meanings only emerge in contrast with what they are not *simultaneous* to what they have overcome. Hence African royalty, primitive techniques, and rude societies constitute a tacit geographical and cultural background that has been transcended with the advent of modernity. Second, alongside this illusory fixity is the unacknowledged perspective from which these concepts acquire their valence. The invisible standpoint is the singularity of capital. Practices of specialization, productivity, or accumulation are projected as totally and self-evidently positive. There is little examination of what the pursuit of efficiency through automated, repetitive activity means for the individual actually performing it. Or, what the effect of accumulation is for those who do not accumulate, not to mention those for whom it entails displacement and dispossession. Instead, a sly universality allows contingent circumstances to acquire the hue of inexorable and inevitable benefit writ large. Finally, the relations Smith describes are presented as largely harmonious. Dizzying ensembles of individuals—butchers and bakers, the crew required to produce a coat, the multitude making those ubiquitous pins—proceed as sounds rather than players in an orchestra. Friction is

nearly undetectable. There is thus remarkably little room for discord or deviance, much less defiance, in the plethora of entanglements that constitute Smith's modern society.

Perhaps the clearest expression of the consequences of this petrified logic is Smith's account of different kinds of labor. Society is made up of either productive or unproductive individuals. On the one hand are manufacturing workers who add value to the materials they work with and thereby generate both their own wages and profits for the capitalist. The labor of what Smith interestingly calls "menial servants," on the other hand, "adds to the value of nothing." Clearly he cannot be imaginatively anticipating people like Chaugutta from Chapter 4, working as a siri alongside Tehl Singh in Ferozepur in the early twentieth century. The colonial incommensurability of "menial" across languages and centuries nearly parallels that of "peasant." For Smith, productivity is determined by a particular evaluation of the ability of labor to produce a surplus. It is at this point that an abstract quality is wedded to a material requirement. All productive labor, Smith says, results in some "vendible commodity," while the results of unproductive labor "generally perish in the very instant of their performance." The occupants of the first category along this material and temporal axis are, predictably, workers employed by a capitalist. More diverse are those of the second, as they range from "the gravest" to the "most frivolous": menials accompanied by "churchmen," "lawyers," and "men of letters of all kinds" to "players, buffoons [and] musicians."[100] Whatever their status within society, the ephemeral quality of their labors do not generate the surplus required for the reproduction not only of themselves but of a capitalist as well. Smith follows this with didactic advice: "A man grows rich by employing a multitude of manufacturers; he grows poor by maintaining a multitude of menial servants." Workers and menials therefore appear as a binary based on a supposedly objective criterion inherent within all modern societies.

How Marx addresses this formulation is equally instructive. He first asks several questions about the criteria itself: What about supervisors, engineers, managers, clerks, and other personnel? Are they not required for material production just as much as workers? Does lack of working with one's hands or a machine automatically exclude one from being productive?

He then disputes the definition's point of departure with his own scenarios. If a cook in a hotel producing mutton chops for its proprietor to sell to patrons is productive, is the same cook hired to produce the same meal by an individual in their home unproductive? Or a seamstress employed in a factory but also called to the house of a neighbor to sew a shirt? Finally, Marx confronts the relationship between tangible and intangible forms of labor. Are the immaterial, temporary labors of actors, musicians, and prostitutes not productive, and indeed profitable, for the owners of theaters, concert halls, and brothels? And although the services of schoolteachers and doctors seem not to result in a "vendible commodity," is there any doubt that education and healthcare are implicated in the ability of labor to produce and reproduce?[101]

Through this set of queries, Marx develops a wider challenge to the concept of what makes labor productive. He unravels the assumptions and contradictions that underpin Smith's formula. A divide between productive and unproductive labor is meaningless unless the position from which this division is made is first established. It is vital to recognize that Smith's binary proceeds from *"the standpoint of the capitalist,* not from that of the *workman."*[102] Smith's entire exposition is thereby shaped by this undeclared specificity. Furthermore, as Marx explains, a capitalist is nothing more than the personification of capital, an agent that itself is but a name given for the dynamic that coheres into the pursuit of surplus-value. For this value to be realized, the various activities of individuals in a particular condition must be congealed into the form of the commodity. This is what separates a seamstress sewing a shirt for a neighbor to wear and for a wage paid by a capitalist who then sells shirts. The second kind of shirt is a commodity because its sale provides the capitalist both wages to pay the seamstress and profit for themselves. Here Marx also emphasizes a critical distinction between the commodity of labor-power and all other commodities. Only the former has the ability to generate a value greater than its own expense, while the latter necessarily circulate as bearers of surpluses that capitalists seek to realize.[103] "The same labour can be productive when I buy it as a capitalist, as a producer, in order to create more value," Marx explains, "and unproductive when I buy it as a consumer, a sender of revenue."[104] In every market alongside "meat and wheat" there exists sex and legal advice as commodities that compete equally for consumers. Yet only "prostitutes" and "lawyers"—as the equivalent of manufacturing workers—are deployed by their proprietors as commodities themselves to produce recurring surpluses. Fractured in these ways, Smith's account of labor productivity is undermined to the point of ceasing itself to be productive.

What then remains of the explanatory value of classical political economy? Marx distills his critique into a few succinct themes. The problem stems from taking certain relational qualities as "characteristics attributable to things."[105] Elsewhere in the *Grundrisse* he exposes how political economy relies on bourgeois relations "smuggled in as the inviolable natural laws on which society in the abstract is founded." The result is that "capital is conceived as a thing, not as a relation."[106] In a broader sense, what Smith does is attribute essences to material objects from a solitary perspective that assigns permanence to ever-changing dynamics. Not only in the measure of productivity, but any number of other idioms in his repertoire undergo a fixing that ultimately constrains their ability to adequately describe shifting relations of production and consumption. And it is this inadequacy, moreover, that betrays a distinct politics to the task of conceptual analysis. Against the seamless logic produced through these essentialisms, Marx repeatedly emphasizes how analytic categories are always flexible, evolving angles that reflect a specific location that illuminates certain functions within a given context. There is no comprehensive, panoptic, or redemptive perch from which the mysteries of any society can observably and predictably unfold.

HISTORY AND THE PECULIARITY OF EUROPE

From this critique emerges a different set of terms to understand the fluidity of labor, production, and surplus. Marx introduces a distinction between use and exchange to mark the transformation of productive activity and the rise of the commodity under the rule of capital. An object has a use-value when production coincides with consumption, when it is produced to fulfill a particular purpose intrinsic to itself, when its value is realized through its use. In this sense, anything produced through labor to satisfy the needs of either the "stomach or the imagination" is a use-value.[107]

Pins, coats, a meal, shirts, whatever, are all use-values insofar as they are made to be used. A profound change occurs, however, when purposeful activity is directed not toward producing objects that fulfill discrete uses but commodities destined to be sold at a profit. Exchange-value marks a moment in the emergence of capital—a new dimension, orientation, and organization of the dynamics of production and consumption. Value is now determined by the exchange of an object independent of its use. For the capitalist owner of a pin-making factory, pins themselves are irrelevant; the same capitalist could produce coats or shirts or any other commodity just as long as their production generates a surplus. What therefore connects use- and exchange-value is the advent of labor itself becoming its own unique commodity.[108] The only quality of importance for the capitalist is the surplus-value generated through appropriating unpaid labor-time during the production process. As Marx explains, a capitalist's "aim is to produce not only a use-value, but a commodity; not only use-value, but value; and not just value, but also surplus-value."[109] The interplay between use and exchange is thus a constant novel presence in the life of a commodity.

The point of explicating Marx's understanding of the commodification of labor is not to substitute Smith's ideas with a supposedly superior theory more appropriate for the modern age. There is little theoretical merit in merely restaging battles over competing visions of economic change from the nineteenth century. Instead, it is to show the specificity of the making of that particular notion of modernity, the claims inherent to its conceptualization, and the occlusions built into the very definitions that give it meaning. Marx makes clear that his engagement with the discipline of political economy is an exercise of posing questions, uncovering assumptions, and bringing contradictions to the fore—and not a corrective, historically more accurate account of the *actual* relations between workers and capitalists. "In order to develop the laws of bourgeois economy," he famously states, "it is not necessary to write the *real history of the relations of production*."[110] What is required is to inhabit and follow the logic produced by Smith—presented as timeless, rational, and idyllic—in order to reveal how it fails to fulfill even his own standards. The politics of generating surplus value through the exploitation of workers and its naturalized expropriation by capitalists are uncomfortable presences produced by his narrative yet at the same time rendered silent. The unspoken, exclusionary universality of bourgeois economics is therefore exposed rather than presumptively replaced because so much hinges on that very silence.

This is how the critique of political economy addresses the question of agriculture, though perhaps in a manner more fortuitous than deliberate. On at least two occasions in *Capital*, Marx mentions his intent to analyze in detail the question of "the English agricultural proletariat" in relation to small farmers, famine conditions, and the Poor Laws.[111] Both times, however, the editor of the book notes that Marx "appears not to have pursued this idea," leaving what seems to be a void in developing the laws of feudal or agrarian economy.[112] Yet to interpret this unfinished task as a sign of the unfortunate incompletion of Marx's oeuvre—and thus a lost opportunity to apply Marx's analysis of English agriculture to the peasantry of colonial India—misses a central lesson of the very critique of political economy. It is not a matter of application, of taking Marx's insights, translating them into a criterion with a predictable outcome, and then charting their unfolding in a radically different context. Indeed, this approach is what informs the many earlier studies noted in Chapter 1 that tabulate the differences of the Panjabi peasant as indications of the continuity of semi-feudalism or quasi-capitalism into the nineteenth and even twentieth century. Instead, just as the critique of the hierarchies generated by industrial production in some parts of Europe need not take place empirically on every factory floor in all contexts and periods, so too are the hierarchies of agricultural production conditioned by the specificities from which they emerge. An analysis of the colonial agrarian economy therefore entails questioning the dominant assumptions of the elements within the field of activity called "agriculture."

THE PAROCHIAL PEASANT IN UNIVERSAL GUISE
The key indication of the ongoing influence of Smith's narrative of agriculture as the other of industry is that despite Marx's critique of the foundations of political economy, two of the most famous Marxists of the early twentieth century adopted many of the same attitudes toward the peasantry and its ultimate demise. If Marx discovered in *The Wealth of*

Nations an attempt to conceal the production and extraction of surplus-value through the manufacturing process, the text more surreptitiously popularized the notion of agriculture as ancient, backward, and transitory. Smith's constant civilizational comparisons appear as innocent contrasts yet implicitly generate a new logic of temporal and material inferiority, seemingly too obvious to contest. Although not a preoccupation of Marx, this set of themes is what informed many of the urgent debates over the peasant question in a rapidly industrializing Europe and elsewhere.[113] Even as Lenin explicitly focused his investigation on rural Russia, and thus to an extent limited the universalism of his conclusions, he nevertheless shared with Kautsky a vision of the future where peasants would eventually become workers. The actual viability of agriculture—of not only whether cultivation could effectively generate disparate surpluses but of how the parameters of efficacy are chosen in different contexts—is hardly questioned. For a long time a key part of the definition of modernity, along with the ostensible complexity, efficiency, and wealth it was expected to bring, was the creation of a new global society based on the very problematic that has animated this book: an expectant end to the peasantry.

The discourses of backwardness and progress have a particular resonance for histories of colonial India. Establishing the inferiority of native society was crucial to the exercise of British rule as well as its subsequent justificatory claims. "The nineteenth-century project of universal comparison," writes Karuna Mantena, "framed and limited by the attempt to chart the unique trajectory of Western modernity, shaped a new vision of the relationship between past and present and thereby contributed to a fundamental rethinking of the idea of the primitive."[114] While many officials dedicated tremendous energies toward conjuring up and cataloguing various cultural deficiencies, religious superstitions, and abhorrent social practices, the domain of material relations was equally important for marking difference-as-inferiority. But here the nature of the subordination could take an unusual turn. The language for essentialist denigration camouflaged as straightforward observation, with perhaps a perverse tinge of praise. Panjab's "greatest blessing," according to its most quoted official, "is that it is the land of peasant proprietors," a group that "constitute as fine raw material as can be found in any part of India."[115] Such a sweeping statement has repeatedly been taken as a given, reproduced, and internalized by scholars and the general public alike well after the formal end of colonialism. Automatically identifying the rural population as timeless peasants engaged in age-old cultivation denied the contemporaneousness of colonizer and colonized by confirming the stagism of India's nineteenth-century present as an equivalent of England's sixteenth-century past. It also reduced incredibly complex human beings and their varied relationships to simplistic occupations to be plotted along an economic scale of civilization. Hence the commonsense assumption that while the English peasant *disappeared*, the Panjabi peasant *remained*—or, from the other end of the process, that while the English proletariat had appeared, a proper Panjabi proletariat had yet to emerge.

In this way, British rule could claim itself a project of benevolence precisely because Panjabis could be depicted as static and archaic peasants in need of transitioning to a preordained future. Of course additional impediments peculiar to the subcontinent—caste, religion, tribe, gender, and climate, along with all of the afflicting irrationalities they entailed—permanently deferred the false promise of making Panjab and India modern. Nonetheless, "[c]olonial governance made some European ideas [. . .] a part of social practice" in the colony, points out Christopher Hill, which is why certain groups such as the Arains of Muzaffargarh or the Bahrupias of Gujrat or the Mazhabis of Lyallpur petitioned to acquire the status of agricultural tribe.[116] The larger point is that categories used to describe Panjabi economic relations contain much of the same prejudices as those used to depict its social relations. While the latter has received more scholarly attention than the former, rarely are the two seen in unison, as part of a single if contradictory system of domination. The agrarian "nature" of Panjab and its diligent and loyal "peasantry" is as much a product of colonial rule as the "natural" propensity of certain Panjabis to violence, laziness, or deceit.

The broader challenge of a new economic history of colonial agriculture—of repoliticizing political economy—is that the very category "peasant" did not emerge out of the ideological vocabulary and political experience of Panjabi society. While conceived in tandem with the proletariat by certain intellectuals in Europe, colonial officials deployed the designation of peasant in isolation both selectively and comprehensively to underscore the obviousness of native inadequacy.[117] This is why Williams's definition of a worldwide peasant disjuncture is less a reflection of actual differences in the economic evolution of societies. It shows instead how the power of universalizing notions developed in classic political economy generated implicit expectations in another midcentury Marxist thinker. At the same time, a straightforward recourse to the vernacular is far from a sufficient response to this predicament. Simply replacing "peasant" with *kisan* or even *kheti karn vala* neither attends to the history of colonial difference-making nor overcomes the enduring burdens of that global inheritance. The specter of comparison continues to haunt the discipline of political economy. That Marx's own critique of this tradition is aimed at the bourgeois mode of production and its internal claims of coherence and rationality is therefore not a sign of its inapplicability. Rather, it provides a vital means to interrogate any social and economic order presented as self-evident and natural. The true task of history-writing might then be to give what appears as timeless a timeline, in order to develop a critique of the presuppositions that impute logic and reason onto relations that are but riven with contingency, conflict, and unpredictability. From that conceptual breach might emerge alternative concepts and values worthy of the future.

CONCLUSION

GLOBAL HISTORY AND THE IMPERMANENCE OF HIERARCHY

> To cultivate the ground was the original destination of man.
> —ADAM SMITH

> Men made clothes for thousands of years, under the compulsion of the need for clothing, without a single man ever becoming a tailor.
> —KARL MARX

PERHAPS THE RIOT OF Isa Khel can now be understood as a different kind of fragment. In the wake of the chapters of this book, returning to an episode of violence in this small town along the Indus River at the end of the nineteenth century offers greater insight into the ordering of the past as well as our attempts to apprehend it. According to Gyanendra Pandey, a fragment is a perspective that "resists the drive for a shallow homogenization" to instead provide new vantage into the contestations present but concealed in all historical narratives.[1] He made this argument in the context of trying to describe the difficulty of writing about sectarian strife in post-independence India. To counter colonialist and chauvinist depictions of the inherent hatred between communities with nationalist platitudes about their inherent goodwill is a retreat from the duty of analysis. Relying on such tropes is "an unacceptable history" for Pandey not only because it is reductive and rhetorical but because it "essentializes 'communalism'" into a static anomaly that can be conveniently isolated and then ignored rather than confronted.² Violence between communities is thus rendered an aberration and an absence in the main drama of the nation.

The received framing of Isa Khel operates in a parallel yet distinctive way. Here officials actually spurred the question of religion to identify the violence as a result of acute financial distress. Muslim peasants falling deeper into debt to Hindu moneylenders led to an almost naturalistic outburst of savagery and larceny, to which the British were left with the task of restoring calm. Such a narrative achieves a remarkable double slight of history. On the one hand, it absolves colonialism of culpability in the greater violence of perpetuating domination and division, so that the government is only presented as benevolently acting against habitually unruly locals. On the other hand, it essentializes capitalism by positioning economic volatility and the desperation is generates as normal features of life outside of time and shorn of agency. Taken together, this incident is reduced to yet another minor affair in the grand project of colonial governance, confirming existing assumptions and therefore unworthy of sustained attention.

As a fragment, however, Isa Khel resists the retelling of such state- and capital-centric narratives. What officials described as "local" and "unimportant" was in fact spectrally global and of utmost if unusual importance to both history and historiography. Its significance can be traced by refracting the main features of the event through a few of the characters encountered in this book. From the onset, a Richard Temple would have used the science of the day to carefully measure the human qualities of different kinds of Muslim cultivators and Hindu traders to assign their proper value to the government. With people like Hazara's Dost Muhammad Khan likely empathizing with those facing insolvency, a Robert Maconachie could have tried to translate their purported war cry from the vernacular. Against the renewed exhortations of *The New York Times*, a figure such as Septimus Thorburn would loudly reiterate the need for special legislation regardless of the self-interested objections of a Harnam Singh Ahluwalia. Yet Mangoo Ram might have cast suspicion at the apparent cooperation between "zamindars" and "low-caste" men, even as their victims sadly recited Bulleh Shah's poetic lament. No doubt scores of kisans, siris, and kamins contemplated and enacted small and even large plots of their own against a variety of targets over the decades. From afar, it is possible that Kautsky would have denounced the violence as opportunism, just as Lenin may have anticipated a greater upsurge around the corner, while Marx might have taken it as an opportunity to ask even more penetrating questions about the political economy of British rule. Ranajit Guha's programmatic statement thus remains decisive: There was "nothing in the militant movements" of colonial India "that was not political."[3]

Within the wider landscape of colonial Panjab, Isa Khel exemplifies how the domains of culture and economy were disrupted, reordered, and intertwined to produce a new set of relations, processes, and hierarchies. Studies of colonialism have usually segregated the two—writings on knowledge practices, social categories, and popular perceptions remain apart from cropping patterns, debt ratios, and household expenses. Cultural politics are dissonant with the politics of economic life, an intellectually and historically specious divide. This book has proceeded differently, starting with a challenge to the dominant historiographical premise of a stalwart and self-evident peasantry enduring and even prospering under a benevolent colonialism. Rather than inverting this theme by insisting on immiseration and underdevelopment, however, I have attempted to bring the history of ideological and material conditions and contestations involved in making such an assumption to the fore. Central to this project has been an unsettling of the commonsense binary of colonizer and colonized. Just as the colonial state was more complex and contradictory than a simple monolithic authority exercising force to achieve rational ends, so too was Panjabi society riven with changing differences of caste, class, and religion as well as deliberate political affiliation. Officials put forward opposing opinions to implement conflicting racial, fiscal, and juridical policies that resulted in a variety of incongruent and unpredictable outcomes. Certain caste and religious groups became relatively empowered through the designation of agricultural tribes and gained exclusive access to a new land market, while others became relegated to the status of menial laborers and were denied entitlements to ownership and resources. These processes produced the figure of the hereditary landowning masculine caste peasant and positioned it at the top of a new yet volatile capitalist agrarian order. The habit of automatically referring to unmarked aggregate groups—Panjabis and Indians as much as Nigerians, Colombians, and Americans—should no longer be tenable.

The five chapters of this book have taken up different themes to investigate the historical emergence of this hierarchy. In Chapter 1, I showed how the oft-repeated claim of colonial benevolence operated to conceal the disrupting and reconfiguring of the relationship between caste identity, labor activity, and land ownership. A "moderate" revenue demand enabled a more invasive process of surveillance and settlement, which for the first time aligned specific castes with the duality of land rights and revenue responsibilities. There was no already assembled generic group of equal landholding peasants in Panjabi society in the nineteenth century. Rather, the colonial state had to work zealously yet arbitrarily to identify the particular characteristics of religious, caste, and tribal groups deemed best suited for exclusive ownership. This inaugurated a new kind of primitive accumulation different from its standard history in Western Europe. The outcome was not a violent separation of "peasants" from their surroundings and displacement into cities. Instead, individuals from certain groups among the rural population came to be entrenched in the countryside, attached to discrete parcels of land through the very processes of being labeled "members of an agricultural tribe." The birth of the historical difference of the Panjabi peasant lies in the novel imposition of the category within the disparate political economy of the colony.

Chapter 2 traced the fractious epistemology for both the figure of the peasant and the various practices of cultivation. The vocabularies from nineteenth century dictionaries and proverbs show that there was no single, widely accepted equivalent for *peasant* in Panjabi or Urdu. A variety of terms such as *kisan, kashtkar*, and *hulwaee kurne wala*—not necessarily corresponding to caste or religion—circulated among the different aspects of cultivation according to region, dialect, and discrete task. However, the advent of the colonial censuses in 1855, 1868, and especially 1881 inaugurated the classification of agricultural and non-agricultural tribes, a pairing that found material expression in the 1901 Punjab Alienation of Land Act. This legislation produced a definition of an agriculturalist based on a mixture of originary descent, caste membership, and a verifiable claim to landholding in order to restrict access to the land market. Importantly, certain caste groups contested the denial of status, petitioning officials to gain admittance into the ranks of agricultural tribes. Far from an ancient feature of Panjabi society, the notion of a hereditary caste peasant owning land is thus a demonstrably new phenomenon born of the contradictions of colonial jurisprudence, language politics, and local initiative.

In Chapter 3, I uncovered the political entanglements surrounding peasant debt and its multiplying remedies. The colonial accounting of indebtedness shifted rather whimsically from generic excessive spending, to the fragmentation of land, to the specific forced sale of land by caste peasants. In developing different legislative solutions to this ever-changing problem, officials normalized a strikingly novel imposition: casted-based private property. At the same time, they used notions of cultural extravagance and irrationality to conceal the consequences of the volatility and precariousness now structurally built into the agrarian economy. As debt became defined as a function of the poor management of resources, its remedy came to be a juridical paternalism based on managing a supposedly habitual profligacy. What this achieved was not the elimination of indebtedness or a cessation of land sales but a restricting of the land-debt market to a select group of participants. Circumscribing eligibility to conduct exchange thereby empowered a rising class within the castes of agricultural tribes to achieve relative dominance in the countryside.

Chapter 4 examined a longer history of lower-caste assertion amid the changing relationship between landed peasants and landless laborers. Using Bhimrao Ambedkar's undelivered "Annihilation of Caste" speech from Lahore as an entry point, I revealed the distinct possibilities and limitations for caste emancipation through religious conversion in early twentieth-century Panjab. Exclusion and exploitation of Chamars and Churhas occurred in the absence of a millennia-old division of laborers based on the authority of Brahminical Hinduism. A critique of caste made by Guru Nanak and early Sikh institutions, as well as Bhakti poets such as Kabir, Ravidas, and Namdev, overturned several elements of conventional Hindu orthodoxy and gave rise to a different form of precolonial rural hierarchy. In the 1920s, Mangoo Ram and the Ad Dharm movement selectively invoked these traditions to create a separate religious community for untouchables. They achieved remarkable success not only in demonstrating the power of lower-caste mobilization but also in acquiring an unprecedented level of dignity and self-empowerment. On the other hand, I put these developments alongside the ongoing subordination of agricultural laborers working as contracted siris to landowning peasants. While this relationship fractures the myth of the singular peasant monopolizing agriculture, it also reflects the persistence of rural inequity and discrimination. A new caste-based agrarian hierarchy developed through the *economy* as opposed to the *religiosity* of untouchability operating under colonial capitalism.

In Chapter 5, I explored how the internal logic of the discipline of political economy generated the universal category "peasant" in tandem with the proletariat. Instead of a simple, sequential progression from one to the other, I showed the simultaneity of their conceptual development. This invokes a classic insight by the anthropologist Robert Redfield from 1953: "There were no peasants before the first cities."[4] In other words, it took the specific concentration of populations in urban centers for the contrast with "the countryside" to emerge. My argument here is that only with the rise of industrial workers in Europe did it become possible, and indeed necessary, to define and describe their opposite: rural peasants. Moreover, the valorization of the coming of manufacturing meant relegating cultivation as an antecedent and inferior condition in the writings of Adam Smith as well as Karl Kautsky and Vladimir Lenin, to which Karl Marx provides an immanent critique. In this way, the global peasant came to be invested with qualities of inadequacy, backwardness, and the need for transformation. Histories of economic change in colonial Panjab must therefore grapple with the advent of a peasantry in the absence of a proletariat. By excavating this intellectual conjuncture, I reveal how the broader ideological and material agenda of colonialism in South Asia is inextricable from a global burden of comparison.

Together these varied themes demonstrate the contestations inherent in the history of one of the most naturalized features of rural society, the division of labor. The lucid serenity of the phrase itself conceals a world of struggles, both grand and quotidian. As the first epigraph to this conclusion from Smith signals, the originary (and masculine) status of agriculture and its linear progress is fundamental to the political imagination in the West. I have attempted to show that in fact there was nothing inevitable about the nature of the agrarian hierarchy in even the most celebrated of agricultural provinces in the British Empire. A series of divisions enacted through different conceptual, racial, juridical, fiscal, cultural, and material spheres restructured and petrified social and economic relations in nineteenth- and early twentieth-century Panjab. Hereditary peasants with exclusive land rights and overwhelming class power were an explicitly modern product, one that emerged out of a colonial imbrication of "primordial" identity and practical activity. The selective use of caste, religion, and tribe ensured that this transformation would affect Panjabi society unevenly, privileging some groups while discriminating against others, yet all the while appearing in conformity with so-called native culture and ancient tradition. The power of the new division of labor with the peasant at its pinnacle is a result of the simultaneity of change and its denial.

At the same time, this book has provided an opportunity to revisit understandings of both the expectations and operations of capital in the colonial world. With an awareness that capitalism does not produce uniformity across the globe, differences in the political economy of colonial Panjab cease to be indications of inferiority or remnants of backwardness with a given trajectory toward correction.[5] Agricultural production and the relationship between peasants and laborers were neither vestiges of a frozen precolonial culture nor variants of a kind of feudalism marked by stagism ("semi," "quasi," "pseudo"). By demonstrating the historical production of these differences, not only is their fixity undone but so too is the perception that they are simply impediments to a preordained future. Indeed, part of my argument is that the specific emergence of the Panjabi "peasant" precludes its inclusion within the rubric of a worldwide and transhistorical "peasantry," a category still seen by some as "the largest class in world history."[6] Instead, I have described how a colonial accumulation of attachments provided certain castes with land ownership, while juridical processes aligned identities with occupations and fiscal policies restricted access to the land market, all amid a discourse of paternalism that naturalized the volatility of the new agrarian economy. Marx in the second epigraph to this conclusion also points to the specificity of a novel combination of knowledge categories, productive relations, and the commodity form. In Panjab fields were plowed, crops grown, and grain harvested for hundreds of years without any fixed notion of "the peasant." That subject—singular, exclusive, masculine, caste-based—emerged only at the particular conjuncture of colonial technologies of rule instigating an internal contest for social and economic primacy among different groups of Panjabis.

Perhaps a more diffuse contribution of this book lies in its reinterpretation of the nature of hierarchy through the prism of history. Contemporary Panjab on both sides of the 1947 border is riven with a myriad of divisions as well as entanglements and aspirations shared with many other parts of the world. Struggles over land ownership, caste conflict, and gender roles take place alongside religious polarization and ecological degradation amid competing designs from New Delhi and Islamabad. At the same time, east Panjab in particular has an unmistakably egalitarian public culture drawing on its radical heritage along with one of the lowest reported rates of caste-based crimes in comparison with other states in India.[7] Beset by numerous crises, its cultivators are nevertheless far from the brink of disappearance. Debates abound on redefining the future of agriculture while recognizing that following the supposed trajectory of Europe is neither possible nor desirable.[8] All of these issues are further implicated in global circuits of capital, from shaping the commodity prices of wheat, rice, and cotton to turning human beings into commodified migrants for the pitiless economies of the West. The results are hardly distributed evenly or arbitrarily: certain groups find ways to benefit, while others are by and large excluded and exploited.

Yet the overriding explanation of these hierarchies—class, caste, nation—is the simple persistence of beliefs and practices from time immemorial, at most unfortunate but by and large inescapable. Through this book, however, I suggest a more recent and therefore less permanent inheritance. Shorn of the solidity of antiquity, the peasant along with the splintered logics of colonialism and capitalism from which it emerged are made to confront the sheer mutability of modernity. By giving this division of labor a history, I have tried to show that it was neither timeless nor inevitable, and thus will not last forever. The power of demonstrating historical change is therefore to bring contingency and unpredictability to our understanding of the past in the making of the present, in order to at least create spaces to think through different possibilities for forging emancipatory horizons. Perhaps as Baba Farid indicated at the very beginning of this book, one must have faith that the ultimate reward for effort lies beyond its obvious outcome.

NOTES

Introduction

Epigraph: *Sri Guru Granth Sahib Ji*, Ang 1379. I am using the online version from <www.srigranth.org> accessed on April 15, 2022. It uses the exegesis by Sahib Singh, *Sri Guru Granth Sahib Darpan* (Jalandhar: Raj Publishers, 1962–64) and is translated by Sant Singh Khalsa. Keeping the transliteration mostly intact but without diacritics, I have slightly adjusted the translation. Here the *dakh bijurian* refers to the small grapes found in Bajaur, a mountainous Panjabi region north of Peshawar in the present-day Khyber Pakhtunkhwa province of Pakistan.

1. The details in this and the previous paragraph are from Report by H. A. Casson, "Riot Isakhel Bannu Dashera," December 28, 1893, Revenue and Agriculture Department (Land Revenue), file 215, no. 18 (B), May 1895, National Archives of India (hereafter NAI), New Delhi, India. See also *Gazetteer of the Bannu District* (Calcutta: Central Press Company, 1883), 176–78, 207–8.

2. Report from H. A. Casson, "Riot Isakhel Bannu Dashera," December 28, 1893, 2.

3. Report from H. A. Casson, "Riot Isakhel Bannu Dashera," December 28, 1893, 13.

4. One exception is a short article by Ikram Ali Malik published in 1984 that summarizes much of the Casson report. See Malik, "Isa Khel Riot of 1893," *Journal of the Pakistan Historical Society*, vol. 23, part 1 (January 1984): 13–21. There remains the possibility of pursuing oral accounts, memories, or alternative archives of this event through interviews in the area, located in the Mianwali district of Punjab in present-day Pakistan. For an analysis of another episode of lopsided mass violence between Muslims, Hindus and Sikhs thirty years later in the nearby district of Kohat, see Neeti Nair, *Changing Homelands: Hindu Politics and the Partition of India* (Cambridge: Harvard University Press, 2011), ch. 2.

5. This is counter to the usual colonial practice of designating conflicts between different communities as the result of inherent and unceasing religious antagonism. See Gyanendra Pandey, *The Construction of Communalism in Colonial North India* (New Delhi: Oxford University Press, 1990); cf. C. A. Bayly, "The Pre-History of 'Communal'? Religious Conflict in India, 1700–1860," *Modern Asian Studies* 19, no. 2 (1985): 177–203.

6. Letter from R. I. Bruce, Commissioner and Superintendent, Derajat Division, to the Chief Secretary to the Government of Punjab, January 15, 1894, 3, in "Riot Isakhel Bannu Dashera."

7. Report from H. A. Casson, "Riot Isakhel Bannu Dashera," December 28, 1893, 12. For a study of the longer history of debt, power, and agriculture in Gujarat—invoking

precisely this trope of the "grasping banniah"—see David Hardiman, *Feeding the Baniya: Peasants and Usurers in Western India* (New Delhi: Oxford University Press, 1996).

8. Malcolm Lyall Darling, *The Punjab Peasant in Prosperity and Debt* (London: Humphrey Milford, 1928), xii–xiii, xvi. For an analysis of the politics of reading ostensibly sympathetic colonial writers such as Darling as historical sources, see Navyug Gill, "Peasant as Alibi: An Itinerary of the Archive in Colonial Panjab," in *Unarchived Histories: The "Mad" and the "Trifling" in the Colonial and Postcolonial World*, ed. Gyanendra Pandey (London: Routledge, 2014), 24–28, 36–37.

9. The 2011 Census of India calculated Dalits as 31.9 percent of the population of Panjab. See *Census of India 2011*, Release of Primary Census Abstract Data Highlights, Dr. C. Chandramouli, April 30, 2013, 11. Estimates of the Jatt population range from 25 to 40 percent. See Ronki Ram, "Beyond Conversion and Sanskritisation: Articulating an Alternative Dalit Agenda in East Punjab," *Modern Asian Studies* 46, no. 3 (May 2012): 659; Paramjit S. Judge, "Caste Hierarchy, Dominance, and Change in Punjab," *Sociological Bulletin* 64, no. 1 (January–April 2015): 61–66; and Surinder Singh Jodhka, "Caste and Untouchability in Rural Punjab," *Economic and Political Weekly* 37, no. 19 (May 11–17, 2002): 1823.

10. On conditions in Pakistani west Panjab, see Aasim Sajjad Akhtar, "The State as Landlord in Pakistani Punjab: Peasant Struggles on the Okara Military Farms," *Journal of Peasant Studies* 33, no. 3 (2006): 479–501; and Mubbashir A. Rizvi, *The Ethics of Staying: Social Movements and Land Rights Politics in Pakistan* (Stanford: Stanford University Press, 2019), chs. 1–3. On caste politics in the southeast portion of Panjab, which in 1966 became the Indian state of Haryana, see Prem Chowdhry, "Jat Domination in South-East Punjab: Socio-Economic Basis of Jat Politics in a Panjab District," *Indian Economic and Social History Review* 19, no. 3–4 (July 1982): 325–346.

11. See Henry Bernstein and Terence J. Byres, "From Peasant Studies to Agrarian Change," *Journal of Agrarian Change* 1, no. 1 (January 2001): 1–56.

12. On the 2020–21 farmer-laborer protest in India, see Pritam Singh, "BJP's Farming Policies: Deepening Agrobusiness Capitalism and Centralisation," *Economic and Political Weekly* 55, no. 41 (October 10, 2020): 14–17; Shreya Sinha, "The Agrarian Crisis in Punjab and the Making of the Anti-Farm Law Protest," *India Forum*, December 4, 2020; and Navyug Gill, "A Popular Upsurge against Neoliberal Arithmetic in India," *Al Jazeera*, December 11, 2020.

13. See Rupa Viswanath, *The Pariah Problem: Caste, Religion, and the Social in Modern India* (New York: Columbia University Press, 2014); Anupama Rao, *The Caste Question: Dalits and the Politics of Modern India* (Berkeley: University of California Press, 2009); Ramnarayan S. Rawat, *Reconsidering Untouchability: Chamars and Dalit History in North India* (Bloomington: Indiana University Press, 2011); and P. Sanal Mohan, *Modernity of Slavery: Struggles against Caste Inequality in Colonial Kerala* (New Delhi: Oxford University Press, 2015). For a poignant critique of the project of mainstream Indian nationalism, see G. Aloysius, *Nationalism Without a Nation in India* (New Delhi: Oxford University Press, 1997).

14. See Aidan Foster-Carter, "The Modes of Production Controversy," *New Left Review* I, no. 107 (February 1978): 47–77; and Robert J. Holton, "Marxist Theories of Social Change and the Transition from Feudalism to Capitalism," *Theory and Society* 10, no. 6 (November 1981): 833–867. On capitalism and U.S. slavery, see James Oakes,

"Capitalism and Slavery and the Civil War," *International Labor and Working-Class History*, no. 89 (Spring 2016): 195–220.

15. See Harry Harootunian, *Marx After Marx: History and Time in the Expansion of Capitalism* (New York: Columbia University Press, 2015); and Dipesh Chakrabarty, *Provincializing Europe: Postcolonial Thought and Historical Difference* (Princeton: Princeton University Press, 2000). See also Irfan Habib, "Marx's Perception of India," in *Essays in Indian History: Towards a Marxist Perception* (New Delhi: Tulika Books, 1995); Sudipta Kaviraj, "On the Status of Marx's Writings on India," *Social Scientist* 11, no. 9 (September 1983): 26–46; and Pranav Jani, "Karl Marx, Eurocentrism, and the 1857 Revolt in British India," in *Marxism, Modernity, and Postcolonial Studies*, ed. Crystal Bartolovich and Neil Lazarus (Cambridge: Cambridge University Press, 2002), 81–97.

16. Antonio Gramsci, "The Revolution Against *Capital*," in *The Gramsci Reader: Selected Writings 1916–1935*, ed. David Forgacs (New York: New York University Press, 2000), 33.

17. Eric R. Wolf, *Peasants* (Englewood Cliffs: Prentice-Hall, 1966), vii.

18. Karl Marx, *Capital: Volume I: A Critique of Political Economy*, trans. Ben Fowkes (London: Penguin Books, 1976), 89.

19. This sense of absence and un-making is an inversion of E. P. Thompson's classic argument about the working class being "present at its own making." See Thompson, *The Making of the English Working Class* (New York: Vintage Books, 1963), 9 and *passim*.

20. See Teodor Shanin, ed., *Defining Peasants: Essays Concerning Rural Societies, Expolary Economics, and Learning from Them in the Contemporary World* (Oxford: Basil Blackwell, 1990).

21. See Sumanta Banerjee, *In the Wake of Naxalbari: A History of the Naxalite Movement in India* (Calcutta: Subarnarekha, 1980).

22. This potential of peasantries in the twentieth century to remake their societies stands in contrast to Eric Hobsbawm's depiction of the limits of peasants as social bandits in nineteenth-century Europe. "Banditry itself is therefore not a programme for peasant society," he writes, "but a form of self-help to escape it in particular circumstances. Bandits, except for their willingness or capacity to refuse individual submission, *have no ideas other than those of the peasantry* (or the section of the peasantry) of which they form a part." Eric Hobsbawm, *Bandits* (Harmondsworth: Penguin Books, 1972), 24, emphasis added.

23. See Daniel Thorner, "Capitalist Farming in India," *Economic and Political Weekly* 4, no. 52 (December 27, 1969): 211–212; Wolf Ladejinsky, "The Green Revolution in Punjab: A Field Trip," *Economic and Political Weekly* 4, no. 26 (June 28, 1969): 73–82; and M. S. Randhawa, *Green Revolution* (New York: John Wiley & Sons, 1974). For an influential ethnography of village life in the midst of these changes, see Murray J. Leaf, *Song of Hope: The Green Revolution in a Panjab Village* (New Brunswick: Rutgers University Press, 1984). On long-term consequences, see Francine R. Frankel, *India's Green Revolution: Economic Gains and Political Costs* (Princeton: Princeton University Press, 1971), ch. 2; Sucha Singh Gill, "The Farmer's Movement and Agrarian Change in the Green Revolution Belt of North-West India," *Journal of Peasant Studies*, 21, no. 3–4 (1994): 195–211; and Sukhpal Singh, "Crisis in Punjab Agriculture," *Economic and Political Weekly* 35, no. 23 (June 3–9, 2000): 1889–1892.

24. See the three-part article: Ashok Rudra, A. Majid, and B. D. Talib, "Big Farmer of the Punjab: Some Preliminary Findings of a Sample Survey," *Economic and Political Weekly* 4, no. 39 (September 27, 1969): 145; Rudra, "Big Farmers of Punjab: Second Installment of Results," *Economic and Political Weekly* 4, no. 52 (December 27, 1969): 213–219; and Rudra, "In Search of the Capitalist Farmer," *Economic and Political Weekly* 5, no. 26 (July 27, 1970): 85–87.

25. See Utsa Patnaik, "Capitalist Development in Agriculture: A Note," *Economic and Political Weekly* 6, no. 39 (September 25, 1971): 125 and *passim*.

26. A few of the notable contributions are Jairus Banaji, "For a Theory of Colonial Modes of Production," *Economic and Political Weekly* 7, no. 52 (December 23, 1972): 2498–2502; Andre Gunder Frank, "On 'Feudal' Modes, Models, and Methods of Escaping Capitalist Reality," *Economic and Political Weekly* 8, no. 1 (January 6, 1973): 36–37; Hamza Alavi, "India and the Colonial Mode of Production," *Economic and Political Weekly* 10, no. 33 (August 1975): 1235–1262; Gail Omvedt, "Capitalist Agriculture and Rural Classes in India," *Economic and Political Weekly* 16, no. 52 (December 26, 1981): 140–159; and Amiya Kumar Bagchi, "Colonialism and the Nature of 'Capitalist' Enterprise in India," *Economic and Political Weekly* 23, no. 31 (July 30, 1988): 38–50.

27. Perhaps most revealing in this literature is that while the peasant was usually a *historical* category for European scholars, it was undeniably a *contemporary* figure for those living and working in what was then known as the Third World. See Foster-Carter, "Modes of Production Controversy"; Holton, "Marxist Theories of Social Change"; and Sven Beckert and Seth Rockman, eds., *Slavery's Capitalism: A New History of American Economic Development* (Philadelphia: University of Pennsylvania Press, 2016).

28. Eric Stokes, "The Return of the Peasant to South Asian History," *The Peasant and the Raj: Studies in Agrarian Society and Peasant Rebellion in Colonial India* (Cambridge: Cambridge University Press, 1978), 268–70.

29. Stokes, "Return of the Peasant," 269.

30. Stokes, "Return of the Peasant," 289.

31. See Ranajit Guha, *Elementary Aspects of Peasant Insurgency in Colonial India* (New Delhi: Oxford University Press, 1983), introduction and ch. 3.

32. See Dipesh Chakrabarty, "A Small History of Subaltern Studies," *Habitations of Modernity: Essays in the Wake of Subaltern Studies* (Chicago: University of Chicago Press, 2002).

33. Ranajit Guha, "On Some Aspects of the Historiography of Colonial India," *Subaltern Studies I: Writings on South Asian History and Society*, ed. Ranajit Guha (New Delhi: Oxford University Press, 1982), 5.

34. Guha, *Elementary Aspects*, 3.

35. See Gyanendra Pandey, *The Ascendancy of the Congress in Uttar Pradesh, 1926–34: A Study in Imperfect Mobilization* (New Delhi: Oxford University Press, 1978); David Hardiman, *Peasant Nationalists of Gujarat, Kheda District 1917–1934* (New Delhi: Oxford University Press, 1981); Shahid Amin, *Sugarcane and Sugar in Gorakhpur: An Inquiry into Peasant Production for Capitalist Enterprise in Colonial India* (New Delhi: Oxford University Press, 1984); Partha Chatterjee, *Bengal 1920–1947: The Land Question* (Calcutta: K. P. Bagchi & Co., 1984); and Gyan Prakash, *Bonded Histories: Genealogies of Labor Servitude in Colonial India* (Cambridge: Cambridge University Press, 1990).

36. See David Ludden, *Peasant History in South India* (Princeton: Princeton University Press, 1985); Sugata Bose, *Agrarian Bengal: Economy, Social Structure, and Politics, 1919–1947* (Cambridge: Cambridge University Press, 1986); and Sumit Guha, *The Agrarian Economy of the Bombay Deccan, 1818–1941* (New Delhi: Oxford University Press, 1986).

37. See Vinayak Chaturvedi, *Peasant Pasts: History and Memory in Western India* (Berkeley: University of California Press, 2007); Vinay Gidwani, *Capital, Interrupted: Agrarian Development and the Politics of Work in India* (Minneapolis: University of Minnesota Press, 2008); and Rawat, *Reconsidering Untouchability*.

38. Norman G. Barrier, *The Punjab Alienation of Land Bill of 1900* (Durham: Duke University Press, 1966), iii.

39. See P.H.M. van den Dungen, *The Punjab Tradition: Influence and Authority in Nineteenth Century India* (London: Allen & Unwin, 1972); J. Royal Roseberry, *Imperial Rule in Punjab: The Conquest and Administration of Multan, 1818–1881* (New Delhi: Manohar Publications, 1987); and Clive Dewey, *Anglo-Indian Attitudes: The Mind of the Indian Civil Service* (London: Hambledon Press, 1993).

40. Imran Ali, *The Punjab under Imperialism, 1885–1947* (Princeton: Princeton University Press, 1988), viii, 10.

41. Ali, *Panjab under Imperialism*, 62. See also M. Mufakharul Islam, *Irrigation, Agriculture, and the Raj: Punjab, 1887–1947* (New Delhi: Manohar Publications, 1997); David Gilmartin, "Scientific Empire and Imperial Science: Colonialism and Irrigation Technology in the Indus Basin," *Journal of Asian Studies* 53, no. 4 (November 1994): 1127–1149; Elizabeth Whitcombe, *Agrarian Conditions in Northern India: The United Provinces under British Rule, 1860–1900* (Berkeley: University of California Press, 1972); and Ian Stone, *Canal Irrigation in British India: Perspectives on Technological Change in a Peasant Economy* (New York: Cambridge University Press, 1984).

42. Tai Yong Tan, *The Garrison State: The Military, Government, and Society in Colonial Punjab, 1849–1947* (New Delhi: Sage, 2005), 31. See also Rajit K. Mazumder, *The Indian Army and the Making of Punjab* (New Delhi: Permanent Black, 2003); and Kate Imy, *Faithful Fighters: Identity and Power in the British Indian Army* (Stanford: Stanford University Press, 2019).

43. Neeladri Bhattacharya, *The Great Agrarian Conquest: The Colonial Reshaping of a Rural World* (Ranikhet: Permanent Black, 2018), 109.

44. See Richard Saumarez Smith, *Rule by Records: Land Registration and Village Custom in Early British Punjab* (New Delhi: Oxford University Press, 1996); and Tom Kessinger, *Vilyatpur, 1848–1968: Social and Economic Change in a North Indian Village* (Berkeley: University of California Press, 1974).

45. See Harjot Oberoi, *The Construction of Religious Boundaries: Culture, Identity, and Diversity in the Sikh Tradition* (Chicago: University of Chicago Press, 1994); cf. Richard G. Fox, *Lions of the Punjab: Culture in the Making* (Berkeley: University of California Press, 1985); and J. S. Grewal, *Recent Debates in Sikh Studies: An Assessment* (New Delhi: Manohar, 2011). See also Kenneth W. Jones, *Arya Dharm: Hindu Consciousness in 19th-Century Punjab* (Berkeley: University of California Press, 1976); David Gilmartin, *Empire and Islam: Punjab and the Making of Pakistan* (Berkeley: University of California Press, 1988); Christopher Harding, *Religious Transformation in South Asia: The Meanings of Conversion in Colonial Punjab* (Oxford: Oxford University Press, 2008); and Rajbir

Singh Judge, "Reform in Fragments: Sovereignty, Colonialism and the Sikh Tradition," *Modern Asian Studies*, 56, no. 4 (July 2022): 1125–1152.

46. See Prem Chowdhry, *The Veiled Women: Shifting Gender Equations in Rural Haryana 1880–1900* (New Delhi: Oxford University Press, 1994); Anshu Malhotra, *Gender, Caste, and Religious Identities: Restructuring Class in Colonial Punjab* (New Delhi: Oxford University Press, 2002); and Farina Mir, *The Social Space of Language: Vernacular Culture in British Colonial Punjab* (Berkeley: University of California Press, 2010).

47. See Naved Hamid, "Dispossession and Differentiation of the Peasantry in the Punjab during Colonial Rule," *Journal of Peasant Studies* 10, no. 1 (1982): 52–72; Neeladri Bhattacharya, "The Logic of Tenancy Cultivation: Central and South-East Punjab, 1870–1935," *The Indian Economic and Social History Review* 20, no. 2 (1983): 121–170; and Bhattacharya, "Agricultural Labour and Production: Central and South-East Punjab, 1870–1940," in *The World of the Rural Labourer in Colonial India*, ed. Gyan Prakash (New Delhi: Oxford University Press, 1992).

48. Chakrabarty, "Small History," 19.

49. Sugata Bose, *Peasant Labour and Colonial Capital: Rural Bengal since 1770* (Cambridge: Cambridge University Press, 1993), 64. See also B. R. Tomlinson, *The Economy of Modern India: From 1860 to the Twenty-First Century* (Cambridge: Cambridge University Press, 2013), 65–68.

Chapter 1

1. Bernard Cohn, "Law and the Colonial State in India," *Colonialism and Its Forms of Knowledge: The British in India* (Princeton: Princeton University Press, 1996), 65. See also C. A. Bayly, *Indian Society and the Making of the British Empire* (Cambridge: Cambridge University Press, 1988); Seema Alavi, *The Sepoys and the Company: Tradition and Transition in Northern India, 1770–1830* (New Delhi: Oxford University Press, 1998); and Robert Travers, *Ideology and Empire in Eighteenth-Century India: The British in Bengal* (Cambridge: Cambridge University Press, 2007).

2. *General report on the administration of the Punjab territories, from 1854–55 to 1855–56 inclusive* (hereafter *General Report 1854–55 to 1855–56*) (Lahore: Punjabee Press, 1858), 21–22.

3. "It is worth while calling attention to the absence of great landlords in the Panjab," writes Baden Henry Baden-Powell, a colonial judge and author of a three-volume treatise on land relations in British India. The main reason for this difference is that "neither the Muhammadan empire nor the Pathan conquerors, nor the later Sikh rulers, ever allowed the local chiefs such power as belonged to the Taluqdar of Oudh or the Zamindar of Bengal; consequentially, they never grew into landlords." At the same time, however, "the bulk of land is *not* cultivated by tenants." Rather, "petty proprietors, co-sharers in village estates—holding fractional shares, or according to some other rule—cultivate their own lands, with their sons and cousins, and often their wives." Revenue policy in Panjab therefore "developed on special lines." See Baden-Powell, *The Land-Systems of British India*, vol. 2 (Oxford: Clarendon Press, 1892), 3:617–18, 569, emphasis in original. Another explanation for the absence of large zamindars in Panjab in comparison with other parts of north India is that they were effectively dismantled and dispersed by the insurgency of Banda Singh Bahadur and its aftermath in the early eighteenth century. In many contemporary

oral and popular accounts, especially among Sikhs, this is regarded as the origins of a small-holding yet self-cultivating peasantry. See Ganda Singh, *Life of Banda Singh Bahadur: Based on Contemporary and Original Sources* (Amritsar: The Sikh History Research Department, 1935); Muzaffar Alam, "Sikh Uprisings under Banda Bahadur 1708–1715," *Proceedings of the Indian History Congress*, vol. 39 (1978): 509–22; and J. S. Grewal, *The Sikhs of the Punjab*, rev. ed. (Cambridge: Cambridge University Press, 1990), ch. 5.

4. Norman G. Barrier, *The Punjab Alienation of Land Bill of 1900* (Durham: Duke University Press, 1966), 4–5.

5. For instance, see P.H.M. van den Dungen, *The Punjab Tradition: Influence and Authority in Nineteenth-Century India* (London: George Allen & Unwin, 1972); Richard G. Fox, *Lions of the Punjab: Culture in the Making* (Berkeley: University of California Press, 1985); Clive Dewey, *Anglo-Indian Attitudes: The Mind of the Indian Civil Service* (London: Hambledon Press, 1993); and Mark Condos, *The Insecurity State: Punjab and the Making of Colonial Power in British India* (Cambridge: Cambridge University Press, 2017), ch. 2.

6. Neeladri Bhattacharya, *The Great Agrarian Conquest: The Colonial Reshaping of a Rural World* (Ranikhet: Permanent Black, 2018), 35, 52.

7. Imran Ali, *The Punjab Under Imperialism, 1885–1947* (Princeton: Princeton University Press, 1988), 238. See also M. Mufakharul Islam, *Irrigation, Agriculture, and the Raj: Punjab, 1887–1947* (New Delhi: Manohar Publishers, 1997).

8. Veena Talwar Oldenburg, *Dowry Murder: The Imperial Origins of a Cultural Crime* (New York: Oxford University Press, 2002), 13, 129. See also David Gilmartin, *Empire and Islam: Punjab and the Making of Pakistan* (Oakland: University of California Press, 1988), chs. 1–2.

9. It is this paradox of Marxists calling for more capitalism that led Andre Gunder Frank to bluntly state that "the historical mission and role of the bourgeoisie in Latin America [. . .] is finished," and thus begin a critique of the linearity of economic progress by examining the simultaneity of development and underdevelopment. See Frank, *Capitalism and Underdevelopment in Latin America* (Harmondsworth: Penguin Books, 1969), 16 and *passim*.

10. The parameters of the debate are from Paul M. Sweezy, "The Transition from Feudalism to Capitalism," *Science and Society* 14, no. 2 (Spring 1950): 134–167; Immanuel Wallerstein, *The Modern World-System: Capitalist Agriculture and the Origins of the European World-Economy in the Sixteenth Century* (New York: Academic Press, 1974); Maurice Dobbs, *Studies in the Development of Capitalism* (New York: International Publishers, 1947); and Robert Brenner, "The Origins of Capitalist Development: A Critique of Neo-Smithian Marxism," *New Left Review* 1, no. 104 (August 1977): 25–92. For a review, see Alice Thorner, "Semi-Feudal or Capitalism? Contemporary Debate on Classes and Modes of Production in India," *Economic and Political Weekly* 17, nos. 49, 50, and 51 (December 4, 11 and 18, 1982): 1961–1968, 1993–1999 and 2061–2066; and more recently Nikhil Pal Singh, "On Race, Violence, and So-Called Primitive Accumulation," *Social Text* 34, no. 3 (September 2016): 27–50.

11. See Eugen Weber, *Peasants into Frenchmen: The Modernization of Rural France, 1870–1914* (Stanford: Stanford University Press, 1976), chs. 12–20.

12. For summaries, see Aidan Foster-Carter, "The Modes of Production Controversy," *New Left Review* 1, no. 107 (February 1978): 47–77; and Robert J. Holton, "Marxist

Theories of Social Change and the Transition from Feudalism to Capitalism," *Theory and Society* 10, no. 6 (November 1981): 833–867. The question of peasant/wage laborer transition is traced in Henry Bernstein and Terence J. Byres, "From Peasant Studies to Agrarian Change," *Journal of Agrarian Change* 1, no. 1 (January 2001): 8–13, 17–35.

13. See Frank Perlin, "Proto-Industrialization and Pre-Colonial South Asia," *Past and Present* no. 98 (February 1983): 30–95; David Washbrook, "Law, State, and Agrarian Society in Colonial India," *Modern Asian Studies* 15, no. 3 (1981): 649–721; David Washbrook, "Progress and Problems: South Asian Economic and Social History c. 1720–1860," *Modern Asian Studies* 22, no. 1 (1988): 57–96; and Partha Chatterjee, *The Nation and Its Fragments: Colonial and Postcolonial Histories* (Princeton: Princeton University Press, 1993), ch. 2.

14. This vast literature usually begins with Eric Williams, *Capitalism and Slavery* (Chapel Hill: University of North Carolina Press, 1944). For a review of recent works, see James Oakes, "Capitalism and Slavery and the Civil War," *International Labor and Working-Class History*, no. 89 (Spring 2016): 195–220. See also Sven Beckert and Seth Rockman, eds., *Slavery's Capitalism: A New History of American Economic Development* (Philadelphia: University of Pennsylvania Press, 2016). The classic problem of categorizing slave labor was provocatively questioned in Sidney W. Mintz, "Was the Plantation Slave a Proletarian?" *Review* (Fernand Braudel Center) 2, no. 1 (Summer 1978): 81–98.

15. See Ritu Birla, *Stages of Capital: Law, Culture, and Market Governance in Late Colonial India* (Durham: Duke University Press, 2009), 3–4 and introduction.

16. Two of the earliest accounts of Panjab and its Sikh rulers that came to influence Company officials are James Browne, *India Tracts: Containing a Description of the Jungle Terry Districts, their Revenues, Trade, and Government: With a Plan for the Improvement of Them. Also an History of the Origin and Progress of the Sicks* (London: Logographic Press, 1788); and George Forster, *A Journey from Bengal to England, through the northern part of India, Kashmire, Afghanistan, and Persia, and into Russia, by the Caspian-Sea*, 2 vols. (London: Faulder, 1798).

17. See "Treaty with the Rajah of Lahore, 1809," in *A Collection of Treaties, Engagements, and Sanads Relating to India and Neighbouring Countries*, vol. 9, compiled by C. U. Aitchison (Calcutta: Office of the Superintendent of Government Printing, 1892), 23.

18. See Amarpal S. Sidhu, *The First Anglo-Sikh War* (Stroud: Amberley Publishing, 2010); Priya Atwal, *Royals and Rebels: The Rise and Fall of the Sikh Empire* (London: Hurst, 2020), chs. 4–5; and Sunit Singh, "The Sikh Kingdom," in *The Oxford Handbook on Sikh Studies*, ed. Pashaura Singh and Louis E. Fenech (Oxford: Oxford University Press, 2014). For the disputed firsthand account of Alexander Gardner, an American who traveled in Central Asia and briefly served in Ranjit Singh's army, see John Keay, *The Tartan Turban: In Search of Alexander Gardner* (London: Kashi House, 2017).

19. On the 1846 Treaty of Lahore, see *The Imperial Gazetteer of India*, vol. 11, ed. William Wilson Hunter (London: Trubner & Co., 1886), xi, 265. The full list of conditions included: "[T]he surrender, in full sovereignty of the territory, hill and plain, lying between the Sutluj and Beas rivers; the payment of one crore and a half of rupees [15,000,000], as indemnity for the expenses of the war; the disbandment of the present Sikh army, and its re-organization under the system and regulations with regard to pay

which existed in the time of Runjeet Singh; the arrangement for limiting the extent of the force which might be henceforth employed to be determined on in communication with the British Government; the surrender of all the guns that had been pointed against [the Company]; the entire regulation and control of both banks of the river Sutluj, to be ceded to [the Company], and such other arrangements for settling the future boundaries of the Sikh state, and the organization of its administration, as might be determined on at Lahore." Henry James Prinsep, *History of the Punjab, and of the Rise, Progress, and Present Condition of the Sect and Nation of the Sikhs*, vol. 2 (London: W. H. Allen & Co., 1846), 359–60.

20. See Amarpal S. Sidhu, *The Second Anglo-Sikh War* (Stroud: Amberley Publishing, 2016).

21. "Proclamation by the Governor-General," enclosure 11 in no. 51, in *Papers relating to the Punjab, 1847–49* (London: Harrison and Son, 1849), 655.

22. "With the conquest of Scinde [Sind] and the Punjaub," Marx explains in an article discussing the 1857 revolt, "the Anglo-Indian empire had not only reached its natural limits, but it had trampled out the last vestiges of independent Indian States. All warlike native tribes were subdued, all serious internal conflicts were at an end, and the late incorporation of Oude proved satisfactorily that the remnants of the so-called independent Indian principalities exist on sufferance only. Hence a great change in the position of the East Indian Company. It no longer attacked one part of India by the help of another part, but found itself placed at the head, and the whole of India at its feet." See Marx, "The Revolt in the Indian Army," *New York Daily Tribune*, July 15, 1857, in Marx and Friedrich Engels, *On Colonialism* (Moscow: Progress Publishers, 1968): 130, emphasis in original.

23. For a discussion of the personalities and politics of early colonial rule, see Dewey, *Anglo-Indian Attitudes*, chs. 5–7; Dungen, *The Punjab Tradition*, chs. 2–3; and Bhattacharya, *Great Agrarian Conquest*, ch. 1.

24. For studies of the 1857 uprising, see Thomas Metcalf, *The Aftermath of Revolt: India 1857–1970* (Princeton: Princeton University Press, 1964); Eric Stokes, *The Peasant Armed: The Indian Revolt of 1857*, ed. C. A. Bayly (Oxford: Clarendon Press, 1986); and Kim A. Wagner, *Rumours and Rebels: A New History of the Indian Uprising of 1857* (London: Peter Lang, 2016).

25. Karuna Mantena, *Alibis of Empire: Henry Maine and the Ends of Liberal Imperialism* (Princeton: Princeton University Press, 2010), 5.

26. For the quotations used in this paragraph, see "Proclamation by the Governor-General," 707.

27. For an argument to extend the Company's empire to the Indus River, see Montague Gore, *Remarks on the Present State of the Punjaub* (London: James Ridgway, 1849); for a return to the Sutlej River border, see John Briggs, *What Are We to Do with the Punjab?* (London: James Madden, 1849).

28. "Proclamation by the Governor-General," 707.

29. "Proclamation by the Governor-General," 707. The emphasis on respecting religion while demanding disarmament reflects the colonial inability to comprehend the integral place of weapons in the Sikh tradition. See Arvind-Pal S. Mandair, *Violence and the Sikhs* (Cambridge; Cambridge University Press, 2022).

30. "Governor-General to the Secret Committee," no. 52 in *Papers relating to the Punjab, 1847–49*, 714.
31. "Governor-General to the Secret Committee," 714.
32. "Governor-General to the Secret Committee," 714–15.
33. An influential text, central to instigating what became known as the "Great Game" between Britain and Russia, is Alexander Burns's three-volume *Travels into Bokhara: Being the Account of a Journey from India to Cabool, Tartary, and Persia* (London: John Murray, 1834). See also David Hopkins, *The Dangers of British India, from French Invasion and Missionary Establishments* (London: Black, Parry and Kingsbury, 1809); and G. T. Vigne, *A Personal Narrative of a Visit to Ghuzni, Kabul, and Afghanistan, and of a Residence at the Court of Dost Mohamed; with Notices of Runjit Sing, Khiva, and the Russian Expedition* (London: Whittaker & Co., 1840).
34. See Browne, *India Tracts*; John Malcolm, *Sketch of the Sikhs; A Singular Nation, Who Inhabit the Province of the Penjab, Situated Between the Rivers Jumna and Indus* (London: John Murray, 1812); Henry T. Prinsep, *Origin of the Sikh Power in the Punjab, and Political Life of Muha-Raja Runjeet Singh* (Calcutta: Military Orphan Press, 1834); W.G. Osborne, *Court and Camp of Runjeet Sing* (London: Henry Colburn, 1840); and Briggs, *What Are We to Do with the Punjab?* See also Amandeep Singh Madra and Parmjit Singh, *Sicques, Tigers, or Thieves: Eyewitness Accounts of the Sikhs (1606–1809)* (London: Palgrave Macmillan, 2004).
35. R. Baird Smith, *Agricultural Resources of the Punjab* (London: Smith, Elder and Co., 1849), 15, emphasis in original. On the preeminent role of cotton in shaping global capitalism, see Sven Beckert, *Empire of Cotton: A Global History* (New York: Vintage, 2014).
36. Smith, *Agricultural Resources of the Punjab*, 14, 17, 23, 14.
37. Smith, *Agricultural Resources of the Punjab*, 24–25.
38. Smith, *Agricultural Resources of the Punjab*, 26–28.
39. Smith, *Agricultural Resources of the Punjab*, 30, 32.
40. Smith, *Agricultural Resources of the Punjab*, 24–25, 27.
41. Smith, *Agricultural Resources of the Punjab*, 15, 16.
42. Smith, *Agricultural Resources of the Punjab*, 15.
43. "Governor-General to the Secret Committee," 664.
44. Smith, *Agricultural Resources of the Punjab*, 36.
45. *General report upon the administration of the Punjab proper for the years 1849–50 and 1850–51, being the two first years after annexation; with a supplementary notice of the cis and trans-Sutlej territories* (hereafter *General Report 1849–50 and 1850–51*) (London: J & H Cox, 1854), 20–21. See also Bhattacharya, *Great Agrarian Conquest*, ch. 2.
46. See Dewey, *Anglo-Indian Attitudes*, ch. 1; and Dungen, *Punjab Tradition*, ch. 2.
47. Mantena, *Alibis of Empire*, 120. "It may be stated at once," writes Baden-Powell, "that the Land Revenue has, *under every form of Government, and at all times,* been so essentially the mainstay of the State income, and its administration has so necessarily involved a network of local jurisdictions and a graded staff of local officers, that the Land Revenue local jurisdiction *is the basis of all other administration divisions* of the territory." See Baden-Powell, *A Short Account of the Land Revenue and its Administration in British India; with a Sketch of the Land Tenures* (Oxford: Clarendon Press, 1907), 21, emphasis added.

48. C. A. Bayly, *Empire and Information: Intelligence Gathering and Social Information in India, 1780–1870* (Cambridge: Cambridge University Press, 1996), 151.

49. Even this book, Robert Needham Cust, *Manual for the Guidance of Revenue Officers in the Punjab* (Lahore: Koh-i-Noor Press, 1866), relied extensively on an amalgamation of materials from earlier texts. The next substantial iterations were D. G. Barkley, *Directions for Revenue Officers in the Punjab* (Lahore: Central Jail Press, 1875), followed by James Douie, *Panjab Settlement Manual* (Lahore: Civil and Military Gazette Press, 1899).

50. James Thomason, *Remarks on the System of Land Revenue Administration Prevalent in the North Western Provinces of Hindoostan* (Calcutta: Baptist Mission Press, 1850). See also Bhattacharya, *Great Agrarian Conquest*, 73.

51. See Ranajit Guha, *A Rule of Property for Bengal: An Essay on the Idea of Permanent Settlement* (Paris: Mouton & Co., 1963); Sugata Bose, *Peasant Labour and Colonial Capital: Rural Bengal Since 1770* (Cambridge: Cambridge University Press, 1993); and Peter Robb, *Ancient Rights and Future Comforts: Bihar, the Bengal Tenancy Act of 1885, and British Rule in India* (Surrey: Curzon Press, 1997).

52. Cust, *Manual*, 66–68.

53. Baden-Powell, *Land-Systems of British India*, vol. 1, 1:211; See also Baden-Powell, "The Permanent Settlement of Bengal," *English Historical Review* 10, no. 38 (April 1895): 276–92.

54. Henry Steinbach, *The Punjaub: Being a Brief Account of the Country of the Sikhs* (London: Smith, Elder & Co., 1845), 67–69. In particular, he describes the "Akalees" as "religious fanatics" who "acknowledge no ruler or laws but their own; think nothing of robbery, or even murder, should they happen to be in the humour for it. [. . .] They move about constantly armed to the teeth, insulting everybody they meet, particularly Europeans." See also Henry Lawrence, *Adventures of an Officer in the Punjaub*, 2 vols. (London: Henry Colburn, 1846).

55. "Governor-General to the Secret Committee," 716, emphasis added.

56. On the politics of military recruitment, see Rajit K. Mazumder, *The Indian Army and the Making of Punjab* (New Delhi: Permanent Black, 2003); Tai Yong Tan, *The Garrison State: The Military, Government, and Society in Colonial Punjab, 1849–1947* (New Delhi: Sage Publishers, 2005); and Kate Imy, *Faithful Fighters: Identity and Power in the British Indian Army* (Stanford: Stanford University Press, 2019).

57. *General Report 1849–50 and 1850–51*, paragraph 89.

58. See Faiz Ahmed, *Afghanistan Rising: Islamic Law and Statecraft between the Ottoman and British Empires* (Cambridge: Harvard University Press, 2017), chs. 2–3; M. Hasan Kakar, *A Political and Diplomatic History of Afghanistan* (Leiden: Brill, 2006), chs. 2–3, 10; and B. D. Hopkins, *The Making of Modern Afghanistan* (London: Palgrave Macmillan, 2008), chs. 2–3.

59. See Baden-Powell, *A Short Account of the Land Revenue*, 148–213; and Baden-Powell, *The Land-Systems of British India*, vol. 1, 1:154–59. See also Eric Stokes, *The Peasant and the Raj: Studies in the Agrarian Society and Peasant Rebellion in Colonial India* (Cambridge: Cambridge University Press, 1978), chs. 1, 2, 4, 9; Tom Kessinger, *Vilyatpur, 1848–1968: Social and Economic Change in a North Indian Village* (Berkeley: University of California Press, 1974), ch. 2; and Bhattacharya, *Great Agrarian Conquest*, ch. 2.

60. *General Report 1849–50 and 1850–51*, 66.

61. The name *Panjab* is widely mistranslated as the "land of the five rivers" from an imprecise conjugation of the words *panj*, meaning five, and *ab*, thought to mean rivers or waters but actually referring to the alluvial tract between two rivers. In that sense, Panjab is better understood as the land of the five inter-river tracts—between the Indus and the Sutlej or even Yamuna—which, as the course of rivers shift, might more closely reflect the changing boundaries between and across them. See Grewal, *Sikhs of the Punjab*, 1–2.

62. *General Report 1849–50 and 1850–51*, 57. On the revenue system under Ranjit Singh, see Indu Banga, *Agrarian System of the Sikhs: Late Eighteenth and Early Nineteenth Century* (New Delhi: Manohar Publishers, 1978), chs. 4–5; and Indu Banga and J. S. Grewal, *Maharaja Ranjit Singh: The State and Society* (Amritsar: Guru Nanak Dev University Press, 2001).

63. *General Report 1849–50 and 1850–51*, 64.

64. *General Report 1849–50 and 1850–51*, 64.

65. Minute by the Honourable J. Lowis, Esq., 9 June 1853, in *General Report 1849–50 and 1850–51*, 322–23.

66. Minute by the Honourable J. Dorin, Esq., 15 June 1853, in *General Report 1849–50 and 1850–51*, 328.

67. Foreign Department, no. 52, letter to the Honourable the Court of Directors of the East-India Company, 2 July 1853, by Dalhousie, J. Lowis and J. Dorin, in *General Report 1849–50 and 1850–51*, iii.

68. Political Department, no. 42, letter from the Court of Directors of the East-India Company to the Governor-General of India in Council, 26 October 1853, by R. Ellice and J. Oliphant, in *General Report 1849–50 and 1850–51*, v–vi.

69. The more notable divisions include the creation of a separate North-West Frontier Province in 1901, the separation of Delhi after it was designated the capital of British India in 1912, the partition of the remainder of Panjab between India and Pakistan in 1947, and the creation of the states of Haryana and Himachal Pradesh from East Panjab in 1966.

70. *General report on the administration of the Punjab territories, comprising the Punjab proper and the cis and trans-Sutlej States, 1851–52 to 1852–53* (hereafter *General Report 1851–52 to 1852–53*) (Calcutta: Calcutta Gazette Office, 1854), 93.

71. *General Report 1851–52 to 1852–53*, 138. While "In train of liquidation" meant that an agreement had been reached to pay the outstanding balance in installments, and "Nominal" meant an amount legitimately excused under existing rules, the other two categories were an admission of the losses the colonial state was willing to endure.

72. *General Report 1851–52 to 1852–53*, 131; see also Kessinger, *Vilyatpur*, 31–32.

73. *General Report 1854–55 to 1855–56*, 24–25.

74. *General Report 1856–57 to 1857–58*, 20.

75. *General Report 1851–52 to 1852–53*, 131.

76. See, for instance, Dungen, *The Punjab Tradition*; Fox, *Lions of the Punjab*; and Condos, *The Insecurity State*, ch. 3.

77. See Rupa Viswanath, *The Pariah Problem: Caste, Religion, and the Social in Modern India* (New York: Columbia University Press, 2014), ch. 5.

78. *General Report 1849–50 and 1850–51*, 5.

79. *General Report 1849–50 and 1850–51*, 56–57.
80. *General Report 1849–50 and 1850–51*, 6.
81. Richard Temple, *Report on the settlement, under regn. IX, of 1833, of the district of Jullundhur, Trans-Sutlej states* (Lahore: Chronicle Press, 1852), 17. See also Bhattacharya, *Great Agrarian Conquest*, 75–83.
82. Temple, *Report*, 69. One rupee contains sixteen annas.
83. H. Davidson, *Report on the revised settlement of the district of Ludhiana in the Cis-Sutlej states* (Lahore: Punjabee Press, 1859), 51.
84. G. C. Barnes et al., *Report on the revised settlement of the Oonah, Hushiarpur, Gurshunkur, and Hurriana purgunahs of the Hushiarpur district in the Trans-Sutlej states* (Lahore: Punjabee Press, 1860), 29.
85. Davidson, *Report*, 51.
86. Temple, *Report*, "Produce Statement No. I." 1 maund equals approximately 82.2 pounds.
87. Temple, *Report*, "Produce Statement No. I."
88. Temple, *Report*, "Produce Statement No. II."
89. E. L. Brandreth, *Report on the revised settlement of the district of Ferozpoor in the Cis-Satlej states* (Lahore: Chronicle Press, 1859), 44.
90. See Guha, *Rule of Property for Bengal*, chs. 1, 4.
91. On the politics of water management in colonial Panjab, see David Gilmartin, *Blood and Water: The Indus River Basin in Modern History* (Oakland: University of California Press, 2015), ch. 3.
92. Brandreth, *Report*, 44.
93. Brandreth, *Report*, 44.
94. See David Gilmartin, "Scientific Empire and Imperial Science: Colonialism and Irrigation Technology in the Indus Basin," *Journal of Asian Studies* 53, no. 4 (November 1994): 1127–49. See also Timothy Mitchell, *Rule of Experts: Egypt, Techno-Politics, Modernity* (Berkeley: University of California Press, 2002), ch. 3; Tania Li, *The Will to Improve: Governmentality, Development, and the Practice of Politics* (Durham: Duke University Press, 2007), ch. 1; and Vinay Gidwani, *Capital, Interrupted: Agrarian Development and the Politics of Work in India* (Minneapolis: University of Minnesota Press, 2008), ch. 1.
95. On colonial irrigation schemes, see Elizabeth Whitcombe, *Agrarian Conditions in Northern India: The United Provinces under British Rule, 1860–1900* (Berkeley: University of California Press, 1972); Ali, *Punjab Under Imperialism*; and Gilmartin, *Blood and Water*, ch. 5.
96. *Punjab Report in Reply to the Inquiries Issued by the Famine Commission* (hereafter *Punjab Reply*), vol. 2 (Lahore: Central Jail Press, 1878–79), 601.
97. *Punjab Reply*, 601, emphasis added.
98. The report concludes with a subtle warning: "Any attempt to ignore this principle [of difference] in our assessments in favour of theoretical equality would not only be financially injurious, but it would be distinctly opposed to the common feeling of the country." *Punjab Report in Reply*, 601.
99. Davidson, *Report*, 56.
100. Davidson, *Report*, 7, 14.

101. Davidson, *Report*, 14.
102. Davidson, *Report*, 14.
103. R.H. Davies and W. Blyth, *Report on the revised settlement of the Umritsur, Sowrian, and Turun Tarun pergunnahs of the Umritsur district in the Umritsur division* (Lahore: Hope Press, 1860), 2, 65.
104. Brandreth, *Report*, 5, 21, 23.
105. See Gyanendra Pandey, "'The Bigoted Julaha,'" *Economic and Political Weekly* 18, no. 5 (January 29, 1983): 27.
106. A crucial assumption of these reports is the equating of peasants with men, to the elision of the many labors of women in agricultural production. See Prem Chowdhry, *The Veiled Women: Shifting Gender Equations in Rural Haryana, 1880–1990* (New Delhi: Oxford University Press, 1994); and Bina Agarwal, *A Field of One's Own: Gender and Land Rights in South Asia* (Cambridge: Cambridge University Press, 1994).
107. Cf. Nicholas B. Dirks, *Castes of Mind: Colonialism and the Making of Modern India* (Princeton: Princeton University Press, 2001), 43–44.
108. See Banga, *Agrarian System of the Sikhs*, ch. 5; Grewal, *Sikhs of the Punjab*, ch. 6; and Anne Murphy, *The Materiality of the Past: History and Representation in Sikh Tradition* (New York: Oxford University Press, 2012), chs. 5–6. While eighteenth- and early nineteenth-century Panjab shared certain features with other regions of the decentralizing Mughal Empire, it is not adequately captured with the telos of an embryonic capitalism or the stagism of a prolonged feudalism. See Irfan Habib, "Potentialities of Capitalistic Development in the Economy of Mughal India," *Journal of Economic History* 29, no. 1 (March 1969): 32–78; and Jairus Banaji, "Trajectories of Accumulation or 'Transitions' to Capitalism?" in *Theory as History: Essays on Modes of Production and Exploitation* (Leiden: Brill, 2010), 336.
109. See Shahid Amin, *Sugarcane and Sugar in Gorakhpur: An Inquiry into Peasant Production for Capitalist Enterprise in Colonial India* (New Delhi: Oxford University Press, 1984); and David Hardiman, *Feeding the Baniya: Peasants and Usurers in Western India* (New Delhi: Oxford University Press, 1996). For an analysis of the relationship among indebtedness, thriftlessness and landlessness in Panjab, see Chapter 3.
110. Gilmartin, *Blood and Water*, 72. See also David Ludden, *Peasant History in South India* (Princeton: Princeton University Press, 1985), ch. 4.
111. The well-known general difficulty in accessing materials for the study of rural life from previous centuries is compounded for the colonial world due precisely to the question of capital through the emergence of the modern state and its official archives. See Dipesh Chakrabarty, *Habitations of Modernity: Essays in the Wake of Subaltern Studies* (Chicago: University of Chicago Press, 2002), ch. 1; Gayatri Chakravorty Spivak, "Can the Subaltern Speak?" in *Marxism and the Interpretation of Culture*, ed. Cary Nelson and Lawrence Grossberg (Urbana: University of Illinois Press, 1988), 275–91, 294–306; and Ranajit Guha, "The Prose of Counter-Insurgency," in *Subaltern Studies II: Writings on South Asian History and Society*, ed. Ranajit Guha (New Delhi: Oxford University Press, 1983), 1–40. On the politics of grappling with archival silences and absences, see Anjali Arondekar, *For the Record: On Sexuality and the Colonial Archive in India* (Durham: Duke University Press, 2009); and Durba Mitra, *Indian Sex Life: Sexuality and the Colonial Origins of Modern Social Thought* (Princeton: Princeton University Press, 2020).

112. Letter from Captain D. Ross, Commissioner and Superintendent, Leia Division, to P. Melvill, esq., Secretary to the Board of Administration, Lahore, 5 June 1851, in *General report 1849–50 and 1850–1*, 237.

113. *General Report 1851–52 to 1852–53*, 106.

114. *General Report 1851–52 to 1852–53*, 145, emphasis in original.

115. See Andrew Sartori, *Liberalism in Empire: An Alternative History* (Oakland: University of California Press, 2014), ch. 1.

116. *General Report 1849–50 and 1850–51*, 20.

117. See *General Report 1849–50 and 1850–51*, 83–86. See also Grewal, *Sikhs of the Punjab*, 96, 106–9, 135–36.

118. "The ease and quiet with which this measure was carried out is worthy of remark," notes the report in one of the many moments of self-congratulation. "That large bodies of brave men, once so turbulent and formidable as to overawe their Government and wield the destinies of their country, should lay down their arms, receive their arrears, and retire from an exciting profession to till the ground, without in any place creating a disturbance, is indicative of the effect which had been produced by the British power, of the manly forbearance which characterizes the Sikhs, and of the satisfaction felt at the justice of the Government." *General Report 1849–50 and 1850–51*, 22.

119. Letter from Edward Thornton, esq., Commissioner and Superintendent, Jhelum division, to P. Melvill, esq., Secretary to the Board of Administration, Lahore, 25 September 1851, in *General Report 1849–50 and 1850–51*, 210–11.

120. Jairus Banaji argues against the dominance of this narrative, while acknowledging the challenge to move beyond it: "The entrenched orthodoxy that England's history supplies us with an archetype of capitalist agriculture is a myth. It is much less credible today as historians begin to map the very different ways in which capitalism evolved in agriculture and continues to do so. There is no 'pure' agrarian capitalism." See Banaji, "Trajectories of Accumulation or 'Transitions' to Capitalism?" 335.

121. On the ideology that informed classical political economists, see Michael Perelman, *The Invention of Capitalism: Classical Political Economy and the Secret History of Primitive Accumulation* (Durham: Duke University Press, 2000).

122. Karl Marx, *Capital: Volume I: A Critique of Political Economy*, trans. Ben Fowkes (London: Penguin Books, 1976), 876, emphasis added.

123. See Marx, *Capital: Volume I*, 878–96.

124. Marx, *Capital: Volume I*, 899. It is the disciplining of these vagabonds, delinquents, and migrants that Michel Foucault explores in detail in *Madness and Civilization: A History of Insanity in the Age of Reason*, trans. Richard Howard (London: Routledge, 2001), chs. 1–2. See also Perelman, *Invention of Capitalism*, ch. 1.

125. Rosa Luxemburg, *The Accumulation of Capital*, trans. Agnes Schwarzschild (London: Routledge, 2003), 348.

126. Capital, Luxemburg states, "must begin by planning for the systematic destruction and annihilation of all the non-capitalist social units which obstruct its development. With that we have passed beyond the stage of primitive accumulation; this process is still going on. Each new colonial expansion is accompanied, as a matter of course, by a relentless battle of capital against the social and economic ties of the natives, who are also forcibly robbed of their means of production and labour power." Later, she adds

that "capital cannot accumulate without the aid of non-capitalist organisations, nor, on the other hand, can it tolerate their continued existence side by side with itself. Only the continuous and progressive disintegration of non-capitalist organisations makes accumulation of capital possible." Luxemburg, *Accumulation of Capital*, 350, 397.

127. See David Harvey, *The New Imperialism* (Oxford: Oxford University Press, 2003), 87–89. See also David Harvey, *Spaces of Capital: Towards a Critical Geography* (Edinburgh: Edinburgh University Press, 2001), chs. 12–15.

128. Harvey, *New Imperialism*, 141.

129. Harvey, *New Imperialism*, 148.

130. See, for instance, Michael Levien, Michael Watts, and Yan Hairong, eds., Special Issue, *The Journal of Peasant Studies* 45, no. 5–6 (2018); and cf. William Clare Roberts, "What Was Primitive Accumulation? Reconstructing the Origin of a Critical Concept," *European Journal of Political Theory* 19, no. 4 (2020): 532–52. See also Silvia Federici, *Caliban and the Witch: Women, the Body, and Primitive Accumulation*, 2nd rev. ed. (Brooklyn: Autonomedia, 2014); and Maria Mies, *Patriarchy and Accumulation on a World Scale: Women in the International Division of Labour* (London: Zed Books, 1986).

131. See Gidwani, *Capital, Interrupted*, ch. 5; Achin Chakraborty and Anthony D'Costa, eds., *The Land Question in India: State, Dispossession, and Capitalist Transition* (Oxford: Oxford University Press, 2017).

132. Harvey, *New Imperialism*, 140, emphasis added. On capitalism and noncapitalist differences in postcolonial India, see Kalyan Sanyal, *Rethinking Capitalist Development: Primitive Accumulation, Governmentality, and Post-colonial Capitalism* (London: Routledge, 2007).

133. For the Patnaiks, this is the "basic difference" of how capitalism treated the peasantry in the colonized world as compared to Europe: "In the latter, they were destroyed as a class to be reincarnated in another avatar, while in the former, they continued to *linger on* despite the fact that their incomes were increasingly compressed by capitalism." See Utsa Patnaik and Prabhat Patnaik, *A Theory of Imperialism* (New York: Columbia University Press, 2017), 149, emphasis added.

134. See Dipesh Chakrabarty, "Small History of Subaltern Studies."

135. Louis Althusser, "The Errors of Classical Economics: An Outline for a Concept of Historical Time," in Althusser and Étienne Balibar, *Reading Capital*, trans. Ben Brewster (London: Verso, 2009), 128.

136. Althusser, "The Errors of Classical Economics," 129, emphasis in original.

137. Althusser makes explicit the need to revise our expectations of Marx. The complex, actual history of English capitalism is something "Marx did not propose to study in *Capital*" even if it is relevant to Marxist theory. Instead, "we must recognize what Marx actually gave us and what he enabled us to obtain for ourselves, although he could not give it to us." See Althusser, "Appendix: On the 'Ideal Average' and the Forms of Transition," in Althusser and Balibar, *Reading Capital*, 218–19, emphasis in original.

138. "It is not clear precisely how industrialized Britain was in the 1830s," argues Angela Zimmerman, "or even exactly how one would measure "industrialization."" See A. Zimmerman, "The Ideology of the Machine and the Spirit of the Factory: Remarx on Babbage and Ure," *Cultural Critique*, no. 37 (Autumn 1997): 6. On the historical

transformation of labor and capital relations in the English countryside, see Robert C. Allen, *Enclosure and the Yeoman: The Agricultural Development of the South Midlands, 1450–1850* (Oxford: Clarendon Press, 1992); Mark Overton, *Agricultural Revolution in England: The Transformation of the Agrarian Economy, 1500–1850* (Cambridge: Cambridge University Press, 1996); and Jane Whittle, ed., *Landlords and Tenants in Britain, 1440–1660: Tawney's Agrarian Problem Revisited* (Woodbridge: The Boydell Press, 2013).

139. Dipesh Chakrabarty argues that, as opposed to the sources available to Marx, the unique priorities of the colonial state created a different archive from which to apprehend the culture of the proletariat in early twentieth-century Calcutta: "We are not reading Marx as a historian of England, and this is not an exercise in comparative history." See Chakrabarty, "Conditions for Knowledge of Working-Class Conditions: Employers, Government, and the Jute Workers of Calcutta, 1890–1940," in *Subaltern Studies II: Writings on South Asian History and Society*, ed. Ranajit Guha (New Delhi: Oxford University Press, 1983), 260. Similarly, Harry Harootunian explains that Marx focused on tracing the presuppositions of capital's present, an intrinsically nonlinear and discordant history "[a]ppearing from the ruins of universal history." "By limiting Marx's account of primitive accumulation to Western Europe," he argues, "it becomes possible to uncover the existence of multiple different routes to development elsewhere." See Harootunian, *Marx After Marx: History and Time in the Expansion of Capitalism* (New York: Columbia University Press, 2015), 45–46.

140. See Jason Read, *The Micro-Politics of Capital: Marx and the Prehistory of the Present* (Albany: State University of New York Press, 2003), ch. 1; Harootunian, *Marx After Marx*, introduction and ch. 1; and Marcello Musto, "The Writing of *Capital*: Genesis and Structure of Marx's Critique of Political Economy," *Critique: Journal of Socialist Theory* 46, no. 1 (2018): 11–26.

141. Marx, *Capital: Volume I*, 873, emphasis added.

142. Marx, *Capital: Volume I*, 349 fn15, emphasis added.

143. Marx, *Capital: Volume I*, 376.

144. Marx, *Capital: Volume I*, 353.

145. Marx, *Capital: Volume I*, 412–13. For an alternative reading of this period, see Cedric J. Robinson, *Black Marxism: The Making of the Black Radical Tradition* (Chapel Hill: University of North Carolina Press, 2000), chs. 1–3.

146. See the chapter "The General Law of Capitalist Accumulation," in Marx, *Capital: Volume I*, esp. 834–54. See also Arthur Young, *The Farmer's Tour through the East of England*, 4 vols. (London: W. Strahan, 1771).

147. Marx, *Capital: Volume I*, 866.

148. Marx, *Capital: Volume I*, 356, 830.

149. "The industrial bourgeoisie," Marx points out, "was seething with wrath at the denunciations of the factory system made by the landed aristocracy." Marx, *Capital: Volume I*, 830. On the politics surrounding the repeal of the Corn Laws in England, see Overton, *Agricultural Revolution in England*, ch. 4; Cheryl Schonhardt-Bailey, *From the Corn Laws to Free Trade: Interests, Ideas, and Institutions in Historical Perspective* (Cambridge: MIT Press, 2006); and Paul A. Pickering and Alex Tyrrell, *The People's Bread: A History of the Anti-Corn Law League* (London: Leicester University Press, 2000).

150. The *Morning Herald* actually sent special commissioners into agricultural districts not only to research general conditions and gather statistics but also to publish the names of laborers and their landlords. Marx, *Capital: Volume I*, 831.

151. Marx, *Capital: Volume I*, 830–31.

152. Sartori, *Liberalism in Empire*, 206. Sartori goes on to suggest a different set of stakes for reading Marx. Instead of trying to measure correctness, it is "rather a question of whether the concept of 'primitive accumulation,' that ubiquitous trope of Marxist analysis of the agrarian question, is an adequate point of departure for thinking about the relationship of metropolitan capitalism in the nineteenth and twentieth centuries to the far-flung and diverse words with which it interacted." See Sartori, *Liberalism in Empire*, 206–8. See also Jairus Banaji, "The Fictions of Free Labour: Contract, Coercion, and So-Called Unfree Labour," in *Theory as History*, 272.

153. See Teodor Shanin, ed., *Late Marx and the Russian Road: Marx and "the Peripheries of Capitalism"* (New York: Monthly Review Press, 1983); and Kevin Anderson, *Marx at the Margins: On Nationalism, Ethnicity, and Non-Western Societies* (Chicago: University of Chicago Press, 2010).

154. For a critique of the practice of comparison, see Gyanendra Pandey, *A History of Prejudice: Race, Caste, and Difference in India and the United States* (New York: Cambridge University Press, 2013), 8–10. See also Gidwani, *Capital, Interrupted*, xv–xvii; and Philippa Levine, "Is Comparative History Possible?" *History and Theory* 53, no. 3 (October 2014): 331–47.

155. This is why the contrast here is between the writings of colonial officials on Panjab and Marx's narrative of accumulation and not English administrators on England. The apparent incommensurability of the genres is what offers new conceptual rather than empirical insights. See Kenneth Pomeranz, *The Great Divergence: China, Europe, and the Making of the Modern World Economy* (Princeton: Princeton University Press, 2000), 3–10; and Dipesh Chakrabarty, *Provincializing Europe: Postcolonial Thought and Historical Difference* (Princeton: Princeton University Press, 2000), 30–37.

156. Perhaps the most influential accounts of this period, relying largely on an alternative archive, are E. P. Thompson, *The Making of the English Working Class* (New York: Vintage Books, 1963), chs. 7, 15; and Eric Hobsbawm and George Rudé, *Captain Swing* (London: Lawrence and Wishart, 1969), chs. 1–4.

157. See Ranajit Guha, *Dominance without Hegemony: History and Power in Colonial India* (New Delhi: Oxford University Press, 1998), chs. 1, 3; and Bayly, *Empire and Information*, chs. 2, 6.

158. Marx does make an occasional caveat: "The English agricultural labourer receives only a quarter as much milk, and half as much bread, as the Irish. [. . .] The reason is simply this, that the poor Irish farmer is incomparably more humane than the rich English," and therefore provides somewhat more food to those in his employ. Marx, *Capital: Volume I*, 895 fn97.

159. Frantz Fanon, *The Wretched of the Earth*, trans. Richard Philcox (New York: Grove Press, 2004), 5.

160. See Partha Chatterjee, *Nationalist Thought and the Colonial World: A Derivative Discourse?* (London: Zed Books, 1986), ch. 2.

Chapter 2

1. See Richard Temple, *Report on the Census, taken on the 1st of January 1855, of the Population of the Punjab Territories*, in *Selections from the Records of the Government of India* (hereafter *1855 Census*) (Calcutta: Calcutta Gazette Office, 1856), 13–14

2. Temple, *1855 Census*, 20.

3. See Christopher Shackle, "Punjabi in Lahore," *Modern Asian Studies* 4, no. 3 (1970): 239–40; and cf. Denzil Ibbetson, *Report on the Census of the Panjab, taken on the 17th of February 1881*, vol. 1 (Calcutta: Superintendent of Government Printing, 1883), 155–60. Important segments of the population also spoke Bilochi, Pashto, Kashmiri, and Tibetan, Ibbetson notes, while adding that "most of the vagrant and criminal tribes have dialects of their own and intelligible only to themselves."

4. Farina Mir, *The Social Space of Language: Vernacular Culture in British Colonial Punjab* (Berkeley: University of California Press, 2010), 47–49. On the evolution of modern Panjabi in East Panjab after 1947, see Paul R. Brass, *Language, Religion, and Politics in North India* (Cambridge: Cambridge University Press, 1974), ch. 6.

5. On Singh's court, see Tariq Rahman, "Panjabi Language during British Rule," *Journal of Punjab Studies* 14, no. 1 (Spring 2007): 28. On British incentives for suppressing Panjabi generally, see Mir, *Social Space of Language*, 49–53 and ch. 1.

6. H. Davidson, *Report on the revised settlement of the district of Ludhiana in the cis-Sutlej states* (Lahore: The Punjabee Press, 1859), 29.

7. Bernard S. Cohn, "The Command of Language and the Language of Command," in *Subaltern Studies IV: Writings on South Asian History and Society*, ed. Ranajit Guha (New Delhi: Oxford University Press, 1985), 276, 283.

8. Cohn, "Command of Language," 316.

9. Cohn, "Command of Language," 322.

10. E. P. Thompson, for instance, marshalled an array of newspapers, legal proceedings, personal memoirs and letters, rural travelogues, parliamentary debates, and published reports to produce an intimate history of class formation in nineteenth-century England; while Eric Hobsbawm and George Rudé culled a wide body of rural county and health inspector reports, personal letters and newspapers, legal records, and Poor Law commissions to provide an account of the violent unmaking of the rural poor a century earlier. See E. P. Thompson, *The Making of the English Working Class* (New York: Vintage Books, 1963); and Eric Hobsbawm and George Rudé, *Captain Swing* (London: Lawrence and Wishart, 1969).

11. On the different possibilities for history-writing in the colony, see Dipesh Chakrabarty, "Conditions for Knowledge of Working-Class Conditions: Employers, Government and the Jute Workers of Calcutta, 1890–1940," in *Subaltern Studies II: Writings on South Asian History and Society*, ed. Ranajit Guha (New Delhi: Oxford University Press, 1983).

12. See Ranajit Guha, *Elementary Aspects of Peasant Insurgency in Colonial India* (Durham: Duke University Press, 1999), 13–15; and Ranajit Guha, "The Prose of Counter-Insurgency," in *Subaltern Studies II: Writings on South Asian History and Society*, ed. Ranajit Guha (New Delhi: Oxford University Press, 1983).

13. Guha, *Elementary Aspects*, 3.

14. James C. Scott, *Weapons of the Weak: Everyday Forms of Peasant Resistance* (New Haven: Yale University Press, 1985), xvi–xvii.

15. Quotation from Scott, *Weapons of the Weak*, ch. 1. On the politics of paternalism amid exploitation, see Jan Breman, *Patronage and Exploitation: Changing Agrarian Relations in South Gujarat, India* (Berkeley: University of California Press, 1974), chs. 2, 4; Gyan Prakash, *Bonded Histories: Genealogies of Labor Servitude in Colonial India* (Cambridge: Cambridge University Press, 1990), chs. 4–5; and cf. Eugene D. Genovese, *Roll, Jordan, Roll: The World the Slaves Made* (New York: Vintage Books, 1976), parts 1–2.

16. Samuel Cross Starkey, *A Dictionary, English and Punjabee, Outlines of Grammar, also Dialogues, English and Punjabee, with Grammar and Explanatory Notes* (Calcutta: D'Rozario and Co., 1849). To maintain consistency and fidelity, I have retained Starkey's spellings of Panjabi words even where incorrect. Also, the last portion of his dialogues appears to be taken directly from the influential Orientalist and Company doctor John Borthwick Gilchrist's *A Collection of Dialogues, English and Hindoostanee* (Calcutta: The Hindoostanee Press, 1804).

17. On the relationship between Maharaja Ranjit Singh, the Company, and smaller local kingdoms in the early nineteenth century, see Chapter 1.

18. Starkey, *Dictionary*, 7, 64, 110.

19. Starkey, *Dictionary*, 7, 64, 110.

20. Starkey, *Dictionary*, 189.

21. Starkey, *Dictionary*, 162, 44, 206.

22. On Christian missionary activity in Panjab, see Christopher Harding, *Religious Transformation in South Asia: The Meanings of Conversion in Colonial Punjab* (Oxford: Oxford University Press, 2008).

23. J. Newton and L. Janvier, *A Dictionary of the Panjabi Language, Prepared by a Committee of the Lodiana Mission* (Ludhiana: The Mission Press, 1854), iii–iv; and James Massey, "Presbyterian Missionaries and the Development of Punjabi Language and Literature, 1834–1984," *Journal of Presbyterian History* 62, no. 3 (Fall 1984): 258–61.

24. On the advent of dotted letters to distinguish the sounds *sh, z,* and *f* from *s, j,* and *ph,* respectively, see Christopher Shackle, "Some Observations on the Evolution of Modern Standard Punjabi," in *Institutions and Ideologies: A SOAS South Asia Reader*, ed. David Arnold and Peter Robb (Surrey: Curzon Press, 1993), 71 and *passim*.

25. Newton and Janvier, *Dictionary*, 120.

26. Newton and Janvier, *Dictionary*, 190.

27. Newton and Janvier, *Dictionary*, 90–91.

28. See Starkey, *Dictionary*, 284, 70, 166, 171.

29. On the conversion of lower-caste groups in colonial Panjab, see Mark Juergensmeyer, *Religion as Social Vision: The Movement against Untouchability in 20th Century Punjab* (Berkeley: University of California Press, 1981); Harding, *Religious Transformation in South Asia*; and Chapter 4.

30. Cf. Nonica Datta, *Forming an Identity: A Social History of the Jats* (New Delhi: Oxford University Press, 1999).

31. Newton and Janvier, *Dictionary*, 180.

32. Newton and Janvier, *Dictionary*, 180.

33. H. H. Wilson, *A Glossary of the Judicial and Revenue Terms, and of Useful Words Occurring in Official Documents Relating to the Administration of the Government of British India* (London: William H. Allen and Co., 1855), i.

34. While most of the responses from the different Presidencies were paltry, Wilson acknowledges the extremely detailed submission by Henry Elliot from the North West Provinces. That text was also published earlier as Henry Elliot, *Supplement to the Glossary of Indian Terms, A–J* (Agra: Orphan Press, 1845).

35. The languages and scripts Wilson includes are Arabic, Persian, and Urdu (in the Nastaliq script); Sanskrit, Hindi, and Marathi (in Devanagari); and Gujarati, Bengali, Oriya, Telugu, Kannada, Tamil, and Malayalam in their own scripts.

36. Wilson, *A Glossary of the Judicial and Revenue Terms*, 284, 290. The term *jotadar* also appears as "farmer" or "cultivator."

37. Wilson, *Glossary*, 253.

38. Wilson, *Glossary*, 234.

39. Wilson, *Glossary*, ii. Also, the entire world of colloquial uses of words, their creative alternations and even inversions, is all but lost to the modern historian. The contemporary word *dope*, to take a trivial example, would usually be given in a conventional dictionary as a narcotic. Yet *dope* as a term widely used in certain communities for positive approval and strong adulation, on the other hand, would all but evade the official record.

40. N. Gerald Barrier, ed., "Introduction" in *The Census in British India: New Perspectives* (Delhi: Manohar Publishers, 1981), vi.

41. See T. Gordon Walker, *Final Report of the Revision of Settlement (1878–83) of the Ludhiana District in the Panjab* (Calcutta: Central Press, 1884), 171–72; and E. L. Brandreth, *Report on the revised settlement of the district of Ferozepur, in the cis-Satlej states* (Lahore: Chronicle Press, 1859), 25.

42. On the politics of census operations across British India, see Bernard S. Cohn, "The Census, Social Structure, and Objectification in South Asia," in *An Anthropologist among the Historians and Other Essays* (New Delhi: Oxford University Press, 1987); Sudipta Kaviraj, "The Imaginary Institution of India," in *Subaltern Studies VII: Writings on South Asian History and Society*, ed. Partha Chatterjee and Gyanendra Pandey (New Delhi: Oxford University Press, 1992); Arjun Appadurai, "Number in the Colonial Imagination," in *Orientalism and the Postcolonial Predicament: Perspectives on South Asia*, ed. Carol A. Breckenridge and Peter van der Veer (Philadelphia: University of Pennsylvania Press, 1993); Nicholas B. Dirks, *Castes of Mind: Colonialism and the Making of Modern India* (Princeton: Princeton University Press, 2001), chs. 3, 10; and Sumit Guha, "The Politics of Identity and Enumeration in India c. 1600–1990," *Comparative Studies in Society and History* 45, no. 1 (January 2003): 148–67. On the census in Panjab, see Kenneth W. Jones, "Religious Identity and the Indian Census," *The Census in British India*; Richard Saumarez Smith, "Rule-by-Records and Rule-by-Reports: Complimentary Aspects of the British Imperial Rule of Law," *Contributions to Indian Sociology* 19, no. 1 (1985): 153–76; and Brian P. Caton, "Social Categories and Colonisation in Panjab, 1849–1920," *Indian Economic and Social History Review* 41, no. 1 (February 2004): 33–50.

43. Mir and Caton, for instance, both discount the censuses of 1855 and 1868 in favor of the 1881 iteration. See Mir, *Social Space of Language,* 47–49; and Caton, "Social Categories," 43–44.

44. See P.H.M. van den Dungen, *The Punjab Tradition: Influence and Authority in Nineteenth-Century India* (London: George Allen & Unwin Ltd., 1972), 147–48, 176–77, 201.

45. Jones, "Religious Identity," 73.

46. Temple, *1855 Census,* 4.

47. On the role of instructions as a means to discipline colonial functionaries, see Appadurai, "Number in the Colonial Imagination," 324.

48. Temple, *1855 Census,* 5.

49. Temple, *1855 Census,* 6–7. On the concern of colonial officials toward popular opposition to the census, and especially the role of rumors, see Dirks, *Castes of Mind,* 201.

50. Temple, *1855 Census,* 7.

51. There is no comprehensive count of Sikhs throughout Panjab in this census, with Temple declaring that since "Sikhism is politically defunct," the "return" of its members to Hinduism is all but inevitable. See Temple, *1855 Census,* 24. Cf. Jones, "Religious Identity," 79; on the status of Sikhs in the 1881 census, see Harjot Oberoi, *The Construction of Religious Boundaries: Culture, Identity, and Diversity in the Sikh Tradition* (Chicago: University of Chicago Press, 1994), 210–12.

52. Cf. Temple, *1855 Census,* 9, 22. There is an unexplained discrepancy of twenty-nine people between the total number and the sum of the two categories, a slight error that undercuts boasts of British reason and the problem of endemic native dishonesty and abstraction.

53. Temple, *1855 Census,* 22–23.

54. On the prehistory of the census in British India, see Cohn, "Census, Social Structure," 231–34, and Appadurai, "Number in the Colonial Imagination," 329.

55. Extract from a dispatch by the Court of Directors to all local administrations, dated June 3, 1846, in A. Shakespear, *Memoir on the Statistics of the North Western Provinces of the Bengal Presidency* (Calcutta: Baptist Mission Press, 1848), 4–5.

56. Circular from J. Thornton to all Collectors of Land Revenue in the NWP, dated 22 October 1846, in Shakespear, *Memoir,* 8, emphasis added.

57. Circular from J. Thornton to all Collectors of Land Revenue in the NWP, dated 15 November 1847, in Shakespear, *Memoir,* 14, emphasis added.

58. Circular no. 2990, from W. Muir to all Collectors and Magistrates of the NWP, dated 22 July 1852, in G. J. Christian, *Report on the Census of the North West Provinces of the Bengal Presidency, taken on the 1st of January, 1853* (Calcutta: Baptist Mission Press, 1854), 10.

59. Cohn, "Census, Social Structure," 236. See also Daniel Thorner and Alice Thorner, *Land and Labour in India* (London: Asia Publishing House, 1962).

60. See Shakespear, *Memoir,* 8, 47. The problem of defining a house is also mentioned in Barrier, "Introduction," x, and Cohn, "Census, Social Structure," 236.

61. See Shakespear, *Memoir,* 7, 9, 31, 176; and Christian, *Report,* 10, 435. Cohn also mentions the problems of determining the transition from childhood to adulthood. See Cohn, "Census, Social Structure," 236–37.

62. Circular by Thornton, dated 22 October 1846, in Shakespear, *Memoir,* 7, 8, 10.
63. Shakespear, *Memoir,* 173.
64. W. Muir, "Instructions for the Formation of the Census of January 1st, 1853," in Christian, *Report,* 9.
65. See "Statement of Castes referred to in Para. 21," in Shakespear, *Memoir,* 30.
66. On the cancellation of the 1864 Panjab census and the planned all-India census of 1861, see Jones, "Religious Identity," 78; and Dirks, *Castes of Mind,* 43.
67. J.A.E. Miller, *Report on the Census of the Punjab, taken on 10th January 1868* (hereafter *1868 Census*) (Lahore: Indian Public Opinion Press, 1870), 1–2.
68. Miller, *Report,* 2, emphasis added.
69. Appadurai, "Number in the Colonial Imagination," 325.
70. The report states that this classification is based on the English system of Register General Dr. Farr and adopted in the NWP, with significant reductions. The six classes were: I. Professional, II. Domestic, III. Commercial, IV. Agricultural, V. Industrial, and VI. Independent etc. See Miller, *Report,* 25–26.
71. This is the first census that counts Sikhs as a separate religion, at 6.5% of the population to 53% Muslim and 34.8% Hindu, with a ubiquitous 5.7% for "Others." See Miller, *Report,* 22.
72. Miller, *Report,* 23. For a study of Churhas, see Vijay Prashad, *Untouchable Freedom: A Social History of a Dalit Community* (New York: Oxford University Press, 2001); on the Chamars, see Ramnarayan S. Rawat, *Reconsidering Untouchability: Chamars and Dalit History in North India* (Bloomington: Indiana University Press, 2001).
73. "Appendix to No. III A: Details of 'Chumar' Population in the Punjab," in Miller, *Report,* n.p.
74. For these figures, see the series of charts under "General Statement No. IV: Population according to occupation" in Miller, *Report,* n.p.
75. Miller, *Report,* 34.
76. See Miller, *Report,* 27, 28, 33.
77. Henry Waterfield, *Memorandum of the Census of British India of 1871–72* (London: George Edward Eyre and William Spottiswoode, 1875), 5. Cf. Dirks, *Castes of Mind,* 201.
78. Cohn, "Census, Social Structure," 238.
79. See Waterfield, *Memorandum,* 22–23.
80. See Waterfield, *Memorandum,* 36–37.
81. Waterfield, *Memorandum,* 38.
82. Waterfield, *Memorandum,* 33.
83. "It was the act of questioning the need for an explanation," writes Cohn, "which lies at the heart of the process" of the objectification of Indian culture. See Cohn, "Census, Social Structure," 230.
84. See R. H. Davies and W. Blyth, *Report on the Revised Settlement of the Umritsur, Sowrian, and Turun Tarun Purgunnahs of the Umritsar District in the Umritsar Division* (Lahore: Home Press, 1860); and G. C. Barnes et al., *Report on the revised settlement of the Oonah, Hushiarpur, Gurshunkur, and Hurriana purgunahs, of the Hushiarpur district, in the Trans-Sutlej States* (Lahore: Punjabee Press, 1860).
85. See Richard C. Temple, ed., *Punjab Notes and Queries, a monthly periodical, devoted to the systematic collection of authentic notes and scraps of information regarding the country*

and the people (Allahabad: Pioneer Press, 1886); C. L. Tupper, *Punjab Customary Law*, vol. 1–3 (Calcutta: Office of the Superintendent of Government Printing, 1881); Lepel H. Griffin, *The Panjab Chiefs: Historical and biographical notices of the principal families in the territories under the Panjab Government* (Lahore: Chronicle Press, 1865); and, for instance, *Gazetteer of the Ferozepure District, 1883–4* (Lahore: The Civil and Military Gazette Press, 1884).

86. This quote comes from Captain Edward Cuttle, a fictional character in Charles Dickens's novel *Dombey and Son* (1847), which served as the epigram for Temple's *Punjab Notes and Queries*.

87. See Neeladri Bhattacharya, *The Great Agrarian Conquest: The Colonial Reshaping of a Rural World* (Ranikhet: Permanent Black, 2018), 240 and ch. 5 *passim*.

88. Perhaps the most famous in this genre are William Crooke, *A Rural and Agricultural Glossary of the North-Western Provinces and Oudh* (Allahabad: Superintendent of Government Printing, 1888); George A. Grierson, *Bihar Peasant Life: Being a discursive catalogue of the surroundings of the people of the province* (Calcutta: The Bengal Secretariat Press, 1885); and Henry Yule and Arthur C. Burnell, *Hobson-Jobson: A glossary of Anglo-Indian colloquial words and phrases, and of kindred terms, etymological, historical, geographical and discursive* (London: John Murray, 1886). See also Shahid Amin's introduction to William Crooke, *A Glossary of North Indian Peasant Life*, ed. Shahid Amin (New Delhi: Oxford University Press, 1989).

89. S. W. Fallon, *A Dictionary of Hindustani Proverbs, including many Marwari, Panjabi, Maggah, Bhojpuri and Tirhuti Proverbs, Sayings, Emblems, Aphorisms, Maxims and Similes*, ed. Richard Temple (Banaras: Medical Hall Press, 1886), ii.

90. Robert Maconachie, ed., *Selected Agricultural Proverbs of the Panjab* (Delhi: Imperial Medical Hall Press, 1890), v–viii.

91. E. O'Brian, ed., *Glossary of the Multani Language compared with Punjabi and Sindhi* (Lahore: Punjab Government Civil Secretariat Press, 1881), ix.

92. Guha, *Elementary Aspects*, 14–15.

93. O'Brian, *Glossary*, xi–xiii.

94. While leaving the transliterations intact, I have modified the translations in some places to better reflect both the meaning and rhythm of each proverb. The respective subjects, however, remain as translated by Maconachie and are underlined. For the original rendition, see the page numbers in parenthesis in Maconachie, *Selected Agricultural Proverbs*.

95. Appadurai, "Number in the Colonial Imagination," 327–29.

96. Ibbetson, *Report*, 2, 10.

97. Cohn, "Census, Social Structure," 242.

98. Ibbetson, *Report*, 2, 10.

99. See the charts titled "Statistics of Census Agency" and "Number and Size of Census Blocks for Districts" in Ibbetson, *Report*, 427–28, 435, 3. The first order for the census was issued on August 7, 1880, and the report was completed in October 1882, though it remained unpublished due to a printing backlog until August 1883.

100. Ibbetson, *Report*, 12.

101. Ibbetson explains an even greater degree of complexity with rendering these seemingly simple terms into Panjabi. "Now the first difficulty we encounter was the

Notes to Chapter 2   287

translation of these headings. In the east *quam* is used for religion and *zat* for caste; in the west *quam* for caste, *zat* for tribe or clan. In the east *got* is the universal word for tribe among the peasantry, insomuch that the Rajputs call their royal races not *kuls* but *gots*; everywhere it is used by Brahmans, Banyas and the like for the Brahminical *gotras*; in the west it is unknown save in the latter sense. As for the local term for smaller tribes or clans they vary almost from district to district and from caste to caste. After consulting Commissioners we [eventually] translated our headings as '*asl quam,*' '*zat ya firqah,*' [and] '*got ya shakh.*'" Ibbetson, *Report*, 188.

102. See "Abstract No. 122, showing Occupations of Males for Divisions and Towns and Villages," and "Abstract No. 125, showing Occupations for Females for Divisions," in Ibbetson, *Report*, 380, 388.

103. Dirks, *Castes of Mind*, 43, 220.

104. Ibbetson, *Report*, 172.

105. On Ibbetson's conceptualization of caste, see Mir, *Social Space of Language*, 130–31. It is most striking in comparison with other British officers such as W. C. Plowden and Henry Waterfield who favored the fourfold *varna* system, and, notably, H. H. Risley, who inaugurated the notion of caste as racialized difference, as well as missionaries such as M. A. Sherring who thought of caste as a Brahmin invention. For more, see Dirks, *Castes of Mind*, 46–50, 203–6.

106. Ibbetson, *Report*, 173.

107. Ibbetson, *Report*, 176.

108. This notion of a functional purpose behind caste as occupation was dramatically reversed by Risley in favor of a racialist correspondence based on the new science of anthropometry in subsequent censuses, detailed in Dirks, *Castes of Mind*, 218–19. See also Karuna Mantena, *Alibis of Empire: Henry Maine and the Ends of Liberal Imperialism* (Princeton: Princeton University Press, 2010), chs. 2–3; and Uday Singh Mehta, *Liberalism and Empire: A Study in Nineteenth-Century British Liberal Thought* (Chicago: University of Chicago Press, 1999), chs. 3–4.

109. See "Abstract No. 64, showing the General Distribution of Castes for Districts and States," in Ibbetson, *Report*, 186. It is notable that the first two categories invoke caste names while the last uses occupational designations.

110. Ibbetson, *Report*, 208.

111. See Ibbetson, *Report*, 225, 227, 227, respectively.

112. Ibbetson, *Report*, 313.

113. Ibbetson, *Report*, 319, 320, respectively.

114. Ibbetson, *Report*, 376, 383, emphasis added.

115. Dirks, *Castes of Mind*, 50.

116. Ibbetson, *Report*, 377, emphasis in original.

117. See Dirks, *Castes of Mind*, 44 and *passim*.

118. On the canal colonies and property relations in colonial Panjab, see David Gilmartin, *Blood and Water: The Indus River Basin in Modern History* (Oakland: University of California Press, 2015); Imran Ali, *The Punjab under Imperialism, 1885–1947* (Princeton: Princeton University Press, 1988); M. Mufakharul Islam, *Irrigation, Agriculture, and the Raj: Punjab, 1887–1947* (New Delhi: Manohar Publishers, 1997); Naved Hamid, "Dispossession and Differentiation of the Peasantry in the Punjab during

Colonial Rule," *Journal of Peasant Studies* 10, no. 1 (1982): 52–72; and Pervaiz Nazir, "Transformation of Property Relations in the Punjab," *Economic and Political Weekly* 16, no. 8 (February 21, 1981): 281–285.

119. On the Deccan riots, see Thomas R. Metcalf, "The British and the Moneylender in Nineteenth Century India," *Journal of Modern History* 34, no. 4 (December 1962): 390–397; Neil Charlesworth, "The Myth of the Deccan Riots of 1875," *Modern Asian Studies* 6, no. 4 (1972): 401–421; and David Hardiman, *Feeding the Baniya: Peasants and Usurers in Western India* (New Delhi: Oxford University Press, 1996). Thorburn's most influential published work on peasant debt in Panjab from this period is *Musalmans and Money-Lenders in the Punjab* (London: William Blackwood & Sons, 1886).

120. From the "Statement of Objects and Reasons" in Gurcharn Singh, ed., *The Punjab Alienation of Land Act (XIII of 1900), with Notes, Notifications, Rules and Circulars* (Lahore: Albion Press, 1901), 74. This text provides a complete version of the Act from the year of its inception, as well as a useful commentary by Gurcharn Singh, a lawyer and examiner at the Punjab University Law College in Lahore, and appendixes of important ancillary materials. For the version modified after the changes that were implemented in 1907, see "The Punjab Alienation of Land Act, 1900," in *Punjab Land Administration Acts and Rules Having the Force of Law Thereunder*, vol. 1 (Lahore: Superintendent of Government Printing, 1933). For a more extensive commentary of the post-1907 version by another early twentieth-century lawyer, see Shadi Lal, ed., *The Punjab Alienation of Land Act XIII of 1900 with Comments and Notes of Cases*, second edition (Lahore: Addison Press, 1907). The scholarly consensus, on the other hand, largely echoes the official narrative. The Act, according to Norman Barrier, simply "prohibited the transfer of land from the Punjabi agriculturalist to the non-agriculturalist moneylender." See Norman G. Barrier, *The Punjab Alienation of Land Bill of 1900* (Durham: Duke University Press, 1966), iii.

121. On the idiom of "tribe" in colonial Panjab, see David Gilmartin, *Empire and Islam: Punjab and the Making of Pakistan* (Berkeley: University of California Press, 1988), ch. 1.

122. *The Punjab Alienation of Land Act (XIII of 1900)*, section 3 (1).

123. See *The Punjab Alienation of Land Act (XIII of 1900)*, section 6 for mortgage limits, section 16 (2) for forced land sales, and sections 9 and 14 for the ultimate authority of district commissioners.

124. *The Punjab Alienation of Land Act (XIII of 1900)*, section 2 (1).

125. See the notification chart published in the *Punjab Gazette Extraordinary*, dated May 25, 1901, found in *The Punjab Alienation of Land Act (XIII of 1900)*, 20–24. The list of tribes notified in specific districts would change considerably over the course of the following two decades.

126. Circular No. 9, dated Lahore, the 20th November 1903, from Director of Land Records and Agriculture, Punjab, to all Commissioners, Deputy Commissioners, Settlement Officers and Colonisation Officers in the Punjab, in *Handbook of Alienation of Land Acts and Circular Orders* (Lahore: no publisher, no date), 24–25, serial 533, Punjab State Archives, Chandigarh, India (hereafter PSA).

127. Circular No. 6, dated 13th December 1906, from the Financial Commissioner to all Revenue Officers in the Punjab, in Lal, ed., *The Punjab Alienation of Land Act XIII of 1900 with Comments and Notes of Cases*, lxxix.

128. "Certificate granted to persons who claim to be 'agriculturalists' as defined in Section 2 (1) of Act XIII of 1900," in *Handbook of Alienation of Land Acts and Circular Orders*, 26.

129. Circular No. 9, in *Handbook of Alienation of Land Acts and Circular Orders*, 24.

130. On the inversed version of the concept of genealogy, see Michel Foucault, "Nietzsche, Genealogy, History," in *The Foucault Reader*, ed. Paul Rabinow (New York: Pantheon Books, 1984).

131. See Barrier, *The Punjab Alienation of Land Bill of 1900*, 96–102; Imran Ali, "Malign Growth? Agricultural Colonization and the Roots of Backwardness in the Punjab," *Past and Present* no. 114 (February 1987): 131; and M. Mufakharul Islam, "The Punjab Land Alienation Act and the Professional Moneylenders," *Modern Asian Studies* 29, no. 2 (May 1995): 274, 290.

132. Financial Commissioner's Circular Letter No. 3441, dated Lahore, the 5th of June 1901, to all Commissioners and Deputy Commissioners in the Punjab, in *Handbook of Alienation of Land Acts and Circular Orders*, 11.

133. "Inclusion of Arains in the Muzaffargarh district in the list of agricultural tribes," November 1907, Punjab Government Civil Secretariat, Revenue and Agriculture Department, proceedings A, file 49, 1, serial R/838, PSA.

134. "Inclusion of the Awans in the list of agricultural tribes of the Muzaffargarh District," June 1914, Punjab Government Civil Secretariat, Revenue and Agriculture Department, proceedings A, file 27, 1, serial R/882, PSA.

135. See "Decision that all Ahairs in the Delhi Division are eligible to participate in the Military allotment of land on the Jhelum Canal," November 1903, Punjab Government Civil Secretariat, Revenue and Agriculture Department, proceedings A, no. 7–9, file 3, 1, serial R/2104, PSA; "Inclusion of the Koreshis of the Gujranwala district and the Khaggas, Bodlas and Koreshis of the Montgomery district in the list of agricultural tribes," July 1908, Punjab Government Civil Secretariat, Revenue and Agriculture Department, proceedings A, file 31, 1–4, serial R/2445, PSA; and "Notification of the Kakezais of the Jhelum district as an agricultural tribe," April 1910, Punjab Government Civil Secretariat, Revenue and Agriculture Department, proceedings A, file 16, 1–2, serial R/811, PSA.

136. "Memorial from Sardar Dost Muhammad Khan, Rais of Bathar, Hazara District," July 1901, Punjab Government Civil Secretariat, Revenue and Agriculture Department, proceedings A, no. 1–2, file 7, 1, serial R/848, PSA.

137. This would have entailed a reduced revenue responsibility, as castes were assessed different rates based on the belief of inherently dissimilar aptitudes for agriculture. For more, see Chapter 1.

138. "Inclusion of the Gujrat Bahrupias in the list of Agricultural Tribes notified under the Punjab Alienation of Land Act," January 1913, Punjab Government Civil Secretariat, Revenue and Agriculture Department, proceedings A, no. 1–3, file 1, 1, serial R/817, PSA.

139. "Inclusion of the Gujrat Bahrupias," 1.

140. "Inclusion of the Gujrat Bahrupias," 1.

141. "Inclusion of Mazhbi Sikhs of the Gujranwala and Lyallpur districts in the list of agricultural tribes," October 1911, Punjab Government Civil Secretariat, Revenue and Agriculture Department, proceedings A, no. 17–25, file 34, 2, serial R/811, PSA.

142. "Inclusion of Mazhbi Sikhs," 1.
143. "Inclusion of Mazhbi Sikhs," 1. See Ali, *Punjab under Imperialism, 1885–1947*, ch. 4.
144. On the potential polarizing of agrarian relations, see Breman, *Patronage and Exploitation*; Prakash, *Bonded Histories*; and Rupa Viswanath, *The Pariah Problem: Caste, Religion, and the Social in Modern India* (New York: Columbia University Press, 2014).
145. For an administrative account of this episode, see N. Gerald Barrier, "The Punjab Disturbances of 1907: The Response of the British Government in India to Agrarian Unrest," *Modern Asian Studies* 1, no. 4 (1967): 353–83.
146. Vinay Gidwani, *Capital, Interrupted: Agrarian Development and the Politics of Work in India* (Minneapolis: University of Minnesota Press, 2008), 148, emphasis removed.
147. On the debate over the rule of difference and colonial capitalism, see David Washbrook, "Law, State, and Agrarian Society in Colonial India," *Modern Asian Studies* 15, no. 3 (1981): 649–721; and Partha Chatterjee, *The Nation and Its Fragments: Colonial and Postcolonial Histories* (Princeton: Princeton University Press, 1993), ch. 2.

Chapter 3

1. "Spendthrifts Ruin India," *The New York Times*, October 7, 1900.
2. "Spendthrifts Ruin India."
3. "Spendthrifts Ruin India."
4. Eric Stokes, *The Peasant and the Raj: Studies in Agrarian Society and Peasant Rebellion in Colonial India* (Cambridge: Cambridge University Press, 1978), 10.
5. See Tom Kessinger, *Vilyatpur, 1848–1968: Social and Economic Change in a North Indian Village* (Berkeley: University of California Press, 1974), 137; David Hardiman, *Feeding the Baniya: Peasants and Usurers in Western India* (New Delhi: Oxford University Press, 1996), ch. 5; and Neil Charlesworth, *Peasants and Imperial Rule: Agriculture and Agrarian Society in the Bombay Presidency, 1850–1935* (Cambridge: Cambridge University Press, 1985), 86.
6. Sugata Bose, *Agrarian Bengal: Economy, Social Structure, and Politics, 1919–1947* (Cambridge: Cambridge University Press, 1986), 99.
7. Eric Stokes, *The Peasant Armed: The Indian Revolt of 1857*, ed. C. A. Bayly (Oxford: Clarendon Press, 1986), 10. Bernard Cohn too identifies the widely held assumption that "it was the British who destroyed the old land control system by establishing an absolute, heritable, and salable right in land." See Cohn, "Structural Change in Indian Rural Society," in *Land Control and Social Structure in Indian History*, ed. Robert Eric Frykenberg (Madison: University of Wisconsin Press, 1969), 55.
8. Thus for instance, in an otherwise detailed and careful historical ethnography, Kessinger follows colonial writers such as Malcolm Darling to argue that "The right of outright sale brought about a rise in land prices and gave landowners *unused to participation in the market* a substantial base for credit which *they could not manage*." Kessinger, *Vilyatpur, 1848–1968*, 135, emphasis added.
9. E. B. Steedman, *Report on the Revised Settlement of the Jhang District of the Punjab, 1874–1880* (Lahore: W. Ball, 1882), 131.

10. See Ranajit Guha, *A Rule of Property for Bengal: An Essay on the Idea of Permanent Settlement* (Paris: Mouton & Co., 1963); Burton Stein, *Thomas Munro: The Origins of the Colonial State and His Vision of Empire* (New Delhi: Oxford University Press, 1995); and Thomas R. Metcalf, "Social Effects of British Land Policy in Oudh," in *Land Control and Social Structure in Indian History*, ed. Robert E. Frykenberg (Madison: University of Wisconsin Press, 1969).

11. Raymond West, *The Land and the Law in India* (Bombay: Education Society Press, 1873), 1.

12. On West, see Rachel Sturman, *The Government of Social Life in Colonial India: Liberalism, Religious Law, and Women's Rights* (Cambridge: Cambridge University Press, 2012), 81–84; and Charlesworth, *Peasants and Imperial Rule*, 63, 119.

13. West, *Land and the Law*, 1.

14. See Ritu Birla, *Stages of Capital: Law, Culture, and Market Governance in Late Colonial India* (Durham: Duke University Press, 2009), 35–37 and ch. 1; and Karuna Mantena, *Alibis of Empire: Henry Maine and the Ends of Liberal Imperialism* (Princeton: Princeton University Press, 2010), ch. 4.

15. West, *Land and the Law*, 2–3.

16. West, *Land and the Law*, 4.

17. West, *Land and the Law*, 4. For more on the politics of producing the "agriculturalist" as a hereditary caste occupation, see Chapter 2.

18. West, *Land and the Law*, 4.

19. West, *Land and the Law*, 7.

20. West, *Land and the Law*, 9, emphasis added.

21. West, *Land and the Law*, 9.

22. West, *Land and the Law*, 14–15. For amounts over five hundred rupees, however, West believed the contracting party would have enough intelligence to understand the ramifications of whatever interest rate they agreed upon, thereby quantifying an intellectual threshold for wealth accumulation.

23. West, *Land and the Law*, 17–18.

24. See Hardiman, *Feeding the Baniya*, 202–12.

25. Since the peasants did not merely target grain hoarder or profiteers, Hardiman critiques Charlesworth's claim that the incident in 1875 was nothing more than a "minor grain riot" that provided a "safety valve for local tensions." Instead, because they "intended to destroy account books and debt-bonds held by sahukars," the peasants were engaging in a unique and organized form of revolt, which they in fact termed *band* in Marathi. See Hardiman, *Feeding the Baniya*, 217–19 and ch. 10. Cf. Charlesworth, *Peasants and Imperial Rule*, ch. 4; and I. J. Catanach, *Rural Credit in Western India, 1875–1930: Rural Credit and the Co-operative Movement in the Bombay Presidency* (Berkeley: University of California Press, 1970), ch. 1.

26. Hardiman, *Feeding the Baniya*, 214.

27. In addition to *Musalmans and Money-Lenders in the Punjab*, Thorburn published *Bannu; or, our Afghan Frontier* (London: Trubner & Co., 1876); *Asiatic Neighbours* (Edinburgh: William Blackwood and Sons, 1895) and *The Punjab in Peace and War* (Edinburgh: William Blackwood and Sons, 1904), among several other titles.

28. For a critique of the notion that "direct" experience provides authentic and thereby "incontestable" and "truthful" evidence for social scientific claims, see Joan W. Scott, "The Evidence of Experience," *Critical Inquiry* 17, no. 4 (Summer 1991): 773–797.

29. See Navyug Gill, "Peasant as Alibi: An Itinerary of the Archive of Colonial Panjab," in *Unarchived Histories: The "Mad" and the "Trifling" in the Colonial and Postcolonial World*, ed. Gyanendra Pandey (London: Routledge, 2014).

30. "Indebtedness of the Muhammadan population of the Dera Ismail Khan district," by S. S. Thorburn, Home Department (Judicial), B proceedings, October 1885, no. 252–54, 8, National Archives of India, New Delhi, India (hereafter NAI).

31. "Indebtedness," 9.

32. "Indebtedness," 11

33. See the chart on the state of indebtedness in "Indebtedness," 12.

34. See chart on the area transferred in "Indebtedness," 10.

35. On the changing discrepancy over the concept of "agriculturalist" in relation to both Panjabi terms for those who cultivate and British legal categories for agricultural and non-agricultural tribes, see Chapter 2.

36. "Indebtedness," 18. The warning of the dangers of Muslim disloyalty was earlier raised in William Wilson Hunter's *The Indian Musalmans: Are They Bound in Conscience to Rebel Against the Queen?* (London: Trubner and Co., 1871).

37. "Indebtedness," 23.

38. See "Indebtedness," 13–23.

39. Letter from J. A. Grant, Esquire, Offig. Junior Secretary to Financial Commissioner, Punjab, to the Offig. Secretary to Government, Punjab, no. 1189, dated Lahore, 24 October 1884, Home Department (Judicial), B proceedings, October 1885, no. 252–54; 4, NAI.

40. Letter from J. A. Grant, 5–6.

41. Letter from H. C. Fanshawe, Offig. Junior Secretary to Government, Punjab and its Dependencies, to J. A. Grant, Esquire, Offig. Junior Secretary to Financial Commissioner, Punjab, no. 507, dated Simla, 23 May 1885, Home Department (Judicial), B proceedings, October 1885, no. 252–54, 1, NAI.

42. Thorburn, *Musalmans and Money-Lenders*, 96, 74.

43. Thorburn, *Musalmans and Money-Lenders*, 62.

44. "Throughout Eastern Europe," writes Thorburn on the first page of his book, "the Jews are hated and persecuted rather because they are successful aliens and professors of an old-world faith than because they are successful [alone]. So with the Bunniahs [baniyas] of Western Panjab. They offend not only because they thrive on the misfortunes of monotheistic agriculturalists, but because they are interlopers and polytheists, if not idolators [sic]." See Thorburn, *Musalmans and Money-Lenders*, 1. Muddled and denigrating comparisons with Jews such as this are common in much of the colonial commentary on debt.

45. Thorburn, *Musalmans and Money-Lenders*, 40.

46. George Campbell, *Memoirs of My Indian Career*, vol. 1, ed. Charles E. Bernard (London: Macmillan and Co., 1893), 279.

47. Brenna Bhandar, *Colonial Lives of Property: Law, Land, and Racial Regimes of Ownership* (Durham: Duke University Press, 2018), 6.

48. Karl Marx, *Capital: Volume I: A Critique of Political Economy*, trans. Ben Fowkes (London: Penguin Books, 1976), 187 and esp. ch. 3. See also Marx, *Grundrisse: Foundations of the Critique of Political Economy*, trans. Martin Nicolaus (London: Penguin Books, 1973), 246.

49. "Agricultural Indebtedness in the Punjab," Keep With Papers (Not for Records), Revenue and Agriculture Department, proceedings no. 1–8, May 1891, 8, NAI.

50. Letter from H. C. Fanshawe, Esquire, Offig. Junior Secretary to Government, Punjab and its Dependencies, to Sir E. C. Buck, Secretary to the Government of India, Revenue and Agriculture Department, dated 7 November 1888, in "Agricultural Indebtedness in the Punjab," 1; and "Agricultural Indebtedness in the Punjab," Keep With Papers (Not for Records), 9.

51. "Agricultural Indebtedness in the Punjab," Keep With Papers (Not for Records), 4.

52. Note by His Excellency the Viceroy on Agricultural Indebtedness in the Punjab, dated 23 January 1890, "Agricultural Indebtedness in the Punjab," Keep With Papers (Not for Records), 13. The Secretary of State and Viceroy also may have been responding to issues raised in Hunter's *The Indian Musalmans*.

53. Letter from H. C. Fanshawe, "Agricultural Indebtedness in the Punjab," 6. Thorburn too noted that in 1871 the Lieutenant-Governor mentioned in a report that "there do not appear to be any statistics available for showing the amount of land which generally, since annexation, or during any particular year, has been sold or mortgaged to money-lenders by zemindars." Thorburn, *Musalmans and Money-Lenders*, 93.

54. See Clive Dewey, "Patwari and Chaukidar: Subordinate Officials and the Reliability of India's Agricultural Statistics," in *The Imperial Impact: Studies in the Economic History of Africa and India*, ed. Clive Dewey and A. G. Hopkins (London: The Athlone Press, 1978).

55. The eighteen eastern districts of Panjab are given as: Delhi, Gurgaon, Karnal, Hissar, Rohtak, Sirsa, Amballa, Ludhiana, Simla, Jalandhar, Hoshiarpur, Kangra, Amritsar, Sialkot, Gurdaspur, Lahore, Ferozpur, and Gujranwala; while the fourteen western districts were: Rawalpindi, Jhelum, Gujarat, Shahpur, Multan, Jhang, Montgomery, Muzaffargarh, Dera Ismail Khan, Dera Ghazi Khan, Bannu, Peshawar, Kohat, and Hazara. As with many documents from this period, the definition of *agriculturalist*, and its difference from *moneylender*, is not explained.

56. For the figures used in this paragraph, see the chart "Abstract Statement of Sales and Mortgages in the Punjab from 1865 to 1886: I. Sales," in "Agricultural Indebtedness in the Punjab," Enclosure no. II, 2–5.

57. I appreciate Kavita Sivaramakrishnan for emphasizing to me both a critique of the validity of colonial numbers over descriptions, and yet the inescapability of working with such historical materials.

58. For this paragraph's figures, see "Abstract Statement of Sales and Mortgages in the Punjab from 1865 to 1886: II. Mortgages," and "Abstract Statement of Sales and Mortgages in the Punjab from 1865 to 1886: General Abstract by Years," in "Agricultural Indebtedness in the Punjab," Enclosure no. II, 6–9 and 10–11.

59. For these figures, see "I. Statement of Sales in the Eastern Districts of the Punjab, 1865–1886" and "II. Statement of Sales in the Western Districts of the Punjab, 1865–1886," in "Agricultural Indebtedness in the Punjab," Enclosure no. II, 1–5 and 1–5.

294   Notes to Chapter 3

60. See "Statement of Lands Mortgaged and Lands Redeemed from Mortgage in the Eastern Districts of the Punjab, 1874–84," and "Statement of Lands Mortgaged and Lands Redeemed from Mortgage in the Western Districts of the Punjab, 1874–84," in "Agricultural Indebtedness in the Punjab," Enclosure no. III B. and IV B., 2–9 and 2–9.

61. Civil Judgement of the Chief Court of the Punjab, no. 110 of 1879, Ramdhan and Another (Plaintiffs) Appellants, versus Jiwan Khan (Defendant) Respondent, appellate side of case no. 1194 of 1878, in "Agricultural Indebtedness in the Punjab," Keep With Papers (Not for Records), Revenue and Agriculture Department, proceedings no. 1–8, May 1891; Enclosure no. IV, 1, NAI, New Delhi, India.

62. Ramdhan and Another (Plaintiffs) Appellants, versus Jiwan Khan (Defendant) Respondent, 1.

63. Ramdhan and Another (Plaintiffs) Appellants, versus Jiwan Khan (Defendant) Respondent, 2, emphasis added.

64. Ramdhan and Another (Plaintiffs) Appellants, versus Jiwan Khan (Defendant) Respondent, 2.

65. On civil courts and landowners, see P.H.M. van den Dungen, *The Punjab Tradition: Influence and Authority in Nineteenth-Century India* (London: George Allen & Unwin Ltd., 1972), 34–35, 67–68, 85–89.

66. See Hardiman, *Feeding the Baniya*, chs. 3, 9, 13; and Bose, *Agrarian Bengal*, chs. 4, 6.

67. Birla, *Stages of Capital*, 58.

68. Letter to Lord George F. Hamilton, Her Majesty's Secretary of State for India, from C. M. Rivaz et. al., Simla, 27 July 1899, Department of Revenue and Agriculture, no. 50 of 1899, in "Proposals for undertaking legislation with the object of checking the transfer of land from the agricultural classes in the Punjab," Legislative Department, proceeding no. 36, September 1899, 3, NAI.

69. Statement of Objects and Reasons, Appendix A19, in "The Punjab Alienation of Land Act, 1900 (XIII of 1900)," (hereafter The Act of 1900), Legislative Department, proceeding no. 11-68, October 1900; 1, NAI.

70. This process is discussed in greater detail in Chapter 2. See also Norman G. Barrier, *The Punjab Alienation of Land Bill of 1900* (Durham: Duke University Press, 1966); M. Mufakharul Islam, "The Punjab Alienation Act and the Professional Moneylenders," *Modern Asian Studies* 29, no. 2 (May 1995): 271–291; and Neeti Nair, *Changing Homelands: Hindu Politics and the Partition of India* (Cambridge: Harvard University Press, 2011), ch. 1.

71. See Statement of Objects and Reasons, in The Act of 1900, 1.

72. "Note on the Punjab Alienation of Land Bill, 1899," by C. L. Tupper, dated 5 February 1900, 1–8; and Letter from J. Wilson, Esquire, Settlement Commissioner, Punjab, to the Senior Secretary to the Financial Commissioner, Punjab, dated 28 December 1899, 9, both in The Act of 1900.

73. Remarks recorded by Mr. Justice Clark, Chief Judge on a Bill to amend the law relating to agricultural land in the Punjab," 1 January 1900, 1; Letter from Captain A. E. Barton, Deputy Commissioner, Jullundhur, to The Commissioner and Superintendent, Jullundhur Division, 8 January 1900, 55; Memorandum by the Honourable the

Lieutenant-Governor of the Punjab on the provisions of the Bill to amend the law relating to agricultural land in the Punjab, 15 May 1900, 5, from The Act of 1900.

74. Letter from Maulvi Inam Ali, Divisional Judge, Sialkot Division, to The Registrar, Chief Court, Punjab, 12 February 1900, 28–29; Comment on Land Alienation bill by Ghazanfar Ali, Tahsildar, Rawalpindi, 18 December 1899, 33–34; Opinion of Subedar-Major Sardar Bahadur Ghulam Hussain, Honorary Magistrate, Jullundur, 8 January 1900, 61–62, from The Act of 1900.

75. Memorial of Zamindars of Amritsar, Gurdaspur and Jullundur Districts (with 3,283 signatures) to His Honour Sir W. Mackworth Young, K.C.S.I., Lieutenant-Governor of the Punjab and its Dependencies, 19 April 1900, Appendix A25, in The Act of 1900, 1.

76. Memorial of Zamindars of Amritsar, Gurdaspur and Jullundur Districts, 2.

77. Memorial from Khan Bahadur Muhammad Barkat Ali Khan, General Secretary, Anjuman-i-Islamia, Punjab, to Secretary to Government of India, Legislative Department, 22 July 1900, Appendix A36, in The Act of 1900, 1.

78. Memorial from Khan Bahadur Muhammad Barkat Ali Khan, 2.

79. Petition from Maulvi Muharram Ali Chisiiti, Editor, *Rafiq-i-Hind*, Lahore, to Chief Secretary to Government, Punjab, 25 June 1900, Appendix A37, in The Act of 1900, 1.

80. Petition from Maulvi Muharram Ali Chisiiti, 2.

81. On the early politics of the Indian National Congress, see Briton Martin Jr., "Lord Dufferin and the Indian National Congress, 1885–1888," *Journal of British Studies* 7, no. 1 (November 1967): 68–96.

82. From the Members of a Committee of the Fifteenth Indian National Congress, Bombay, to Secretary to Government of India, Home Department, 31 December 1899, Appendix A21, in The Act of 1900, 1–2.

83. Translation of Petition from Jowahir Singh, Lal Chand, Krori Mal and 108 others, residents of Shabkadar in Peshawar District, 26 March 1900, Appendix A23, in The Act of 1900, 1.

84. Translation of Petition from Pundit Jia Lal Chaudhri, Ajudhia Parshad and 85 others of Farukhnagar, District Gurgaon, no date, Appendix A23, in The Act of 1900, 2.

85. There are over a dozen versions with almost the exact same wording of this petition claiming to be from other districts of Panjab included within the file The Act of 1900.

86. Memorial of certain Inhabitants of Lahore district to His Excellency the Right Honorable Lord Curzon of Kedleston, PC, GMSI, GMIE, Viceroy and Governor-General of India in Council, 17 May 1900, Appendix A22, in The Act of 1900, 6.

87. Memorial, 6.
88. Memorial, 6.
89. Memorial, 7.
90. Memorial, 7.

91. From R. Humphreys, Esquire, Deputy Commissioner, Hissar, to The Commissioner and Superintendent, Delhi Division, 7 February 1900, Appendix A24, in The Act of 1900, 12.

92. Note on the Land Alienation Bill by Diwan Narindra Nath, 5 March 1900, Appendix A24, in The Act of 1900, 13.
93. Bhandar, *Colonial Lives of Property*, 181.
94. On Sir Harnam Singh Ahluwalia's career and the intrigue surrounding the Kapurthala royal family, see the brief reflections of his grandson in Arjan Singh, *The Legend of the Maneater* (New Delhi: Ravi Dayal Publishers, 1993), ch. 1.
95. See Minute of Dissent by Harnam Singh Ahluwalia, 6 August 1900, Appendix A44, in The Act of 1900, 5–6.
96. Minute of Dissent by Harnam Singh Ahluwalia, 7.
97. Comment by the Honourable Mr. Rivaz, Extract from the Proceedings of the Council of the Governor General of India, assembled for the purpose of making Laws and Regulations under the provisions of the Indian Councils Act, 1861 and 1892, Panjab Alienation of Land Bill, 19 October 1900, Appendix A63, in The Act of 1900, 1, emphasis added.
98. Comment by the Honourable Mr. Rivaz, 2.
99. Comment by the Honourable Mr. Rivaz, 2.
100. Comment by the Honourable Mr. Rivaz, 2, emphasis added.
101. Comment by the Honourable Mr. Rivaz, 37.
102. Comment by the Honourable Mr. Rivaz, 37–38.
103. See Ian Talbot, *Punjab and the Raj, 1849–1947* (New Delhi: Manohar, 1988), 51, 101–2; and David Gilmartin, *Empire and Islam: Punjab and the Making of Pakistan* (Berkeley: University of California Press, 1988), 146–47. For brief familial reminiscences on the Khattar clan by another of its descendants, see Tariq Ali, *The Clash of Fundamentalisms: Crusades, Jihads, and Modernity* (London: Verso, 2002), 8–9.
104. Comment by the Honourable Nawab Muhammad Hayat Khan, Extract from the Proceedings of the Council of the Governor General of India, assembled for the purpose of making Laws and Regulations under the provisions of the Indian Councils Act, 1861 and 1892, Panjab Alienation of Land Bill, 19 October 1900, Appendix A63, in The Act of 1900, 5–6.
105. Comment by the Honourable Nawab Muhammad Hayat Khan, 9.
106. Comment by the Honourable Mr. Rivaz, 38.
107. *Annual Report of the Working of the Punjab Alienation of Land Act, XIII of 1900, for the year ending 30th September 1903* (hereafter *Annual Report 1903*) (Lahore: The Civil and Military Gazette Press, 1904), 13, emphasis added.
108. See *Annual Report of the Working of the Punjab Alienation of Land Act, XIII of 1900, For the year ending 30th September 1904* (hereafter *Annual Report 1904*) (Lahore: The Civil and Military Gazette Press, 1905), 10; and *Annual Report 1903*, 7, 10.
109. See *Annual Report 1903*, 1, 4–5; and *Annual Report of the Working of the Punjab Alienation of Land Act, XIII of 1900, For the year ending 30th September 1905* (Lahore: The Civil and Military Gazette Press, 1906), 9.
110. For changes in the price of land, see *Annual Report on the Punjab Alienation of Land Act XIII of 1900, as amended by Punjab Act I of 1907, For the year ending the 30th September 1907* (hereafter *Annual Report 1907*) (Lahore: The Civil and Military Gazette Press, 1908), 8. For the omnipresent desire for land, see *Annual Report of the Working of*

the Punjab Alienation of Land Act, XIII of 1900, For the year ending 30th September 1906 (Lahore: The Civil and Military Gazette Press, 1907), 7.

111. *Annual Report 1907*, 11.

112. *Annual Report on the Working of the Punjab Alienation of Land Act XIII of 1900, For the year ending 30th September 1901* (Lahore: The Civil and Military Gazette, 1902), 6.

113. *Annual Report on the Punjab Alienation of Land Act, XIII of 1900, as amended by the Punjab Act I of 1907, For the year ending the 30th September 1908* (Lahore: The Civil and Military Gazette, 1909), 1, 2, 7.

114. *Annual Report 1904*, 17, emphasis added.

115. On indebtedness in post-independence east Panjab, see P. Satish, "Institutional Credit, Indebtedness and Suicides in Punjab," *Economic and Political Weekly* 41, no. 26 (June 30–July 7, 2006): 2754–2761; Vishav Bharti, "Indebtedness and Suicide: Field Notes on Agricultural Labourers of Punjab," *Economic and Political Weekly* 46, no. 14 (April 2–8, 2011): 35–40; and Sukhpal Singh and Shruti Bhogal, "Punjab's Small Peasantry: Thriving or Deteriorating?," *Economic and Political Weekly* 49, no. 26–27 (June 28–July 5, 2014): 95–100. See also P. Sainath, *Everyone Loves a Good Drought: Stories from India's Poorest Districts* (New Delhi: Penguin Books, 1996).

116. Steedman, *Report*, 132.

117. See Malcolm Lyall Darling, *The Punjab Peasant in Prosperity and Debt* (London: Humphrey Milford, 1925), esp. chs. 1, 8–9, 12.

118. From C. A. Roe, *Report on the Revised Settlement of the Multan District of the Punjab, 1873–1880* (Lahore: W. Ball, 1883), quoted in "Agricultural Indebtedness in the Punjab," 27.

119. W. E. Purser, *Final Report on the Revised Settlement of the Jullundur District in the Punjab* (Lahore: The Civil and Military Gazette Press, 1892), 71–72.

120. W. E. Purser and H. C. Fanshawe, *Report on the Revised Land Revenue Settlement of the Rohtak District of the Hissar Division in the Punjab, 1873–1879* (Lahore: W. Ball, 1880), 63.

121. See Ranajit Guha, "The Prose of Counter-Insurgency," *Subaltern Studies II: Writings on South Asian History and Society*, ed. Ranajit Guha (New Delhi: Oxford University Press, 1983); and Ranajit Guha, *Elementary Aspects of Peasant Insurgency in Colonial India* (Durham: Duke University Press, 1999), chs. 1–2.

122. Sardar Kartar Singh, *Family Budgets, 1932–33, of Four Tenant-Cultivators in the Lyallpur District*, Board of Economic Inquiry Publication No. 40 (Lahore: The Civil and Military Gazette Press, 1934), v.

123. See Imran Ali, *The Punjab under Imperialism, 1885–1947* (Princeton: Princeton University Press, 1988).

124. Kartar Singh, *Family Budgets, 1932–33*, 2.

125. Kartar Singh, *Family Budgets, 1932–33*, 21, 3–4.

126. Kartar Singh and Ajaib Singh, *Family Budgets, 1933–34, of Six Tenant-Cultivators in the Lyallpur District*, Board of Economic Inquiry Publication No. 44 (Lahore: The Civil and Military Gazette Press, 1935), 27–29.

127. Labh Singh and Ajaib Singh, *Family Budgets, 1934–35*, iii.

128. Labh Singh and Ajaib Singh, *Family Budgets, 1935–36, of Six Tenant-Cultivators in the Lyallpur District*, Board of Economic Inquiry Publication No. 59 (Lahore: The Civil and Military Gazette Press, 1938), 19–20, 4, iii.

129. Labh Singh and Ajaib Singh, *Family Budgets, 1936–37, of Eleven Cultivators in the Punjab*, Board of Economic Inquiry Publication No. 62 (Lahore: The Civil and Military Gazette Press, 1939), 10–11, 34, 41.

130. Labh Singh and Ajaib Singh, *Family Budgets, 1937–38, of Ten Cultivators in the Punjab*, Board of Economic Inquiry Publication No. 67 (Lahore: The Civil and Military Gazette Press, 1939), 9, 30–32.

131. Labh Singh, Ajaib Singh, and Faiz Ilahi, *Family Budgets, 1938–39, of Twenty-Six Cultivators in the Punjab*, Board of Economic Inquiry Publication No. 72 (Lahore: The Civil and Military Gazette Press, 1941), 9, 30, 50–52.

132. Labh Singh et al., *Family Budgets, 1938–39*, 30–32, 48, 51, 61.

133. All of the studies make claims to the representative quality of the participating families as above average. The fourth in the series, for instance, states that "[t]hese tenants fall, with respect to their income and social status, midway between ordinary tenants and the peasant proprietors in the Canal Colonies, but compared with the Punjab farmers as a whole, they may be assumed to be a little above the average." At the same time, the sixth study further specifies that "[i]t is not claimed that the families whose accounts appear in these pages are typical of the general run of peasants in the Punjab" since they "work under department supervision, using superior seeds and implements, and the area worked by them is also fairly large." One must therefore imagine the conditions and trajectory of the large majority of cultivators that were not as privileged. See Labh Singh and Ajaib Singh, *Family Budgets, 1935–36*, vii–viii; and Labh Singh and Ajaib Singh, *Family Budgets, 1937–38*, iii.

134. On the politics of marriage in colonial north India, see Veena Talwar Oldenburg, *Dowry Murder: The Imperial Origins of a Cultural Crime* (New York: Oxford University Press, 2002), ch. 1; and Anshu Malhotra, *Gender, Caste, and Religious Identities: Restructuring Class in Colonial Punjab* (New Delhi: Oxford University Press, 2002), chs. 2–3.

135. For a recent account of debt as a grand, global phenomenon across several millennia, see David Graeber, *Debt: The First 5,000 Years* (New York: Melville House, 2011).

136. "Indebtedness," 8.

Chapter 4

1. On the life and politics of Ambedkar, see the classic Dhananjay Keer, *Dr. Ambedkar: Life and Mission* (Bombay: Popular Prakashan, 1954); Eleanor Zelliot, *Ambedkar's World: The Making of Babasaheb and the Dalit Movement* (New Delhi: Navayana, 2013); Gail Omvedt, *Ambedkar: Towards an Enlightened India* (New Delhi: Penguin, 2004); and more recently Anand Teltumbde and Suraj Yengde, eds., *The Radical in Ambedkar: Critical Reflections* (Gurgaon: Allen Lane, 2018).

2. Bhimrao Ramji Ambedkar, "Annihilation of Caste," in *Dr. Babasaheb Ambedkar: Writings and Speeches*, vol. 1, ed. Vasant Moon (Bombay: Education Department of the Government of Maharashtra, 1979), 27.

3. Ambedkar, "Annihilation of Caste," 34–35.

4. The publication of an annotated edition of this text renewed debates over Ambedkar's relationship to Hinduism, nationalism, and caste emancipation. See Bhimrao Ramji Ambedkar, *Annihilation of Caste: The Annotated Critical Edition* (New Delhi: Navayana Publishers, 2014), and especially the controversial introduction by Arundhati Roy. In an endorsement on the front flap of this edition, the writer and activist Anand Teltumbde states: "What *Communist Manifesto* is to the capitalist world, *Annihilation of Caste* is to caste India."

5. Ambedkar, "Annihilation of Caste," 41, 46.
6. Ambedkar, "Annihilation of Caste," 47.
7. Ambedkar, "Annihilation of Caste," 68.
8. Ambedkar, "Annihilation of Caste," 78.

9. In 1931, Panjab had a total population of 28,490,857, of which 23,580,852 (82.8%) were under direct British rule and 4,910,005 (17.2%) under seventeen different subordinate princely states. The overwhelming majority lived in the countryside rather than cities: 87.6% rural to 12.4% urban. In terms of religion, officially Hindus were 37.6%, Muslims 51.9%, Sikhs 7.3%, Christians 1.9%, and "Others" 1.3% of the total population. Yet in rural areas, Hindus dropped to 29.1%, Muslims remained at 52.5%, and Sikhs rose to 15.3%. See Khan Ahmad Hasan Khan, *Census of India, 1931: Volume XVII, Punjab, Part 1—Report* (Lahore: The Civil and Military Gazette Press, 1933), 11, 89, 96, 98.

10. Out of a depressed class population estimated at 1,422,009 in 1931, the official figure for followers of Ad Dharm is 418,789, including 113,580 from Jalandhar, 111,829 from Hoshiarpur, 50,718 from Lyallpur, and 36,262 from Ferozepur. Ahmad Hasan Khan, the author of the census report, briefly mentions that a "tug-of-war" started in some districts between Ad Dharmi activists and Hindu and Sikh landowners over the religion lower castes were declaring to census enumerators. See Khan, *Census of India, 1931*, Part 1—Report, 374, 318, 294, and iii–iv.

11. See Surinder Singh Jodhka, "Prejudice without Pollution? Scheduled Castes in Contemporary Punjab," *Journal of Indian School of Political Economy* 12, no. 3–4 (2000): 381–403; Harish Puri, "Scheduled Castes in Sikh Community: A Historical Perspective," *Economic and Political Weekly* 38, no. 26 (June 28–July 4, 2023): 2693–2701; and Ronki Ram, "Untouchability in India with a Difference: Ad Dharm, Dalit Assertion, and Caste Conflicts in Punjab," *Asia Survey* 44, no. 6 (2004): 895–912.

12. Ambedkar is unequivocal in drawing the two together in order to condemn Hindu scripture: "You must take the stand that Buddha took. You must take the stand which Guru Nanak took. You must not only discard the *Shastras*, you must deny their authority, as did Buddha and Nanak." On the other hand, he mentions historical incidents of forced conversions to Islam (and Christianity) but does so to further lambaste the violence of indifference in Hinduism. "I have no hesitation in saying that if the Mohammedan has been cruel the Hindu has been mean and meanness is worse than cruelty." Ambedkar, "Annihilation of Caste," 69, 54.

13. See Nicholas B. Dirks, *Castes of Mind: Colonialism and the Making of Modern India* (Princeton: Princeton University Press, 2001), chs. 3, 5; C. J. Fuller, "Ethnographic Inquiry in Colonial India: Herbert Risley, William Crooke, and the Study of Tribes and Castes," *Journal of the Royal Anthropological Institute* 23, no. 3 (September 2017): 603–621;

and Neeladri Bhattacharya, *The Great Agrarian Conquest: The Colonial Reshaping of a Rural World* (Ranikhet: Permanent Black, 2018), ch. 1.

14. A. Zimmerman, *Anthropology and Antihumanism in Imperial Germany* (Chicago: University of Chicago Press, 2001), 7 and ch. 10.

15. See Peter Mayer, "Inventing Village Tradition: The Late 19th Century Origins of the North Indian 'Jajmani System,'" *Modern Asian Studies* 27, no. 2 (May 1993): 358.

16. William H. Wiser, *The Hindu Jajmani System: A Socio-Economic System Interrelating Members of a Hindu Village Community in Services* (Lucknow: Lucknow Publishing House, 1936), 5.

17. Charlotte V. Wiser and William H. Wiser, *Behind Mud Walls* (New York: Richard R. Smith, 1930), 18.

18. Wiser, *Hindu Jajmani System*, 10.

19. Wiser, *Hindu Jajmani System*, 11.

20. On the advent of area studies in the post-1945 era, see Harry Harootunian, *History's Disquiet: Modernity, Cultural Practice, and the Question of Everyday Life* (New York: Columbia University Press, 2002).

21. Oscar Lewis, "Caste and the Jajmani System in a North Indian Village," *The Scientific Monthly* 83, no. 2 (August 1956): 71. For a complete account of Lewis's relationships and experiences in Rampur, see Oscar Lewis, *Village Life in Northern India: Studies in a Delhi Village* (Urbana: University of Illinois Press, 1958).

22. Bernard S. Cohn, "The Changing Status of a Depressed Caste," in *Village India: Studies in the Little Community*, ed. McKim Marriott (Chicago: University of Chicago Press, 1955), 67 and *passim*. Cohn returned to Madhopur twice in the late 1950s to document the ongoing changes experienced by Chamars. See also "Changing Traditions of a Low Caste" and "Madhopur Revisited" in Bernard S. Cohn, *An Anthropologist among the Historians and Other Essays* (New Delhi: Oxford University Press, 1987).

23. See Harold A. Gould, "The Hindu Jajmani System: A Case of Economic Particularism," *Southwestern Journal of Anthropology* 14, no. 4 (Winter 1958): 428; and Harold A. Gould, "A Jajmani System of North India: Its Structure, Magnitude, and Meaning," *Ethnology* 3, no. 1 (January 1964): 31, emphasis added.

24. On the religious-based assumptions of village labor studies, see Simon Commander, "The Jajmani System of North India: An Examination of its Logic and Status across Two Centuries," *Modern Asian Studies* 17, no. 2 (1983): 283–311.

25. Gould, "Jajmani System," 18–19.

26. Cohn, "Changing Status," 64.

27. See M. N. Srinivas, "The Indian Village: Myth and Reality," in *The Dominant Caste and Other Essays* (New Delhi: Oxford University Press, 1987); Arjun Appadurai, "Is Homo Hierarchicus?" *American Ethnologist* 13, no. 4 (November 1986): 745–761; and R.S. Khare, ed., *Caste, Hierarchy, and Individualism: Indian Critiques of Louis Dumont's Contributions* (New Delhi: Oxford University Press, 2006).

28. See Dirks, *Castes of Mind*, chs. 3, 6, 10.

29. See Susan Bayly, *Caste, Society, and Politics in India from the Eighteenth Century to the Modern Age* (New York: Cambridge University Press, 1999); M.S.S. Pandian, *Brahmin and Non-Brahmin: Genealogies of the Tamil Political Present* (New Delhi: Permanent Black, 2007); Rupa Viswanath, *The Pariah Problem: Caste, Religion, and the Social*

in *Modern India* (New York: Columbia University Press, 2014); and P. Sanal Mohan, *Modernity of Slavery: Struggles against Caste Inequality in Colonial Kerala* (New Delhi: Oxford University Press, 2015).

30. See Jan Breman, *Patronage and Exploitation: Changing Agrarian Relations in South Gujarat, India* (Berkeley: University of California Press, 1974); Gyan Prakash, *Bonded Histories: Genealogies of Labor Servitude in Colonial India* (Cambridge: Cambridge University Press, 1990); Vijay Prashad, *Untouchable Freedom: A Social History of a Dalit Community* (New York: Oxford University Press, 2000); Vinay Gidwani, *Capital, Interrupted: Agrarian Development and the Politics of Work in India* (Minneapolis: University of Minnesota Press, 2008); Anupama Rao, *The Caste Question: Dalits and the Politics of Modern India* (Berkeley: University of California Press, 2009); Ramnarayan S. Rawat, *Reconsidering Untouchability: Chamars and Dalit History in North India* (Bloomington: Indiana University Press, 2011); and Chinnaiah Jangam, *Dalits and the Making of Modern India* (New Delhi: Oxford University Press, 2017).

31. See Sumit Guha, *Beyond Caste: Identity and Power in South Asia, Past and Present* (Leiden: Brill, 2013).

32. Wiser and Wiser, *Behind Mud Walls*, 69, 71.

33. Lewis, "Caste and the Jajmani System," 2.

34. Although Maharaja Ranjit Singh reigned until his death in 1839 and his kingdom remained nominally independent for another decade, some portions of Panjab such as the Lahore region came under different misl leaders as early as 1765, while other areas in the west and south were not incorporated until the 1830s. See Muzaffar Alam, *The Crisis of Empire in Mughal North India: Awadh and the Punjab, 1707–48* (New Delhi: Oxford University Press, 1986), chs. 4–5; J. S. Grewal, *The Sikhs of the Punjab*, rev. ed. (Cambridge: Cambridge University Press, 1998), chs. 5–6; and Purnima Dhavan, *When Sparrows Become Hawks: The Making of the Sikh Warrior Tradition, 1699–1799* (New York: Oxford University Press, 2011).

35. Kessinger emphasizes the importance of this decision. "This change represents more than the substitution of *zamindars* from one particular family, lineage, caste, or religious group for those drawn from a different background—a process common in other parts of India in the pre-British period. The elimination of the position of *zamindar* constituted a fundamental change in the structure of rural society in the Punjab." See Kessinger, *Vilyatpur 1848–1968: Social and Economic Change in a North India Village* (Berkeley: University of California Press, 1974), 27–29. See also note 3 on pages 268–269.

36. Kessinger explains that while *zamindar* denoted an individual officially authorized to collect revenue in Mughal times and continues to convey a sense of superiority and large landholding across north India, in Panjab it simply meant "cultivator." Kessinger, *Vilyatpur 1848–1968*, 19 fn29. In fact, *zamindar* existed alongside other words such as *kisan* and *khetikar* that could mean cultivator as well as several other analogous categories. This heterogeneity came to an end with colonial legislation deploying the categories of "agriculturalist" and "agricultural tribes" to structure access to land. For more, see Chapter 2.

37. See Karine Schomer and W. H. McLeod, eds., *The Sants: Studies in a Devotional Tradition of India* (New Delhi: Motilal Banarsidass, 1987).

38. John S. Hawley and Mark Juergensmeyer, *Songs of the Saints of India* (New Delhi: Oxford University Press, 2004), 35.

39. *Sri Guru Granth Sahib Ji* (hereafter *SGGS*), Ang 1102–03. All of the following verses in this chapter are from the online version <www.srigranth.org> accessed on April 13, 2022 and translated by Sant Singh Khalsa. I have removed the diacritics and modified a few of the transliterations, translations, and spacings. For a slightly different rendering of this verse from Kabir, see Hawley and Juergensmeyer, *Songs of the Saints of India*, 51.

40. *SGGS*, Ang 324. For a very different translation based on the *Kabirgranth*, see Hawley and Juergensmeyer, *Songs of the Saints of India*, 54.

41. Eleanor Zelliot and Rohini Mokashi-Punekar, eds., *Untouchable Saints: An Indian Phenomenon* (New Delhi: Manohar Publishers, 2005), 35. See also Brij Mohan Sagar, *Songs of Ravi Das* (Chandigarh: Publication Bureau of Panjab University, 2003), 1–17.

42. *SGGS*, Ang 525. See also Hawley and Juergensmeyer, *Songs of the Saints of India*, 26.

43. *SGGS*, Ang 345. See also Hawley and Juergensmeyer, *Songs of the Saints of India*, 32.

44. On Ravidas and his concept of Begampura, see Gail Omvedt, *Seeking Begampura: The Social Vision of Anticaste Intellectuals* (New Delhi: Navayana Publishers, 2008), ch. 4.

45. Susan Prill, "Representing Sainthood in India: Sikh and Hindu Visions of Namdev," *Material Religion* 5, no. 2 (July 2009): 159. See also Nirmal Dass, ed., *Songs of the Saints from the Adi Granth* (Albany: State University of New York Press, 2000), 26.

46. *SGGS*, Ang 1292. See also Dass, ed., *Songs of the Saints*, 78.

47. On the process of incorporating verses from different Bhagats in the *Adi Granth*, see Gurinder Singh Mann, *The Making of Sikh Scripture* (New Delhi: Oxford University Press, 2001), ch. 7; and Pashaura Singh, *The Bhagats of the Guru Granth Sahib: Sikh Self-Definition and the Bhagat Bani* (New Delhi: Oxford University Press, 2003), chs. 1, 6.

48. See J. S. Grewal, *Guru Nanak in History* (Chandigarh: Publication Bureau of Panjab University, 1969); W. H. McLeod, *Guru Nanak and the Sikh Religion* (Oxford: Clarendon Press, 1968); and cf. Arvind-Pal S. Mandair, *Religion and the Specter of the West: Sikhism, India, Postcoloniality, and the Politics of Translation* (New York: Columbia University Press, 2009), chs. 3, 4, 6.

49. See Nikky-Guninder Kaur Singh, "Introduction," in Guru Nanak, *Poems from the Guru Granth Sahib*, ed. and trans. Nikky-Guninder Kaur Singh (Cambridge: Harvard University Press, 2022), xiii, emphasis in original.

50. *SGGS*, Ang 142; Ang 7; and Ang 15.

51. All four of these early Sikhs were killed along with dozens of others in the Battle of Chamkaur against Mughal forces in 1704. On Guru Gobind Singh and the Khalsa initiation, see Grewal, *The Sikhs of the Punjab*, 77; and Louis Fenech, *The Cherished Five in Sikh History* (New York: Oxford University Press, 2021). On Jiwan Singh and other Dalit Sikhs, see Raj Kumar Hans, "Making Sense of Dalit Sikh History," in *Dalit Studies*, ed. Ramnarayan S. Rawat and K. Satyanarayana (Durham: Duke University Press, 2016), 135–40.

52. See Jodhka, "Prejudice without Pollution?" 385.

53. Hans, "Making Sense of Dalit Sikh History," 138.

54. See Christopher Hill, *The World Turned Upside Down: Radical Ideas During the English Revolution* (London: Penguin, 1991); and Ranajit Guha, *Elementary Aspects of Peasant Insurgency in Colonial India* (New Delhi: Oxford University Press, 1983), ch. 2;

and cf. Mikhail Bakhtin, *Rabelais and His World*, trans. Helene Iswolsky (Bloomington: Indiana University Press, 1984), ch. 3.

55. This poem is part of an unwritten oral tradition called *kafi* and therefore does not have a single, standard Panjabi rendering. I have made my own translation based on the Gurmukhi version from Bullhe Shah, *Sufi Lyrics*, ed. and trans. Christopher Shackle (Cambridge: Harvard University Press, 2015), 9–10. See also Kartar Singh Duggal's translation as "Strange are the Times" from Shahmukhi online at <www.apnaorg.com/poetry/bulleheng>, accessed April 19, 2020. For a very different version, see Taufiq Rafat translation as "A Topsy-Turvey World," in *Bulleh Shah: A Selection* (Lahore: Vanguard Publications, 1982), 66.

56. See Jagjit Singh, *Percussions of History: The Sikh Revolution, In the Caravan of Revolutions* (SAS Nagar: Nanakshahi Trust, 2006), especially chs. 11, 12, 16, 18.

57. See the early eighteenth-century descriptions in "Banda Bahadur's Rebellion, 1710–16" from Muhammad Hadi Kamwar Khan's *Tazkiratu's Salatin Chaghata* and "Banda Bahadur and his Followers" from Khafi Khan's *Muntakhabu'l Lubab*, both translated in J. S. Grewal and Irfan Habib, eds. *Sikh History from Persian Sources* (New Delhi: Tulika, 2001), 143, 157. On the distinction between inter- and intra-class warfare in the Mughal period, Wilfred Cantwell Smith famously argued that conflicts between classes were "always bitter, fierce, brutal; they usually ended in pillage, massacre, and a devastation that makes many upper-class wars of the time seem picnics." See Smith, "Lower-class Uprisings in the Mughal Empire," in *The Mughal State, 1526–1750*, ed. Muzaffar Alam and Sanjay Subrahmanyam (New Delhi Oxford University Press, 1988), 328.

58. See Chetan Singh, *Region and Empire: Panjab in the Seventeenth Century* (New Delhi: Oxford University Press, 1991), ch. 7; Hardip Singh Syan, *Sikh Militancy in the Seventeenth Century: Religious Violence in Mughal and Early Modern India* (New York: I.B. Tauris, 2013), ch. 4; and Purnima Dhavan, "Reading the Texture of History and Memory in Early-Nineteenth-Century Punjab," *Comparative Studies of South Asia, Africa, and the Middle East* 29, no. 3 (2009): 515–527.

59. See Raj Kumar Hans, "Sant Poet Wazir Singh: A Window for Reimagining Nineteenth Century Punjab," *International Journal of Punjab Studies* 20, no. 1–2 (January 2013): 137.

60. Anshu Malhotra, "Bhakti and the Gendered Self: A Courtesan and a Consort in Mid Nineteenth Century Punjab," *Modern Asian Studies* 46, no. 6 (November 2012): 1508–32. See also Anshu Malhotra, *Piro and the Gulabdasis: Gender, Sect, and Society in Punjab* (New Delhi: Oxford University Press, 2017).

61. See Ali Raza, *Revolutionary Pasts: Communist Internationalism in Colonial India* (Cambridge: Cambridge University Press, 2020), 155 and ch. 5.

62. Leslie S. Saunders, *Report on the revised land revenue settlement of the Lahore district in the Lahore division of the Panjab, 1865–69* (Lahore: Central Jail Press, 1873), 61–62.

63. A well-known description of the lack of Brahmin power in rural Panjab at the turn of the century comes from the autobiography of Prakash Tandon, a son of an Khatri engineer who received his education in England and went on to become a top manager in a large multinational company. "That they [Brahmins] could be the leaders of society, in a position of privilege," he writes, "I only discovered when I went to live outside the Punjab. With us the Brahmins were an unprivileged class and exercised

little influence on the community." And later: "The very address 'oh Pandita' or 'oh Brahmina' had a gentle sarcasm about it." On the other hand, speaking of Jatts he noted that "the farmer boys among whom I grew up were a remarkable lot, well made, self-confident and fearless." See Prakash Tandon, *Punjabi Century: 1857–1947* (Berkeley: University of California Press, 1968), 76–77, 52. See also the remarkable autobiography of Gurnam S. S. Brard, *East of Indus: My Memories of Old Punjab* (New Delhi: Hemkunt Publishers, 2007).

64. See Paramjit S. Judge, "Hierarchical Differentiation among Dalits," *Economic and Political Weekly* 38, no. 28 (July 12–18, 2003): 2990.

65. The Chamar Mahan Sabha, or "Grand Chamar Society," is a prominent Jalandhar-based organization that advocates on behalf of scheduled castes in Panjab, particularly Ravidasias. In recent years, a number of songs with titles such as "Putt Chamaran De" (Sons of Chamars) and lyrics boasting of the physical strength, material possessions, and self-respect of Chamars have become popular in certain circles. The title and content of these songs can be seen as mimetic responses to perhaps one of the most famous Panjabi songs, "Putt Jattan De" ("Sons of Jatts") by Surinder Shinda from 1983.

66. See Bernard Cohn, "The Census, Social Structure and Objectification in South Asia," in *An Anthropologist among the Historians and Other Essays* (New Delhi: Oxford University Press, 1987); Arjun Appadurai, "Number in the Colonial Imagination," in *Orientalism and the Postcolonial Predicament,* ed. Carol Breckenridge and Peter van der Veer (Philadelphia: University of Pennsylvania Press, 1993); and Kenneth Jones, "Religious Identity and the Indian Census," in *The Census in British India: New Perspectives,* ed. N. Gerald Barrier (New Delhi: Manohar Publishers, 1981).

67. In 1881, the census shows Chamars numbered 1,072,699 in addition to 349,272 Mochis, while Churhas were 1,078,739. The figures for others castes are: Jatts 4,432,750, Rajputs 1,677,569, Brahmins 1,084,193, Pathans 859,582, Gujars 627,304, and Khatris 419,139 out of a total population of 22,712,120. See Denzil Ibbetson, *Report on the Census of the Panjab, taken in the 17th of February 1881,* vol. 2 (Lahore: Superintendent of the Central Gaol Press, 1883), Table No. VII A, "Statement showing the Distribution of the People by Tribe, Caste, and Religion," 4–10.

68. For details about this traumatic episode and the evolving tensions between the Arya Samaj and the Singh Sabha, see Kenneth W. Jones, "Ham Hindu Nahin: Arya-Sikh Relations, 1877–1905," *Journal of Asian Studies* 32, no. 3 (May 1973): 465–74.

69. See Kenneth W. Jones, *Arya Dharm: Hindu Consciousness in 19th Century Punjab* (Berkeley: University of California Press, 1976); Harjot Oberoi, *The Construction of Religious Boundaries: Culture, Identity, and Diversity in the Sikh Tradition* (Chicago: University of Chicago Press, 1994); and Christopher Harding, *Religious Transformation in South Asia: The Meanings of Conversion in Colonial Punjab* (New York: Oxford University Press, 2008).

70. In the 1921 census there were 1,139,741 Chamars, 434,682 Mochis, and 165,164 Dagis, while there were 749,687 Churhas, 366,098 Mussalis, 281,946 Christians (without a specified caste), and 65,004 Mazhabis. The religious proportions are given within each caste category. See L. Middleton and S. M. Jacob, *Census of India, 1921: Punjab and Delhi,* vol. 15, part II (Lahore: The Civil and Military Gazette Press, 1922), Table XIII,

"Caste or Tribe," 194–254; and Table XV, "Territorial Distribution of the Christian Population by Sect and Race," 264–72.

71. See Harish K. Puri, *Ghadar Movement: Ideology, Organization, and Strategy* (Amritsar: Guru Nanak Dev University Press, 1993); Maia Ramnath, *Haj to Utopia: How the Ghadar Movement Charted Global Radicalism and Attempted to Overthrow the British Empire* (Berkeley: University of California Press, 2011); J. S. Grewal, Harish K. Puri, and Indu Banga, eds., *The Ghadar Movement: Background, Ideology, Action, and Legacies* (Patiala: Publication Bureau of Punjabi University, 2013); and Parmbir Singh Gill, "A Different Kind of Dissidence: The Ghadar Party, Sikh History, and the Politics of Anticolonial Mobilization," *Sikh Formations: Religion, Culture, Theory* 10, no. 1 (2014): 23–41.

72. See Mark Juergensmeyer, *Religion as Social Vision: The Movement against Untouchability in 20th Century Punjab* (Berkeley: University of California Press, 1982), Appendix A: "The Early Life of Mangoo Ram," 283–89.

73. Juergensmeyer, *Religion as Social Vision*, 44.

74. Juergensmeyer, *Religion as Social Vision*, 45.

75. See Juergensmeyer, *Religion as Social Vision*, Appendix B: "The Report of the Ad Dharm Mandal, 1926–1931," 299–302. See also Ram, "Untouchability in India with a Difference," 900–902.

76. See Cassie Adcock, *The Limits of Tolerance: Indian Secularism and the Politics of Religious Freedom* (New York: Oxford University Press, 2013), ch. 5.

77. Puri, "Scheduled Castes in Sikh Community," 2697; Hans, "Making Sense of Dalit Sikh History," 142–47; and Surinder Singh Jodhka, "Caste and Untouchability in Rural Punjab," *Economic and Political Weekly* 37, no. 19 (May 11–17, 2002): 1814–1820.

78. Juergensmeyer, *Religion as Social Vision*, 76.

79. Giani Ditt Singh, *Nakli Sikh Prabodh* [False Sikhs Redeem Yourselves], (Lahore, 1895) and Kahn Singh Nabha, *Ham Hindu Nahin* [We are not Hindus], (Amritsar, 1899); from Puri, "Scheduled Castes in Sikh Community," 2697.

80. Middleton and Jacob, *Census of India, 1921*, Table XIII: Caste or Tribe, 254.

81. Ambedkar, "Annihilation of Caste," 35.

82. Gandhi's opposition to the possibility of Ambedkar converting to Sikhi is mentioned in Kapur Singh's reflections, published in 1972. See Kapur Singh, *Sachi Sakhi* [True Story] (Jalandhar: Raj Roop Prakashan, 1972), 58.

83. Singh, *Sachi Sakhi*, 58.

84. Puri, "Scheduled Castes in Sikh Community," 2698.

85. The original account and extended explanation in Panjabi is in Singh, *Sachi Sakhi*, 59 (my translation). See also Puri, "Scheduled Castes in Sikh Community," 2698; and the compendium by Mal Singh, *Sikh Mission ate Dr. Bhim Rao Ambedkar* [The Sikh Mission and Dr. Bhim Rao Ambedkar] (Patiala: Gracious Books, 2020). The Darbar Sahib is the gurduara complex in Amritsar containing the Akal Takht and Harimandir Sahib, the latter which is sometimes referred to in English as "the Golden Temple" due to its upper portion having been encased in gold plate by Maharaja Ranjit Singh in the early nineteenth century.

86. See Juergensmeyer, *Religion as Social Vision*, Appendix B, 301.

87. Khan, *Census of India, 1931*, Part 1—Report, iv.

88. Juergensmeyer, *Religion as Social Vision*, 77.

89. Khan, *Census of India, 1931,* Part 2—Tables, Table XVII—"Race, Tribe or Caste," 282–302.

90. Juergensmeyer, *Religion as Social Vision,* 77.

91. Juergensmeyer, *Religion as Social Vision,* 162. See also Gauri Viswanathan, *Outside the Fold: Conversion, Modernity, and Belief* (Princeton: Princeton University Press, 1988), ch. 7; Ajay Skaria, "Ambedkar, Marx, and the Buddhist Question," *South Asia: Journal of South Asian Studies* 38, no. 3 (2015): 450–65; Aishwary Kumar, *Radical Equality: Ambedkar, Gandhi, and the Risk of Democracy* (Stanford: Stanford University Press, 2015), ch. 5; and Nathaniel Roberts, *To Be Cared For: The Power of Conversion and the Foreignness of Belonging in an Indian Slum* (Oakland: University of California Press, 2016), ch. 4.

92. This task was left to an independent network of shrines and educational institutions. See Juergensmeyer, *Religion as Social Vision,* 152–55; Ronki Ram, "Ravidass Deras and Social Protest: Making Sense of Dalit Consciousness in Punjab (India)," *Journal of Asian Studies* 67, no. 4 (November 2008): 1341–1364; and Ram, "Untouchability in India with a Difference," 905–912.

93. Juergensmeyer, *Religion as Social Vision,* 80. See also David Gilmartin, *Empire and Islam: Punjab and the Making of Pakistan* (Berkeley: University of California Press, 1988), chs. 4–6.

94. For a critique of the notion of Chamars as leather workers, see Rawat, *Reconsidering Untouchability,* chs. 2–3. On the evolution of Churha identity in the Delhi region, see Prashad, *Untouchable Freedom.*

95. Juergensmeyer, *Religion as Social Vision,* Appendix B, 300–301.

96. On this pivotal piece of colonial legislation, see Norman G. Barrier, *The Punjab Alienation of Land Bill of 1900* (Durham: Duke University Press, 1966); M. Mufakharul Islam, "The Punjab Land Alienation Act and the Professional Moneylenders," *Modern Asian Studies* 29, no. 2 (May 1995): 274, 290; and Pervaiz Nazir, "Origins of Debt, Mortgage, and Alienation of Land in Early Modern Punjab," *Journal of Peasant Studies* 27, no. 3 (2000): 82; as well as Chapters 2 and 3.

97. R. K. Seth and Faiz Ilahi, *An Economic Survey of Durrana Langana, a Village in the Multan District of the Punjab,* Punjab Village Surveys No. 11 (Lahore: The Civil and Military Gazette Press, 1938), 30–31, emphasis added. The labors of women disappear into the masculine assumptions built around the categories "cultivator," "peasant," and "kisan." On the gendered politics of agriculture, see Prem Chowdhry, *The Veiled Women: Shifting Gender Equations in Rural Haryana, 1880–1900* (New Delhi: Oxford University Press, 1994); Bina Agarwal, *A Field of One's Own: Gender and Land Rights in South Asia* (Cambridge: Cambridge University Press, 1994); and Govind Kelkar and Maithreyi Krishnaraj, eds., *Women, Land and Power in Asia* (New Delhi: Routledge, 2013).

98. Randhir Singh, *An Economic Survey of Kala Gaddi Thamman (Chak 73 G.B), a Village in the Lyallpur District of the Punjab,* Punjab Village Surveys No. 4 (Lahore: The Civil and Military Gazette Press, 1932), Appendix A to Chapter 1, 17–18.

99. See Neeladri Bhattacharya, "Agricultural Labour and Production: Central and South-East Punjab, 1870–1940," in *The World of the Rural Labourer in Colonial India,* ed. Gyan Prakash (New Delhi: Oxford University Press, 1992), 154–65; Kessinger, *Vilyatpur 1848–1968,* 56–75; and Jodhka, "Caste and Untouchability on Rural Punjab," 1814, 1816, 1822.

100. See Rajit K. Mazumder, *The Indian Army and the Making of Punjab* (New Delhi: Permanent Black, 2003); and Kate Imy, *Faithful Fighters: Identity and Power in the British Indian Army* (Stanford: Stanford University Press, 2019).

101. The siri relationship differed sharply from the indentured or enslaved laborers in north India explored in Prakash's *Bonded Histories*, the "pariahs" of Tamil Nadu in Viswanath's *The Pariah Problem*, or the slave castes in Mohan's *Modernity of Slavery*. Cf. Jodhka, "Caste and Untouchability in Rural Punjab," 1816; and Ram, "Untouchability in India with a Difference," 899.

102. Sardar Gian Singh, *An Economic Survey of Gaggar Bhana, a Village in the Amritsar District of the Punjab*, Punjab Village Surveys No. 1 (Lahore: The Civil and Military Gazette Press, 1928), 25.

103. Perhaps the most vivid depiction of contemporary lower-caste siri laborers is from the poem "Jatt te Siri da Haal" (The Condition of a Jatt and a Siri) by the revolutionary poet Sant Ram Udasi from the late 1970s. See Rajinder Rahi, ed., *Sant Ram Udasi: Jeevan ate Samuchi Rachna* [Sant Ram Udasi: Life and Collected Work] (Ludhiana: Chetna Parkashan, 2001), 174.

104. See Lajpat Rai Dawar, *An Economic Survey of Suner, a Village in the Ferozepore District of the Punjab*, Punjab Village Surveys No. 9 (Lahore: The Civil and Military Gazette Press, 1936), Appendix B to Chapter 1: "Specimen of agreement between cultivating owner and his siri," 24.

105. See Gian Singh, *Economic Survey of Gaggar Bhana*, 33–36.

106. See Dawar, *Economic Survey of Suner*, 170–71; Randhir Singh, *Economic Survey of Kala Gaddi Thamman*, 153–57; Gian Singh, *Economic Survey of Gaggar Bhana*, 182–83; and Seth and Ilahi, *Economic Survey of Durrana Langana*, 266–70. Cultivators also enjoyed greater access to gheo and milk because they owned more and better-producing buffalo.

107. There is a discrepancy in the specific numbers used for Farmer A's income and expenses over five pages of calculations and the summary chart on the last page of this section. The occupier rate of Rs. 69 is also not included in the land revenue figure. In the summary, gross income is Rs. 1,602 and expenses are Rs. 1,014 for a profit of Rs. 588. See Raj Narain, *An Economic Survey of Gijhi, a Village in the Rohtak District of the Punjab*, Punjab Village Surveys No. 2 (Lahore: The Civil and Military Gazette Press, 1932), 199–203, 213–22.

108. Men belonging to the cultivating classes consumed the following amount of wheat in ounces per day for the following age groups: 26.64 oz. for 11–15 years, 32.44 oz. for 16–25 years, and 34.5 oz. for 26–50 years. Non-cultivating men, on the other hand, consumed significantly less: 22.5 oz. for 11–15 years, 26.26 oz. for 16–25 years, and 30 oz. for 26–50 years. See Gian Singh, *Economic Survey of Gaggar Bhana*, 191.

109. Gian Singh, *Economic Survey of Gaggar Bhana*, 185.

110. Narain, *Economic Survey of Gijhi*, 16, emphasis added.

111. Narain, *Economic Survey of Gijhi*, 17.

112. Dawar, *Economic Survey of Suner*, 88.

113. See Guha, *Elementary Aspects*, ch. 2; and James C. Scott, *Weapons of the Weak: Everyday Forms of Peasant Resistance* (New Haven: Yale University Press, 1985), chs. 1–2.

114. Ram Lall Bhalla, *Report on Economic Survey of Bairampur in the Hoshiarpur District* (Lahore: Superintendent of Government Printing, 1922), 142.

115. On the ongoing legacy of Ad Dharm, see Juergensmeyer, *Religion as Social Vision*, 152–54; and Ronki Ram, "Social Exclusion, Resistance, and Deras: Exploring the Myth of Casteless Sikh Society in Punjab," *Economic and Political Weekly* 42, no. 40 (October 6–12, 2007): 4066–4074.

116. Karl Marx, "On the Jewish Question," in *The Marx-Engels Reader*, 2nd ed., ed. Robert C. Tucker (New York: W.W. Norton & Company, 1978), 34.

117. Marx, "On the Jewish Question," 32. See also Aamir Mufti, *Enlightenment in the Colony: The Jewish Question and the Crisis of Postcolonial Culture* (Princeton: Princeton University Press, 2007), ch. 1; Rao, *Caste Question*, 21–26; and Ritu Birla, *Stages of Capital: Law, Culture, and Market Governance in Late Colonial India* (Durham: Duke University Press, 2009), 24–27.

118. Marx, "On the Jewish Question," 33, 34, emphasis in original.

119. Marx, "On the Jewish Question," 35.

120. Marx, "On the Jewish Question," 46.

121. See Partha Chatterjee, *The Nation and Its Fragments: Colonial and Postcolonial Histories* (Princeton: Princeton University Press, 1993), ch. 2; and Birla, *Stages of Capital*, chs. 4–5.

122. Kessinger, *Vilyatpur 1848–1968*, 219.

123. On the current political situation of Dalits in east Panjab, see Harish K. Puri, ed., *Dalits in Regional Context* (Jaipur: Rawat Publishers, 2004); and Amandeep Sandhu, *Panjab: Journeys Through Fault Lines* (Chennai: Westland, 2019), chs. 9, 11. On west Panjab, see Aasim Sajjad Akhtar, "The State as Landlord in Pakistani Punjab: Peasant Struggles on the Okara Military Farms," *Journal of Peasant Studies* 33, no. 3 (2006): 479–501; and Mubbashir Rizvi, *The Ethics of Staying: Social Movements and Land Rights Politics in Pakistan* (Stanford: Stanford University Press, 2019).

Chapter 5

1. Raymond Williams, *Keywords: A Vocabulary of Culture and Society* (London: Fontana Press, 1976), 231.

2. Williams, *Keywords*, 232. The first sentence of Eric Hobsbawm and George Rudé's seminal 1969 study of English farm laborers concurs: "Agricultural England in the 19th century presented a unique and amazing spectacle to the enquiring foreigner: *they had no peasants*." See Hobsbawm and Rudé, *Capitan Swing* (London: Lawrence and Wishart, 1969), 23, emphasis added. Even earlier, in 1893 Friedrich Engels begins his account of the peasant question with a similar observation: "In Britain proper big landed estates and large-scale agriculture have totally displaced the self-supporting peasant." See Engels, *The Peasant Question in France and Germany* (Moscow: Foreign Languages Publishing House, 1955), 5.

3. Williams, *Keywords*, 232.

4. Samuel Moyn and Andrew Sartori, "Approaches to Global Intellectual History," in *Global Intellectual History*, ed. Samuel Moyn and Andrew Sartori (New York: Columbia University Press, 2013), 11.

5. See Andrew Sartori, "Global Intellectual History and the History of Political Economy," in *Global Intellectual History*, ed. Moyn and Sartori, 124 and *passim*.

6. For an overview of the debate, see Henry Bernstein and Terence J. Byres, "From Peasant Studies to Agrarian Change," *Journal of Agrarian Change* 1, no. 1 (January 2001): 1–56. Another angle is Kenneth Pomeranz, *The Great Divergence: China, Europe, and the Making of the Modern World Economy* (Princeton: Princeton University Press, 2000); and Prasannan Parthasarathi, *Why Europe Grew Rich and Asia Did Not: Global Economic Divergence, 1600–1850* (Cambridge: Cambridge University Press, 2011). Both respond to arguments first raised in Andre Gunder Frank, *Capitalism and Underdevelopment in Latin America* (Harmondsworth: Penguin Books, 1969); and Walter Rodney, *How Europe Underdeveloped Africa* (London: Bogle-L'Ouverture Publications, 1972).

7. See Daniel Thorner, "Chayanov's Concept of Peasant Economy" in *A.V. Chayanov on the Theory of Peasant Economy*, ed. Daniel Thorner, Basile Kerblay, and R.E.F. Smith (Madison: University of Wisconsin Press, 1986), xi.

8. I read Lenin's and Kautsky's investigations of the peasant question without the automatic and narrow imposition of the future. That kind of an exercise might entail locating both texts within the larger body of work of each author and along the arch of their public and personal careers. Or it could mean attempting to decide, by recourse to empirical studies of the subsequent few decades, who answered the peasant question more correctly. As a result, however, the focus would become a question of Lenin and a question of Kautsky; of their orthodoxy, revisionism, prescience, ignorance, innovation, or any other partisan adjective. For my purposes, the texts of 1899 need not be implicated the fate of their authors or by what came after. It is important, in other words, to avoid having the characters of Lenin and Kautsky overwhelm the specificity of their historical projects and historiographical consequences.

9. A short collection of articles by Lenin was also published in 1901 as Vladimir Ilich Lenin, *The Agrarian Question and the "Critics of Marx"* (Moscow: Foreign Languages Publishing House, 1954).

10. "The 'agrarian question,'" writes Terence J. Byres in a summary of the debate at the turn of the century, "was, in essence, the 'peasant question.'" See Byres, "The Agrarian Question, Forms of Capitalist Agrarian Transition and the State: An Essay with Reference to Asia," *Social Scientist* 14, no. 11–12 (December 1986): 8.

11. On the different meanings of the agrarian/peasant question, see Henry Bernstein, "Agrarian Questions Then and Now," *Journal of Peasant Studies* 24, no. 1–2 (1996): 23–38.

12. On the politics of formulating specific differences (as prejudices) into questions, see Gyanendra Pandey, *A History of Prejudice: Race, Caste, and Difference in India and the United States* (Cambridge: Cambridge University Press, 2013), ch. 2.

13. Louis Althusser, "On the Young Marx," in *For Marx*, trans. Ben Brewster (London: Verso, 2005), 67 fn30, emphasis in original.

14. See David McLellan, *Karl Marx: His Life and Thought* (London: Macmillan, 1973); and Gareth Stedman Jones, *Karl Marx: Greatness and Illusion* (London: Allen Lane, 2018).

15. Althusser, "On the Young Marx," 62.

16. "It is not the material reflected on that characterizes and qualifies a reflection, but, at this level the *modality of the reflection,* the actual relation the reflection has with

its objects, that is, the *basic problematic* that is the starting-point for the reflection of the objects of the thought." See Althusser, "On the Young Marx," 68, emphasis in original.

17. Karl Marx, "On the Jewish Question," in *The Marx-Engels Reader*, 2nd ed., ed. Robert C. Tucker (New York: W.W. Norton & Company, 1978), 40.

18. W.E.B. Du Bois, *The Souls of Black Folk* (New York: Alfred A Knopf, 1976), 15, 7.

19. Karl Kautsky, *The Agrarian Question*, trans. Pete Burgess (London: Zwan Publications, 1988), 2.

20. Kautsky, *Agrarian Question*, 10.

21. Vladimir Ilich Lenin, *The Development of Capitalism in Russia*, 2nd ed. (Moscow: Progress Publishers, 1964), 313.

22. Kautsky, *Agrarian Question*, 20.

23. Lenin, *Development of Capitalism in Russia*, 382, 316.

24. Lenin, *Development of Capitalism in Russia*, 313.

25. Kautsky, *Agrarian Question*, 13.

26. Lenin, *Agrarian Question and the "Critics of Marx,"* 62.

27. Lenin, *Agrarian Question and the "Critics of Marx,"* 62.

28. Kautsky, *Agrarian Question*, 111.

29. Kautsky, *Agrarian Question*, 114. The notion of peasant self-exploitation is more fully elaborated by the Soviet agrarian economist A. V. Chayanov. See Teodor Shanin, "Chayanov's Message: Illuminations, Miscomprehensions, and the Contemporary 'Development Theory,'" in *A. V. Chayanov on the Theory of Peasant Economy*, ed. Thorner, Kerblay, and Smith.

30. Kautsky, *Agrarian Question*, 112–18.

31. Kautsky, *Agrarian Question*, 112.

32. It is of course evident that such definitive statements presuppose what are now disputable assumptions about progress, equality, and rationality; they also resemble colonialist discourses of backward native societies in need of discipline, upliftment, and tutelage. Yet not only is such a critique anachronistic, but it misses the importance of how these particular understandings of capitalism shaped the narrative of the global peasant. In other words, rather than dismiss Lenin and Kautsky as inaccurate, it is more important to consider the productivity of their arguments irrespective of veracity.

33. Lenin, *Development of Capitalism in Russia*, 382.

34. Kautsky, *Agrarian Question*, 17.

35. Lenin, *Development of Capitalism in Russia*, 173, emphasis in original.

36. Lenin, *Development of Capitalism in Russia*, 174.

37. Lenin, *Development of Capitalism in Russia*, 181.

38. Kautsky, *Agrarian Question*, 11.

39. See Kautsky, *Agrarian Question*, 59, 96, 145, 311.

40. Hamza Alavi and Teodor Shanin recognize this ambivalence in Kautsky's argument in their introduction, pointing out that "Kautsky's analysis nearly turns full circle. Having started with a presumption of a general tendency on the part of capitalist development to dissolve and eliminate the peasantry, he finds himself explaining the opposite, namely why such a tendency does not prevail; why the peasantry may even persist within the general framework of capitalism." See Alavi and Shanin,

"Introduction to the English Edition: Peasantry and Capitalism," in Kautsky, *Agrarian Question*, xiii
41. Kautsky, *Agrarian Question*, 324.
42. Kautsky, *Agrarian Question*, 330.
43. Kautsky, *Agrarian Question*, 330–31, emphasis added.
44. Lenin, *Development of Capitalism in Russia*, 220, 595–98.
45. "The agrarian question may be defined," according to Byres, "as the *continuing* existence in the countryside of poor countries of substantive obstacles to an unleashing of the forces capable of generating economic development." He goes on to state that this continuity "represents a *failure* of accumulation to proceed adequately in the countryside—that impinging powerfully upon the town; an intimately related *failure* of class formation in the countryside, appropriate to that accumulation; and a *failure* of the state to mediate successfully those transitions." See Terence J. Byres, "Political Economy, the Agrarian Question, and the Comparative Method," *Journal of Peasant Studies* 22, no. 4 (1995): 569 and *passim*, emphasis added. It is precisely this sense of continuity and failure that marks the stagism of the category peasant and the impossible burdens it entails for non-European histories.
46. The inaccuracy of Lenin's assessment, though not relevant here, is beyond dispute. "The major fact of Russian rural history in the first quarter of the century," according to Shanin, "is that the predicted development both of the class structure and of the political response of the peasants did not happen." See Teodor Shanin, *The Awkward Class: Political Sociology of Peasantry in a Developing Society, Russia 1910–1925* (Oxford: Clarendon Press, 1972), 2. On Lenin's empirical errors, see Esther Kingston-Mann, *Lenin and the Problem of Marxist Peasant Revolution* (New York: Oxford University Press, 1983), ch. 3.
47. Lenin, *Development of Capitalism in Russia*, 33, emphasis added. One might even add "Lenin" and several others to "Marx" in this passage to deepen the critique of using quotations from select European thinkers to conduct predictive arguments about the social and economic trajectory of the rest of the world.
48. From the mid-nineteenth century onward, a debate has ensued—interestingly sometimes termed the "Adam Smith Problem"—over the apparent contradiction between the differing conceptions of human nature in Smith's *The Theory of Moral Sentiments* (1759) and *The Wealth of Nations* (1776). See Russell Nieli, "Spheres of Intimacy and the Adam Smith Problem," *Journal of the History of Ideas* 47, no. 4 (October–December 1986): 611–24; and Dogan Göçmen , *The Adam Smith Problem: Human Nature and Society in "The Theory of Moral Sentiments" and "The Wealth of Nations"* (London: Tauris Academic Studies, 2007).
49. See Amartya Sen, "Capitalism Beyond the Crisis," *The New York Review of Books*, March 26, 2009; Murray Milgate and Shannon C. Stimson, *After Adam Smith: A Century of Transformation in Politics and Political Economy* (Princeton: Princeton University Press, 2009), 2; and Nieli, "Spheres of Intimacy," 611.
50. See Edwin Cannan's "Editor's Introduction" in Adam Smith, *An Inquiry into the Nature and Causes of the Wealth of Nations* (hereafter *The Wealth of Nations*), ed. Edwin Cannan (Chicago: University of Chicago Press, 1976).
51. See Emma Rothschild, "Adam Smith and Conservative Economics," *Economic History Review* 45, no. 1 (1992): 74–96; Amartya Sen and Emma Rothschild, "Adam

Smith's Economics," in *The Cambridge Companion to Adam Smith*, ed. Knud Haakonssen (Cambridge: Cambridge University Press, 2006), 319–65; and Amartya Sen, "Adam Smith and the Contemporary World," *Erasmus Journal of Philosophy and Economics* 3, no. 1 (2010): 50–67.

52. Although Smith did not use the term "political economy" in his title, Cannan explains that this was probably due to an attempt to differentiate his work from James Steuart's *An Inquiry into the Principles of Political Economy: being an Essay on the Science of Domestic Policy in Free Nations*, published nine years earlier in 1767.

53. Smith, *The Wealth of Nations*, 1:2.

54. The gesture of implicating economic theory with civilizational hierarchy, particularly through the colonial encounter between Europeans and indigenous societies in the Americas, is explored in Ronald L. Meek, *Social Science and the Ignoble Savage* (Cambridge: Cambridge University Press, 1976).

55. Smith, *The Wealth of Nations*, 1:2.

56. Smith, *The Wealth of Nations*, 1:2.

57. Smith, *The Wealth of Nations*, 1:16.

58. Smith, *The Wealth of Nations*, 1:15; For a depiction of these interrelations in the form of a chart, see Gavin Kennedy, *Adam Smith: A Moral Philosopher and His Political Economy* (New York: Palgrave Macmillan, 2008), 106.

59. Smith, *The Wealth of Nations*, 1:15.

60. Smith, *The Wealth of Nations*, 1:85, emphasis added.

61. Smith, *The Wealth of Nations*, 2:383; see also 2:450.

62. David McNally, *Political Economy and the Rise of Capitalism: A Reinterpretation* (Berkeley: University of California Press, 1988), 210. See Cannan's discussion of the phrase "the division of labour" in Smith, *The Wealth of Nations*, 1:7 fn1. Incidentally, Edwin Cannan was Ambedkar's doctoral supervisor at the London School of Economics in 1923.

63. Smith, *The Wealth of Nations*, 1:8–9.

64. Smith, *The Wealth of Nations*, 1:9.

65. Smith, *The Wealth of Nations*, 1:17.

66. Smith, *The Wealth of Nations*, 1:17.

67. Smith, *The Wealth of Nations*, 1:19–20.

68. Smith, *The Wealth of Nations*, 1:18; and cf. Nieli, "Spheres of Intimacy."

69. Smith, *The Wealth of Nations*, 1:19.

70. David Ricardo, in sustained conversation with Smith's ideas, articulated the use of (unmarked) labor in relation to rent and profit to measure true value. See David Ricardo, *Principles of Political Economy and Taxation* (London: J. M. Dent and Sons, 1911), chs. 1, 5 and 28.

71. Smith, *The Wealth of Nations*, 1:19.

72. Smith, *The Wealth of Nations*, 1:276.

73. Smith, *The Wealth of Nations*, 1:277–78.

74. Smith, *The Wealth of Nations*, 2:291.

75. Smith, *The Wealth of Nations*, 1:21.

76. Smith, *The Wealth of Nations*, 1:21.

77. Smith, *The Wealth of Nations*, 1:183.

78. Smith, *The Wealth of Nations*, 1:182–83.
79. Smith, *The Wealth of Nations*, 1:10–11.
80. Smith, *The Wealth of Nations*, 1:9.
81. On Smith and slavery, see Charles L. Griswold, *Adam Smith and the Virtues of Enlightenment* (Cambridge: Cambridge University Press, 1999); and Ronald L. Meek, *Smith, Marx, and After: Ten Essays in the Development of Economic Thought* (London: Chapman & Hall, 1977). On the debate over slavery and capitalism in the Americas, see Eric Williams, *Capitalism and Slavery* (Chapel Hill: University of North Carolina Press, 1944); David Brion Davis, *The Problem of Slavery in the Age of Revolution* (Ithaca: Cornell University Press, 1975); Eugene D. Genovese, *Roll, Jordan, Roll: The World the Slaves Made* (New York: Vintage Books, 1976); and, more recently, Walter Johnson, *River of Dark Dreams: Slavery and Empire in the Cotton Kingdom* (Cambridge: The Belknap Press, 2013); and Sven Beckert, *Empire of Cotton: A Global History* (New York: Vintage, 2014).
82. Smith, *The Wealth of Nations*, 1:90.
83. Smith's ignoring of the mediation between slavery and free labor is at least in part why Marx explicates at length both the necessity of doubly free labor and the conditions that produce it.
84. Smith, *The Wealth of Nations*, 3:411–12.
85. Smith, *The Wealth of Nations*, 1:90.
86. Smith, *The Wealth of Nations*, 1:12.
87. Smith, *The Wealth of Nations*, 1:12.
88. Smith, *The Wealth of Nations*, 2:294.
89. Smith, *The Wealth of Nations*, 2:295.
90. Both Engels and Lenin, however, deemed this text the fourth volume of *Capital*, instigating an ongoing debate on its placement and status within Marx's oeuvre. Originally edited and published in German by Kautsky in selections from 1905 to 1910, it first appeared in English in substantial length in 1952, and then re-arranged and reissued in full by the Institute of Marxism-Leninism in Moscow in 1963. On the history of this volume, including an incendiary critique of Kautsky, see S. Ryazanskaya's "Preface" in Karl Marx, *Theories of Surplus-Value*, vol. 1, ed. S. Ryazanskaya, trans. Emile Burns (Moscow: Progress Publishers, 1963), 13–20.
91. See John Eaton's review of the 1952 edition edited by G. A. Bonner and Emile Burns in *Science and Society* 18, no. 3 (Summer 1954): 274–75.
92. "If among a nation of hunters," writes Smith, "it usually costs twice the labour to kill a beaver which it does to kill a deer, one beaver should naturally exchange for or be worth two deer. It is natural that what is usually the produce of two days or two hours labour, should be worth double of what is usually the produce of one day's or one hour's labour." See Smith, *The Wealth of Nations*, 1:53; also cf. Marx, *Theories of Surplus-Value*, 78.
93. Marx, *Theories of Surplus-Value*, 80.
94. Marx, *Theories of Surplus-Value*, 80.
95. Marx, *Theories of Surplus-Value*, 84.
96. Marx, *Theories of Surplus-Value*, 87.
97. Marx, *Theories of Surplus-Value*, 88.
98. Marx, *Theories of Surplus-Value*, 88, emphasis added.
99. Marx, *Theories of Surplus-Value*, 103, emphasis added.

100. Smith, *The Wealth of Nations*, 2:351–52.

101. See Marx, *Theories of Surplus-Value*, 164–67. Questions such as these are part of what animate Paul Willis's seminal study of class reproduction among schoolchildren in England. See Willis, *Learning to Labor: How Working Class Kids Get Working Class Jobs* (New York: Columbia University Press, 1977).

102. Marx, *Theories of Surplus-Value*, 158, emphasis in original. As an especially immanent example these days, Marx adds that "a writer is a productive labourer not in so far as he produces ideas, but in so far as he enriches the publisher who publishes his works."

103. "If the commodity the worker sells the capitalist were an inanimate object, there could be no surplus value," points out Martin Nicolaus in his preface to the *Grundrisse*. "'[B]ut because it exists not as a thing, but as the capacity of a living being,' a surplus value can be extracted from 'it,' day after day, as long as the worker is alive and able-bodied." See Karl Marx, *Grundrisse: Foundations of the Critique of Political Economy*, trans. Martin Nicolaus (London: Penguin Books, 1973), 21.

104. Marx, *Theories of Surplus-Value*, 165.

105. Karl Marx, *Capital: Volume II: The Process of Circulation of Capital*, trans. David Fernbach (London: Penguin Books, 1978), 282 and ch. 10.

106. Marx, *Grundrisse*, 87, 258.

107. Karl Marx, *Capital: Volume I: A Critique of Political Economy*, trans. Ben Fowkes (London: Penguin Books, 1976), 125.

108. See Sartori, "Global Intellectual History," 112.

109. Marx, *Capital: Volume I*, 293.

110. Marx, *Grundrisse*, 460, emphasis in original.

111. See Marx, *Capital: Volume I*, 363 fn54, 869–70 fn41.

112. For an attempt to piece together Marx's scattered writings on agrarian societies, see Teodor Shanin, ed., *Late Marx and the Russian Road: Marx and the 'Peripheries of Capitalism'* (New York: Monthly Review Press, 1983); and cf. Eric Hobsbawm, "Introduction," in Karl Marx, *Pre-Capitalist Economic Formations*, ed. Eric Hobsbawm (New York: International Publishers, 1965). See also Kevin Anderson, *Marx at the Margins: On Nationalism, Ethnicity, and Non-Western Societies* (Chicago: University of Chicago Press, 2010).

113. A classic statement is Clifford Geertz, "Studies in Peasant Life: Community and Society," *Biennial Review of Anthropology* 2 (1961): 1–41. Cf. Alex Weingrod and Emma Morin, "Post Peasants: The Character of Contemporary Sardinian Society," *Comparative Studies in Society and History* 13, no. 3 (July 1971): 301–324; and Mariko Tamanoi, "Reconsidering the Concept of Post-Peasantry: The Transformation of the Masoveria System in Old Catalonia," *Ethnology* 22, no. 4 (October 1983): 295–305.

114. Karuna Mantena, *Alibis of Empire: Henry Maine and the Ends of Liberal Imperialism* (Princeton: Princeton University Press, 2010), 57.

115. Malcolm L. Darling, *The Punjab Peasant in Prosperity and Debt* (London: Humphrey Milford, 1928), xii–xiii. It is often overlooked that in the very next sentence, Darling adds that this same peasant is "[i]gnorant, no doubt, and unimaginative, and with a mind that is often empty as the horizon that surrounds him."

116. Christopher L. Hill, "Conceptual Universalization in the Transnational Nineteenth Century," in *Global Intellectual History*, ed. Moyn and Sartori, 145.

117. "Fundamentally," writes Andrew Sartori about the distinct emergence of the critique of capitalism in modern Europe as opposed to the twelfth- or fourteenth-century Islamic world, "this indifference to the problematics of political economy stemmed from the fact that the object for which political economy was developed—capitalist social relations—simply did not exist as a problematic calling for systematic conceptualization." See Sartori, "Global Intellectual History," 120.

Conclusion

Epigraphs: Adam Smith, *An Inquiry into the Nature and Causes of the Wealth of Nations*, ed. Edwin Cannan (Chicago: University of Chicago Press, 1976), 403; Karl Marx, *Capital: Volume I: A Critique of Political Economy*, trans. Ben Fowkes (London: Penguin Books, 1976), 133.

1. Gyanendra Pandey, "In Defense of the Fragment: Writing about Hindu-Muslim Riots in India Today," *Representations* no. 37 (Winter 1992): 28.
2. Pandey, "In Defense of the Fragment," 41.
3. Ranajit Guha, *Elementary Aspects of Peasant Insurgency in Colonial India* (Durham: Duke University Press, 1999), 6.
4. Robert Redfield, *The Primitive World and Its Transformation* (Ithaca: Cornell University Press, 1953), 31.
5. See Dipesh Chakrabarty, "A Small History of Subaltern Studies," *Habitations of Modernity: Essays in the Wake of Subaltern Studies* (Chicago: University of Chicago Press, 2002), 13; and cf. Vinay Gidwani, *Capital, Interrupted: Agrarian Development and the Politics of Work in India* (Minneapolis: University of Minnesota Press, 2008); Ritu Birla, *Stages of Capital: Law, Culture, and Market Governance in Late Colonial India* (Durham: Duke University Press, 2009); and Kalyan Sanyal, *Rethinking Capitalist Development: Primitive Accumulation, Governmentality, and Post-colonial Capitalism* (London: Routledge, 2007).
6. Earlier, Teodor Shanin stated, "Peasants have existed for millennia as the massive majority of mankind and were still its majority when their recognition so forcefully struck social scientists." See Shanin, ed., *Peasants and Peasant Societies*, 2nd ed. (Oxford: Basil Blackwell, 1987), 1. More recently, James C. Scott mentions his disillusionment with revolutions both in France and Russia as well as Vietnam, China, and Cambodia in terms of what they "meant for the largest class in world history: the peasantry." See Scott, *Decoding Subaltern Politics: Ideology, Disguise, and Resistance in Agrarian Politics* (London: Routledge, 2013), 2 and *passim*.
7. See "State/UT-wise Cases Registered In Police Stations and Cr.PC (156 3) under Crimes against SCs During 2021," *Crimes in India 2021*, National Crimes Record Bureau, Ministry of Home Affairs, Government of India, <https://ncrb.gov.in/en/Crime-in-India-2021>, accessed March 23, 2023.
8. See Sukhpal Singh, "Punjab Agriculture: Pinning Hopes on Private Sector for Revival," *Economic and Political Weekly* 56, no. 2 (January 9, 2021): 10–12; Devinder Sharma, "A Battle Only Half Won," *The Tribune*, November 22, 2021; and Navyug Gill, "Gramsci at the Delhi Border: Indian Farmers and the Revolution against Inevitability," *Antipode Online*, June 14, 2021.

BIBLIOGRAPHY

Board of Economic Inquiry
Singh, Sardar Kartar. *Family Budgets, 1932–33, of Four Tenant-Cultivators in the Lyallpur District*. Board of Economic Inquiry Publication No. 40. Lahore: The Civil and Military Gazette Press, 1934.
Singh, Kartar, and Ajaib Singh. *Family Budgets, 1933–34, of Six Tenant-Cultivators in the Lyallpur District*. Board of Economic Inquiry Publication No. 44. Lahore: The Civil and Military Gazette Press, 1935.
Singh, Labh, and Ajaib Singh. *Family Budgets, 1935–36, of Six Tenant-Cultivators in the Lyallpur District*. Board of Economic Inquiry Publication No. 59. Lahore: The Civil and Military Gazette Press, 1938.
Singh, Labh, and Ajaib Singh. *Family Budgets, 1936–37, of Eleven Cultivators in the Punjab*. Board of Economic Inquiry Publication No. 62. Lahore: The Civil and Military Gazette Press, 1939.
Singh, Labh, and Ajaib Singh. *Family Budgets, 1937–38, of Ten Cultivators in the Punjab*. Board of Economic Inquiry Publication No. 67. Lahore: The Civil and Military Gazette Press, 1939.
Singh, Labh, Ajaib Singh, and Faiz Ilahi. *Family Budgets, 1938–39, of Twenty-Six Cultivators in the Punjab*. Board of Economic Inquiry Publication No. 72. Lahore: The Civil and Military Gazette Press, 1941.

Census Reports
Census of India 2011, Release of Primary Census Abstract Data Highlights, Dr. C. Chandramouli, April 30, 2013.
Christian, G. J. *Report on the Census of the North West Provinces of the Bengal Presidency, taken on the 1st of January, 1853*. Calcutta: Baptist Mission Press, 1854.
Ibbetson, Denzil. *Report on the Census of the Panjab, taken on the 17th of February 1881*. Volume 1. Calcutta: Superintendent of Government Printing, 1883.
Ibbetson, Denzil. *Report on the Census of the Panjab, taken in the 17th of February 1881*. Volume 2. Lahore: Superintendent of the Central Gaol Press, 1883.
Khan, Khan Ahmad Hasan. *Census of India, 1931: Volume XVII, Punjab*. Part 1—Report. Lahore: The Civil and Military Gazette Press, 1933.
Middleton, L., and S. M. Jacob. *Census of India, 1921: Punjab and Delhi*. Volume 15, Part II. Lahore: The Civil and Military Gazette Press, 1922.
Miller, J.A.E. *Report on the Census of the Punjab, taken on 10th January 1868*. Lahore: Indian Public Opinion Press, 1870.

Shakespear, A. *Memoir on the Statistics of the North Western Provinces of the Bengal Presidency*. Calcutta: Baptist Mission Press, 1848.

Temple, Richard. *Report on the Census, taken on the 1st of January 1855, of the Population of the Punjab Territories*. In *Selections from the Records of the Government of India*. Calcutta: Calcutta Gazette Office, 1856.

Waterfield, Henry. *Memorandum of the Census of British India of 1871–72*. London: George Edward Eyre and William Spottiswoode, 1875.

Government Reports

Annual Report on the Working of the Punjab Alienation of Land Act XIII of 1900, For the year ending 30th September 1901. Lahore: The Civil and Military Gazette, 1902.

Annual Report of the Working of the Punjab Alienation of Land Act, XIII of 1900, for the year ending 30th September 1903. Lahore: The Civil and Military Gazette Press, 1904.

Annual Report of the Working of the Punjab Alienation of Land Act, XIII of 1900, For the year ending 30th September 1904. Lahore: The Civil and Military Gazette Press, 1905.

Annual Report of the Working of the Punjab Alienation of Land Act, XIII of 1900, For the year ending 30th September 1905. Lahore: The Civil and Military Gazette Press, 1906.

Annual Report of the Working of the Punjab Alienation of Land Act, XIII of 1900, For the year ending 30th September 1906. Lahore: The Civil and Military Gazette Press, 1907.

Annual Report on the Punjab Alienation of Land Act XIII of 1900, as amended by Punjab Act I of 1907, For the year ending the 30th September 1907. Lahore: The Civil and Military Gazette Press, 1908.

Annual Report on the Punjab Alienation of Land Act, XIII of 1900, as amended by the Punjab Act I of 1907, For the year ending the 30th September 1908. Lahore: The Civil and Military Gazette, 1909.

Crimes in India 2021. National Crimes Record Bureau, Ministry of Home Affairs, Government of India.

General report upon the administration of the Punjab proper for the years 1849–50 and 1850–51, being the two first years after annexation; with a supplementary notice of the cis and trans-Sutlej territories. London: J & H Cox, 1854.

General report on the administration of the Punjab territories, comprising the Punjab proper and the cis and trans-Sutlej States, 1851–52 to 1852–53. Calcutta: Calcutta Gazette Office, 1854.

General report on the administration of the Punjab territories, from 1854–55 to 1855–56 inclusive. Lahore: Punjabee Press, 1858.

General report on the administration of the Punjab territories, from 1856–57 to 1857–58 inclusive, together with a brief account of the administration of the Delhi territory, from the re-occupation of Delhi up to May 1858. Lahore: The Chronicle Press, 1858.

General report on the Punjab and its dependencies, for 1858–59. Lahore: Hope Press, 1859.

Historical Publications

Baden-Powell, Baden Henry. *The Land-Systems of British India*. Volume 2. Oxford: Clarendon Press, 1892.

Baden-Powell, Baden Henry. "The Permanent Settlement of Bengal." *English Historical Review* 10, no. 38 (April 1895): 276–292.

Bibliography   319

Baden-Powell, Baden Henry. *A Short Account of the Land Revenue and its Administration in British India; with a Sketch of the Land Tenures.* Oxford: Clarendon Press, 1907.

Briggs, John. *What Are We to Do with the Punjab?* London: James Madden, 1849.

Browne, James. *India Tracts: Containing a Description of the Jungle Terry Districts, their Revenues, Trade, and Government: With a Plan for the Improvement of Them. Also an History of the Origin and Progress of the Sicks.* London: Logographic Press, 1788.

Burns, Alexander. *Travels into Bokhara: Being the account of a journey from India to Cabool, Tartary, and Persia.* London: John Murray, 1834.

Campbell, George. *Memoirs of My Indian Career.* Volume 1. Edited by Charles E. Bernard. London: Macmillan and Co., 1893.

Darling, Malcolm Lyall. *The Punjab Peasant in Prosperity and Debt.* London: Humphrey Milford, 1928.

Douie, James. *The Panjab, North-West Frontier Province and Kashmir.* Cambridge: Cambridge University Press, 1916.

Elliot, Henry. *Supplement to the Glossary of Indian Terms, A–J.* Agra: Orphan Press, 1845.

Fallon, S. W. *A Dictionary of Hindustani Proverbs, including many Marwari, Panjabi, Maggah, Bhojpuri and Tirhuti Proverbs, Sayings, Emblems, Aphorisms, Maxims and Similes.* Edited by Richard Temple. Banaras: Medical Hall Press, 1886.

Forster, George. *A Journey from Bengal to England, through the northern part of India, Kashmire, Afghanistan, and Persia, and into Russia, by the Caspian-Sea.* 2 Volumes. London: Faulder, 1798.

Gilchrist, John Borthwick. *A Collection of Dialogues, English and Hindoostanee.* Calcutta: The Hindoostanee Press, 1804.

Gore, Montague. *Remarks on the Present State of the Punjaub.* London: James Ridgway, 1849.

Grierson, George A. *Bihar Peasant Life: Being a discursive catalogue of the surroundings of the people of the province.* Calcutta: The Bengal Secretariat Press, 1885.

Hopkins, David. *The Dangers of British India, from French Invasion and Missionary Establishments.* London: Black, Parry, and Kingsbury, 1809.

Hunter, William Wilson. *The Indian Musalmans: Are They Bound in Conscience to Rebel Against the Queen?* London: Trubner and Co., 1871.

Lawrence, Henry. *Adventures of an Officer in the Punjaub.* 2 Volumes. London: Henry Colburn, 1846.

Maconachie, Robert, ed. *Selected Agricultural Proverbs of the Panjab.* Delhi: Imperial Medical Hall Press, 1890.

Malcolm, John. *Sketch of the Sikhs; A singular nation, who inhabit the province of the Penjab, situated between the rivers Jumna and Indus.* London: John Murray, 1812.

Newton, J., and L. Janvier. *A Dictionary of the Panjabi Language, Prepared by a Committee of the Lodiana Mission.* Ludhiana: The Mission Press, 1854.

O'Brian, E., ed. *Glossary of the Multani Language compared with Punjabi and Sindhi.* Lahore: Punjab Government Civil Secretariat Press, 1881.

Osborne, W. G. *Court and Camp of Runjeet Sing.* London: Henry Colburn, 1840.

Prinsep, Henry James. *History of the Punjab, and of the rise, progress and present condition of the sect and nation of the Sikhs.* Volume 2. London: W. H. Allen & Co., 1846.

Prinsep, Henry T. *Origin of the Sikh Power in the Punjab, and Political Life of Muha-Raja Runjeet Singh.* Calcutta: Military Orphan Press, 1834.

Smith, R. Baird. *Agricultural Resources of the Punjab.* London: Smith, Elder and Co., 1849.

"Spendthrifts Ruin India." *The New York Times.* October 7, 1900.

Sri Guru Granth Sahib Ji, <www.srigranth.org> accessed on April 15, 2022.

Starkey, Samuel Cross. *A Dictionary, English and Punjabee, Outlines of Grammar, also Dialogues, English and Punjabee, with Grammar and Explanatory Notes.* Calcutta: D'Rozario and Co., 1849.

Steinbach, Henry. *The Punjaub: Being a brief account of the country of the Sikhs.* London: Smith, Elder & Co., 1845.

Thorburn, Septimus. *Asiatic Neighbours.* Edinburgh: William Blackwood and Sons, 1895.

Thorburn, Septimus. *Bannu; or, our Afghan Frontier.* London: Trubner & Co., 1876.

Thorburn, Septimus. *Musalmans and Money-Lenders in the Punjab.* London: William Blackwood & Sons, 1886.

Thorburn, Septimus. *The Punjab in Peace and War.* Edinburgh: William Blackwood and Sons, 1904.

Vigne, G. T. *A personal narrative of a visit to Ghuzni, Kabul, and Afghanistan, and of a residence at the court of Dost Mohamed; with notices of Runjit Sing, Khiva, and the Russian expedition.* London: Whittaker & Co., 1840.

West, Raymond. *The Land and the Law in India.* Bombay: Education Society Press, 1873.

Young, Arthur. *The Farmer's Tour through the East of England.* 4 Volumes. London: W. Strahan, 1771.

Yule, Henry, and Arthur C. Burnell. *Hobson-Jobson: A glossary of Anglo-Indian colloquial words and phrases, and of kindred terms, etymological, historical, geographical and discursive.* London: John Murray, 1886.

National Archives of India

"Agricultural Indebtedness in the Punjab." Keep With Papers (Not for Records), Revenue and Agriculture Department, proceedings no. 1–8, May 1891, National Archives of India, New Delhi, India.

"Indebtedness of the Muhammadan population of the Dera Ismail Khan district," by S. S. Thorburn, Home Department (Judicial), B proceedings, October 1885, no. 252–54.

Letter from H. C. Fanshawe, Offig. Junior Secretary to Government, Punjab and its Dependencies, to J. A. Grant, Esquire, Offig. Junior Secretary to Financial Commissioner, Punjab, no. 507, dated Simla, 23 May 1885, Home Department (Judicial), B proceedings, October 1885, no. 252–54.

Letter from J. A. Grant, Esquire, Offig. Junior Secretary to Financial Commissioner, Punjab, to the Offig. Secretary to Government, Punjab, no. 1189, dated Lahore, 24 October 1884, Home Department (Judicial), B proceedings, October 1885, no. 252–54.

Letter to Lord George F. Hamilton, Her Majesty's Secretary of State for India, from C. M. Rivaz et. al., Simla, 27 July 1899, Department of Revenue and Agriculture, no. 50 of 1899, in "Proposals for undertaking legislation with the object of checking

the transfer of land from the agricultural classes in the Punjab," Legislative Department, proceeding no. 36, September 1899.
Report by H. A. Casson, "Riot Isakhel Bannu Dashera," dated December 28, 1893, Revenue and Agriculture Department (Land Revenue), file 215, no. 18 (B), May 1895
Statement of Objects and Reasons, Appendix A19, in "The Punjab Alienation of Land Act, 1900 (XIII of 1900)," Legislative Department, proceeding no. 11-68, October 1900.

Official Publications

Aitchison, C. U., ed. *A collection of treaties, engagements, and sanads relating to India and neighbouring countries.* Volume IX. Calcutta: Office of the Superintendent of Government Printing, 1892.
Barkley, D. G. *Directions for Revenue Officers in the Punjab.* Lahore: Central Jail Press, 1875.
Crooke, William. *A Rural and Agricultural Glossary of the North-Western Provinces and Oudh.* Allahabad: Superintendent of Government Printing, 1888.
Cust, Robert Needham. *Manual for the Guidance of Revenue Officers in the Punjab.* Lahore: Koh-i-Noor Press, 1866.
Douie, James. *Panjab Settlement Manual.* Lahore: Civil and Military Gazette Press, 1899.
Gazetteer of the Bannu District. Calcutta: Central Press Company, 1883.
Gazetteer of the Ferozepure District, 1883-4. Lahore: The Civil and Military Gazette Press, 1884.
Griffin, Lepel H. *The Panjab Chiefs: Historical and biographical notices of the principal families in the territories under the Panjab Government.* Lahore: Chronicle Press, 1865.
Hunter, William Wilson, ed. *The Imperial Gazetteer of India.* Volume XI. London: Trubner & Co., 1886.
Lal, Shadi, ed. *The Punjab Alienation of Land Act XIII of 1900 with Comments and Notes of Cases.* 2nd ed. Lahore: Addison Press, 1907.
Papers relating to the Punjab, 1847-49, London: Harrison and Son, 1849.
Punjab Land Administration Acts and Rules Having the Force of Law Thereunder. Volume 1. Lahore: Superintendent of Government Printing, 1933.
Punjab Report in Reply to the Inquiries Issued by the Famine Commission. Volume 2. Lahore: Central Jail Press, 1878-9.
Singh, Gurcharn, ed. *The Punjab Alienation of Land Act (XIII of 1900), with Notes, Notifications, Rules and Circulars.* Lahore: Albion Press, 1901.
Temple, Richard C., ed. *Punjab Notes and Queries, a monthly periodical, devoted to the systematic collection of authentic notes and scraps of information regarding the country and the people.* Allahabad: Pioneer Press, 1886.
Thomason, James. *Remarks on the system of land revenue administration prevalent in the North Western Provinces of Hindoostan.* Calcutta: Baptist Mission Press, 1850.
Tupper, C. L. *Punjab Customary Law.* Volumes 1-3. Calcutta: Office of the Superintendent of Government Printing, 1881.
Wilson, H. H. *A Glossary of the Judicial and Revenue Terms, and of Useful Words Occurring in Official Documents Relating to the Administration of the Government of British India.* London: William H. Allen and Co., 1855.

Punjab State Archives

"Decision that all Ahairs in the Delhi Division are eligible to participate in the Military allotment of land on the Jhelum Canal." November 1903, Punjab Government Civil Secretariat, Revenue and Agriculture Department, proceedings A, no. 7–9, file 3, 1, serial R/2104, Punjab State Archives, Chandigarh, India.

Handbook of Alienation of Land Acts and Circular Orders. Lahore: no publisher, no date. Serial 533.

"Inclusion of Arains in the Muzaffargarh district in the list of agricultural tribes." November 1907, Punjab Government Civil Secretariat, Revenue and Agriculture Department, proceedings A, file 49, 1, serial R/838.

"Inclusion of the Awans in the list of agricultural tribes of the Muzaffargarh District." June 1914, Punjab Government Civil Secretariat, Revenue and Agriculture Department, proceedings A, file 27, 1, serial R/882.

"Inclusion of the Gujrat Bahrupias in the list of Agricultural Tribes notified under the Punjab Alienation of Land Act." January 1913, Punjab Government Civil Secretariat, Revenue and Agriculture Department, proceedings A, no. 1–3, file 1, 1, serial R/817.

"Notification of the Kakezais of the Jhelum district as an agricultural tribe." April 1910, Punjab Government Civil Secretariat, Revenue and Agriculture Department, proceedings A, file 16, 1–2, serial R/811.

"Inclusion of the Koreshis of the Gujranwala district and the Khaggas, Bodlas and Koreshis of the Montgomery district in the list of agricultural tribes." July 1908, Punjab Government Civil Secretariat, Revenue and Agriculture Department, proceedings A, file 31, 1–4, serial R/2445.

"Inclusion of Mazhbi Sikhs of the Gujranwala and Lyallpur districts in the list of agricultural tribes." October 1911, Punjab Government Civil Secretariat, Revenue and Agriculture Department, proceedings A, no. 17–25, file 34, 2, serial R/811.

"Memorial from Sardar Dost Muhammad Khan, Rais of Bathar, Hazara District." July 1901, Punjab Government Civil Secretariat, Revenue and Agriculture Department, proceedings A, no. 1–2, file 7, 1, serial R/848.

Settlement Reports

Barnes, G. C., et al. *Report on the revised settlement of the Oonah, Hushiarpur, Gurshunkur, and Hurriana purgunahs of the Hushiarpur district in the Trans-Sutlej states.* Lahore: Punjabee Press, 1860.

Brandreth, E. L. *Report on the revised settlement of the district of Ferozpoor in the Cis-Satlej states.* Lahore: Chronicle Press, 1859.

Davidson, H. *Report on the revised settlement of the district of Ludhiana in the Cis-Sutlej states.* Lahore: Punjabee Press, 1859.

Davies, R. H., and W. Blyth. *Report on the revised settlement of the Umritsur, Sowrian, and Turun Tarun pergunnahs of the Umritsur district in the Umritsur division.* Lahore: Hope Press, 1860.

Purser, W. E. *Final Report on the Revised Settlement of the Jullundur District in the Punjab.* Lahore: The Civil and Military Gazette Press, 1892.

Purser, W. E., and H. C. Fanshawe. *Report on the Revised Land Revenue Settlement of the Rohtak District of the Hissar Division in the Punjab, 1873–1879.* Lahore: W. Ball, 1880.
Roe, C. A. *Report on the Revised Settlement of the Multan District of the Punjab, 1873–1880.* Lahore: W. Ball, 1883.
Saunders, Leslie S. *Report on the revised land revenue settlement of the Lahore district in the Lahore division of the Panjab, 1865–69.* Lahore: Central Jail Press, 1873.
Steedman, E. B. *Report on the Revised Settlement of the Jhang District of the Punjab, 1874–1880.* Lahore: W. Ball, 1882.
Temple, Richard. *Report on the settlement, under regn. IX, of 1833, of the district of Jullundhur, Trans-Sutlej states.* Lahore: Chronicle Press, 1852.
Walker, T. Gordon. *Final Report of the Revision of Settlement (1878–83) of the Ludhiana District in the Panjab.* Calcutta: Central Press, 1884.

Village Surveys

Bhalla, Ram Lall. *Report on Economic Survey of Bairampur in the Hoshiarpur District.* Lahore: Superintendent of Government Printing, 1922.
Dawar, Lajpat Rai. *An Economic Survey of Suner, a Village in the Ferozepore District of the Punjab.* Punjab Village Surveys No. 9. Lahore: The Civil and Military Gazette Press, 1936.
Narain, Raj. *An Economic Survey of Gijhi, a Village in the Rohtak District of the Punjab.* Punjab Village Surveys No. 2. Lahore: The Civil and Military Gazette Press, 1932.
Seth, R. K., and Faiz Ilahi. *An Economic Survey of Durrana Langana, a Village in the Multan District of the Punjab.* Punjab Village Surveys No. 11. Lahore: The Civil and Military Gazette Press, 1938.
Singh, Randhir. *An Economic Survey of Kala Gaddi Thamman (Chak 73 G.B), a Village in the Lyallpur District of the Punjab.* Punjab Village Surveys No. 4. Lahore: The Civil and Military Gazette Press, 1932.
Singh, Sardar Gian. *An Economic Survey of Gaggar Bhana, a Village in the Amritsar District of the Punjab.* Punjab Village Surveys No. 1. Lahore: The Civil and Military Gazette Press, 1928.

Secondary Sources

Adcock, Cassie. *The Limits of Tolerance: Indian Secularism and the Politics of Religious Freedom.* New York: Oxford University Press, 2013.
Agarwal, Bina. *A Field of One's Own: Gender and Land Rights in South Asia.* Cambridge: Cambridge University Press, 1994.
Ahmed, Faiz. *Afghanistan Rising: Islamic Law and Statecraft between the Ottoman and British Empires.* Cambridge: Harvard University Press, 2017.
Akhtar, Aasim Sajjad. "The State as Landlord in Pakistani Punjab: Peasant Struggles on the Okara Military Farms." *Journal of Peasant Studies* 33, no. 3 (2006): 479–501.
Alam, Muzaffar. *The Crisis of Empire in Mughal North India: Awadh and the Punjab, 1707–48.* New Delhi: Oxford University Press, 1986.
Alam, Muzaffar. "Sikh Uprisings under Banda Bahadur 1708–1715." *Proceedings of the Indian History Congress*, vol. 39 (1978): 509–522.

Alavi, Hamza. "India and the Colonial Mode of Production." *Economic and Political Weekly* 10, no. 33 (August 1975): 1235–1262.

Alavi, Hamza, and Teodor Shanin. "Introduction to the English Edition: Peasantry and Capitalism." In Karl Kautsky, *The Agrarian Question*. Translated by Pete Burgess. London: Zwan Publications, 1988.

Alavi, Seema. *The Sepoys and the Company: Tradition and Transition in Northern India, 1770–1830*. New Delhi: Oxford University Press, 1998.

Ali, Imran. "Malign Growth? Agricultural Colonization and the Roots of Backwardness in the Punjab." *Past and Present* no. 114 (February 1987): 110–132.

Ali, Imran. *The Punjab under Imperialism, 1885–1947*. Princeton: Princeton University Press, 1988.

Ali, Tariq. *The Clash of Fundamentalisms: Crusades, Jihads, and Modernity*. London: Verso, 2002.

Allen, Robert C. *Enclosure and the Yeoman: The Agricultural Development of the South Midlands, 1450–1850*. Oxford: Clarendon Press, 1992.

Aloysius, G. *Nationalism Without a Nation in India*. New Delhi: Oxford University Press, 1997.

Althusser, Louis. "On the Young Marx." In *For Marx*. Translated by Ben Brewster. London: Verso, 2005.

Althusser, Louis, and Étienne Balibar. *Reading Capital*. Translated by Ben Brewster. London: Verso, 2009.

Ambedkar, Bhimrao Ramji. "Annihilation of Caste." In *Dr. Babasaheb Ambedkar: Writings and Speeches*. Volume 1. Edited by Vasant Moon. Bombay: Education Department of the Government of Maharashtra, 1979.

Ambedkar, Bhimrao Ramji. *Annihilation of Caste: The Annotated Critical Edition*. New Delhi: Navayana Publishers, 2014.

Amin, Shahid. "Introduction." In William Crooke, *A Glossary of North Indian Peasant Life*. Edited by Shahid Amin. New Delhi: Oxford University Press, 1989.

Amin, Shahid. *Sugarcane and Sugar in Gorakhpur: An Inquiry into Peasant Production for Capitalist Enterprise in Colonial India*. New Delhi: Oxford University Press, 1984.

Anderson, Kevin. *Marx at the Margins: On Nationalism, Ethnicity, and Non-Western Societies*. Chicago: University of Chicago Press, 2010.

Appadurai, Arjun. "Is Homo Hierarchicus?" *American Ethnologist* 13, no. 4 (November 1986): 745–761.

Appadurai, Arjun. "Number in the Colonial Imagination." In *Orientalism and the Postcolonial Predicament: Perspectives on South Asia*. Edited by Carol A. Breckenridge and Peter van der Veer. Philadelphia: University of Pennsylvania Press, 1993.

Arondekar, Anjali. *For the Record: On Sexuality and the Colonial Archive in India*. Durham: Duke University Press, 2009.

Atwal, Priya. *Royals and Rebels: The Rise and Fall of the Sikh Empire*. London: Hurst, 2020.

Bagchi, Amiya Kumar. "Colonialism and the Nature of 'Capitalist' Enterprise in India." *Economic and Political Weekly* 23, no. 31 (July 30, 1988): 38–50.

Bakhtin, Mikhail. *Rabelais and His World*. Translated by Helene Iswolsky. Bloomington: Indiana University Press, 1984.

Banaji, Jairus. "For a Theory of Colonial Modes of Production." *Economic and Political Weekly* 7, no. 52 (December 23, 1972): 2498–2502.
Banaji, Jairus. *Theory as History: Essays on Modes of Production and Exploitation*. Leiden: Brill, 2010.
Banerjee, Sumanta. *In the Wake of Naxalbari: A History of the Naxalite Movement in India*. Calcutta: Subarnarekha, 1980.
Banga, Indu. *Agrarian System of the Sikhs: Late Eighteenth and Early Nineteenth Century*. New Delhi: Manohar Publishers, 1978.
Banga, Indu, and J. S. Grewal. *Maharaja Ranjit Singh: The State and Society*. Amritsar: Guru Nanak Dev University Press, 2001.
Barrier, N. Gerald, ed. *The Census in British India: New Perspectives*. Delhi: Manohar Publishers, 1981.
Barrier, N. Gerald. "The Punjab Disturbances of 1907: The Response of the British Government in India to Agrarian Unrest." *Modern Asian Studies* 1, no. 4 (1967): 353–383.
Barrier, Norman G. *The Punjab Alienation of Land Bill of 1900*. Durham: Duke University Press, 1966.
Bayly, C. A. *Empire and Information: Intelligence Gathering and Social Information in India, 1780–1870*. Cambridge: Cambridge University Press, 1996.
Bayly, C. A. *Indian Society and the Making of the British Empire*. Cambridge: Cambridge University Press, 1988.
Bayly, C. A. "The Pre-History of 'Communal'? Religious Conflict in India, 1700–1860." *Modern Asian Studies* 19, no. 2 (1985): 177–203.
Bayly, Susan. *Caste, Society, and Politics in India from the Eighteenth Century to the Modern Age*. New York: Cambridge University Press, 1999.
Beckert, Sven. *Empire of Cotton: A Global History*. New York: Vintage, 2014.
Beckert, Sven, and Seth Rockman, eds. *Slavery's Capitalism: A New History of American Economic Development*. Philadelphia: University of Pennsylvania Press, 2016.
Bernstein, Henry. "Agrarian Questions Then and Now." *Journal of Peasant Studies* 24, no. 1–2 (1996): 22–59.
Bernstein, Henry, and Terence J. Byres. "From Peasant Studies to Agrarian Change." *Journal of Agrarian Change* 1, no. 1 (January 2001): 1–56.
Bhandar, Brenna. *Colonial Lives of Property: Law, Land, and Racial Regimes of Ownership*. Durham: Duke University Press, 2018.
Bharti, Vishav. "Indebtedness and Suicide: Field Notes on Agricultural Labourers of Punjab." *Economic and Political Weekly* 46, no. 14 (April 2-8, 2011): 35–40.
Bhattacharya, Neeladri. "Agricultural Labour and Production: Central and South-East Punjab, 1870–1940." In *The World of the Rural Labourer in Colonial India*. Edited by Gyan Prakash. New Delhi: Oxford University Press, 1992.
Bhattacharya, Neeladri. *The Great Agrarian Conquest: The Colonial Reshaping of a Rural World*. Ranikhet: Permanent Black, 2018.
Bhattacharya, Neeladri. "The Logic of Tenancy Cultivation: Central and South-East Punjab, 1870–1935." *Indian Economic and Social History Review* 20, no. 2 (1983): 121–170.
Birla, Ritu. *Stages of Capital: Law, Culture, and Market Governance in Late Colonial India*. Durham: Duke University Press, 2009.

Bose, Sugata. *Agrarian Bengal: Economy, Social Structure, and Politics, 1919–1947.* Cambridge: Cambridge University Press, 1986.
Bose, Sugata. *Peasant Labour and Colonial Capital: Rural Bengal since 1770.* Cambridge: Cambridge University Press, 1993.
Brard, Gurnam S. S. *East of Indus: My Memories of Old Punjab.* New Delhi: Hemkunt Publishers, 2007.
Brass, Paul R. *Language, Religion, and Politics in North India.* Cambridge: Cambridge University Press, 1974.
Breman, Jan. *Patronage and Exploitation: Changing Agrarian Relations in South Gujarat, India.* Berkeley: University of California Press, 1974.
Brenner, Robert. "The Origins of Capitalist Development: A Critique of Neo-Smithian Marxism." *New Left Review* 1, no. 104 (August 1977): 25–92.
Byres, Terence J. "The Agrarian Question, Forms of Capitalist Agrarian Transition, and the State: An Essay with Reference to Asia." *Social Scientist* 14, no. 11–12 (November–December 1986): 3–67.
Byres, Terence J. "Political Economy, the Agrarian Question, and the Comparative Method." *Journal of Peasant Studies* 22, no. 4 (1995): 561–580.
Cannan, Edwin. "Editor's Introduction." In Adam Smith, *An Inquiry into the Nature and Causes of the Wealth of Nations.* Edited by Edwin Cannan. Chicago: University of Chicago Press, 1976.
Catanach, I. J. *Rural Credit in Western India 1875–1930: Rural Credit and the Cooperative Movement in the Bombay Presidency.* Berkeley: University of California Press, 1970.
Caton, Brian P. "Social Categories and Colonisation in Panjab, 1849–1920." *Indian Economic and Social History Review* 41, no. 1 (February 2004): 33–50.
Charlesworth, Neil. "The Myth of the Deccan Riots of 1875." *Modern Asian Studies* 6, no. 4 (1972): 401–421.
Charlesworth, Neil. *Peasants and Imperial Rule: Agriculture and Agrarian Society in the Bombay Presidency, 1850–1935.* Cambridge: Cambridge University Press, 1985.
Chakrabarty, Dipesh. "Conditions for Knowledge of Working-Class Conditions: Employers, Government and the Jute Workers of Calcutta, 1890–1940." In *Subaltern Studies II: Writings on South Asian History and Society.* Edited by Ranajit Guha. New Delhi: Oxford University Press, 1983.
Chakrabarty, Dipesh. *Habitations of Modernity: Essays in the Wake of Subaltern Studies.* Chicago: University of Chicago Press, 2002.
Chakrabarty, Dipesh. *Provincializing Europe: Postcolonial Thought and Historical Difference.* Princeton: Princeton University Press, 2000.
Chakraborty, Achin, and Anthony D'Costa, eds. *The Land Question in India: State, Dispossession, and Capitalist Transition.* Oxford: Oxford University Press, 2017.
Chatterjee, Partha. *Bengal 1920–1947: The Land Question.* Calcutta: K. P. Bagchi & Co., 1984.
Chatterjee, Partha. *The Nation and Its Fragments: Colonial and Postcolonial Histories.* Princeton: Princeton University Press, 1993.
Chatterjee, Partha. *Nationalist Thought and the Colonial World: A Derivative Discourse?* London: Zed Books, 1986.

Chaturvedi, Vinayak. *Peasant Pasts: History and Memory in Western India*. Berkeley: University of California Press, 2007.
Chowdhry, Prem. "Jat Domination in South-East Punjab: Socio-Economic Basis of Jat Politics in a Punjab District." *Indian Economic and Social History Review* 19, no. 3–4 (July 1982): 325–346.
Chowdhry, Prem. *The Veiled Women: Shifting Gender Equations in Rural Haryana, 1880–1990*. New Delhi: Oxford University Press, 1994.
Cohn, Bernard S. *An Anthropologist among the Historians and Other Essays*. New Delhi: Oxford University Press, 1987.
Cohn, Bernard S. "The Changing Status of a Depressed Caste." In *Village India: Studies in the Little Community*. Edited by McKim Marriott. Chicago: University of Chicago Press, 1955.
Cohn, Bernard S. "The Command of Language and the Language of Command." In *Subaltern Studies IV: Writings on South Asian History and Society*. Edited by Ranajit Guha. New Delhi: Oxford University Press, 1985.
Cohn, Bernard. "Law and the Colonial State in India." In *Colonialism and Its Forms of Knowledge: The British in India*. Princeton: Princeton University Press, 1996.
Cohn, Bernard. "Structural Change in Indian Rural Society." In *Land Control and Social Structure in Indian History*. Edited by Robert Eric Frykenberg. Madison: University of Wisconsin Press, 1969.
Commander, Simon. "The Jajmani System of North India: An Examination of its Logic and Status across Two Centuries." *Modern Asian Studies* 17, no. 2 (1983): 283–311.
Condos, Mark. *The Insecurity State: Punjab and the Making of Colonial Power in British India*. Cambridge: Cambridge University Press, 2017.
Dass, Nirmal, ed. *Songs of the Saints from the Adi Granth*. Albany: State University of New York Press, 2000.
Datta, Nonica. *Forming an Identity: A Social History of the Jats*. New Delhi: Oxford University Press, 1999.
Davis, David Brion. *The Problem of Slavery in the Age of Revolution*. Ithaca: Cornell University Press, 1975.
Dewey, Clive. *Anglo-Indian Attitudes: The Mind of the Indian Civil Service*. London: Hambledon Press, 1993.
Dewey, Clive. "Patwari and Chaukidar: Subordinate Officials and the Reliability of India's Agricultural Statistics." In *The Imperial Impact: Studies in the Economic History of Africa and India*. Edited by Clive Dewey and A. G. Hopkins. London: The Athlone Press, 1978.
Dhavan, Purnima. "Reading the Texture of History and Memory in Early-Nineteenth-Century Punjab." *Comparative Studies of South Asia, Africa, and the Middle East* 29, no. 3 (2009): 515–527.
Dhavan, Purnima. *When Sparrows Become Hawks: The Making of the Sikh Warrior Tradition, 1699–1799*. New York: Oxford University Press, 2011.
Dirks, Nicholas B. *Castes of Mind: Colonialism and the Making of Modern India*. Princeton: Princeton University Press, 2001.
Dobbs, Maurice. *Studies in the Development of Capitalism*. New York: International Publishers, 1947.

Du Bois, W.E.B. *The Souls of Black Folk*. New York: Alfred A Knopf, 1976.

Dungen, P.H.M. van den. *The Punjab Tradition: Influence and Authority in Nineteenth-Century India*. London: George Allen & Unwin, 1972.

Eaton, John. "Review of *Theories of Surplus Value*, by Karl Marx, G. A. Bonner, & Emile Burns." *Science and Society* 18, no. 3 (Summer 1954): 274–275.

Engels, Friedrich. *The Peasant Question in France and Germany*. Moscow: Foreign Languages Publishing House, 1955.

Fanon, Frantz. *The Wretched of the Earth*. Translated by Richard Philcox. New York: Grove Press, 2004.

Federici, Silvia. *Caliban and the Witch: Women, the Body, and Primitive Accumulation*. 2nd rev. ed. Brooklyn: Autonomedia, 2014.

Fenech, Louis. *The Cherished Five in Sikh History*. New York: Oxford University Press, 2021.

Foster-Carter, Aidan. "The Modes of Production Controversy." *New Left Review* 1, no. 107 (February 1978): 47–77.

Foucault, Michel. *Madness and Civilization: A History of Insanity in the Age of Reason*. Translated by Richard Howard. London: Routledge, 2001.

Foucault, Michel. "Nietzsche, Genealogy, History." In *The Foucault Reader*. Edited by Paul Rabinow. New York: Pantheon Books, 1984.

Fox, Richard G. *Lions of the Punjab: Culture in the Making*. Berkeley: University of California Press, 1985.

Frank, Andre Gunder. *Capitalism and Underdevelopment in Latin America*. Harmondsworth: Penguin Books, 1969.

Frank, Andre Gunder. "On 'Feudal' Modes, Models and Methods of Escaping Capitalist Reality." *Economic and Political Weekly* 8, no. 1 (January 6, 1973): 36–37.

Frankel, Francine R. *India's Green Revolution: Economic Gains and Political Costs*. Princeton: Princeton University Press, 1971.

Fuller, C. J. "Ethnographic Inquiry in Colonial India: Herbert Risley, William Crooke, and the Study of Tribes and Castes." *Journal of the Royal Anthropological Institute* 23, no. 3 (September 2017): 603–621.

Geertz, Clifford. "Studies in Peasant Life: Community and Society." *Biennial Review of Anthropology* 2 (1961): 1–41.

Genovese, Eugene D. *Roll, Jordan, Roll: The World the Slaves Made*. New York: Vintage Books, 1976.

Gidwani, Vinay. *Capital, Interrupted: Agrarian Development and the Politics of Work in India*. Minneapolis: University of Minnesota Press, 2008.

Gill, Navyug. "Gramsci at the Delhi Border: Indian Farmers and the Revolution against Inevitability." *Antipode Online*, June 14, 2021.

Gill, Navyug. "Peasant as Alibi: An Itinerary of the Archive of Colonial Panjab." In *Unarchived Histories: The "Mad" and the "Trifling" in the Colonial and Postcolonial World*. Edited by Gyanendra Pandey. London: Routledge, 2014.

Gill, Navyug. "A Popular Upsurge against Neoliberal Arithmetic in India." *Al Jazeera*, December 11, 2020.

Gill, Parmbir Singh. "A Different Kind of Dissidence: The Ghadar Party, Sikh History and the Politics of Anticolonial Mobilization." *Sikh Formations: Religion, Culture, Theory* 10, no. 1 (2014): 23–41.
Gill, Sucha Singh. "The Farmer's Movement and Agrarian Change in the Green Revolution Belt of North-West India." *Journal of Peasant Studies*, 21, no. 3–4 (1994): 195–211.
Gilmartin, David. *Blood and Water: The Indus River Basin in Modern History*. Oakland: University of California Press, 2015.
Gilmartin, David. *Empire and Islam: Punjab and the Making of Pakistan*. Oakland: University of California Press, 1988.
Gilmartin, David. "Scientific Empire and Imperial Science: Colonialism and Irrigation Technology in the Indus Basin." *Journal of Asian Studies* 53, no. 4 (November 1994): 1127–1149.
Göçmen, Dogan. *The Adam Smith Problem: Human Nature and Society in "The Theory of Moral Sentiments" and "The Wealth of Nations."* London: Tauris Academic Studies, 2007.
Gould, Harold A. "The Hindu Jajmani System: A Case of Economic Particularism." *Southwestern Journal of Anthropology* 14, no. 4 (Winter 1958): 428–437.
Gould, Harold A. "A Jajmani System of North India: Its Structure, Magnitude, and Meaning." *Ethnology* 3, no. 1 (January 1964): 12–41.
Grewal, J. S. *Guru Nanak in History*. Chandigarh: Publication Bureau of Panjab University, 1969.
Grewal, J. S. *Recent Debates in Sikh Studies: An Assessment*. New Delhi: Manohar, 2011.
Grewal, J. S. *The Sikhs of the Punjab*. Rev. ed. Cambridge: Cambridge University Press, 1990.
Grewal, J. S., and Irfan Habib, eds. *Sikh History from Persian Sources*. New Delhi: Tulika, 2001.
Grewal, J. S., Harish K. Puri, and Indu Banga, eds. *The Ghadar Movement: Background, Ideology, Action, and Legacies*. Patiala: Publication Bureau of Punjabi University, 2013.
Graeber, David. *Debt: The First 5,000 Years*. New York: Melville House, 2011.
Gramsci, Antonio. "The Revolution Against *Capital*." In *The Gramsci Reader: Selected Writings 1916–1935*. Edited by David Forgacs. New York: New York University Press, 2000.
Guha, Ranajit. *Dominance without Hegemony: History and Power in Colonial India*. New Delhi: Oxford University Press, 1998.
Guha, Ranajit. *Elementary Aspects of Peasant Insurgency in Colonial India*. New Delhi: Oxford University Press, 1983.
Guha, Ranajit. "On Some Aspects of the Historiography of Colonial India." In *Subaltern Studies I: Writings on South Asian History and Society*. Edited by Ranajit Guha. New Delhi: Oxford University Press, 1982.
Guha, Ranajit. "The Prose of Counter-Insurgency." In *Subaltern Studies II: Writings on South Asian History and Society*. Edited by Ranajit Guha. New Delhi: Oxford University Press, 1983.
Guha, Ranajit. *A Rule of Property for Bengal: An Essay on the Idea of Permanent Settlement*. Paris: Mouton & Co., 1963.

Guha, Sumit. *The Agrarian Economy of the Bombay Deccan, 1818–1941.* New Delhi: Oxford University Press, 1986.
Guha, Sumit. *Beyond Caste: Identity and Power in South Asia, Past and Present.* Leiden: Brill, 2013.
Guha, Sumit. "The Politics of Identity and Enumeration in India c. 1600–1990." *Comparative Studies in Society and History* 45, no. 1 (January 2003): 148–167.
Griswold, Charles L. *Adam Smith and the Virtues of Enlightenment.* Cambridge: Cambridge University Press, 1999.
Habib, Irfan. "Marx's Perception of India." In *Essays in Indian History: Towards a Marxist Perception.* New Delhi: Tulika Books, 1995.
Habib, Irfan. "Potentialities of Capitalistic Development in the Economy of Mughal India." *Journal of Economic History* 29, no. 1 (March 1969): 32–78.
Hamid, Naved. "Dispossession and Differentiation of the Peasantry in the Punjab during Colonial Rule." *Journal of Peasant Studies* 10, no. 1 (1982): 52–72.
Hans, Raj Kumar. "Making Sense of Dalit Sikh History." In *Dalit Studies.* Edited by Ramnarayan S. Rawat and K. Satyanarayana. Durham: Duke University Press, 2016.
Hans, Raj Kumar. "Sant Poet Wazir Singh: A Window for Reimagining Nineteenth Century Punjab." *International Journal of Punjab Studies* 20, no. 1–2 (January 2013): 135–158.
Hardiman, David. *Feeding the Baniya: Peasants and Usurers in Western India.* New Delhi: Oxford University Press, 1996.
Hardiman, David. *Peasant Nationalists of Gujarat, Kheda District 1917–1934.* New Delhi: Oxford University Press, 1981.
Harding, Christopher. *Religious Transformation in South Asia: The Meanings of Conversion in Colonial Punjab.* Oxford: Oxford University Press, 2008.
Harootunian, Harry. *History's Disquiet: Modernity, Cultural Practice, and the Question of Everyday Life.* New York: Columbia University Press, 2002.
Harootunian, Harry. *Marx After Marx: History and Time in the Expansion of Capitalism.* New York: Columbia University Press, 2015.
Harvey, David. *The New Imperialism.* Oxford: Oxford University Press, 2003.
Harvey, David. *Spaces of Capital: Towards a Critical Geography.* Edinburgh: Edinburgh University Press, 2001.
Hawley, John S., and Mark Juergensmeyer. *Songs of the Saints of India.* New Delhi: Oxford University Press, 2004.
Hill, Christopher L. "Conceptual Universalization in the Transnational Nineteenth Century." In *Global Intellectual History.* Edited by Samuel Moyn and Andrew Sartori. New York: Columbia University Press, 2013.
Hill, Christopher. *The World Turned Upside Down: Radical Ideas During the English Revolution.* London: Penguin, 1991.
Hobsbawm, Eric. *Bandits.* Harmondsworth: Penguin Books, 1972.
Hobsbawm, Eric. "Introduction." In Karl Marx, *Pre-Capitalist Economic Formations.* Edited by Eric Hobsbawm. New York: International Publishers, 1965.
Hobsbawm, Eric, and George Rudé. *Captain Swing.* London: Lawrence and Wishart, 1969.

Holton, Robert J. "Marxist Theories of Social Change and the Transition from Feudalism to Capitalism." *Theory and Society* 10, no. 6 (November 1981): 833–867.
Hopkins, B. D. *The Making of Modern Afghanistan*. London: Palgrave Macmillan, 2008.
Imy, Kate. *Faithful Fighters: Identity and Power in the British Indian Army*. Stanford: Stanford University Press, 2019.
Islam, M. Mufakharul. *Irrigation, Agriculture, and the Raj: Punjab, 1887–1947*. New Delhi: Manohar Publications, 1997.
Islam, M. Mufakharul. "The Punjab Land Alienation Act and the Professional Moneylenders." *Modern Asian Studies* 29, no. 2 (May 1995): 271–291.
Jangam, Chinnaiah. *Dalits and the Making of Modern India*. New Delhi: Oxford University Press, 2017.
Jani, Pranav. "Karl Marx, Eurocentrism, and the 1857 Revolt in British India." In *Marxism, Modernity, and Postcolonial Studies*. Edited by Crystal Bartolovich and Neil Lazarus. Cambridge: Cambridge University Press, 2002.
Jodhka, Surinder Singh. "Caste and Untouchability in Rural Punjab." *Economic and Political Weekly* 37, no. 19 (May 11–17, 2002): 1813–1823.
Jodhka, Surinder Singh. "Prejudice without Pollution? Scheduled Castes in Contemporary Punjab." *Journal of Indian School of Political Economy* 12, no. 3–4 (2000): 381–403.
Johnson, Walter. *River of Dark Dreams: Slavery and Empire in the Cotton Kingdom*. Cambridge: The Belknap Press, 2013.
Jones, Kenneth W. *Arya Dharm: Hindu Consciousness in 19th-Century Punjab*. Berkeley: University of California Press, 1976.
Jones, Kenneth W. "Religious Identity and the Indian Census." In *The Census in British India*. Edited by N. Gerald Barrier. Delhi: Manohar Publishers, 1981.
Jones, Gareth Stedman. *Karl Marx: Greatness and Illusion*. London: Allen Lane, 2018.
Judge, Paramjit S. "Caste Hierarchy, Dominance, and Change in Punjab." *Sociological Bulletin* 64, no. 1 (January–April 2015): 55–76.
Judge, Paramjit S. "Hierarchical Differentiation among Dalits." *Economic and Political Weekly* 38, no. 28, (July 12–18, 2003): 2990–2991.
Judge, Rajbir Singh. "Reform in Fragments: Sovereignty, Colonialism, and the Sikh Tradition." *Modern Asian Studies*, 56, no. 4 (July 2022): 1125–1152.
Juergensmeyer, Mark. *Religion as Social Vision: The Movement against Untouchability in 20th Century Punjab*. Berkeley: University of California Press, 1981.
Kakar, M. Hasan. *A Political and Diplomatic History of Afghanistan*. Leiden: Brill, 2006.
Kautsky, Karl. *The Agrarian Question*. Translated by Pete Burgess. London: Zwan Publications, 1988.
Kaviraj, Sudipta. "The Imaginary Institution of India." In *Subaltern Studies VII: Writings on South Asian History and Society*. Edited by Partha Chatterjee and Gyanendra Pandey. New Delhi: Oxford University Press, 1992.
Kaviraj, Sudipta. "On the Status of Marx's Writings on India." *Social Scientist* 11, no. 9 (September 1983): 26–46.
Keay, John. *The Tartan Turban: In Search of Alexander Gardner*. London: Kashi House, 2017.
Keer, Dhananjay. *Dr. Ambedkar: Life and Mission*. Bombay: Popular Prakashan, 1954.
Kelkar, Govind, and Maithreyi Krishnaraj, eds. *Women, Land, and Power in Asia*. New Delhi: Routledge, 2013.

Kennedy, Gavin. *Adam Smith: A Moral Philosopher and His Political Economy.* New York: Palgrave Macmillan, 2008.
Kessinger, Tom. *Vilyatpur, 1848–1968: Social and Economic Change in a North Indian Village.* Berkeley: University of California Press, 1974.
Khare, R. S., ed. *Caste, Hierarchy, and Individualism: Indian Critiques of Louis Dumont's Contributions.* New Delhi: Oxford University Press, 2006.
Kingston-Mann, Esther. *Lenin and the Problem of Marxist Peasant Revolution.* New York: Oxford University Press, 1983.
Kohli, Sita Ram, and Hari Ram Gupta. *Students' Historical Atlas of India.* Allahabad: The Indian Press, 1945.
Kumar, Aishwary. *Radical Equality: Ambedkar, Gandhi, and the Risk of Democracy.* Stanford: Stanford University Press, 2015.
Ladejinsky, Wolf. "The Green Revolution in Punjab: A Field Trip." *Economic and Political Weekly* 4, no. 26 (June 28, 1969): 73–82.
Leaf, Murray J. *Song of Hope: The Green Revolution in a Panjab Village.* New Brunswick: Rutgers University Press, 1984.
Lenin, Vladimir Ilich. *The Agrarian Question and the "Critics of Marx."* Moscow: Foreign Languages Publishing House, 1954.
Lenin, Vladimir Ilich. *The Development of Capitalism in Russia.* 2nd ed. Moscow: Progress Publishers, 1964.
Levien, Michael, Michael Watts, and Yan Hairong, eds. Special issue. *The Journal of Peasant Studies* 45, no. 5–6 (2018).
Levine, Philippa. "Is Comparative History Possible?" *History and Theory* 53, no. 3 (October 2014): 331–347.
Lewis, Oscar. "Caste and the Jajmani System in a North Indian Village." *The Scientific Monthly* 83, no. 2 (August 1956): 66–81.
Lewis, Oscar. *Village Life in Northern India: Studies in a Delhi Village.* Urbana: University of Illinois Press, 1958.
Li, Tania. *The Will to Improve: Governmentality, Development, and the Practice of Politics.* Durham: Duke University Press, 2007.
Ludden, David. *Peasant History in South India.* Princeton: Princeton University Press, 1985.
Luxemburg, Rosa. *The Accumulation of Capital.* Translated by Agnes Schwarzschild. London: Routledge, 2003.
Madra. Amandeep Singh, and Parmjit Singh. *Sicques, Tigers, or Thieves: Eyewitness Accounts of the Sikhs (1606–1809).* London: Palgrave Macmillan, 2004.
Malhotra, Anshu. "Bhakti and the Gendered Self: A Courtesan and a Consort in Mid Nineteenth Century Punjab." *Modern Asian Studies* 46, no. 6 (November 2012): 1506–1536.
Malhotra, Anshu. *Gender, Caste, and Religious Identities: Restructuring Class in Colonial Punjab.* New Delhi: Oxford University Press, 2002.
Malhotra, Anshu. *Piro and the Gulabdasis: Gender, Sect, and Society in Punjab.* New Delhi: Oxford University Press, 2017.
Malik, Ikram Ali. "Isa Khel Riot of 1893." *Journal of the Pakistan Historical Society* 32, part 1 (January 1984): 13–21.

Mandair, Arvind-Pal S. *Religion and the Specter of the West: Sikhism, India, Postcoloniality, and the Politics of Translation.* New York: Columbia University Press, 2009.
Mandair, Arvind-Pal S. *Violence and the Sikhs.* Cambridge; Cambridge University Press, 2022.
Mann, Gurinder Singh. *The Making of Sikh Scripture.* New Delhi: Oxford University Press, 2001.
Mantena, Karuna. *Alibis of Empire: Henry Maine and the Ends of Liberal Imperialism.* Princeton: Princeton University Press, 2010.
Martin, Briton, Jr. "Lord Dufferin and the Indian National Congress, 1885–1888." *Journal of British Studies* 7, no. 1 (November 1967): 68–96.
Marx, Karl. *Capital: Volume I: A Critique of Political Economy.* Translated by Ben Fowkes. London: Penguin Books, 1976.
Marx, Karl. *Capital: Volume II: The Process of Circulation of Capital.* Translated by David Fernbach. London: Penguin Books, 1978.
Marx, Karl. *Grundrisse: Foundations of the Critique of Political Economy.* Translated by Martin Nicolaus. London: Penguin Books, 1973.
Marx, Karl. "On the Jewish Question." In *The Marx-Engels Reader.* 2nd ed. Edited by Robert C. Tucker. New York: W.W. Norton & Company, 1978.
Marx, Karl. *Theories of Surplus-Value.* Volume 1. Edited by S. Ryazanskaya. Translated by Emile Burns. Moscow: Progress Publishers, 1963.
Marx, Karl, and Friedrich Engels. *On Colonialism.* Moscow: Progress Publishers, 1968.
Massey, James. "Presbyterian Missionaries and the Development of Punjabi Language and Literature, 1834–1984." *Journal of Presbyterian History* 62, no. 3 (Fall 1984): 258–261.
Mayer, Peter. "Inventing Village Tradition: The Late 19th Century Origins of the North Indian 'Jajmani System.'" *Modern Asian Studies* 27, no. 2 (May 1993): 357–395.
Mazumder, Rajit K. *The Indian Army and the Making of Punjab.* New Delhi: Permanent Black, 2003.
McLellan, David. *Karl Marx: His Life and Thought.* London: Macmillan, 1973.
McLeod, W. H. *Guru Nanak and the Sikh Religion.* Oxford: Clarendon Press, 1968.
McNally, David. *Political Economy and the Rise of Capitalism: A Reinterpretation.* Berkeley: University of California Press, 1988.
Meek, Ronald L. *Social Science and the Ignoble Savage.* Cambridge: Cambridge University Press, 1976.
Meek, Ronald L. *Smith, Marx, and After: Ten Essays in the Development of Economic Thought.* London: Chapman & Hall, 1977.
Mehta, Uday Singh. *Liberalism and Empire: A Study in Nineteenth-Century British Liberal Thought.* Chicago: University of Chicago Press, 1999.
Metcalf, Thomas. *The Aftermath of Revolt: India 1857–1970.* Princeton: Princeton University Press, 1964.
Metcalf, Thomas R. "The British and the Moneylender in Nineteenth Century India." *Journal of Modern History* 34, no. 4 (December 1962): 390–397.
Metcalf, Thomas R. "Social Effects of British Land Policy in Oudh." In *Land Control and Social Structure in Indian History.* Edited by Robert E. Frykenberg. Madison: University of Wisconsin Press, 1969.

Mies, Maria. *Patriarchy and Accumulation on a World Scale: Women in the International Division of Labour.* London: Zed Books, 1986.

Milgate, Murray, and Shannon C. Stimson. *After Adam Smith: A Century of Transformation in Politics and Political Economy.* Princeton: Princeton University Press, 2009.

Mintz, Sidney W. "Was the Plantation Slave a Proletarian?" *Review* (Fernand Braudel Center) 2, no. 1 (Summer 1978): 81–98.

Mir, Farina. *The Social Space of Language: Vernacular Culture in British Colonial Punjab.* Berkeley: University of California Press, 2010.

Mitchell, Timothy. *Rule of Experts: Egypt, Techno-Politics, Modernity.* Berkeley: University of California Press, 2002.

Mitra, Durba. *Indian Sex Life: Sexuality and the Colonial Origins of Modern Social Thought.* Princeton: Princeton University Press, 2020.

Mohan, P. Sanal. *Modernity of Slavery: Struggles against Caste Inequality in Colonial Kerala.* New Delhi: Oxford University Press, 2015.

Moyn, Samuel, and Andrew Sartori. "Approaches to Global Intellectual History." In *Global Intellectual History.* Edited by Samuel Moyn and Andrew Sartori. New York: Columbia University Press, 2013.

Mufti, Aamir. *Enlightenment in the Colony: The Jewish Question and the Crisis of Postcolonial Culture.* Princeton: Princeton University Press, 2007.

Murphy, Anne. *The Materiality of the Past: History and Representation in Sikh Tradition.* New York: Oxford University Press, 2012.

Musto, Marcello. "The Writing of *Capital*: Genesis and Structure of Marx's Critique of Political Economy." *Critique: Journal of Socialist Theory* 46, no. 1 (2018): 11–26.

Nair, Neeti. *Changing Homelands: Hindu Politics and the Partition of India.* Cambridge: Harvard University Press, 2011.

Nazir, Pervaiz. "Origins of Debt, Mortgage, and Alienation of Land in Early Modern Punjab." *Journal of Peasant Studies* 27, no. 3 (2000): 55–91.

Nazir, Pervaiz. "Transformation of Property Relations in the Punjab." *Economic and Political Weekly* 16, no. 8 (February 21, 1981): 281–285.

Nieli, Russell. "Spheres of Intimacy and the Adam Smith Problem." *Journal of the History of Ideas* 47, no. 4 (October–December 1986): 611–624.

Oakes, James. "Capitalism and Slavery and the Civil War." *International Labor and Working-Class History*, no. 89 (Spring 2016): 195–220.

Oberoi, Harjot. *The Construction of Religious Boundaries: Culture, Identity, and Diversity in the Sikh Tradition.* Chicago: University of Chicago Press, 1994.

Oldenburg, Veena Talwar. *Dowry Murder: The Imperial Origins of a Cultural Crime.* New York: Oxford University Press, 2002.

Omvedt, Gail. *Ambedkar: Towards an Enlightened India.* New Delhi: Penguin, 2004.

Omvedt, Gail. "Capitalist Agriculture and Rural Classes in India." *Economic and Political Weekly* 16, no. 52 (December 26, 1981): 140–159.

Omvedt, Gail. *Seeking Begampura: The Social Vision of Anticaste Intellectuals.* New Delhi: Navayana Publishers, 2008.

Overton, Mark. *Agricultural Revolution in England: The Transformation of the Agrarian Economy 1500–1850.* Cambridge: Cambridge University Press, 1996.

Pandey, Gyanendra. *The Ascendancy of the Congress in Uttar Pradesh, 1926–34: A Study in Imperfect Mobilization*. New Delhi: Oxford University Press, 1978.
Pandey, Gyanendra. "'The Bigoted Julaha.'" *Economic and Political Weekly* 18, no. 5 (January 29, 1983): 19–28.
Pandey, Gyanendra. *The Construction of Communalism in Colonial North India*. New Delhi: Oxford University Press, 1990.
Pandey, Gyanendra. *A History of Prejudice: Race, Caste, and Difference in India and the United States*. New York: Cambridge University Press, 2013.
Pandey, Gyanendra. "In Defense of the Fragment: Writing about Hindu-Muslim Riots in India Today." *Representations* no. 37 (Winter 1992): 27-55.
Pandian, M.S.S. *Brahmin and Non-Brahmin: Genealogies of the Tamil Political Present*. New Delhi: Permanent Black, 2007.
Parthasarathi, Prasannan. *Why Europe Grew Rich and Asia Did Not: Global Economic Divergence, 1600–1850*. Cambridge: Cambridge University Press, 2011.
Patnaik, Utsa. "Capitalist Development in Agriculture: A Note." *Economic and Political Weekly* 6, no. 39 (September 25, 1971): 123–130.
Patnaik, Utsa and Prabhat Patnaik. *A Theory of Imperialism*. New York: Columbia University Press, 2017.
Perelman, Michael. *The Invention of Capitalism: Classical Political Economy and the Secret History of Primitive Accumulation*. Durham: Duke University Press, 2000.
Perlin, Frank. "Proto-Industrialization and Pre-Colonial South Asia." *Past and Present* no. 98 (February 1983): 30–95.
Pickering, Paul A., and Alex Tyrrell. *The People's Bread: A History of the Anti-Corn Law League*. London: Leicester University Press, 2000.
Pomeranz, Kenneth. *The Great Divergence: China, Europe, and the Making of the Modern World Economy*. Princeton: Princeton University Press, 2000.
Prakash, Gyan. *Bonded Histories: Genealogies of Labor Servitude in Colonial India*. Cambridge: Cambridge University Press, 1990.
Prashad, Vijay. *Untouchable Freedom: A Social History of a Dalit Community*. New York: Oxford University Press, 2001.
Prill, Susan. "Representing Sainthood in India: Sikh and Hindu Visions of Namdev." *Material Religion* 5, no. 2 (2009): 156–179.
Puri, Harish K., ed. *Dalits in Regional Context*. Jaipur: Rawat Publishers, 2004.
Puri, Harish K. *Ghadar Movement: Ideology, Organization, and Strategy*. Amritsar: Guru Nanak Dev University Press, 1993.
Puri, Harish. "Scheduled Castes in Sikh Community: A Historical Perspective." *Economic and Political Weekly* 38, no. 26 (June 28–July 4, 2023): 2693–2701.
Rahi, Rajinder, ed. *Sant Ram Udasi: Jeevan ate Samuchi Rachna* [Sant Ram Udasi: Life and Collected Work]. Ludhiana: Chetna Parkashan, 2001.
Rahman, Tariq. "Punjabi Language during British Rule." *Journal of Punjab Studies* 14, no. 1 (Spring 2007): 27–39.
Ram, Ronki. "Beyond Conversion and Sanskritisation: Articulating an Alternative Dalit Agenda in East Punjab." *Modern Asian Studies* 46, no. 3 (May 2012): 639–702.
Ram, Ronki. "Ravidass Deras and Social Protest: Making Sense of Dalit Consciousness in Punjab (India)." *Journal of Asian Studies* 67, no. 4 (November 2008): 1341–1364.

Ram, Ronki. "Social Exclusion, Resistance, and Deras: Exploring the Myth of Casteless Sikh Society in Punjab." *Economic and Political Weekly* 42, no. 40 (October 6–12, 2007): 4066–4074.

Ram, Ronki. "Untouchability in India with a Difference: Ad Dharm, Dalit Assertion, and Caste Conflicts in Punjab." *Asia Survey* 44, no. 6 (2004): 895–912.

Ramnath, Maia. *Haj to Utopia: How the Ghadar Movement Charted Global Radicalism and Attempted to Overthrow the British Empire.* Berkeley: University of California Press, 2011.

Randhawa, M. S. *Green Revolution.* New York: John Wiley & Sons, 1974.

Rao, Anupama. *The Caste Question: Dalits and the Politics of Modern India.* Berkeley: University of California Press, 2009.

Rawat, Ramnarayan S. *Reconsidering Untouchability: Chamars and Dalit History in North India.* Bloomington: Indiana University Press, 2011.

Raza, Ali. *Revolutionary Pasts: Communist Internationalism in Colonial India.* Cambridge: Cambridge University Press, 2020.

Read, Jason. *The Micro-Politics of Capital: Marx and the Prehistory of the Present.* Albany: State University of New York Press, 2003.

Redfield, Robert. *The Primitive World and Its Transformation.* Ithaca: Cornell University Press, 1953.

Ricardo, David. *Principles of Political Economy and Taxation.* London: J. M. Dent and Sons, 1911.

Rizvi, Mubbashir A. *The Ethics of Staying: Social Movements and Land Rights Politics in Pakistan.* Stanford: Stanford University Press, 2019.

Robb, Peter. *Ancient Rights and Future Comforts: Bihar, the Bengal Tenancy Act of 1885, and British Rule in India.* Surrey: Curzon Press, 1997.

Roberts, Nathaniel. *To Be Cared For: The Power of Conversion and the Foreignness of Belonging in an Indian Slum.* Oakland: University of California Press, 2016.

Roberts, William Clare. "What was Primitive Accumulation? Reconstructing the Origin of a Critical Concept." *European Journal of Political Theory* 19, no. 4 (2020): 532–552.

Robinson, Cedric J. *Black Marxism: The Making of the Black Radical Tradition.* Chapel Hill: University of North Carolina Press, 2000.

Rodney, Walter. *How Europe Underdeveloped Africa.* London: Bogle-L'Ouverture Publications, 1972.

Roseberry, J. Royal. *Imperial Rule in Punjab: The Conquest and Administration of Multan, 1818–1881.* New Delhi: Manohar Publications, 1987.

Rothschild, Emma. "Adam Smith and Conservative Economics." *Economic History Review* 45, no. 1 (1992): 74–96.

Rudra, Ashok. "Big Farmers of Punjab: Second Installment of Results." *Economic and Political Weekly* 4, no. 52 (December 27, 1969): 213–219.

Rudra, Ashok. "In Search of the Capitalist Farmer." *Economic and Political Weekly* 5, no. 26 (July 27, 1970): 85–87.

Rudra, Ashok, A. Majid, and B. D. Talib. "Big Farmer of the Punjab: Some Preliminary Findings of a Sample Survey." *Economic and Political Weekly* 4, no. 39 (September 27, 1969): 143–146.

Ryazanskaya, S. "Preface." In Karl Marx, *Theories of Surplus-Value*. Volume 1. Edited by S. Ryazanskaya. Translated by Emile Burns. Moscow: Progress Publishers, 1963.
Sagar, Brij Mohan. *Songs of Ravi Das*. Chandigarh: Publication Bureau of Panjab University, 2003.
Sainath, P. *Everyone Loves a Good Drought: Stories from India's Poorest Districts*. New Delhi: Penguin Books, 1996.
Sandhu, Amandeep. *Panjab: Journeys Through Fault Lines*. Chennai: Westland, 2019.
Sanyal, Kalyan. *Rethinking Capitalist Development: Primitive Accumulation, Governmentality and Post-colonial Capitalism*. London: Routledge, 2007.
Sartori, Andrew. "Global Intellectual History and the History of Political Economy." In *Global Intellectual History*. Edited by Samuel Moyn and Andrew Sartori. New York: Columbia University Press, 2013.
Sartori, Andrew. *Liberalism in Empire: An Alternative History*. Oakland: University of California Press, 2014.
Satish, P. "Institutional Credit, Indebtedness and Suicides in Punjab." *Economic and Political Weekly* 41, no. 26 (June 30–July 7, 2006): 2754–2761.
Schomer, Karine, and W. H. McLeod, eds. *The Sants: Studies in a Devotional Tradition of India*. New Delhi: Motilal Banarsidass, 1987.
Schonhardt-Bailey, Cheryl. *From the Corn Laws to Free Trade: Interests, Ideas, and Institutions in Historical Perspective*. Cambridge: MIT Press, 2006.
Scott, James C. *Decoding Subaltern Politics: Ideology, Disguise, and Resistance in Agrarian Politics*. London: Routledge, 2013.
Scott, James C. *Weapons of the Weak: Everyday Forms of Peasant Resistance*. New Haven: Yale University Press, 1985.
Scott, Joan W. "The Evidence of Experience." *Critical Inquiry* 17, no. 4 (Summer 1991): 773–797.
Sen, Amartya. "Adam Smith and the Contemporary World." *Erasmus Journal of Philosophy and Economics* 3, no. 1 (2010): 50–67.
Sen, Amartya. "Capitalism Beyond the Crisis." *New York Review of Books*. March 26, 2009.
Sen, Amartya, and Emma Rothschild. "Adam Smith's Economics." In *The Cambridge Companion to Adam Smith*. Edited by Knud Haakonssen. Cambridge: Cambridge University Press, 2006.
Shackle, Christopher. "Punjabi in Lahore." *Modern Asian Studies* 4, no. 3 (1970): 239–267.
Shackle, Christopher. "Some Observations on the Evolution of Modern Standard Punjabi." In *Institutions and Ideologies: A SOAS South Asia Reader*. Edited by David Arnold and Peter Robb. Surrey: Curzon Press, 1993.
Shah, Bullhe. "Strange are the Times." Translated by Kartar Singh Duggal. From <www.apnaorg.com/poetry/bulleheng>. Accessed April 19, 2020.
Shah, Bullhe. *Sufi Lyrics*. Edited and Translated by Christopher Shackle. Cambridge: Harvard University Press, 2015.
Shah, Bulleh. "A Topsy-Turvey World." In *Bulleh Shah: A Selection*. Translated by Taufiq Rafat. Lahore: Vanguard Publications, 1982.
Shanin, Teodor. *The Awkward Class: Political Sociology of Peasantry in a Developing Society, Russia 1910–1925*. Oxford: Clarendon Press, 1972.

Shanin, Teodor. "Chayanov's Message: Illuminations, Miscomprehensions, and the Contemporary 'Development Theory.'" In *A. V. Chayanov on the Theory of Peasant Economy*. Edited by Daniel Thorner, Basile Kerblay, and R.E.F. Smith. Madison: University of Wisconsin Press, 1986.

Shanin, Teodor, ed. *Defining Peasants: Essays Concerning Rural Societies, Expolary Economics, and Learning from Them in the Contemporary World*. Oxford: Basil Blackwell, 1990.

Shanin, Teodor, ed. *Late Marx and the Russian Road: Marx and "the Peripheries of Capitalism."* New York: Monthly Review Press, 1983.

Shanin, Teodor, ed. *Peasants and Peasant Societies*. 2nd ed. Oxford: Basil Blackwell, 1987.

Sharma, Devinder. "A Battle Only Half Won." *The Tribune*, November 22, 2021.

Sidhu, Amarpal S. *The First Anglo-Sikh War*. Stroud: Amberley Publishing, 2010.

Sidhu, Amarpal S. *The Second Anglo-Sikh War*. Stroud: Amberley Publishing, 2016.

Singh, Arjan. *The Legend of the Maneater*. New Delhi: Ravi Dayal Publishers, 1993.

Singh, Chetan. *Region and Empire: Panjab in the Seventeenth Century*. New Delhi: Oxford University Press, 1991.

Singh, Ganda. *Life of Banda Singh Bahadur: Based on Contemporary and Original Sources*. Amritsar: The Sikh History Research Department, 1935.

Singh, Jagjit. *Percussions of History: The Sikh Revolution, In the Caravan of Revolutions*. SAS Nagar: Nanakshahi Trust, 2006.

Singh, Kapur. *Sachi Sakhi* [True Story]. Jalandhar: Raj Roop Prakashan, 1972.

Singh, Khushwant. *The Sikhs*. London: George Allen and Unwin, 1953.

Singh, Mal. *Sikh Mission ate Dr. Bhim Rao Ambedkar* [The Sikh Mission and Dr. Bhim Rao Ambedkar]. Patiala: Gracious Books, 2020.

Singh, Nikhil Pal. "On Race, Violence, and So-Called Primitive Accumulation." *Social Text* 34, no. 3 (September 2016): 27–50.

Singh, Nikky-Guninder Kaur. "Introduction." In Guru Nanak, *Poems from the Guru Granth Sahib*. Edited and Translated by Nikky-Guninder Kaur Singh. Cambridge: Harvard University Press, 2022.

Singh, Pashaura. *The Bhagats of the Guru Granth Sahib: Sikh Self-Definition and the Bhagat Bani*. New Delhi: Oxford University Press, 2003.

Singh, Pritam. "BJP's Farming Policies: Deepening Agrobusiness Capitalism and Centralisation." *Economic and Political Weekly* 55, no. 41 (October 10, 2020): 14–17.

Singh, Sukhpal. "Crisis in Punjab Agriculture." *Economic and Political Weekly* 35, no. 23 (June 3–9, 2000): 1889-1892.

Singh, Sukhpal. "Punjab Agriculture: Pinning Hopes on Private Sector for Revival." *Economic and Political Weekly* 56, no. 2 (January 9, 2021): 10–12.

Singh, Sukhpal, and Shruti Bhogal. "Punjab's Small Peasantry: Thriving or Deteriorating?" *Economic and Political Weekly* 49, no. 26–27 (June 28–July 5, 2014): 95–100.

Singh, Sunit. "The Sikh Kingdom." In *The Oxford Handbook on Sikh Studies*. Edited by Pashaura Singh and Louis E. Fenech. Oxford: Oxford University Press, 2014.

Sinha, Shreya. "The Agrarian Crisis in Punjab and the Making of the Anti-Farm Law Protest." *The India Forum*, December 4, 2020.

Skaria, Ajay. "Ambedkar, Marx and the Buddhist Question." *South Asia: Journal of South Asian Studies* 38, no. 3 (2015): 450–465.

Smith, Adam. *An Inquiry into the Nature and Causes of the Wealth of Nations.* Edited by Edwin Cannan. Chicago: University of Chicago Press, 1976.
Smith, Richard Saumarez. *Rule by Records: Land Registration and Village Custom in Early British Punjab.* New Delhi: Oxford University Press, 1996.
Smith, Richard Saumarez. "Rule-by-Records and Rule-by-Reports: Complimentary Aspects of the British Imperial Rule of Law." *Contributions to Indian Sociology* 19, no. 1 (1985): 153–176.
Smith, Wilfred Cantwell. "Lower-class Uprisings in the Mughal Empire." In *The Mughal State, 1526–1750.* Edited by Muzaffar Alam and Sanjay Subrahmanyam. New Delhi: Oxford University Press, 1988.
Spivak, Gayatri Chakravorty. "Can the Subaltern Speak?" In *Marxism and the Interpretation of Culture.* Edited by Cary Nelson and Lawrence Grossberg. Urbana: University of Illinois Press, 1988
Srinivas, M. N. "The Indian Village: Myth and Reality." In *The Dominant Caste and Other Essays.* New Delhi: Oxford University Press, 1987.
Stein, Burton. *Thomas Munro: The Origins of the Colonial State and His Vision of Empire.* New Delhi: Oxford University Press, 1995.
Stokes, Eric. *The Peasant and the Raj: Studies in the Agrarian Society and Peasant Rebellion in Colonial India.* Cambridge: Cambridge University Press, 1978.
Stokes, Eric. *The Peasant Armed: The Indian Revolt of 1857.* Edited by C. A. Bayly. Oxford: Clarendon Press, 1986.
Stone, Ian. *Canal Irrigation in British India: Perspectives on Technological Change in a Peasant Economy.* New York: Cambridge University Press, 1984.
Sturman, Rachel. *The Government of Social Life in Colonial India: Liberalism, Religious Law, and Women's Rights.* Cambridge: Cambridge University Press, 2012.
Syan, Hardip Singh. *Sikh Militancy in the Seventeenth Century: Religious Violence in Mughal and Early Modern India.* New York: I.B. Tauris, 2013.
Sweezy, Paul M. "The Transition from Feudalism to Capitalism." *Science and Society* 14, no. 2 (Spring 1950): 134–167.
Talbot, Ian. *Punjab and the Raj, 1849–1947.* New Delhi: Manohar, 1988.
Tamanoi, Mariko. "Reconsidering the Concept of Post-Peasantry: The Transformation of the Masoveria System in Old Catalonia." *Ethnology* 22, no. 4 (October 1983) 295–305.
Tan, Tai Yong. *The Garrison State: The Military, Government, and Society in Colonial Punjab, 1849–1947.* New Delhi: Sage, 2005.
Tandon, Prakash. *Punjabi Century: 1857–1947.* Berkeley: University of California Press, 1968.
Teltumbde, Anand, and Suraj Yengde, eds. *The Radical in Ambedkar: Critical Reflections.* Gurgaon: Allen Lane, 2018.
Thompson, E. P. *The Making of the English Working Class.* New York: Vintage Books, 1963.
Thorner, Alice. "Semi-Feudal or Capitalism? Contemporary Debate on Classes and Modes of Production in India." *Economic and Political Weekly* 17, nos. 49, 50, and 51 (December 4, 11 and 18, 1982): 1961–1968, 1993–1999 and 2061–2066.

Thorner, Daniel. "Capitalist Farming in India." *Economic and Political Weekly* 4, no. 52 (December 27, 1969): 211–212.
Thorner, Daniel. "Chayanov's Concept of Peasant Economy." In *A. V. Chayanov on the Theory of Peasant Economy*. Edited by Daniel Thorner, Basile Kerblay, and R.E.F. Smith. Madison: University of Wisconsin Press, 1986.
Thorner, Daniel, and Alice Thorner. *Land and Labour in India*. London: Asia Publishing House, 1962.
Tomlinson, B. R. *The Economy of Modern India: From 1860 to the Twenty-First Century*. Cambridge: Cambridge University Press, 2013.
Travers, Robert. *Ideology and Empire in Eighteenth-Century India: The British in Bengal*. Cambridge: Cambridge University Press, 2007.
Viswanath, Rupa. *The Pariah Problem: Caste, Religion, and the Social in Modern India*. New York: Columbia University Press, 2014.
Viswanathan, Gauri. *Outside the Fold: Conversion, Modernity, and Belief*. Princeton: Princeton University Press, 1988.
Wagner, Kim A. *Rumours and Rebels: A New History of the Indian Uprising of 1857*. London: Peter Lang, 2016.
Wallerstein, Immanuel. *The Modern World-System: Capitalist Agriculture and the Origins of the European World-Economy in the Sixteenth Century*. New York: Academic Press, 1974.
Washbrook, David. "Law, State, and Agrarian Society in Colonial India." *Modern Asian Studies* 15, no. 3 (1981): 649–721.
Washbrook, David. "Progress and Problems: South Asian Economic and Social History c. 1720–1860." *Modern Asian Studies* 22, no. 1 (1988): 57–96.
Weber, Eugen. *Peasants into Frenchmen: The Modernization of Rural France, 1870–1914*. Stanford: Stanford University Press, 1976.
Weingrod, Alex, and Emma Morin. "Post Peasants: The Character of Contemporary Sardinian Society." *Comparative Studies in Society and History* 13, no. 3 (July 1971): 301–324.
Whitcombe, Elizabeth. *Agrarian Conditions in Northern India: The United Provinces under British Rule, 1860–1900*. Berkeley: University of California Press, 1972.
Whittle, Jane, ed. *Landlords and Tenants in Britain, 1440–1660: Tawney's Agrarian Problem Revisited*. Woodbridge: The Boydell Press, 2013.
Williams, Eric. *Capitalism and Slavery*. Chapel Hill: University of North Carolina Press, 1944.
Williams, Raymond. *Keywords: A Vocabulary of Culture and Society*. London: Fontana Press, 1976.
Willis, Paul. *Learning to Labor: How Working Class Kids Get Working Class Jobs*. New York: Columbia University Press, 1977.
Wiser, William H. *The Hindu Jajmani System: A Socio-Economic System Interrelating Members of a Hindu Village Community in Services*. Lucknow: Lucknow Publishing House, 1936.
Wiser, Charlotte V., and William H. Wiser. *Behind Mud Walls*. New York: Richard R. Smith, 1930.
Wolf, Eric R. *Peasants*. Englewood Cliffs: Prentice-Hall, 1966.

Zelliot, Eleanor. *Ambedkar's World: The Making of Babasaheb and the Dalit Movement.* New Delhi: Navayana, 2013.
Zelliot, Eleanor, and Rohini Mokashi-Punekar, eds. *Untouchable Saints: An Indian Phenomenon.* New Delhi: Manohar Publishers, 2005.
Zimmerman, A. *Anthropology and Antihumanism in Imperial Germany.* Chicago: University of Chicago Press, 2001.
Zimmerman, A. "The Ideology of the Machine and the Spirit of the Factory: Remarx on Babbage and Ure." *Cultural Critique,* no. 37 (Autumn 1997): 5–29.

INDEX

Page numbers in *italics* indicate illustrations.

Abbott, Evelyn Robins, 111
Abdali, Ahmad Shah (Afghan ruler), 183, 192
accumulation: East India Company in Panjab and narrative of, 56–62; primitive, 24, 25, 56–57, 59–60
Ad Dharm movement, 20, 176, 177, 196, 198–204, 214–16, 218, 258, 299n10
Addiscombe Military Seminary, 36
Adi Granth, 188–89, 191, 200, 302n47
Afghans/Afghanistan: East India Company and, 28, 35, 38–39; Second Anglo-Afghan War (1842), 38; Sikhs in Panjab and, 183, 191; Thorburn on, 129, 131
The Agrarian Question (Kautsky), 222
Agricultural Resources of the Punjab (R. Baird Smith), 33–36
agriculturalists. *See* concept of "peasant;" peasants and global capitalism in colonial Panjab
Ahluwalia, Harnam Singh, 8, 153–57, 164, 255, 296n94
Aitchison, Charles, 133
Alavi, Hamza, 310–11n40
Ali, Shaikh Asghar, 115
Ali, Ghazanfar, 146
Ali, Imran, 16
Ali, Inam, 146
Ali, Tariq, 15
Althusser, Louis, 59, 223–24, 278n137, 309–10n16
Ambedkar, Bhimrao Ramji, 8, 20; alternative religion for untouchables,

search for, 201–5, 213–15; *Annihilation of Caste* speech, 174–76, 179, 213–14, 258, 299n4, 299n12; Buddhism, conversion to, 204; at Columbia University, New York, 198; on division of labor, 176, 182; as law minister of postcolonial India, 217; at London School of Economics, under Cannan, 312n62; Panjab Alienation of Land Act, abolition of, 217
Ambedkar, Yashwant Rao, 201
American Civil War (1861–65), 104
American Presbyterian Church in Panjab, 74, 177
Amritsar, Treaty of (1809), 26
Anderson, Kevin, 62
Anglo-Sikh wars (1845–46 and 1848–49), 55, 67, 277n118
Anjuman-i-Islamia, 148, 154
Annihilation of Caste speech (Ambedkar), 174–76, 179, 213–14, 258, 299n4, 299n12
Appadurai, Arjun, 97
Arains, 51, 52, 111, 167, 168, 220, 252
Arya Samaj, 197, 199–200, 202
Awans, 86, 111–12

Baba Farid (Chishti sufi). *See* Farid
Baden-Powell, Baden Henry, 38, 268n3, 272n47
Bahadur, Banda Singh, 183, 191, 193, 268–69n3, 303n57
Bahrupias, 113, 252
Baloch/Biloch, 100, 106, 133
Banaji, Jairus, 277n120

343

Banga, Indu, 53
baniyas, 128, 134, 142, 158, 164, 292n44
Barnes, George, 46–47
Barrier, Norman, 15–16, 288n129
Barton, Arthur, 145
Bayly, C. A., 37
Begampura, 186–87, 193
Behind Mud Walls (Wiser and Wiser), 177
benevolent colonialism. *See* colonial benevolence
Bengal's *zamindari* (landlord) settlement compared to Panjab, 37–38, 39
Bentham, Jeremy, 232
Bhagat Kabir. *See* Kabir
Bhagat Namdev. *See* Namdev
Bhagat Ravidas. *See* Ravidas
Bhai Jaita (Jiwan Singh), 191, 302n51
bhaiachara (brotherhood) or *mahalwari* (estate) settlements, 39
Bhakti movement, 20, 177, 183–88, 193, 194, 258
Bhandar, Brenda, 135
Bhangis, 182, 216
Bhattacharya, Neeladri, 17, 91
Biloch/Baloch, 100, 106, 133
Birla, Ritu, 18, 143
Blyth, William, 51
Board of Economic Inquiry, 165–71, *166*, 205–6
Bonaparte, Napoleon, 38
Bose, Sugata, 123
Brahmins: Bhakti movement and, 185, 188; caste viewed as invention of, 287n105; census enumerations of, 86, 99, 100; as moneylenders, 128; Panjab, lack of influence in, 195, 303–4n63; as percentage of population, 197, 304n67; in *siri* relationships, 211
Brandreth, Edward, 48–49, 52
Brayne, Frank, 129, 177
Briggs, John, 33
British Indian Army, 16, 38, 115, 198; revolt of 1857, 29, *43*, 125, 271n22

British rule, peasant Panjab under. *See* peasants and global capitalism in colonial Panjab
Browne, James, 32
Bruce, Richard, 3
Buddhism, 176, 204, 299n12
Buxar, Battle of (1764), 22
Byres, Terence J., 311n45

canals and irrigation, 4, 16, 23, 33–34, 46, 48–49
Cannan, Edwin, 312n62
Capital (Marx), 24, 56, 59–62, 97, 243, 244, 250, 313n90
capital accumulation. *See* accumulation
capitalism, global. *See* peasants and global capitalism in colonial Panjab
Casson, Herbert A., 2–3
caste, 20, 174–218, 258–59; Ad Dharm movement and, 20, 176, 177, 196, 198–204, 214–16, 218, 258, 299n10; Ambedkar's speech on, 174–76; Bhakti movement challenging, 20, 177, 183–88, 193, 194; in censuses, 82, 86–89, 98–99, 197; colonial and Panjabi terms for, 194–96, 286–87n101; conversion out of Hinduism and, 20, 176, 177, 182, 195, 196–98, 201–2, 213–16; difficulty of escaping strictures of, 177, 182, 200, 217; division of labor/laborers, as, 175, 176, 177–83; early anthropological writings on Indian system of, 177–83; East India Company, classification of cultivators by, 50–53; fourfold *varna* caste system, 99, 156–57, 287n105; Ibbetson on, 97–104, 286–87n101, 287n105; indebtedness and caste, 126, 133–34; *langar* (inter-caste and inter-faith cooking and eating), 191; occupation [mis]aligned with, 4–5, 18, 69, 88, 89, 99–104, 106, 117–19, 156–57, 204–5, 216; in Panjab cultural milieu, 176, 183–94; in Panjabi dictionaries, 73, 74–75; property rights and, 215, 216–17;

proverbs and, 93, 95–96; Punjab Alienation of Land Act and, 257–58; racialized view of, 287n105, 287n108; [re]framing the caste question, 213–18; Sikh attitudes toward, 188–89, 191, 192, 200–202, 213, 218, 258; *siri* relationship between landed cultivators and landless laborers, 206–13, *208*, 307n103; technological environment, effects of evolution of, 216–17. *See also* hereditary caste identity/peasantry, idea of; *specific castes*
census in Panjab: caste, enumeration of, 82, 86–89, 98–99, 197; census of 1881, 97–104, *99*, 108, 286n99, 304n67; census of 1921, 304–5n70; census of 1931, caste and religious identity in, 202–4, 299n9; early censuses, 78–91, *83*, *84*, 108, 284n43; popular opposition to, 284n49; religious identity, enumeration of, 80, 82, *83*, *84*, 87, 90, 98, 197
Césaire, Aimé, 7
Chakrabarty, Dipesh, 18, 63, 279n139
Chamar Mahan Sabha (Grand Chamar Society), 304n65
Chamars: Ad Dharm movement and, 198; census enumerations of, 4, 88, 100, 103, 197; Cohn's study of, 180, 181; contemporary Dalit use of term, 196, 304n65; illegality of term, in postcolonial India, 196, 215; as landless laborers in Panjab, 4–5; as non-agricultural, under Punjab Alienation of Land Act, 110, 116; occupation and identity, [mis]alignment of, 5, 117, 204, 306n94; as percentage of population, 4, 197–98, 202–3, 304n67, 304n70; in Punjabi caste vocabulary, 195–96; "Ravidasia," as surname for, 185, 195–96; religious identities of, 197–98, 203, 216; as *siris*, 206, 207, 213
Chamkaur, Battle of (1704), 302n51
Chand, Lal, 150
Charlesworth, Neil, 291n25

Chaudhri, Jia Lal, 150
Chaugutta, son of Karmun, 207–9, *208*, 212, 217
Chayanov, A. V., 310n29
Children's Employment Commissions (England), 60
Chinese Revolution, 11
Chisiiti, Muharram Ali, 148–49
Christian, G. J., *84*, 103
Christians and Christianity: American Presbyterian Church in Panjab, 74, 177; forced conversions, 299n12; lower caste conversion to, 75, 182, 195, 196, 197–98, 203, 213, 216; Marx's "On the Jewish Question," 214–15; as percentage of population, 197–98, 203, 299n9, 304n70
Churhas: census enumerations of, 88, 100–103, 197; illegality of term, in postcolonial India, 196, 215; as non-agricultural, under Punjab Alienation of Land Act, 110, 116; occupation and identity, [mis]alignment of, 204, 207; as percentage of population, 197–98, 203, 304n67, 304n70; in Punjabi caste vocabulary, 195–96; religious identities of, 197–98, 202, 203; as *siris*, 206, 207, 213
Clark, William, 145, 149
Cohn, Bernard, 69–70, 82, 89, 180, 181, 284n61, 285n83, 290n7, 300n22
collective nature of agriculturalist enterprise, 205–6, 213, 216
collective nature of labor generally, 235–36
colonial benevolence, 4, 255, 256; East India Company's claims of, 22–24, 39, 40, 65–66, 67, 70, 257; indebtedness, problem of, 132, 146, 158, 162, 165; theories of peasant inadequacy and, 236, 252
colonial Panjab. *See* peasants and global capitalism in colonial Panjab
colonial paternalism. *See* paternalism, colonial

comparison, 63, 66, 79, 203, 220, 222, 241–42, 251, 253, 259, 261, 268n3, 280n154
concept of "peasant," 5–6, 20, 67–119, 257–58; census of 1881 and, 97–104, *99*, 108, 286n99; collective nature of agriculturalist enterprise, 205–6, 213, 216; definition of agriculturalist, in Punjab Alienation of Land Act, 105; early censuses, "agriculturalist" and other categories in, 78–91, *83*, *84*, 108, 284n43; early Panjabi dictionaries on, 71–78, 116–17, 220; etymology of term, 219; genealogical determination of, in Punjab Alienation of Land Act, 107–9, *108*, *109*; indebtedness issue and, 152; language, politics of, 67–70; market and non-market forces, interplay of, 118–19; occupation and caste identity, [mis]alignment of, 4–5, 18, 69, 88, 89, 99–104, 106, 117–19; occupation and identity, lack of [mis]alignment between, 18, 69, 70–78; petitions for agriculturalist status after 1901, 110–16, *114*, 205; proverbs, collection of, 91–96; Punjab Alienation of Land Act (1901) and, 70, 104–10, *107*, *109*, 115, 118, 152, 157, 288n120; scientific enumeration under colonial rule and, 117
conversion out of Hinduism by lower castes, 20, 176, 177, 182, 195, 196–98, 201–2, 213–16
Corn Laws (England), 61–62, 279n149
Cornwallis, Charles, 37, 124–25
Crooke, William, 177
Cross, Richard A., 136
Cuban Revolution, 11
Curzon, Lord, 122
Cust, Robert, 37

Dagis, 195, 197, 202, 203, 304n70. *See also* Chamars
Dalhousie, James Broun-Ramsay, Marquess of, 28, 30–32, 35, 38, 40–41,
Dalits, 174–76; Ad Dharm movement and, 20, 176, 177, 196, 198–204, 214–16, 218,

258, 299n10; Bhakti movement and, 185; caste in Punjab cultural milieu and, 177, 185, 191, 194, 213; *Chamar*, use of, 196, 304n65; identity reformation, efforts at, 20; as percentage of Panjab population, 4, 264n9. *See also* caste
Dante's *Inferno*, 61
Darbar Sahib, 202, 305n85
Darling, Malcolm, 129, 162, 177, 290n8, 314n115
Davidson, Henry, 47, 51, 52, 69, 73
Davies, Robert, 51
debt. *See* indebtedness
Deccan Riots (1875), 104, 127–29, 291n25
The Development of Capitalism in Russia (Lenin), 222
Dickens, Charles, 286n86
dictionaries, 8, 70, 72–74, 76, 116–17, 257
Dirks, Nicholas, 103, 181
division of labor: Ambedkar on, 176, 182; caste and, 175, 176, 177–83; history of, 5–9; Adam Smith on, 234–39; undivided labor, Adam Smith on condition of, 237–39
Dombey and Son (Dickens), 286n86
Dorin, Joseph, 41
Dost Mohammed Khan (ruler of Kabul), 38, 255
Douglas, Montagu W., 113–15
Du Bois, W. E. B., 224, 228
Dumont, Louis, 181
Dussehra Festival, 2
Dutt, Romesh Chunder, 149

East India Company in Panjab, 20, 22–66, 257; administrative system and revenue settlement, 28, 36–40; agricultural capacity and potential, assessing, 44–49; annexation (1856), 22, 28, 30–32; boundaries and territories, establishment of, 40, 42, 274n61, 274n69; capitalism, manifestation of, 23–25; caste and religious identities, classification of cultivators by, 50–53; civilizing mission, annexation portrayed as,

30–32, 36, 39–40; colonial benevolence claimed by, 22–24, 39, 40, 65–66, 67, 70, 257; conquest of Panjab, 22, 26–30; differentiated from European peasant narrative, 62–66; heterogeneity of Panjab, issues raised by, 67–68; indebtedness and, 124–25; irrigation and canals, 23, 33–34, 46; land revenue demanded and collected by, 22, 28, 36–37, 40–44, *43*, 50, 55, 124–25, 272n49; language, politics of, 67–70, 76; maps, *27*, *29*; martial capacities of Panjabis, evocations of, 31, 35, 38, 41, 273n54; Marx's narrative of accumulation and, 56–62; property and money, tethering of, 53–56; revenue possibilities, pre-annexation calculations of, 32–36; revocation of charter (1859), 29–30; revolts against, 28, 29, 30, 40, 125; Maharaja Ranjit Singh, kingdom of, 26–28, *27*
Engels, Friedrich, 308n2, 313n90
European peasant history, universalization from, 7–11, 18–19, 56–63, 219, 221, 230, 245, 250–53

Factory Acts (England), 60
Famine Commission (1878), 50, 136
Fanon, Frantz, 7, 64
Fanshawe, Herbert, 164
Farid, Baba, 1, 21, 117, 189, 262
Faridkot, kingdom of, 26
feudalism, 10, 13, 16, 64, 250, 260, 276n108; feudal, 19, 23–24, 135
Feuerbach, Ludwig, 223
food and consumption: cultivating versus non-cultivating men, 307n108; *langar* (inter-caste and inter-faith cooking and eating), 191, 200; in rural family budget survey, 165–71, *166*, 298n133; *siri* relationships and, 210–12; Adam Smith on food production, 238–39, 254, 259–60, 313n92
Ford Foundation, 11, 179
Fort William College, 36
Foucault, Michel, 109, 277n124

Frank, Andre Gunder, 269n9
French Revolution, 11
Friedman, Milton, 232

Gait, Edward, 177
Gandhi, Mohandas Karamchand, 174, 201, 202, 204
Gardner, Alexander, 270n18
Gazetteers, 91
gender. *See* women and gender
genealogical determination of agriculturalist status, in Punjab Alienation of Land Act, 107–9, *108*, *109*
German Social Democratic Party (SPD), 225, 228–29
Ghadar Party, 194, 198
Ghakhars, 106, 166
Gidwani, Vinay, 18, 117
Gilchrist, John Borthwick, 282n16
global capitalism. *See* peasants and global capitalism in colonial Panjab
Glossary of Judicial and Revenue Terms (Wilson), 76–77
Glossary of the Multani Language compared with Punjabi and Sindhi (O'Brian), 92–93
Gould, Harold, 180
Gramsci, Antonio, 7–8
Grant, John Andrew, 132–33
Green Revolution, 12, 15
Griffin, Lepel, 91
Grundrisse (Marx), 248, 314n103
Guha, Ranajit, 14, 71, 93, 191, 256
Gujars, 101, 102, 197, 304n67
Gulabdasi sect, 194
Guru Arjun, 189
Guru Gobind Singh, 183, 191, 302n51
Guru Granth Sahib, 192. *See also* Adi Granth
Guru Nanak, 176, 188–90, 193, 197, 200, 218, 258, 299n12

Haileybury College, 36
Ham Hindu Nahin ("We Are Not Hindus;" Kahn Singh Nabha), 200

Hans, Raj Kumar, 194
Hardiman, David, 128, 291n25
Harijans, 174. *See also* Dalits
Harnis, 101, 102, 107
Harootunian, Harry, 279n139
Harvey, David, 57–58
Hayek, Friedrich von, 232
Hegel, Georg W. F., 223
hereditary caste identity/peasantry, idea of, 5, 21; concept of "caste," analyses of, 175, 176, 182, 185, 190–91, 216, 217; concept of "peasant," analyses of, 89, 105, 109, 117; indebtedness problem and, 126, 134, 144, 147, 148, 158; theories of peasant inadequacy and, 220, 256, 258, 260
Hill, Christopher, 191
The Hindu Jajmani System (William Wiser), 177, 178
Hindus and Hinduism: caste sanctioned by, 175–76; census identification of, 80, 82, *83, 84,* 90, 98, 197, 285n71; Churhas and Chamars identifying as, 197; East India Company, characterization by, 51; efforts to retain lower castes within, 197; indebtedness of Muslims to Hindu money, 130–35; Isa Khel riot and, 2–3, 263n5; lower-caste conversion out of, 20, 176, 177, 182, 195, 196–98, 201–2, 213–16; as percentage of population, 197–98, 203, 299n9; Sikh presence in Panjab complicating binary narrative of Hindu-Muslim relations, 17
historical versus contemporary category, treatment of peasant as, 266n27
Hobbes, Thomas, 243
Hobsbawm, Eric, 265n22, 281n10, 308n2
Homo Hierarchicus (Dumont), 181
Hume, David, 232
Hunter, Henry, 61
Hunter, William Wilson, 133, 177
Hussain, Ghulam, 146, 147
Hutcheson, Francis, 232

Ibbetson, Denzil, 79, 97–104, 110, 116, 117, 133, 286–87n101, 287n105
identity: landed property, conflation with, 126. *See also* caste; occupation and identity; "peasant," concept of; religion and religious identity
Ilahi, Faiz, 165, 205
inadequacy, theories of. *See* theories of peasant inadequacy
indebtedness, 20, 120–73, 258; caste and, 126, 133–34; civil suits involving, 139–43, *140*; data and statistics, compilation of, 136–39; essential precariousness of agricultural life and, 165, 169–73; government/legislative intervention in, 124, 127, 135–36, 143–44; identity and landed property, conflation of, 126; landed property transfers, shift in focus to, 136; *The New York Times* article of 1900 on, 120–22, *121,* 161; as object of inquiry, 120–23, 124–28; paternalistic attributions to peasant indiscipline, 120, 122, 129, 133–34, 161–65, 172–73; property rights and, 123–24, 173, 290nn7–8; Punjab Alienation of Land Act and, 124, 144–61, 172 (*See also* Punjab Alienation of Land Act); religion and, 126, 130–35; revolts and violence associated with, 125, 127–29, 131; rural family budget survey, 165–71, *166,* 298n133; scholarship on debt crisis, 122–24; Thorburn's analysis of Muslim indebtedness for Hindu money, 129–36
indentured laborers, 307n101
India, postcolonial: agency of peasants, discovery of, 12–15; Ambedkar as law minister of, 217; illegality of untouchable caste terms in, 196, 215; Naxalbari peasant uprising (1967), 11; Punjab Alienation of Land Act (1901), abolition of, 217
The Indian Musalmans (Hunter), 133
Indian National Congress, 149, 175
Inferno (Dante), 61

An Inquiry into the Nature and Causes of the Wealth of Nations (Adam Smith), 231–32, 250–51, 312n54
irrigation and canals, 4, 16, 23, 33–34, 46, 48–49
Isa Khel riot (1893), 1–4, 8, 21, 127, 254–56, 263n4
Islam. *See* Hindu-Muslim relations; Muslims

jagirs, 41, 45, 55
"Jai Guru Dev" greeting, 199
jajmani system, 178–83. *See also* caste
Janvier, Levi, 74
Jat-Pat Todak Mandal ("Association for the Breaking of Caste"), 174, 199, 201
Jatts: census enumeration of, 86, 100–101, 102, 103, 197; East India Company, characterization by, 51–52; Baba Farid on, 1, 117; in Ghadar Party, 198; indebtedness and, 133; martial prowess/peasant qualities attributed to, 16; as misl leaders, 193; in Panjabi dictionaries, 73, 75–76, 77, 117; peasants, identification with, 5, 69, 75–76, 77, 220; as percentage of population, 5, 197, 264n9, 304n67; in proverbs, 93, 95–96; Punjab Alienation of Land Act (1901) and, 106; in rural family budget survey, 167, 168; as Sikhs, 200, 201; in *siri* relationships with lower castes, 210, 213
Jews and Judaism, 134, 214–15, 223–24, 292n44
Jind, kingdom of, 26
Jones, Kenneth, 79
Journal of Agrarian Change, 6
The Journal of Peasant Studies, 6
Juergensmeyer, Mark, 198, 204
Julahas, 52, 100, 195, 196, 210, 216

Kabir (Bhakti poet), 176, 184–85, 188, 190, 193, 196, 199, 201, 203, 213, 218, 258
Kabir-panthis, 196

kafi, 303n55
Kant, Immanuel, 223, 232
Kautsky, Karl, 8, 20, 221–31, 242–43, 250–51, 256, 259, 309n8, 310–11n40, 310n32, 313n90
Kessinger, Tom, 17, 183, 216, 290n8, 301n35
Keywords (Williams), 219–21
Khalsa, 191, 200
Khalsa, Sant Singh, 302n39
Khan, Ahmad Hasan, 299n9-10
Khan, Dost Muhammad (petitioner for agriculturalist status), 112, 255
Khan, Dost Mohammed (ruler of Kabul), 38
Khan, Jiwan, civil suit against (1878), 139–42, *140*, 161, 169, 173
Khan, Muhammad Barkat Ali, 148
Khan, Muhammad Hayat, 8, 156–57, 173
Khatiks, 102, 103
Khatris, 190, 197, 200, 211, 213, 303n63, 304n67
Kirti Kisan Party, 194
Kolis, 106, 195. *See also* Chamars
Kumhars, 195, 205, 211, 216
Kutanas, 101, 196. *See also* Churhas

Lahore, Treaty of (1846), 28, 30, 270–71n19
Lall, Isa Charan, 111–12
The Land and the Law in India (West), 125–27
landed property: civil suits involving transfers of, 139–43, *140*; conflation of identity with, 126; data and statistics on transfers of, 136–39; East India Company, demands for/collection of land revenue by, 22, 28, 36–37, 40–44, *43*, 50, 55, 124–25, 272n49; indebtedness problem and shift in focus to land transfers, 136; *siri* relationship between landed cultivators and landless laborers, 206–13, *208*, 307n103. *See also* property rights; Punjab Alienation of Land Act (1901)
landlords. *See* zamindars

langar (Sikh inter-caste and inter-faith cooking and eating), 191, 200
language: of Bhagats, 189; colloquial usage, loss of, 283n39; Panjabi and its dialects, 68–69, 192–93, 281n3; Panjabi dictionaries, 73, 74–75; politics of, 67–70, 76; spoken in Panjab, 68–69, 281n3; Urdu in Panjab, official imposition of, 68–69
Lansdowne, Henry Petty-Fitzmaurice, Marquess of, 136
Lawrence, Charles, 28
Lawrence, John, 22, 28, 30, 36, 39–40, 42–44, 54, 79, 88, 129
Lenin, Vladimir, 8, 20, 221–31, 242–43, 250–51, 256, 259, 309n8, 310n32, 311n46, 313n90
Lewis, Oscar, 179–80, 182
loans and moneylenders. *See* indebtedness
Locke, John, 232
Lohar, 195, 206
Lowis, John, 41
Luxemburg, Rosa, 57, 277–78n126
Lyall, James, 135–36

Maconachie, Robert, 92, 94–96, 255, 286n94
mahalwari (estate) or *bhaiachara* (brotherhood) settlements, 39
Maharaja Dalip Singh. *See* Singh, Dalip
Maharaja Ranjit Singh. *See* Singh, Ranjit
Mal, Krori, 150
Malcolm, John, 32
Malhotra, Anshu, 194
Malthus, Thomas, 243
Mandeville, Bernard, 232
Mansel, Charles, 28
Mantena, Karuna, 30, 251
Manu (lawgiver), 99, 175, 179, 199, 217
Manusmriti, 175, 179
Marathis, 127, 128, 291n25
martial prowess attributed to Panjabis, 16, 31, 35, 38, 41, 273n54

Marx, Karl, 7–8, 20; on East India Company, 28, 271n22; homogenizing approach to peasantry, 64; Lenin/Kautsky and, 242–43, 250–51; narrative of accumulation, analysis of, 56–62, 279n139, 279n149, 280n152, 280n155, 280n158; on occupation and identity, 254; Panjab peasant narrative differentiated from, 62–63; political economy, critique of, 245–50, 256, 259; on primitive accumulation, 24, 25, 56–57, 59–60; on property rights, 215; "questions" in public discourse and, 223–24; on Adam Smith, 232, 242–48, 250, 313n83; theories of peasant inadequacy and, 20, 222; on writers and publishing, 314n102
Marx, Karl, works: *Capital*, 24, 56, 59–62, 97, 243, 244, 250, 313n90; *Grundrisse*, 248, 314n103; "On the Jewish Question," 214–15, 224; *Theories of Surplus-Value*, 243–45, 313n90
Marxism: East India Company in Panjab and, 24; Lenin and Kautsky as Marxists, 243, 250–51; neo-Marxist historians, 13; on peasantry, 9–11, 12; of Raymond Williams, 253
Masihs, 196, 203. *See also* Churhas
Maynard, John, 113
Mazhabis, 4–5, 113–16, *114*, 196, 197, 200, 201, 203, 217, 252, 304n70. *See also* Churhas
McNally, David, 234
Meek, Ronald L., 312n54
Mehras, 195, 205, 217
"menials," as term, 70, 75, 100, 101, 103, 110, 116–18, 124, 180, 195–96, 216, 246
Mill, John Stuart, 232
Miller, John Andrew Erasmus, 87–89
Mochis, 195, 197, 203, 304n67, 304n70. *See also* Chamars
moneylenders and loans. *See* indebtedness
Montmorency, Geoffrey F. de, 115
Morning Chronicle (newspaper), 61
Morning Herald (newspaper), 280n150

Mughal Empire, 29, 183, 191–93, 276n108, 301n36, 302n51, 303n57
Muir, William, 82, 85
Munro, Thomas, 125
Musalmans and Money-Lenders in the Punjab (Thorburn), 133–34, 135–36
Muslims: census identification of, 80, 82, *83, 84*, 90, 98, 285n71; Churhas and Chamars identifying as, 197; East India Company, characterization by, 51, 52; forced conversions, 299n12; indebtedness of Muslims to Hindu money, 130–35; Isa Khel riot and, 2–3, 263n5; lower caste conversion to Islam, 195, 196, 197–98, 213; as percentage of population, 197, 203, 299n9; Sikh presence in Panjab complicating binary narrative of Hindu-Muslim relations, 17
Mussalis, 101, 196, 197, 203, 217, 304n70. *See also* Churhas

Nabha, Kahn Singh, 200
Nabha, kingdom of, 26
Nais, 195, 211, 216
Nakli Sikh Prabodh ("False Sikhs Redeem Yourselves;" Ditt Singh), 200, 202
Namdev (Bhakti poet), 176, 187–88, 199, 201, 203, 258
naming the peasant. *See* concept of "peasant"
Nath, Raja Deena, 40
Native States, 26, 28, 29, 40, 67, 72, 104, 144
Naxalbari peasant uprising (1967), India, 11
neo-Machiavellian/neo-Marxist historians, 13
The New York Times (newspaper), 120–22, *121*, 161, 173, 255
Newton, John, 74–76, 77
Nicolaus, Martin, 314n103
North West Provinces (NWP): census in, 79, 81, 83, 86, 89, 90, 285n70; East India Company and, 29, 33–35, 36, 37, 39; Hindustani language used in, 76; indebtedness in, 136; Urdu language adopted by British officers and service in, 68

Oberoi, Harjit, 17
O'Brian, Edward, 92–93
occupation and identity: caste, [mis]alignment of occupation with, 4–5, 18, 69, 88, 89, 99–104, 106, 117–19, 156–57, 204–5, 216; census, enumeration and categorization by, 78–91, *83, 84*, 98–104; early anthropological writings on *jajmani* caste system and, 177–83; lack of alignment between, in Panjabi dictionaries, 18, 69, 70–78; Marx on, 254; Punjab Alienation of Land Act leading to alignment of, 220, 257
"On the Jewish Question" (Marx), 214–15, 224
Osborne, W. G., 32

Paine, Thomas, 232
Pandey, Gyanendra, 52, 254
Pandits, 94, 205, 304n63
Panjab. *See* peasants and global capitalism in colonial Panjab
Panjab, meaning/etymology of, 274n61
The Panjab Chiefs (Griffin), 91
Panjab school of administration, 23, 44, 146
Panjabi language and dialects, 68–69, 192–93, 281n3
paternalism, colonial: of East India Company, 23; indebtedness eliciting, 120, 122, 129, 133–34, 161–65, 172–73; scholarly assertion of, 15
Pathans, 16, 41, 86, 100, 102, 106, 133, 197, 220, 268n3, 304n67
Patiala, kingdom of, 26, 201
Patnaik, Prabhat, 58–59, 278n133
Patnaik, Utsa, 12, 58–59, 278n133
patriarchy of rural households, 17, 82, 83, 106, 108–9, 117, 127, 163, 227

peasants and global capitalism in colonial Panjab, 1–21, 254–62; agency of peasants in India, discovery of, 12–15; alternative genealogy for global capital, proposing, 7–8; benevolent colonialism, myth of, 4, 255, 256 (*See also* colonial benevolence); birth of peasant via modern politics, 18–19, 65, 257–58; caste and, 20, 174–218, 258–59 (*See also* caste); colonizer/colonized binary, investigating, 6–7, 256–57; concept of "peasant," investigating, 5–6, 20, 67–119, 257–58 (*See also* concept of "peasant"); demise/dormancy of peasantry, assumptions about, 9–12, 56–57, 228–31, 252, 265n22, 266n27 (*See also* theories of peasant inadequacy); division of labor, as history of, 5–9; East India Company and, 20, 22–66, 257 (*See also* East India Company in Panjab); European peasant history, universalization from, 7–11, 18–19, 56–63, 219, 221, 230, 245, 250–53; hereditary peasant status, 5, 21 (*See also* hereditary caste identity/peasantry, idea of); historical versus contemporary category, treatment of peasant as, 266n27; homogenization of peasantry, 6–7, 64; indebtedness and, 20, 120–73, 258 (*See also* indebtedness); Isa Khel riot (1893), interpretations of, 1–4, 8, 21, 127, 254–56, 263n4; occupation and identity, ahistorical [mis]alignment of, 4–5, 18 (*See also* occupation and identity); revolutionary movements, involvement of peasants in, 11–12; scholarship on Panjab peasants, 15–18; scope and approach to historical sources, 8–9, 276n111; theories of peasant inadequacy and, 20–21, 219–53, 258 (*See also* theories of peasant inadequacy)
Petty, William, 243
Physiocrats, 243
Pioneer Press, Allahabad, 134

Piro (from Gulabdasi sect), 194
Plowden, W. C., 287n105
political economy, 6, 9, 19-21, 59, 64, 116, 118, 183, 196, 211-13, 221-22, 231, 243, 245, 248-50, 253, 256-57, 259-60; repoliticizing, 252
Pomeranz, Kenneth, 63
postcolonial India. *See* India, postcolonial
primitive accumulation, 24, 25, 56–57, 58–60, 65, 257, 277–78n126, 279n139, 280n152
Prinsep, Henry, 32
private property. *See* landed property; property rights
property rights: caste and, 215, 216–17; indebtedness and, 123–24, 173, 290nn7–8; Marx on, 215; money and property, East India Company's tethering of, 53–56. *See also* landed property
proverbs, collection of, 91–96
Public Health reports (England), 61
Punjab Agricultural College (Lyallpur), 165
Punjab Alienation of Land Act (1901): abolition of, 217; caste, implications for, 257–58; colonial measures of success of, 157–61, 173; concept of "peasant" and, 70, 104–10, *107*, *109*, 115, 118, 152, 157, 288n120; final draft proceedings, 153–57; hypothecation of agricultural produce banned by, 145; indebtedness and, 124, 144–61, 172; initial draft and comments, 144–53; occupation and identity, leading to alignment of, 220, 257; passage of, 157; permanent alienations, requiring official sanction for, 144; petitions for agriculturalist status after passage of, 110–16, *114*, 205; text and commentary, 288n120; usufructuary mortgages, limits on, 144–45
Punjab Customary Law series (Tupper), 91, 145
Punjab Gazette, 106

Punjab Notes and Queries (Temple), 91, 286n86
Punjab Revenue Act (1887), 104
Punjab Tenancy Act (1887), 104
Puranas, 175
Puri, Harish, 201
Purser, William, 163

Quesnay, François, 232
"questions" in public discourse, 223–24, 311n47

racialism: caste, racialized view of, 287n105, 287n108; indebtedness, colonialist analyses of, 135
Rafiq-i-Hind (newspaper), 148–49
Rahitas, 196, 197
Raike, Charles, 51
raiyatwari (cultivator) settlements, 39
Rajputs, 16, 51, 100–101, 106, 107, 113, 133, 197, 199, 287n101, 304n67
Ram, Atma, 208, 209
Ram, Mangoo, 8, 198–200, 202, 203–4, 205, 218, 255, 258
Ram, Sant, 174
Ramdasia, 196, 200, 203. *See also* Chamars
Ramdhan, civil suit of (1878), 139–42, 161, 173
Rangreta, Bir Singh, 191
Ravidas (Bhakti poet), 185–87, 188–89, 190, 193, 194, 195, 199, 201, 203, 214, 258
Ravidasia Sikh, 185, 195–96, 200, 201, 203, 304n65. *See also* Chamars
Raza, Ali, 194
Redfield, Robert, 259
religion and religious identity: Ad Dharm movement, 20, 176, 177, 196, 198–204, 214–16, 218, 258, 299n10; caste and conversion out of Hinduism, 20, 176, 177, 182, 195, 196–98, 201–2, 213–16; census identification of, 80, 82, *83, 84,* 87, 90, 98, 197; East India Company, classification of cultivators by, 50–53; indebtedness and, 126, 130–35; *langar* (inter-caste and inter-faith cooking and eating), 191, 200; proverbs and, 93. *See also specific religious groups*
Reports from the Poor Law Inspectors (England), 61
Reports of the Inspectors of Factories (England), 60
Ricardo, David, 232, 243, 312n70
Risalewala Government Agricultural Farm, 167
Rishi Valmiki. *See* Valmiki
Risley, Herbert H., 178, 287n105, 287n108
Rivaz, Charles, 143, 154–56, 157, 161, 162, 164, 171
Rizvi, Mubbashir, 15
Rohilla rulers, 35–36
Ross, David, 54
Roy, Arundhati, 299n4
Rudé, George, 281n10, 308n2
Rudra, Ashok, 12
Russell, Robert, 177
Russian Revolution, 11

sahukars (moneylenders). *See* indebtedness
Sarkar-i-Khalsa, kingdom of, 26
Sartori, Andrew, 18, 220, 280n152, 315n117
scheduled castes. *See* Dalits
Scott, James C., 72, 315n6
Scottish Enlightenment, 232
Second Anglo-Afghan War (1842), 38
Second Anglo-Sikh War (1848-49), 55, 67, 277n118
Selected Agricultural Proverbs of the Panjab (Maconachie), 92, 94–96, 286n94
Sen, Amartya, 231
sepidari system, 205
Seth, R. K., 205
Shaftesbury, Antony Ashley Cooper, Earl of, 62
Shah, Bulleh (poet), 191–92, 255, 303n55
Shah, Nadir (Persian ruler), 183
Shanin, Teodor, 62, 310–11n40, 311n46, 315n6
Shastras, 175, 176, 299n12
Sherring, M. A., 287n105
Shiromani Akali Dal, 194

Swami Shraddhanand, 197
Sikhs and Sikhi: Ad Dharm movement and, 200; *Adi Granth*, 188, 189, 191, 192; Ambedkar and, 201–2, 204; Anglo-Sikh wars (1845-46 and 1848-49), 55, 67, 277n118; caste, attitudes toward, 188–89, 191, 192, 200–202, 213, 218, 258; census identification of, 80, 82, *83, 84*, 90, 284n51, 285n71; Churhas and Chamars identifying as, 197; founding and development of Sikh faith, 188, 191; Hindu-Muslim relations, complicating binary narrative of, 17; Khalsa, 191, 200; lower-caste conversion to Sikhi, 195, 196, 201–2, 213; martial prowess/peasant qualities attributed to, 16; Panjab, effects of Sikh rule in, 183; as percentage of population, 197–98, 203, 299n9; Ravidasia Sikh, 185, 195–96, 200, 201, 203, 304n65; weapons, traditional integral place of, 271n29
Singh, Ajaib, 165
Singh, Baldev, 201
Singh, Bussawa, 72
Singh, Dalip (Maharaja), 28, 30-32
Singh, Giani Ditt, 200, 202
Singh, Sardar Gian, 207
Singh, Gurcharn, 288n120
Singh, Sardar Harjit, 112
Singh, Himmat, 191
Singh, Jiwan (Bhai Jaita), 191, 302n51
Singh, Jowahir, 150
Singh, Kapur, 8, 202
Singh, Kartar, 165, 171
Singh, Labh, 165
Singh, Mohkam, 191
Singh, Nikky-Guninder Kaur, 189
Singh, Ranjit (Maharaja), 17, 26–28, *27*, 30, 37, 38, 40, 45, 68, 150, 183, 193, 271n19, 301n34, 305n85
Singh, Sahib, 191
Singh, Master Tara, 201
Singh, Tehl, 207–9, *208*, 212, 217, 246
Singh, Wazir, 194

Singh Sabha movement, 200–201
siri relations, 206–13, *208*, 307n103
slaves/slavery, 24, 126, 199, 240–41, 270n14, 307n101, 313n81, 313n83
Smith, Adam, 8, 20, 221–22, 231–47, 259; the "Adam Smith problem," 311n48; on division of labor, 234–39; on food production, 238–39, 254, 259–60, 313n92; foundational nature of political economy of, 231–34; Marx on, 232, 242–48, 250, 313n83; on travails of undivided labor, 237–39; wealth, conceptualization of idea of, 232–34; *Wealth of Nations*, 231–32, 250–51, 312n54; on workers versus slaves and peasants, 240–42, 313n83
Smith, Henry Alexander, 113
Smith, R. Baird, 33–36, 37
Smith, Richard Saumarez, 17
Smith, Wilfred Cantwell, 303n57
Smyth, John, 141–43
Social Democratic Party (SPD), Germany, 225, 228–29
The Souls of Black Folk (Du Bois), 224, 228
Starkey, Samuel, 72–74, 76–77, 282n16
Steedman, Edward, 162, 164
Steinbach, Henry, 273n54
Steuart, James, 243, 312n52
Stokes, Eric, 13, 122
Subaltern Studies/subaltern, 14, 70, 196

Tandon, Prakash, 303–4n63
Tarkhan, 194–95, 206, 211, 217
Temple, Richard, 45–46, 47, 80, 86, 91–92, 103, 117, 129, 255, 286n86
theories of peasant inadequacy, 20–21, 219–53, 259; demise/dormancy of peasantry, assumptions about, 228–31; etymology of "peasant" and, 219–21; European peasant history, universalization from, 7–11, 18–19, 56–63, 219, 221, 230, 245, 250–53; Kautsky on, 8, 20, 221–31, 242–43, 250–51, 256, 259, 309n8, 310–11n40, 310n32, 313n90; Lenin on, 8, 20, 221–31, 242–43,

250–51, 256, 259, 309n8, 310n32, 311n46, 313n90; Marx and, 20, 222, 242–53 (*See also* Marx, Karl); "questions" in public discourse, 223–24, 311n47; Adam Smith and, 8, 20, 221–22, 231–47 (*See also* Smith, Adam); tracing trajectory of impact of capital on peasant society, 225–28
Theories of Surplus-Value (Marx), 243–45, 313n90
Thomason, James, 37
Thompson, E. P., 265n19, 281n10
Thorburn, Septimus: concept of "peasant" and, 104, 288n119; death of, 171; on indebtedness, 129–36, 142, 149, 154, 161, 163, 164, 255, 292n44, 293n53
Thornton, Edward, 55–56
Thornton, John, 81, 82, 85
Tupper, Charles, 91, 145

Udasi, Sant Ram, 307n103
untouchables. *See* caste; Dalits; *specific untouchable castes*
Urdu language imposed on Panjab, 68–69

Valmiki, 196, 199
Valmikis, 196. *See also* Churhas
Varaich, 101, 102, 103
varna system, 99, 156–57, 287n105
Vedas, 175, 213
Viswanath, Rupa, 15, 44

Wace, Edward, 92
Waterfield, Henry, 89–90, 287n105
Wealth of Nations (Adam Smith), 231–32, 250–51, 312n54
Weber, Eugen, 24
West, Raymond, 125–27, 128, 134, 161, 291n22

William Blackwood & Sons, Edinburgh, 134
Williams, Raymond, 219–21, 253
Willis, Paul, 314n101
Wilson, Horace H., 76–77, 283n34–35
Wilson, James, 145
Wiser, William and Charlotte, 177–79, 180, 182, 205, 206
Wolf, Eric, 9
Wollstonecraft, Mary, 232
women and gender: agriculture, masculinist assumptions about, 259, 276n106, 306n97; Ambedkar, Sikh marriage considered by, 201; census identification of, *83–84*, 84–85, 87, 98; indebtedness and, 163; patriarchy of rural households, 17, 82, 83, 106, 108–9, 117, 127, 163, 227; proverbs and, 93, 95; seclusion of wives and caste practices, 180
World Bank, 11

Young, William, 145–46

zamindari (landlord) settlements, 37–38, 39
zamindars (landlords): civil court cases involving indebtedness and land transfers, 139–43, *140*; East India Company and, 48, 49, 54; government officials and, 146; indiscipline attributed to, 162, 164, 165, 172–73; Panjab society, absence from, 183, 268–69n3, 301nn35–36; in Panjabi dictionaries, 69, 73, 74; Punjab Alienation of Land Act and, 146–52, 160; *siri* relationships and, 212
Zimmerman, A., 178, 278n138

ALSO PUBLISHED IN THE SOUTH ASIA IN MOTION SERIES

Qaum, Mulk, Sultanat: Citizenship and National Belonging in Pakistan
Ali Usman Qasmi

Boats in a Storm: Law, Migration, and Decolonization in South and Southeast Asia, 1942–1962
Kalyani Ramnath

Colonizing Kashmir: State-building under Indian Occupation
Hafsa Kanjwal

Life Beyond Waste: Work and Infrastructure in Urban Pakistan
Warqas H. Butt

Dust on the Throne: The Search for Buddhism in Modern India
Douglas Ober

Mother Cow, Mother India: A Multispecies Politics of Dairy in India
Yamini Narayanan

The Vulgarity of Caste: Dalits, Sexuality, and Humanity in Modern India
Shailaja Paik

Delhi Reborn: Partition and Nation Building in India's Capital
Rotem Geva (2022)

The Right to be Counted: The Urban Poor and the Politics of Resettlement in Delhi
Sanjeev Routray (2022)

Protestant Textuality and the Tamil Modern: Political Oratory and the Social Imaginary in South Asia
Bernard Bate, Edited by E. Annamalai, Francis Cody, Malarvizhi Jayanth, and Constantine V. Nakassis (2021)

Special Treatment: Student Doctors at the All India Institute of Medical Sciences
Anna Ruddock (2021)

From Raj to Republic: Sovereignty, Violence, and Democracy in India
Sunil Purushotham (2021)

The Greater India Experiment: Hindutva Becoming and the Northeast
Arkotong Longkumer (2020)

Nobody's People: Hierarchy as Hope in a Society of Thieves
Anastasia Piliavsky (2020)

Brand New Nation: Capitalist Dreams and Nationalist Designs in Twenty-First-Century India
Ravinder Kaur (2020)

Partisan Aesthetics: Modern Art and India's Long Decolonization
Sanjukta Sunderason (2020)

Dying to Serve: the Pakistan Army
Maria Rashid (2020)

In the Name of the Nation: India and Its Northeast
Sanjib Baruah (2020)

Faithful Fighters: Identity and Power in the British Indian Army
Kate Imy (2019)

Paradoxes of the Popular: Crowd Politics in Bangladesh
Nusrat Sabina Chowdhury (2019)

The Ethics of Staying: Social Movements and Land Rights Politics in Pakistan
Mubbashir A. Rizvi (2019)

Mafia Raj: The Rule of Bosses in South Asia
Lucia Michelutti, Ashraf Hoque, Nicolas Martin, David Picherit, Paul Rollier, Arild Ruud and Clarinda Still (2018)

For a complete listing of titles in this series, visit the Stanford University Press website, www.sup.org.

Printed in the USA
CPSIA information can be obtained
at www.ICGtesting.com
JSHW080341281023
50996JS00006B/6